Geography and the Urban Environment

Progress in Research and Applications

Volume IV

Edited by

D. T. HERBERT

Professor of Geography
University College of Wales, Swansea

and

R. J. JOHNSTON

Professor of Geography
University of Sheffield

JOHN WILEY & SONS

Chichester · New York · Brisbane · Toronto

British Library Cataloguing in Publication Data:
Geography and the urban environment.
  Vol. 4
  1. Cities and towns
  I. Herbert, D T.
  II. Johnston, R. J.
  9.10′.09   GF125

  ISBN 0 471 28051 8

Photosetting by Thomson Press (India) Limited, New Delhi
and printed in Great Britain by Page Bros. (Norwich) Ltd.

Geography
and the
Urban Environment

GEOGRAPHY AND THE URBAN ENVIRONMENT
Progress in Research and Applications

Editors

D. T. HERBERT

Department of Geography, University College of Wales, Swansea

and

R. J. JOHNSTON

Department of Geography, University of Sheffield

Editorial Advisory Board

For
David Aled and Nia Wyn Herbert
and
Chris and Lucy Johnston

List of Contributors

ROBERT J. BENNETT — *Department of Geography, University of Cambridge, Downing Place, Cambridge, CB2 3EN, England*

ROD BURGESS — *Planning Department, Architectural Association School of Architecture, 34–36 Bedford Square, London, WC1B 3ES, England*

TERRY CHRISTENSEN — *Department of Political Science, San José State University, San José, California, 95152, U.S.A.*

MICHAEL P. CONZEN — *Department of Geography, University of Chicago, 5828 S. University Avenue, Chicago, Illinois 60637, U.S.A.*

J. NICHOLAS ENTRIKIN — *Department of Geography, University of California, Los Angeles, California 92004, U.S.A.*

FREDERICK HILL — *The Child in the City Programme, University of Toronto, 455 Spadina Avenue, Toronto, Ontario M5S 2G8, Canada*

WILLIAM A. MICHELSON — *Professor of Social Ecology, University of California, Irvine, California 92664, U.S.A*

DENISE PICHE — *Ecole D'Architecture, Cité Universitaire, Université Laval, Quebec, P. Q., Canada, G1K 7P4*

JOHN P. RADFORD — *Department of Geography, York University, 4700 Keele Street, Downsview, Ontario, M3J 1P3, Canada*

R. ANDREW SAYER — *School of Social Sciences, The University of Sussex, Arts Building, Falmer, Brighton, BN1 9QN, England*

Contents

Preface

Volume IV of Geography and the Urban Environment is basically cast in the same mould as its predecessors in this series. The strand of methodological discussions which we are anxious to maintain from one volume to the next is strongly represented here, with an in-depth discussion of the social construction of concepts which have recently influenced the development of geographical thought on the key topics of regionalism and the meaning of place. The question of values in contemporary geographical research is also covered with a strong emphasis upon the philosophical underpinnings of the wider issue. In both of these themes, of the social construction of ideas and values, the contributions are symptomatic of the willingness of human geographers to extend their terms of reference far beyond the traditional limits and to delve deeply into the philosophies of the social sciences.

The philosophical–methodological focus is maintained in a contribution which although primarily focused upon housing development in Latin America, effectively constitutes a powerful critique of the various theoretical approaches which have been applied to Third World problems and an advocacy of the marxist perspective. Marxist ideas are currently exerting a strong influence on research in the social sciences; it is essential that their roles in geographical studies be fully explored and evaluated.

The remaining six chapters in this volume fall into three 'groups'. First, we have two contributions with a common concern with public policy and the links between state decision-makers and the local consumers of goods and services. Although this common purpose can be recognized, the two contributions are very different. Terry Christensen is essentially concerned with ways in which decisions are made and implemented and in particular with the extent to which the 'affected' public are able to respond to and modify, or change the plans. Covent Garden provides an example of a contested plan in which community action emerged and the bureaucratic machine was forced to reconsider its options. Bob Bennett writes on the role of Central Government finance and in particular the British Rate Support Grant as a central element of state funding. The origins of the present system are explored, its complexities and merits are examined, and some of the alternative mechanisms are discussed. As urban geographers increasingly accept the need to recognize that local environments and their problems have to be placed in the context of the macro-structure of society, more research of this kind will be essential.

One observable feature in current research is the growing tendency to focus upon the 'geographies' of sub-groups within the overall population. A well developed literature on ethnic minorities is one body of work of this type, the geography of the elderly, as discussed in volume 3 of this series, is another. The two contributions on the geography of urban children add another facet to this range. Fred Hill and Bill Michelson report on their wide-ranging 'Child in the City' programme at the University of Toronto. Some of the problems—data collection and otherwise of research in this field are evident in what they say but the usefulness of spatial factors in understanding behaviour and providing facilities for children is also evident. We are also reminded in this chapter of the large literature on child development and some of its concepts are introduced in a detailed manner in Denise Piché's study of children in London. Alternative views on child development are discussed and the main 'stages' are recognized; with these stages Piché's research demonstrates that it is possible to relate progressions in geographical learning and spatial behaviour. Again, this is a topic in which many opportunities for geographical research can be identified.

The final theme in this volume involves the city in the United States. John Radford writes on the emerging social geography of the American city in the nineteenth century, identifying both the social processes at work and the spatial outcomes which appeared. Given the prominent role which the Industrial City in the United States has assumed in influencing much modern urban geography and in providing the concept of spatial models of the city, closer analyses of the antecedents of the 'Burgess city' of the inter-war period are providing a new dimension to our understanding of the urban process. Michael Conzen adds to this perspective by examining the American urban system as a whole in an essay which builds upon the author's previous work in this field and traces the evolution of American cities and their connectivities through a number of distinctive phases of urban development.

Overall, this volume offers a strong statement of our continuing concern to provide a forum for the discussion of broad issues of methodological and philosophical interest and includes a number of specific themes in which examples of recent geographical research can be demonstrated. We should emphasize that our aim is to provide continuity between volumes as well as to provide unity within any one. On both of these aims we are occasionally and inevitably frustrated by the inability of invited writers to meet necessary deadlines or to deliver manuscripts of a standard we eventually find acceptable. This is part of the business of editing and a source of frustration—it can have serious effects upon the planned balance of any one volume. For the most part, however, our authors have met our deadlines and standards with good will and professional competence and we are, as always, extremely grateful to them. Our technical and secretarial back-up has been of the highest quality and our editorial board has continued to provide a source of good ideas and constructive help. We welcome ideas and offers of contributions for future volumes.

DAVID HERBERT
RON JOHNSTON

Geography and the Urban Environment
Progress in Research and Applications, Volume IV
Edited by D. T. Herbert and R. J. Johnston
© 1981 John Wiley & Sons Ltd.

Chapter 1

Philosophical Issues in the Scientific Study of Regions

J. Nicholas Entrikin

The transition between reigning orthodoxies in American geography during the 1950s and the 1960s, in which the spatial theme superceded the regional theme, has often been identified as the period of emergence of a modern social science of geography. Such a characterization has been in part due to the superficial similarities between the methods of the spatial school and those of the physical sciences, but, more importantly, it has been due to the expressed commitment by proponents of this school to the goal of a nomothetic science of geography. Although a similar commitment was expressed by the leading proponent of chorology, Richard Hartshorne (1939, 1959), the primary point of disagreement between the two perspectives concerned the study of the specific region, an essential element of Hartshorne's chorology that did not fit within the spatial school's view of nomothetic science (Sack, 1974, p. 440).

Most attempts to clarify the logical relationship between chorology and spatial analysis have been argued from a positivist (logical positivist, logical empiricist) perspective (e.g. Schaefer, 1953; Bunge, 1962; Berry, 1964; Harvey, 1969; Sack, 1974). Two interpretations have emerged from this single philosophical perspective; they diverge upon the issue of whether the idiographic aspect of Hartshorne's chorology can be regarded as compatible with the positivist conception of the 'logic of science'. The first view, expressed most clearly in the writings of Schaefer (1953) and Harvey (1969), suggests that idiographic studies are based upon intuition and are hence subjective and unscientific. The second view, developed by Sack (1974), regards such studies as compatible with an expanded conception of the logic of science. Both views are based upon arguments concerning explanatory form, and both maintain that chorology as described by Hartshorne involves a greater degree of subjective judgment than is prescribed in the positivist philosophy of science (e.g. Brodbeck, 1963; 1968; Nagel, 1961; Hempel, 1965), but they differ in their assessment of the degree of subjectivity involved in the study of the specific region.

The fact that two such interpretations have been presented is in part a function of the positivistic perspective of the interpreters, in that proponents of this ahistorical philosophy of science posit the existence of a 'logic of science' and any deviations from this logic are considered to be unscientific or to be modified versions of this logic (Keat and Urry, 1975, p. 24; see also Gale, 1972). Such 'rational reconstructions' of the history of geographical thought are evident in the positivists' interpretations of chorological explanations. Schaefer and Harvey view such explanation as intuitionist and unscientific. Sack, however, argues that chorological explanations are explanation sketches, a less complete form of the deductive nomological model (i.e. Hempel's [1965] model of scientific explanation).

The variance of opinion concerning the nature of chorological explanation and hence the logical relationship between chorology and spatial analysis can be attributed to a variety of factors. One important consideration is the difference in the goals of Hartshorne as opposed to those of his interpreters. Hartshorne states in the introduction to his *Perspective on the Nature of Geography* (1959), pp. (10–11) that:

> To eliminate any appearance of deductive reasoning from *a priori* theories concerning either geography or science, this book will proceed inductively, seeking to determine the actual character of geographic work as geographers have viewed that work.

While Hartshorne attempted to derive inductively the nature of geography, Schaefer, Harvey, and Sack began with a conception of the nature of science and discussed how geography conformed to such a view. This difference in orientation has resulted in a situation in which many of Hartshorne's arguments have been ignored or reinterpreted to fit within the concepts and categories of positivistic philosophy of science. Hartshorne's inductive approach and his general reluctance to engage in philosophical debate concerning the nature of science have had, therefore, the consequence of creating a philosophical ambiguity that makes difficult any synthesis of his ideas within a positivistic framework.

This ambiguity is further enhanced by Hartshorne's incorporation of neo-Kantian concepts and arguments (e.g. the idiographic–nomothetic distinction) into his discussions of chorology. These concepts and arguments have been significant in the positivists' analyses of Hartshorne's work and can be viewed as influential in the dual interpretation of the arguments. Neo-Kantian philosophy, similar to positivism, has had a variety of advocates and thus a variety of interpretations. It has been described as a philosophy that contains both positivist and naturalist arguments as well as anti-positivist and anti-naturalist arguments (Giedymin, 1975; Von Rintelen, 1970, pp. 1–35). Selective emphasis of either side of these dichotomies will lead to differing conceptions of the philosophy.

The confluence of the philosophical ambiguity of Hartshorne's work, the difficulties of expressing some of his ideas within a positivist framework, and his incorporation of neo-Kantian arguments are best illustrated in discussions of the critical issue of scientific significance in the study of individual regions. Hartshorne's (1959, pp. 41–47) criteria, such as 'significant to man', appear to be examples of the neo-Kantian premise of value-relevance. Harvey (1969, p. 74) rejects such criteria as unscientific and Sack (1974, p. 443) reinterprets them in stating that:

> Although his [Hartshorne's] criteria of significance for chorological synthesis are vague, a nomothetic model with its commitment to empiricism may be closer to what he intended than other well-known competing system of analysis.

Sack's interpretation has been maintained to a degree in recent comments on the relationship between chorology and spatial analysis by Guelke (1977a; 1977b; 1978) Gregory (1978). Both Guelke and Gregory suggest a revival of the study of individual regions, yet they reject Hartshorne's arguments as a basis for their perspectives in emphasizing the ahistorical, and positivistic, nature of his thought. The concern for disassociating their arguments from those of Hartshorne serves to obscure a commonality of interest that must necessarily exist in discussions of regional geography. Although the proposed regional approaches of Guelke and Gregory differ radically, and each differs from Hartshorne's chorology, all three individuals must address questions concerning criteria of significance, objectivity and other related issues. Each in varying degrees rejects the positivistic basis of significance in minimizing the importance of empirical laws and theories and emphasizes, instead, the importance of human values and interests. Such criteria provide the basis for claims concerning objectivity.

In the sections that follow I will identify some of the neo-Kantian arguments found in Hartshorne's work and discuss the interpretations of these arguments by Schaefer, Harvey, and Sack. I will argue that Hartshorne's inductive approach to studying the nature of geography and the philosophical ambiguity that necessarily results from such an approach precludes the neat categorization of chorology within a positivist or neo-Kantian framework. And, finally, I will illustrate how recent discussions of regional geography once again raise issues that were critical to the debate concerning chorology and spatial analysis.

CHOROLOGY AND NEO-KANTIAN PHILOSOPHY

To argue that Hartshorne's chorology represents a neo-Kantian approach to the study of geography would be an oversimplification of the complexity of his thought as well as a contradiction of Hartshorne's own conception of his work. It is possible, however, to recognize neo-Kantian arguments within his writing, especially when he discusses topics such as the relationship between the sciences and the justification for the study of the unique. Both these topics bear upon the question of explanation in geography. I will introduce briefly Hartshorne's comments on regional geography and then provide a general overview of neo-Kantianism, in order to provide a context for understanding the divergent interpretations of chorology.

According to Hartshorne (1959, p. 21), geography as the study of areal differentiation is to be 'concerned to provide accurate, orderly, and rational description and interpretation of the variable character of the earth surface'. Although he is reluctant to discuss the nature of science, Hartshorne (1959, pp. 146–172) establishes some minimum criteria for a scientific enterprise which include (1) a commitment to empirical observation, (2) objectivity, (3) a concern for universality and thus the development of generic principles, and (4) a concern for the systematic ordering of what is known. Adherence to such criteria would lead to the goal of 'reliable knowledge of reality' (Hartshorne, 1959, p. 169). He concedes that if science were defined strictly in terms of the development of causal laws and theories, not all of geographic research would qualify as scientific, yet it is evident that he, himself, does not accept such a definition (Hartshorne, 1939, p. 449). Geography as the study of areal differentiation and areal integration provides a type of knowledge that is similar to that provided by other sciences and is not equivalent to the types of knowledge associated with common sense, intuition or art (Hartshorne, 1959, pp. 169–70).

As a chorological science, geography is somewhat different from the systematic sciences, such as physics and chemistry, and from chronological sciences, such as history. A chorological science seeks to integrate spatially a wide variety of phenomena and interrelationships between and among phenomena, as opposed to chronological sciences which integrate phenomena over time, and to systematic sciences which concentrate upon developing causal laws representing relationships between classes of phenomena. Such a division is ideal, however, for Hartshorne realized that no science could neglect completely space, time, and causal laws. The division is nonetheless useful in representing differing emphases of the various types of sciences. Among the chorological sciences, geography is distinct in terms of its emphasis upon the study of 'the earth surface, differentiated from place to place by interrelated elements significant to man, . . .' (Hartshorne, 1959, p. 182).

According to Hartshorne, the discipline of geography consists of a systematic and a regional branch, both of which are important for chorological studies. This division does not correspond to an idiographic—nomothetic distinction, however, in that both types of concept formation could be found in each. For example, regional studies could emphasize generic regions (regions of a certain classificatory type) or specific regions (regions based upon an integration of phenomena and their interrelationships as they actually exist in a place). The former emphasizes those aspects common to two or more areas while the latter emphasizes the unique aspects of an area. As Sack (1974, p. 440) notes:

> Although Hartshorne discussed several meanings of regions and how they have been used in the discipline, it is the specific or unique region that is central and indispensible to the chorological view and about which most controversy ensued. The major difficulty arose from discussing in general, methodological terms, what was conceived of as unique.

It is this controversial concept of the specific region that is the center of most of the arguments concerning chorological explanation and thus needs further elaboration.

The regions discussed by geographers are not phenomena, but rather they are constructions, mental entities. Hartshorne (1939, p. 395) states that:

> The area itself is not a phenomenon, any more than a period of history is a phenomenon; it is only an intellectual framework of phenomena, an abstract concept which does not exist in reality.

He also states that:

> In order to cover the world, therefore, we recognize as unit areas—'regions' in the general sense—pieces of area that are distinctive in varying respects. These regions are neither separate from each other, like the heavenly bodies, nor are they even rough approximations of clearly different total complexes, merging only by gradual transition into each other like the colors of the rainbow. For in any one of them important features may be more closely interrelated with the total complex of a neighboring unit area than with that of the area in which they are included. In other words, these unit areas are neither objects nor phenomena but rather creations of the student's mind. Hence, any system of classification and hypotheses based upon them are dependent not on reality but on what is in the student's mind. (Hartshorne, 1959, pp. 159–160)

Regions are thus constructed and can take distinct forms depending upon the dominant mode of concept formation. The generic region has been relatively uncontroversial in that it corresponds with the positivist views on classification, but the specific region, often referred to as the basis of the 'exceptionalist thesis', has been the centre of the controversy surrounding Hartshorne's arguments. Two important elements of this controversy have concerned scientific significance and cause, and thus I will present Hartshorne's ideas on these topics.

The question of scientific significance is linked with the related issue of appropriate criteria of selection. If the goal of a study is the comprehension of the individual case, such analysis precludes complete dependence upon causal laws and theories which elaborate relationships between general concepts. Indeed, one of the positivist criteria for judging a concept scientifically significant is that it must be related in the form of law-like generalizations with other concepts (Brodbeck, 1963, p. 59; 1968, pp. 6–9). By definition, an idiographic approach does not satisfy this criterion. Hartshorne addresses this issue in a neo-Kantian fashion in that significance is stated in terms of values. For example, the choice of an area for study should depend upon such values. He states that:

> If, however, the ultimate purpose is simply to provide maximum knowledge concerning an individual case, the validity of choice of area on which to expend valuable research time and publication facility will depend on the degree of human interest or need for knowledge of that particular area among the innumerable available areas of the world. (Hartshorne, 1959, p. 164)

Other statements by Hartshorne (1939, pp. 242, 475; 1959, pp. 41–47, 89) suggest the same general theme of significance to man, as well as a more specific theme of geographical significance or significance for areal differentiation of the world.

Hartshorne comments briefly on the meaning of significance to man, but he is quite specific in his discussion of geographical significance. In quoting from Hettner's work, Hartshorne (1939, p. 240) presents two conditions that phenomena must satisfy to be geographically significant:

> One condition . . . is the difference from place to place together with the spatial association of things situated beside each other, the presence of geographical complexes or systems—for example, the drainage system, the system of atmospherical circulation, the trade areas and others. No phenomenon of the earth's surface is to be thought of for itself; it is understandable only through the conception of its location in relation to other places on the earth. The second condition is the causal connection between the different realms of nature and their different phenomena united at one place. Phenomena which lack such a connection with the other phenomena of the same place, or whose connection we do not recognize, do not belong in geographical study. Qualified and needed for such a study are the facts of the earth's surfaces which are locally different and whose local differences are significant for other kinds of phenomena, or, as it has been put, are geographically efficacious.

Thus, phenomena not only must be spatially connected to be geographical significant, but also they must be causally connected. Such a connection is between phenomena, however, and is distinct from a causal connection between classes of phenomena, usually referred to as a causal law. Hartshorne (1959, pp. 18–19) noted that:

The connections or causal relationships among the phenomena of geography, as Hettner noted in 1905, are of two kinds: The mutual relationships among different phenomena at one place, and relationships or connections between phenomena at different places.

For Hartshorne (1959, pp. 146–72), the causal connection of importance to geographers is that existing between phenomena, and while causal laws are important in geography, the nature of the subject matter of the field often makes their formulation difficult.

Hartshorne's discussion of idiographic and nomothetic concept formation, and of significance and causality resemble in part discussions by the neo-Kantians, especially those of Heinrich Rickert. This similarity is not surprising in that Hartshorne refers to both Windelband and Rickert in his work, yet such references are usually tempered by an attempt to distinguish his own ideas from those of the two philosophers (Hartshorne, 1939, p. 379; 1955, p. 231n; 1959, p. 149; 1972, p. 78). All such references refer to the division of science into idiographic and nomothetic branches. Hartshorne argues that the neo-Kantians classify sciences as being either idiographic or nomothetic, but he maintains that geographers employ both types of approaches. Although one could gain this impression of a clear separation of the sciences in reading Windelband's (1907) address of 1894, both he and Rickert state that in actuality sciences use both types of concept formation, a view which corresponds with Hartshorne's conception of geography. (Windelband, 1961, p. 57; Rickert, 1962, pp. xi–xix)

According to Rickert, the two different types of concept formation derive from distinct goals of scientists studying the same reality. Rickert (1962, pp. 56–57) states that:

> With the object of making clear and explicit two purely logical, and hence purely formal, concepts of nature and history—by which I mean not two different domains of reality, but the same reality seen from two different points of view—I myself have attempted to formulate the fundamental logical problem of classifying the sciences according to their methods in the following way: Empirical reality becomes nature when we view it with respect to its universal characteristics; it becomes history when we view it as particular and individual.

Neither type of concept merely copies reality, both are constructions, yet each is constructed in accordance with different goals. Associated with these differing goals are two distinct criteria of selection. In the nomothetic view those aspects of phenomena which are common to more than one phenomenon are emphasized, and individual differences are considered as being unimportant. The goal of idiographic studies is the opposite in that the scientist considers the individual aspects of phenomena as essential. Both types of concept formation are found in all the sciences, but it is the nomothetic approach that has led to the development of laws in the natural sciences (Rickert, 1962, pp. 10–61).

Within each approach, concepts are formed through a process of abstraction. In the generalizing method, empirical reality its divided into general 'classes' of phenomena and relations between phenomena. The distinction between scientific concepts and everyday speech concepts is that the goal of scientific concepts is to 'completely overcome the infinite multiplicity of an unlimited universe of concrete facts' (Burger, 1976, p. 25). In overcoming this multiplicity, scientific concepts must be highly general, yet precise, systems of statements identifying the elements and their relationships which constitute the concept. This system of statements, known as the definition of a concept, replaces the ambiguous images which are usually associated with prescientific concepts. These general concepts are phrased in terms that make their scope infinite, despite the fact that they are based upon a finite number of observations. They are thus equivalent to laws of nature. Burger (1976, p. 32) states that:

> Accordingly, Rickert can say: 'The concept of gravity and the law of gravity are just completely identical . . . as far as the content of theoretical knowledge is concerned . . .'. The problem is of course, that general concepts are always formed on the basis of an analysis of only a limited amount of empirical cases. This means that scientists can never be certain that their definitions definitely assert laws of nature. Their generalizations hold for whatever empirical facts they know, i.e., they are 'empirically general'. They cannot be sure, however, whether or not there are some as yet undiscovered instances (like the famous black swans) which cannot be subsumed under the concept without modifying it. That is, they cannot be sure that the existing generalizations are absolutely universal. Now it is obvious that on the basis of empirical knowledge, i.e., within empirical science, there is no way of making the distinction between the empirical and the absolute validity of a general concept, since the latter cannot be known. Empirically general concepts, therefore—whether they describe things or relations of cause and effect—are treated by scientists just as if they were absolutely valid laws of nature.

The other type of concept formation involves an individualizing method which attempts to capture the unique aspects of each phenomenon. Such uniqueness is captured through a process of abstraction similar to that used in the formation of general concepts, but unlike the nomothetic method, the idiographic method chooses to emphasize the aspect of a phenomenon considered to be essential to its individuality. Such an approach attempts to capture the concreteness of a phenomenon, but can never actually achieve such a goal in that knowledge, according to Rickert, can never merely copy an existing reality (Rickert, 1962, p. 30–39).

The immediate problem facing a scientist emphasizing the individual case concerns the objective significance of such knowledge. Significance in the nomothetic sciences is derived from the laws of nature which are developed in these sciences. No such laws are possible for the scientist interested in the unique aspects of culture. According to Rickert (1962, pp. 97–103; Von Rintelen, 1970, pp. 24–28) cultural scientists overcome this problem by selecting phenomena for study which embody general cultural values. For example, the principle of selection in history is that of 'value relevance', which is described by Burger (1976, p. 39; see also Hindess, 1977, pp. 31–34; Rickert, 1962, p. 19) as follows:

> ... its application [the principle of value relevance] results in a selection of those parts of empirical reality which for human observers embody one or several of those general cultural values which are held by people in the society in which the scientific observers live. For the embodiment of these values in those cultural products around whose creation collective life centers—like law, religion, and kinship—has existential significance for everybody living in the society, including the scientific observer. Such phenomena are 'value relevant', or 'culturally significant'.

Rickert (1962, pp. 135–45) acknowledges that values vary among cultures and among different historical periods, but he attempts to avoid relativism in positing transcendental set of universally valid values. Rickert (Burger, 1976, pp. 41–42) states that:

> It is, therefore, not sufficient to exclude the purely individual values and to designate those values as the guiding principles of a historical description which are shared by all members of a particular community. Rather, if history is to compete with the kind of universal validity which natural science claims when it establishes laws of nature, we have to assume that certain values are not only factually valid for all members of certain communities, but that the recognition of values universally can be demanded as necessary and inevitable from every scientific investigator.

Such a set of values allegedly gives to historical knowledge the objectivity and validity that natural laws give to natural science. Both types of concepts consist of abstractions and hence generalizations, yet the aim of the individualizing method is to use general concepts to capture the uniqueness of a phenomenon or of relationships among phenomena.

Similarly, both types of concept formation involve the notion of cause, but in two different senses. Rickert argues that the historian must take into account the fact that all phenomena are caused and, in turn, are causes. He differentiates the above notion, the principle of causality, from causal laws, however (Burger,

1976, pp. 20–21; Rickert, 1962, p. 94). Although the historian must consider causal relationships between phenomena, it is not his role to develop causal laws as the natural scientist does. Such causal laws would be logically impossible due to the individualizing concept formation employed by the historian.

These brief synopses of Hartshorne's chorology and of Rickert's neo-Kantian arguments should illustrate certain similarities between the two viewpoints. These similarities can be listed as follows: (1) that two ideal types of concept formation exist, nomothetic and idiographic, and that all sciences employ both to varying degrees; (2) that the idiographic approach is a means of obtaining objective knowledge of the world that is different from artistic knowing, intuition and common sense; (3) that the basis of this objectivity is found in values which determine criteria of significance and selection; and (4) that although scientists using an idiographic approach do not develop causal laws, they are nonetheless concerned with causal relations between phenomena. In isolating these similarites, I do not intend to suggest an isomorphism between Rickert's philosophy and Hartshorne's discussion of geography. The views of these two individuals diverge on many different subjects. For example, Hartshorne does not suggest that the values which determine the criteria of significance are transcendental nor does he accept an a priori classification of the sciences. While many differences exist, the specification of common elements is essential for clarifying the nature of chorology.

CHOROLOGY AS UNDERSTANDING

Questions concerning subjectivity in regional studies have been raised through-out the history of the discipline of geography, but they take on an added significance when combined with the positivists' conception of an appropriate scientific explanation. The positivists' conception of the 'unity of science' implies that there is one method of science. This conception has been extended to suggest that there is one ideal form of scientific explanation, the deductive nomological, and that other types of explanation are either unscientific or variants of this form. The argument that chorological explanation is unscientific and best understood as a form understanding based upon intuition rather than as a form of explanation is presented most clearly in two important discussions of a positivist geography of spatial organization, Schaefer's (1953) article 'Exceptionalism in geography: A methodological examination', and Harvey's (1969) book *Explanation in Geography*. Both attack the neo-Kantian aspects of Hartshorne's chorology, yet in their final analysis both present a somewhat misleading conclusion that Hartshorne's chorology is similar to, or based upon, Dilthey's idea of 'understanding'.

Schaefer condemned Hartshorne's chorology for its emphasis upon idiographic concept formation and its de-emphasis of the importance of laws in scientific explanation. According to Schaefer, this 'exceptionalist' position had its roots in the Kantian view of geography as perpetuated by Hettner and Hartshorne. Schaefer (1953, pp. 235–36) interprets this position in stating that:

> Both history and geography are essentially chorological. History arranges phenomena in time, geography in space. Both, in contrast to other disciplines, integrate phenomena heterogeneous among themselves. Also, these phenomena are unique. No historical event and historical period is like any other. In geography no two phenomena and no two regions are alike. Thus both fields face the task of explaining the unique. Such explanation is, therefore, unlike all scientific explanation which 'explains' by subsumption under laws. But there are no laws for the unique; little use, then, in looking for historical or geographical laws or prediction. The best one can hope for is, in Dilthey's fashion, some sort of 'understanding' or, more frankly, empathetic understanding.

Although Schaefer is referring to Hettner's arguments in the above quote, he attributes the same 'anti-scientific bias' to Hartshorne when he refers to Hartshorne's historicist roots and states that:

> The argument for the uniqueness of the geographical material stems both logically and historically from historicism. The main protagonist of this line of thought in America is Hartshorne. So it is easily understood why he makes so much of the old Kantian parallelism between history and geography. If history, according to the historicist, deals with unique events and if geography is like history, then geography, too, deals with the unique and must try to 'understand' rather than search for laws. (Schaefer, 1953, p. 238)

The view that chorology is unscientific because of its reliance upon the subjective judgements implied by 'understanding' has been further elaborated by Harvey. He argues that the following inferences are usually drawn from what he refers to as 'Kantian view' of the sciences:

(i) If geography is to treat of the sum of our perceptions in space then there can be no limit placed on the class of objects which geography studies.

(ii) If there is no limit to the factual content of geography then the discipline must be defined by its distinctive method of approach rather than in terms of its subject-matter. Thus, geography is frequently characterized as a 'point of view' rather than a subject which deals with a characteristic subject-matter.

(iii) If we are concerned with the sum total of reality in all its aspects as we perceive it in terms of spatial location, then it follows that we are essentially concerned with unique collections of events or objects, rather than with developing generalizations about classes of events. Locations, it was argued, are unique.

(iv) If locations are unique, then the description and interpretation of what existed at those unique locations could not be accomplished by referring to general laws. It required, rather, understanding in the sense of empathy or 'verstehen', i.e. the employment of the idiographic method. (Harvey, 1969, pp. 70–71)

Thus, both Schaefer and Harvey dismiss chorology as unscientific due to its emphasis on the unique. This unscientific character is associated with the subjectivism which Harvey attributes to the lack of a scientific criterion of significance. Harvey (1969, p. 74) states that:

In practice geographers do not study everything in spatial context, but limit consideration to a selection of phenomena. The question arises as to the grounds of this selection. Hartshorne examines this bothersome problem but the only criterion of significance he could establish was that the phenomena should be 'significant to man'. This criterion can be applied to all knowledge, however, and without further refinement it remains empty of any meaning.

Harvey (1969, p. 75) provides an alternative when he states that the 'problem of significance as defined by Hartshorne has no solution independent of geographic theory'. Such theory 'invests objects and events with significance, it defines the framework (e.g. the coordinate system) into which events and objects may be fitted, and it provides systematic general statements which may be employed in explaining, understanding, describing, and interpreting, events'. (Harvey, 1969, pp. 74–75)

Both Schaefer (1953, pp. 235–36) and Harvey (1969, p. 64) thus relegate chorology to the status of a hermeneutic discipline, interested in understanding and interpretation. This characterization is further reinforced by their association of the ideas of Wilhelm Dilthey with chorology. Dilthey, a philosopher often associated with hermeneutics, shared with Windelband and Rickert a concern for establishing the epistemological basis of the human sciences. He was often, however, in fundamental disagreement with the neo-Kantians (Hodges, 1952; Makkreel, 1975). One area of disagreement concerned the status of empathetic understanding in human science and another concerned the relationship of history and art. For Dilthey, understanding through re-experiencing is fundamental to knowing the past, and artistic understanding is never rigidly separated from the type of understanding employed in history (Makkreel, 1975). For Rickert, however, and similarly for his student Max Weber, understanding is important for gaining ideas for study, yet it is not a process of abstraction, and hence not a means of idiographic concept formation (Burger, 1976, p. 109). Also, Rickert is emphatic in his separation of artistic knowing from historical knowing (Rickert, 1962, pp. 73–79, 112).

Hartshorne's arguments concerning these two issues resemble those of Rickert in that Hartshorne rejects empathetic understanding as a means of doing chorology and is careful to distinguish geographical understanding from artistic understanding, common sense or intuition. Although Hartshorne (1939, pp. 132–33; 1959, pp. 167–72) notes problems of subjective and arbitrary judgment by geographers, he is clear in his belief in chorology as providing objective knowledge of reality. He states that: 'Effective description in geography therefore involves no small degree of art, not in the sense of subjective impressions, but in the objective sense of discernment and insight based on knowledge of those relationship that can be known' (Hartshorne's 1959, pp. 171–2). Such a view would not constitute an art of geography.

Schaefer and Harvey also note Hartshorne's link to Rickert and Windelband, but their emphasis is upon intuition and hence subjective interpretation and understanding in chorology. They mention Hartshorne's discussion of the nomothetic, but they emphasize the idiographic. Thus, in attacking chorology as unscientific they characterize it as a hermeneutic science. In doing so, however, they go considerably beyond Hartshorne's arguments.

CHOROLOGY AS EXPLANATION SKETCH

Harvey (1969, p. 75) concludes part of his discussion of explanation in geography by suggesting that possibly 'explanation sketches' provided a middle ground between the rigorous deductive nomological of the positivist approach and the empathetic understanding of the chorologists' idiographic approach. Sack, however, develops the thesis that the explanatory form of chorology is best represented by such explanation sketches. His argument, still positivistic in orientation, takes a more conciliatory view of the relationship between chorology and spatial analysis. He states that:

Examination of the development of the two positions [chorology and spatial analysis] and elimination of their more fanciful claims reveals a common commitment to empiricism and a shared interest in the physical geometric relationships of facts. (Sack, 1974, p. 439)

In commenting on the types of explanations offered in the two approaches, he states that:

A balanced synthesis should result when the spatial and the chorological schools are seen as two foci of a scale of nomothetic completeness in discourses which concern the geometric connections between facts. (Sack, 1974, p. 440)

Sack is correct in identifying this common emphasis upon empiricism and spatial connectivity of facts, but other aspects of Hartshorne's chorology do not fit neatly into the framework of an explanation sketch. To make chorology fit such a mould, it is necessary for Sack to reinterpret Hartshorne's arguments concerning significance, causality and uniqueness into terms more acceptable to positivist philosophy of science.

The importance of the question of significance in Sack's synthesis is indicated in his statement that:

> If there were a middle ground between hypothesis testing and an abandonment of scientific criteria of significance, there might be a way of formulating the specific region without unnecessarily polarizing the discipline with incommensurable methodologies. (Sack, 1974, p. 448)

Such a middle ground is found in the idea of explanatory incompleteness and more generally in the idea of disciplinary 'immaturity'. Sack recognizes that generalizations concerning the relationships between phenomena are not always available, and thus one must relax the positivists' concept of significance in order to gain an understanding of complex interrelationships between phenomena. He recognizes Hartshorne's distinct criteria in stating that:

> As though to assure that the analysis will not step back into the realm of the nomothetic in the form of hypotheses testing and correcting and thus delimit a place of a general kind, Hartshorne stated throughout that the criteria of significance in geography is not equivalent to the notion of scientifically connected concepts, but is suggested rather by expressions such as significant to areal differentiation and integration, and significant to man. (Sack, 1974, p. 443)

But such criteria have no place within a positivist philosophy of science and thus Sack (1974, p. 443) concludes that:

> Although his criteria of significance for chorological synthesis are vague, a nomothetic model with its commitment to empiricism may be closer to what he intended than other well-known competing systems of analysis [art and metaphysical holism].

While it is true that Hartshorne's criteria are vague, they are nonetheless in keeping with the neo-Kantian arguments concerning value relevance.

Associated with the issue of significance is that of causality. Sack (1974, p. 443) recognizes that Hartshorne's discussion of cause and causal relations does not seem to be equivalent to the concept of cause in scientific laws. This lack of equivalence is due to the difference between the principle of causality and causal laws. As previously noted, one criterion of selection discussed by both Hettner and Hartshorne is that phenomena should be causally connected with one another. This principle of causality does not serve as a criterion of significance or selection within positivist discussions of explanation and thus is not a part of discussion of chorological explanation as explanation sketches. Rather, the role of chorology in discovering spatial linkage between facts is emphasized, and presented as a partial step toward the formation of laws.

The final translation of Hartshorne's chorology into terms more acceptable to positivism can be seen in Sack's discussion of the concept of uniqueness. Hartshorne appears to claim that not only does the complexity of areal integrations make the restatement of these integrations in terms of scientific laws in fact unlikely, but also that such a goal may in principle be impossible. He states that:

> Through genetic study of the development of the particular complex, or through comparative study of the few areas of similar character, we may be able to suggest possible hypotheses, but the description of what is involved in the complexity of the individual case can only be the subject of an individual study, for which general principles, beyond a certain point, *will never* be available. (Hartshorne, 1959, p. 164) [my emphasis]

One can view the relationship of idiographic and nomothetic approaches as ends of a continuum, if it is accepted that idiographic studies gradually give way to nomothetic studies as more knowledge is gained, i.e., as one approaches the goal of 'explanatory completeness'. Such a continuum is broken, however, when it is recognized that the idiographic and nomothetic approaches are defined as two distinct modes of concept formation. Rickert argues that the division of the two orientations is based upon the goals of the researcher, and illustrates this point with reference to geography (Rickert, 1962, p. 131). Hartshorne (1959, p. 164) similarly argues that:

> Whatever degree of integration one studies—from topical to regional—it is pertinent for a student to have in mind from the start whether his purpose is primarily to develop generic conclusions or to examine an individual case.

Such a division does not prohibit the use of generic concepts in individual studies, but it does suggest a greater distinctiveness between the nomothetic and idiographic approaches than can be explained in terms of the stage of development of the human sciences.

Sack is correct in recognizing many of the similarities between chorology and spatial analysis, especially their commitments to empirical science and the importance of the geometric connectivity of facts. The differences of the philosophical context of the two viewpoints make difficult, however, attempts at synthesis based upon explanatory form. In order to view chorology and spatial analysis as two points along a continuum of explanatory completeness, it is necessary to both emphasize the positivistic and naturalistic aspects of Hartshorne's arguments, and to ignore or retranslate arguments that contradict these two philosophical positions. In doing so, however, some of the distinctive aspects of Hartshorne's chorology are lost.

CONTEMPORARY ARGUMENTS CONCERNING REGIONAL GEOGRAPHY

The primary issues in the positivists' interpretations of the relationship between chorology and spatial analysis are fundamental to all discussions of the nature of human science, and thus they have remained prominent in contemporary debate concerning human geography. Questions of scientific significance, validity, objectivity, the role of values, and of empirical laws and theories in geographic research are subjects of continuing controversy, but the tone of the present debate differs from that of the 1950s, 1960s and early 1970s debates in that it is predominantly anti-positivist and anti-naturalist (e.g. see Lay and Samuels, 1978; Gregory, 1978; Gale and Olsson, 1979; Johnston, 1980; pp. 112–189). Similar controversies can be found throughout the social sciences, and although the attacks upon positivism vary from ethical criticisms to logical criticisms, two of the most common are the related issue of: (1) the gap between the expectations of a positivist science of human activity and the results of such a science; and (2) the problem of the 'reflexive', or self-conscious, nature of human action that inhibits the development of empirical laws and theories.

The first issue is best expressed by Bernstein (1976, pp. 227–28) in his analysis of political and social theory. He states that:

It has been projected that the social sciences, as they mature, will discover well-tested bodies of empirical theory which will eventually coalesce in ever more adequate and comprehensive theories. Yet if we judge the results to date of the endeavor to discover such theories, there is no hard evidence that this expectation is being fulfilled. . .
The rationalizations for this disparity between expectation and fulfilment, which play on metaphors of the 'youth', 'immaturity', 'preparadigmatic', and 'paradigmatic' stages of scientific inquiry, have become thin and unconvincing. These rationalizations move in a closed circle. They presuppose what ought to be at issue: whether we have good reason to think that social and political inquiry should follow the development of the natural sciences.

One contributing element in the creation of this gap is the difficulty of establishing laws of human action. For example, Giddens (1977, p. 88) argues that one of the difficulties associated with generalizations in the human sciences is that they are inevitably 'unstable in relation to their subject matter'. Such instability is the direct result of the self-conscious and purposeful nature, or reflexivity of, human activity. In the human sciences reflexivity has a dual aspect in that the scientist attempts to understand the reflexive nature of human activity, as well as recognize that science, as a form of human activity, must itself be reflexive.

Although the number of new perspectives suggested for human geography are in Johnston's (1979, p. 189) terms 'branching toward anarchy', the inappropriateness of empirical laws and theories as goals of human geographers and the need for developing a reflexive human geography are two common themes. For example, in their book on *Humanistic Geography*, Ley and Samuels (1978, pp. 19–20) suggest some of the issues involved in a fully reflexive science in arguing that:

> Reflexivity . . . means that all our cognitive categories are relative. But how relative? and relative to what?
> It goes almost without saying that therein lies the central issue for an understanding of anything known to man and especially for an understanding of the human—our own—condition. To what are our cognitive categories relative? On what empirical grounds and by what criteria are our conceptions, perceptions, ideas, statements, propositions, arguments, or, simply, our notions about the human condition (or anything else) to be judged correct, valid, reasonable, credible, and acceptable? How are these grounds and criteria established? From what do they derive?

They also suggest a direction for addressing such issues when they state that:

> . . . at an epistemological level, a humanistic geography is concerned to restore and make explicit the relation between knowledge and human interests . All social constructions, be they cities or geographic knowledge, reflect the values of a society and an epoch, so that humanistic philosophies reject out of hand any false claim to objectivity and pure theory in the study of man. Such claims, most notably those of contemporary positivism, negate themselves through their lack of reflexivity, their unself-conscious espousal of value positions. (Ley and Samuels, 1978, p. 21)

Among the critics of a positivist and naturalist human geography, who, along with Ley and Samuels, argue for a reflexive human geography are two historical geographers, Guelke (1971; 1977a; 1977b; 1978; 1979) and Gregory (1978). Although their perspectives differ radically, Guelke and Gregory call for the study of historically specific regions, and in presenting their justifications for such studies provide arguments different from the regionalization as classification arguments that have dominated theoretical discussions of regions over the last two decades. Similar to Hartshorne, each briefly addresses the issue of the scientific significance and the objectivity of such knowledge, and each returns to arguments using concepts of human cognitive interests and values. Despite this similarity, both Guelke and Gregory reject Hartshorne as an intellectual ancestor for their regional perspectives, in part because of his alleged positivist orientation.

Gregory sees a close relationship between the chorological approach of Hartshorne and the spatial approach of his positivist critic Schaefer. Gregory (1978, p. 31) states that:

> ... although Bunge described the academic dispute between them [Hartshorne and Schaefer] as 'an argument between Michelson and Newton, or Hegel and Feuerbach'. It is extremely difficult to reconcile this with the emphasis of both models on the geometry of the landscape and their common exclusion of any conception of process from geographical inquiry.

He concludes that the major difference between the two viewpoints appears to be one of ends (specific regions versus morphological laws) rather than means. This conclusion, however, neglects some of the neo-Kantian themes found in Hartshorne's arguments concerning concept formation and criteria of selection that would appear to distinguish a part of the 'means' suggested by Hartshorne from those of Schaefer.

Guelke (1977b, p. 376) reaches similar conclusions, but states them in greater detail. He argues that:

> If one seeks to understand recent developments in geography one must begin with an examination of *The Nature of Geography*. Most subsequent developments, I argue, were not revolutionary, but involved the logical extension of key ideas to be found in that book.

One such 'key idea' was that of the nature of scientific explanation. According to Guelke (1977b, p. 377):

> Although he [Hartshorne] refused to define 'science', he adopted an essentially conventional or logical positivist view of what constituted a scientific explanation.

The basis for Guelke's (1978, p. 42) claims are presented as follows:

> Hartshorne insisted on the unity of physical and human geography and implicitly accepted the basic deductive—nomological model of explanation. He was of the opinion that observation and classification were necessary first stepts in the formulation of geographic laws and theories. All these ideas accorded well with the basic positions of logical positivism.

The main point of divergence between Hartshorne's arguments and logical positivist ideas concerns his 'concessions' to the idealist writings of philosophers 'such as Dilthey and Rickert' (Guelke, 1978, p. 42). Such concessions were related to the division of science into idiographic and nomothetic branches, and were necessary, according to Guelke (1978, p. 42), in order for Hartshorne to account for the actual practice of geography in which few laws had been developed. Guelke (1978, p. 42) states that:

This kind of distinction [idiographic–nomothetic] was completely alien to logical positivists, who insisted that science was indivisible. Neither was this position in accord with Hartshorne's own view that geographers needed laws in their explanations. The use of the nomothetic—idiographic distinction appears to have been an attempt to explain the paucity of laws in both human and physical geography. Yet precisely because Hartshorne accepted the deductive–nomological model of explanation his position on uniqueness was a major barrier in the way of scientific explanations,

Guelke's interpretation of Hartshorne allows him to suggest that:

Schaefer's paper is seen by many as a forceful attack on Hartshorne, as indeed it was, but the two men were closer together on philosophical issues than might at first be imagined. Schaefer, like Hartshorne, accepted the deductive–nomological model of explanation, the unity of science, and most elements of logical positivism, although he has little to say on issues relating to verification. (Guelke, 1978, p. 43)

Although Guelke is correct in suggesting that there are important similarities between views of Hartshorne and Schaefer, his interpretation of the nature of chorology is misleading. His extreme interpretation appears to be a result of his failure to recognize the range of neo-Kantian arguments found in Hartshorne's work, and of his impressionistic accounts of the logical positivism implicit in Hartshorne's views. The first failure is illustrated by Guelke's (1978, p. 42) argument that Hartshorne's 'concession' to Rickert's discussion of the idiographic–nomothetic distinction was necessary in order for Hartshorne to explain the lack of laws in geography, but that it was an appendage, inconsistent with the body of his thought. No evidence appears to exist, however, suggesting that the distinction serves as merely an *ex post facto* rationalization and appendage. Rather, as has been argued in the previous sections of this paper, Hartshorne's discussion of idiographic and nomothetic science is quite consistent with many of his other arguments on the nature of geography.

The impressionisitic nature of some of Guelke's interpretations can be illustrated through several examples drawn from the most recent of his three works cited above. Guelke (1978, p. 42) argues that Hartshorne considered observation and classification to be the first steps toward the formulation of scientific laws and theories, and that such a view is in accord with the logical positivist philosophy of science. Yet one of the positivists noted by Guelke, C. G. Hempel (1966, p. 11), states that such a view of science is 'untenable'. On the same page, Guelke (1978, p. 42) refers to Hartshorne's alleged view that geographers 'needed laws in their explanations'. While Hartshorne (1939, pp. 366–97; 1959, pp. 146–72) recognizes the importance of laws in scientific research, it is incorrect to imply necessity from his statements. A final example is Guelke's (1978, p. 42) claim that Hartshorne 'implicitly accepted' or 'accepted' the deductive nomological form of explanation. Such an assertion, juxtaposed with Hartshorne's alleged belief in the necessity of laws for explanation, seems less defensible than arguments that link chorology to explanation sketches. These and other statements by Guelke represent minor overstatements individually, but taken as a whole they serve to illustrate his exaggeration of the importance of logical positivist ideas in Hartshorne's formulation the nature of geography.

The emphasis by both Guelke and Gregory on the positivistic aspects of Hartshorne's arguments, and their relative neglect of the nonpositivistic aspects, obscures certain common concerns in their suggestions for a regional approach. Although Hartshorne, Guelke, and Gregory express quite disparate goals, philosophies, and considerations as to the essential elements of a successful regional approach, each has acknowledged the importance of studying specific regions. This quite general similarity of interest creates as a common foe positivist philosophers and geographers who have argued that the essence of scientific activity is the ability to explain and predict, that such explanations involve laws, that the significance and validity of scientific concepts derives from their connection with other concepts in the form of laws, and that the abandonment of this criterion of significance would necessarily involve a subjectivism and a relativism that would be incompatible with the ideals of science (Brodbeck, 1963, 1968; Nagel, 1962; Hempel, 1964; Schaefer, 1953; Harvey, 1969).

Opposition to this position by Hartshorne, Guelke and Gregory has been centred upon two related arguments, (1) an 'expansion' of the meaning of science and (2) an adoption of criteria of significance for objective studies of the individual case. I will briefly discuss Hartshorne's views on these two issues and compare them with the views of Guelke and Gregory. Such a comparison will illustrate that Guelke's idealist position more closely resembles Schaefer's (1953) description of an 'exceptionalist' view of geography than does Hartshorne's chorology. Both, however, present similar types of arguments concerning the scientific nature of geography, and the criteria of significance involved in the objective study of the individual case. Gregory's views on these topics diverge from those of the other two, however, due to his incorporation of the philosophical anthropology of Jurgen Habermas (1971; 1973; 1975). Despite the fact that he too adopts a broad conception of science and bases validity and objectivity upon human interests and values, Gregory's adoption of a framework that places science within a social theory significantly alters the meaning of these terms.

As noted previously, Hartshorne (1959, pp. 167–72) attempted to avoid entering into a debate on the nature of science and the application of the term 'science' to the study of geography. Although he reasons that no logical argument precludes a definition of science as the search for general laws, he implies that such a definition would be overly restrictive. If this definition were strictly applied, research that was not law seeking in both the human sciences as well as the natural sciences would be in the awkward position of having 'no positive definition, no rules or standards of study to distinguish it from such forms of knowledge as intuition, common sense, artistic perception, or personal judgment' (Hartshorne, 1959, p. 169). To avoid such a situation, Hartshorne (1959, pp. 169–70) suggests an 'empirical' definition of science, that is, one that accepts as scientific those disciplines which have traditionally been called sciences, those disciplines that have sought to 'establish reliable knowledge of reality'.

According to Hartshorne, the nature of geography's subject matter requires that geographers employ both a nomothetic and an idiographic approach, and while the criteria of significance of the former are tied to the development of laws, those of the latter are based upon values. Although the criteria of significance discussed by Hartshorne are in accord with the general outline of Rickert's philosophy, the transcendental status of such values would seem to be in conflict with the empirical nature of Hartshorne's arguments. A more compatible discussion of value-relevance can be found, however, in the arguments of Rickert's student, Max Weber. Weber (1949, p. 81) suggests that discussions of cultural reality are always tied to 'particular points of view'. According to Goddard (1973, p. 12), Weber eschews the transcendental ego of Kant, and replaces it with:

... an active, but also necessarily evaluating, empirical ego (qua social scientist) which synthesizes or unifies historical data according to their significance from a certain point of view, and in doing so, imparts to them a form of objectivity. And those 'points of view' have their roots in specific cultural milieux of different times and places.

Thus in discussing objectivity Weber (1949, p. 64) states that:

The quality of an event as a 'social economic' event is not something which it possesses 'objectively'. It is rather conditioned by the orientation of our cognitive interest, as it arises from the specific cultural significance which we attribute to the particular event in a given case.

This empirically variable concept of 'significance' and 'interest' appears in Hartshorne's (1959, p. 45) arguments when he states that:

> To accept man's interest as the measuring rod of significance in all parts of geography does not, to be sure, provide a single unitary criterion . . .
>
> It is likewise true that the features of the earth have a different significance for peoples of different cultures, or of different times, and for different groups and individuals within the same time and culture. There is therefore ample room for a great variety of different and incommensurable interests in geography conceived in terms of the interest of man.

Thus a consensus of values and interests, as well as the discovery of laws and theories, appear to serve as criteria of significance within Hartshorne's 'empirical' definition of the science of geography.

Guelke (1971; 1977a; 1977b) accepts studies of regions and of areal differentiation as the core of geography, but he differs from Hartshorne in his emphasis upon studying the thought behind human action and his neglect of the natural environment. Also, his atheoretical idealist approach suggests a regional geography that is almost exclusively idiographic (Guelke, 1977a). Although these and other points of disagreement are evident in comparing the two discussions, Guelke adopts a position similar to that of Hartshorne on the scientific nature of the study of the individual region, and on the view that a consensus of values and interests provides the basic criterion of significance for such studies.

Guelke (1978, p. 53) argues that geographers must adopt a concept of science that is compatible with their 'special problems'. Such a concept would seemingly need to be consistent with Guelke's (1978, p. 59) idealist perspective that 'is premised on understanding concrete situations without laws or theories'. He posits that:

> I think [that] the majority of geographers would agree that geography must remain a science in the broad sense that it should be founded on observation and that explanation should be open to critical analysis. (Guelke, 1978, p. 58)

Guelke (1979, p. 10) recognizes that the adoption of this minimal conception of science means that the idealist geographer must use criteria of significance that are different from those employed in the natural sciences. For example, he argues that:

> A fact or event becomes significant to historical geography in terms of its actual or potential importance in changing the way people construe their situations. (Guelke, 1979, p. 8)

Such a claim raises two related questions: (1) how do we know what facts or events change the way people think?; and (2) what criteria are used for judging between competing interpretations? Guelke (1974, p. 202; 1978, p. 53; 1979, p. 8) is aware of these difficulties and implies that critical analysis by, and consensus among, practising geographers concerning both the strength of the supporting evidence and the coherence of the arguments would provide the basis for settling such disputes. The importance of this consensus is indicated by Guelke's (1977b, p. 384) discussion of 'good explanation' in which he states that:

> What geographers need ask is: Do our explanations further our under-standing? Do they satisfy our intellectual curiosity? Are they concerned with cause rather than function? If geographers can agree in general terms on what a good explanation will involve, the philosophical issue can be treated independently. In other words, whether a good explanation logically derives from laws, from verstehen or rational understanding or from context or synthesis, is a distinct philosophical question of no immediate concern to the practice of geography.

Unfortunately, Guelke appears content to argue that such an agreement can exist, without making explicit the criteria for such a consensus.

Gregory (1978, pp. 144–46; see also 1976) is among the group of Guelke's critics who have expressed discontent with the lack of objective standards for choosing between competing interpretations and explanations (e.g. Billinge, 1977; Chappell, 1976; Watts and Watts, 1978), and he counters Guelke's atheoretical idealist perspective with a critical theorist view of geography. Although Gregory (1978, pp. 75, 171) does not share Guelke's concern for establishing an idiographic human geography, he does suggest that the task of the geographer is the investigation of the 'constitution' of specific, regional 'social formations', 'articulations', and 'transformations'. The validity claims of such a science would be established through rational discourse, a level of communication in which a critical attitude is taken towards accepted beliefs. This critical attitude is somewhat similar to that taken by the phenomenologist towards the natural viewpoints, but, unlike the phenomenologist, the critical theorist argues that the truth of statements and the correctness of norms are established in rational discourse (McCarthy, 1973, p. 139).

A primary goal of Habermas' project is to establish the formal conditions of discourse. For example, he argues that one essential condition is the removal of all constraints from the speech situation that would serve to distort communication, constraints such as an asymmetric power distribution among the participants. This condition is necessary in that it allows for the possibility of a discursively achieved consensus based upon the force of the argument and not upon the force of accidental or imposed constraints on discussion (McCarthy, 1973, p. 145). In using aspects of Habermas' linguistically based critical theory, Gregory attempts to clarify the nature of critical analysis and rational consensus, concepts that are important to, yet unexamined in, Guelke's arguments.

Gregory (1978, p. 171), similar to Hartshorne and Guelke, presents a conception of science in which natural science is only one of several types and in which human interests and values play an important role in determining significance and objectivity, but his view of the relationship between knowledge and interests is quite distinct. His justification for geography as critical science incorporates Habermas' view that all knowledge is founded upon 'quasi-transcendental' (neither empirically contingent nor a product of an ahistorical transcendental ego), knowledge-constitutive interests or cognitive interests. The three primary interests, to which all others may be reduced, are the technical, the practical and the emancipatory, and they are rooted in the existential aspects of social life: work, interaction, and power. These existentially based interests in turn provide the foundation for three distinct types of science, empirical–analytic, historical–hermeneutic and critical. Thus the social relation of work creates the technical interest that is the basis for empirical–analytic science, and this same logic can be repeated tying interaction–practical interests–historical hermeneutic science and power-emancipatory interests-critical science. Gregory (1978, p. 160; see also Habermas 1971, p. 311) notes the role of such interests in stating that:

> The three interests are not barriers to the objectivity of knowledge (as the traditional belief in 'pure theory' presupposes), but the very conditions of objective knowledge, and this is as true of the emancipatory interest as it is of the technical and the practical.

These interests are the basis for scientific objectivity in that it is through them that the objects of science are 'constituted'. Thus Habermas (1973, pp. 1–40, 211) presents a 'classical' view of theory in which theory is derived from, and inextricably linked with, human interests, as opposed to a 'traditional' view in which pure theory is established by a disinterested observer.

The role of shared interests and values as a part of the basis for significance and objectivity in Hartshorne's chorological studies has been noted. Although the interests discussed by Gregory are of a different nature in that they are viewed as quasi-transcendental, universal interests, they appear to serve some of the same functions as those described by Hartshorne. This apparent similarity masks, however, a fundamental antagonism between the two underlying philosophical perspectives. In bridging the logical gap between pure and practical reason, and hence linking fact and value, theory and practice, Habermas has contradicted one of the basic tenets of Kantian and neo-Kantian philosophy (Overend, 1977, p. 120; Bernstein, 1976, pp. 185–236). Both Rickert and Weber have maintained that values are important as criteria of selection for choosing significant phenomena from an infinite reality, but each also argues that scientific activity should be value-neutral. Habermas (1971, pp. 183–84, 303–4, 338–41) rejects the idea of value-neutrality as a misconception based upon an incorrect view of reality and upon a false division of fact from value. Reality is constituted by cognitive interests according to Habermas, and thus cannot be conceived of as independent of such interests. In discussing the relation of fact and value, Habermas (1971, p. 304) states that:

> The very term values, which neo-Kantianism brought into philosophical currency, and in relation to which science is supposed to preserve neutrality, renounces the connection between the two [fact and value] that theory originally intended.

Thus any attempt to suggest a synthesis of critical theory and the neo-Kantian arguments of value-relevance encounters the obstacle of seemingly incompatible ontological and epistemological assumptions (Keat and Urry, 1975, p. 223).

CONCLUSION

Positivist proponents of the spatial analytic tradition have used arguments concerning a single logic of science to undermine the importance of the study of specific regions. In using the deductive nomological form of explanation as the standard by which all explanations are judged, they have argued that the descriptive and subjective characteristics of parts of Hartshorne's chorology did not conform with the ideals of scientific study. More recent positivistic arguments have moderated this criticism by arguing that chorology presents a less complete and less rigorous from of scientific explanation, but that it fits within the general logic of science.

The very conception of an ahistorical logic of science has been criticized in the philosophy of science, the philosophy of social science and more recently in discussion of the nature of geography. Two of the geographers who have criticized this view of science, Guelke and Gregory, have suggested a re-emphasis upon regional studies. The brief and preliminary nature of these two proposals does not allow for speculation concerning an impending revival of regional studies or a 'paradigm-like' shift in human geography. Furthermore any such speculation would be based on the erroneous assumption that regional geography has been dormant since the rise of spatial analysis. While regional studies have continued to be published, relatively few discussions of the philosophical issues underlying the scientific study of specific regions have appeared during this period. The proposals of Guelke and Gregory offer quite distinct viewpoints on this topic, but both serve to indicate that the current dissatisfaction with positivist and naturalist conceptions of geography has been a catalyst for renewed discussion of these issues.

REFERENCES

Bernstein, R. (1976). *The Restructuring of Social and Political Theory*. University of Pennsylvania Press, Philadelphia.

Berry, B. (1964). Approaches to regional analysis, a synthesis. *Annals, Association of American Geographers*, **54**, 2–11.

Billinge, M. (1977). In search of negativism: phenomenology and historical geography. *Journal of Historical Geography*, **3**, 55–67.

Brodbeck, M. (1963). Logic and scientific method in research on teaching. In N. L. Gage (ed.), *Handbook of Research on Teaching*, Rand McNally, Chicago.

Brodbeck, M. (1968). General introduction. In M. Brodbeck (Ed.), *Readings in the Philosophy of the Social Sciences*, Macmillan, New York, pp. 1–11.

Bunge, W. (1962). Theoretical geography. *Lund Studies in Geography, Series C*, No. 1, C. W. K. Gleerup, Lund, Sweden.

Burger, T. (1976). *Max Weber's Theory of Concept Formation*. Duke University Press, Durham, North Carolina.

Chappel, J. E. (1976). Comment in reply. *Annals, Association of American Geographers*, **66**, 169–73.

Gale, S. (1972). On the heterodoxy of explanation, a review of David Harvey's *Explanation in Geography*. *Geographical Analysis*, **4**, 285–322.

Gale, S. and Olsson, G. (eds) (1979). *Philosophy in Geography*. D. Reidel Publishing Co., Dordrecht, Holland.

Giddens, A. (1977). *Studies in Social and Political Theory*. Basic Books, New York.

Giedymin, J. (1975). Antipositivism in contemporary philosophy of social science. *British Journal for the Philosophy of Science*, **26**, 275–301.

Goddard, D. (1973). Max Weber and the objectivity of social science. *History and Theory*, **12**, 1–22.

Gregory, D. (1976). Rethinking historical geography. *Area*, **8**, 295–99.

Gregory, D. (1978). *Ideology, Science, and Human Geography*. Hutchinson and Co. London.

Guelke, L. (1971). Problems of scientific explanation in geography. *Canadian Geographer*, **15**, 38–53.

Guelke, L. (1977a). Regional geography. *The Professional Geographer*, **29**, 1–7.

Guelke, L. (1977b). The role of laws in human geography. *Progress in Human Geography*, **1**, 376–86.

Guelke, L. (1978). Geography and logical positivism. In D. Herbert and R. Johnston (eds.), *Geography and the Urban Environment*, I, John Wiley and Sons, Chichester, pp. 35–61.

Guelke, L. (1979). Historical Geography and Collingwood's Theory of Historical Knowing. Paper Presented at the *IGU Symposium on Research Methods in Historical Geography*, University of Cambridge, Cambridge, England.

Habermas, J. (1971). *Knowledge and Human Interests*. Trans. by Jeremy Shapiro, Beacon Press, Boston.

Habermas, J. (1973). *Theory and Practice*. Trans. by J. Viertel, Beacon Press, Boston.

Habermas, J. (1975). *Legitimation Crisis*. Trans. by T. McCarthy, Beacon Press, Boston.

Hartshorne, R. (1939). *The Nature of Geography*, Association of American Geographers, Lancaster, Pennsylvania.

Hartshorne, R. (1955). 'Exceptionalism in geography' re-examined. *Annals, Association of American Geographers*, **45**, 205–44.

Hartshorne, R. (1959). *Perspective on the Nature of Geography*. Rand-McNally, Chicago.

Hartshorne, R. (1972). Review of *Kant's Concept of Geography* by J. A. May. *Canadian Geographer*, **16**, 77–79.

Harvey, D. (1969). *Explanation in Geography*. Edward Arnold, London.

Hempel, C. G. (1965). *Aspects of Scientific Explanation*. Free Press, New York.

Hempel, C. G. (1966). *Philosophy of Natural Science*. Prentice Hall, Englewood Cliffs, New Jersey.

Hindess, B. (1977). *Philosophy and Methodology in the Social Sciences*. Harvester Press, Hassocks, England.

Hodges, H. A. (1952). *The Philosophy of Wilhelm Dilthey*. Routledge and Kegan Paul, Ltd., London.

Johnston, R. J. (1979). *Geography and Geographers: Anglo-American Human Geography Since 1945*. Edward Arnold, London.

Keat, R. and J. Urry (1975). *Social Theory as Science*. Routledge and Kegan Paul, London.

Ley, D. and M. Samuels (eds). (1978). *Humanistic Geography*. Maaroufa Press, Chicago.

Makkreel, R. (1975). *Dilthey: Philosopher of the Human Studies*. Princeton University Press, Princeton, New Jersey.

McCarthy, T. A. (1973). A theory of communicative competence. *Philosophy of Social Science*, **3**, 135–56.

Nagel, E. (1961). *The Structure of Science*. Harcourt Brace and World, New York.

Overend, T. (1977). Discussion: The socialization of philosophy, two monistic fallacies in Habermas' critique of knowledge. *Philosophy and Phenomenological Research*, pp. 119–24.

Rickert, H. (1962). *Science and History*, translated by G. Reisman. D. Van Nostrand, Co., Princeton, New Jersey.

Sack, R. D. (1974). Chorology and Spatial Analysis. *Annals, Association of American Geographers*, **64**, 439–52.

Schaefer, F. K. (1953). Exceptionalism in geography: A methodological examination. *Annals, Association of American Geographers*, **43**, 226–49.

Von Rintelen, F. J. (1970). *Contemporary German Philosophy*, H. Bouvier and Co., Verlag, Bonn.

Watts, S. and Watts, S. (1978). The idealist alternative in geography and history. *The Professional Geographer*, **30**, 123–27.

Weber, M. (1949). *The Methodology of the Social Sciences*, translated and edited by E. Shils and H. Finnh, Free Press, New York.

Windelband, W. (1907). *Geschichte und Naturwissenschaft*. In W. Windelband (Ed.), Präludien, J. Mohr, Tübingen, Germany, pp. 355–79.

Windelband, W. (1961). *Theories in Logic*, translated by J. Kiernan. The Philosophical Library, New York.

Geography and the Urban Environment
Progress in Research and Applications, Volume IV
Edited by D. T. Herbert and R. J. Johnston

Chapter 2

Defensible Values in Geography: Can Values be Science-free?

R. Andrew Sayer

INTRODUCTION

In the early 1970s, the 'problem of values' was deeply felt and widely discussed in geography. The upshot of those debates was closer to a chaos of unresolved problems than a consensus, and little can be salvaged from them that has gained even limited acceptance. The point of this chapter is to follow through some of the arguments about the problem of values in detail, in order to try to sort out some of these difficulties. I shall first argue that the traditional way of conducting the argument in terms of the logical status and relations of statements is inadequate in that it completely misses the insights on values to be gained by situating them in an active social context. When looked at in this way, values can be shown to be not only unavoidable but also susceptible to rational evaluation. Two implications of this are of crucial importance: that the value-laden character of social science need not be considered as a problem; and that making rationally defended 'value-judgements' is an essential element of any rigorous social inquiry. But first it is necessary to look a little more closely at the disarray that characterizes the current state of the debate in geography.

Elements of the current state of the debate

Harvey's twin assaults on the assumptions of value-freedom, in his discussion of the population debate (1974a) and his contribution to the relevance debate (1974b) created some reverberations in helping to dispel those assumptions, but the response was far from clear. The 'spatial scientists' often conceded that they had values and that their work was in some way value-laden, but felt able to justify a continuing interest in 'positive' or 'status-quo theory' (for example, see King and Golledge, 1978, and Haggett *et al* 1978, p. 24). Harvey and others attacked the 'trivial view that there is one version of some problem that is scientific and a variety of versions which are purely ideological' (Harvey, 1974a,

p. 257), and yet that view persisted, often in a disguised form where non-positivist theories were assumed to be normative. For example, consider the following:

> . . . . there is no proof that one set of assumptions is inherently better as the basis for postulating normative theory than is another. In the last resort, the choice between one set of basic assumptions and another is a metaphysical matter, a question of belief that is not amenable to scientific analysis . . . . The failure to realize that quantitative methods are generally positive in character rather than normative and that competing normative views of the world depend largely upon metaphysical matters of belief, probably underlies the disenchantment that some geographers have expressed. (Chisholm 1975, p. 176)

This is based on the curious notion that radical theories are simply normative and do not also deal with 'what is the case', and on a (popular) misuse of the term 'metaphysical'. Metaphysics concerns the most basic terms in which we think, such as matter, thing, relation, time—terms which are no less basic to science than to normative theory. How we conceive of these basic terms has an important but often unacknowledged effect upon more specific ideas about the real world. This applies no less to positivism, despite its intention of displacing metaphysics: it merely contains a different, unexamined and unacknowledged, metaphysics (cf. Harré, 1972).

Those who acknowledged that values would never be excluded from science usually assumed that nevertheless values constituted a problem for, or a threat to, science and so their intrusion had to be minimized. It was assumed without much discussion that values were somehow beyond the scope of rational defence: a lack of value-freedom in science was assumed to be a problem because of the lack of science in values. The combination of the assumption that values were science-free[1] and the acknowledgement of the inevitability of their presence produced some unfortunate responses, especially in the shape of a relativism in which all possible beliefs had equal claims to truth. As Harvey warned, it is unhelpful:

> . . . . to argue that *all* versions of a problem are ideological, and it is downright misleading to suggest that our views . . . depend merely upon whether we are optimists or pessimists, socialists or conservatives, determinists or possibilists, and the like. (Harvey, 1947a p. 257)

These views have been put forward by people of a variety of political persuasions, and amount to a *refusal of argument*. In fundamental debates between people of widely-differing views, it is always tempting 'in the last resort', as Chisholm so revealingly puts it, to throw in the old discussion-stopper: 'it all depends on your values/ideology/value-judgements'. While this is an obvious way of terminating a debate, the popular and more innocent-sounding appeal to *eclecticism* often had similar effects (e.g. Wilson, 1978; Hay 1979); the claim that all views had something to contribute could easily serve as a protection against criticism and as a way of saying 'you go your way and I'll go mine'.

Awareness of the problem (really several problems) of values had undermined faith in the claims of scientific knowledge, and yet here again Harvey was concerned to stem the tide of relativism and irrationalism by acknowledging the importance of the:

> . . . . spirit of scientific endeavour that seeks to establish 'truth' without invoking subjective personal preferences; to say that there is no such thing as ethical neutrality is not to say that we are reduced to mere personal opinion (Harvey, 1974a, p. 257)

The question 'which values?' had to be faced; but as long as values were assumed to be science-free it could not. It is not clear to me whether Harvey's interest in the matter lay in the general philosophical problems of values, or in particular substantive values, or both. However, three important directions in which the issue might be tackled are given in his work:

(1) by asking the important question 'why these beliefs?' it was implied that values were not an autonomous realm of ideas but were intimately related to material social conditions, such that their origins could be explained (Harvey, 1973);

(2) by finding out how particular sets of values are derived from particular theories, or more generally, approaches or methods (Harvey, 1974a); and

(3) through practice.

The interest in *ideology* which arose later in the 1970s developed (1) and (2) and took values out of their commonly-assumed independence and situated them back in theory and practice. Unfortunately, there is such a baroque variety of concepts of ideology stemming from different epistemologies and theories of society that the debate has not made much progress. I shall argue later that (3) is confused and that although (1) and (2) are extremely important, they leave some central questions still unanswered. In particular, they explain how material and theoretical influences *produced* or *form* values, but not what values themselves *are*. Harvey acknowledges in his essay on the population debate that he does not deal with the question of the nature of rationality. The consequence of either ignoring this or simply putting it under the heading of 'practice' is to conjure away the whole question of the rationale behind making value judgements and reduce it to an apparently simple causal determination in which no reasoning, or evaluation, by the people concerned is involved.

Given the current confused state of the debate, it is necessary to go back and examine some of the main philosophical arguments about the problems of values. Among these, I shall give most prominence to the question of the allegedly science-free nature of values, in order to try to block recurrence of the above-mentioned refusals of arguments. Geographers are not alone in facing the problems of values in social science, and so much of the discussion will not be particularly geographical, but it is no less relevant for that. The philosophical literature on this subject is daunting, to say the least, and to an outsider it almost seems that if one went into it too far, one might never come out again, or, like Gunner Olsson in *Birds in Egg* (1979), one might return to find the audience intrigued but uncomprehending.

The 'fact-value conceptual space'

The fact-value distinction does not stand in isolation, but has commonly been associated with a whole series of parallel distinctions or dichotomies. These are some of the more important ones:

fact	—	value
is	—	ought
means	—	ends
positive	—	normative
fact	—	belief, view
science	—	ideology
descriptive	—	prescriptive
explanation	—	evaluation
objective	—	subjective
logic appraisal	—	moral appraisal

There also are some common alleged *equivalences*, such as 'objectivity'—'impartiality' (on the fact side) and 'subjective'—'evaluative' (on the value side).

Many of these distinctions and equivalences are wrongly drawn and I shall challenge some of them later. However, it is important at the outset to appreciate how fundamental these distinctions are in polarizing much of our thinking into: (1) knowledge which is true or false as a matter of fact or definition; and (2) knowledge which has no factual content and cannot be shown to be true or false but is merely dependent on subjective wants of some kind. What is involved is not just a few isolated distinctions, but a whole conceptual space or network and, as will be argued, a very confused one at that.

Starting points

There are two main types of discussions of the problems of values: those that take most of the above distinctions and equivalences as their starting point;

and those that try to break out of them. The first kind are conducted by examining (usually very simple) statements one by one in terms of their logical properties. The second kind does not accept this abstraction of statements from the context of communication in practical situations. Which of these approches is adopted has a crucial bearing on the answers. Geographers seem to be caught in an uncomfortable position between them because their experience of communication in practical situations suggests answers opposed to those implied by the first type of discussion-framework, which they nevertheless tend to retain in methodological and philosophical discussions.

THE PROBLEM OF VALUES FROM THE STANDPOINT OF THE FACT-VALUE CONCEPTUAL NETWORK

At a simple level, the fact-value distinction can easily be supported by comparing simple possible statements of the kind:

(i) the average journey-to-work trip length was 2.6 km;
(ii) geographers ought not to have advised the US government on its strategy in Indochina.

Although (ii) implies a statement of fact (that geographers did advise the US government on its strategy in Indochina) the presence of 'ought' signals that (ii) is a statement of moral judgement. In no sense can this normative statement be said to be true or false in the same way as (i) can. I argue below that this contrast is not acceptable if it is made into a rigid *dichotomy* of mutually exclusive and entirely dissimilar poles, but I think it stands as a distinction.

There are several well-rehearsed objections to this. One response is to claim that (i) is based upon value judgements and so is not essentially different from (ii). The problem here is that if the concept of a value-judgement is *universalized* so that all our knowledge is based upon them, it ceases to refer to anything specific at all. Yet, although judgements have to be made in asserting (i), they are not of a *moral* kind: they are merely estimates. Nagel (1961) makes the point by contrasting *characterizing* with *appraising* judgements; only the latter involve moral questions. The *correct* point about the response is that it recognizes what many defenders of the fact-value distinction (including, apparently, Chisholm) do not: that knowledge of matters of fact is theory-laden and fallible.

On this issue, sloppy use of those highly ambiguous terms—'objective' and 'subjective'—has been responsible for a catalogue of errors. What these terms characteristically conceal is the difference between, on the one hand, fallibility in knowing what is the case and the necessity of choosing between theories, and on the other hand, making choices not about what is the case but about what we think ought to be the case, where ought implies moral evaluations

of good or bad, right or wrong. As is argued later, the distinction is more difficult
to sustain where social objects are concerned, but I do not see that there are
any such problems in the study of natural (non-human) objects. It can be
readily conceded that any theory is anthropocentric in so far as the definitions
of objects of interest are socially influenced, but it does not follow from this
that we should choose between competing theories of a natural process (e.g.
the movement of the tides) on moral grounds.

A further problem with this particular objection to the fact-value distinction
is that it is thoroughly relativistic. If all knowledge is based on value-judgements
which we can take or leave, there can be no *reason* for preferring any particular
ideas: we are back to our discussion stopper—'it all depends on your values'.
But it does not follow from the fact that all knowledge is fallible, that it is all
equally fallible, nor that fallibility is necessarily due to a grounding of knowledge
in value judgements. Frequently, the relativistic argument is used in an
inconsistent way: having asserted that *all* knowledge is inevitably value-laden,
particular ideas are attacked for *being* value-laden! All that can be argued from
the premise of universal value-ladenness is that the *pretence* of value-freedom is
wrong. Also, relativistic arguments easily backfire on their advocates when
faced with those who have some confidence in their own claims to objectivity
and who are only too happy to concede that their opponents' ideas are based
on ideology, values, mystical conversion experiences, or metaphysical beliefs.
(See again, for example Chisholm, 1975, p. 176.) The thoroughgoing relativist
is trapped within the same conceptual space as the simple-minded objectivist.
Being unable to accept the objectivist belief in knowledge based on unambiguous
facts, the relativist chooses the other pole of pure subjectivism and irrationalism.
Given such a choice it is therefore hardly surprising that the former option is
usually preferred as the lesser of two evils. But it is only if it is argued that
values do have a certain factual or descriptive content and that they are rationally
defensible, thereby breaking with the fact-value dichotomy and its polarized
conceptual space, that this kind of challenge can avoid irrationalism.

Given our provisional acceptance of the orthodox terms of the debate—i.e.
the comparison of simple types of statements and their logical properties—it
appears that the distinction of fact and value is tenable, with the implication
(not explored here) that the other associated dichotomies, such as that between
science and ideology, have some support too. But the most prominent issue in
the debate, and perhaps the trump card of the value-freedom school, concerns
the logical relations *between* statements such as (i) and (ii). We have noted
that evaluative or normative statements may include a factual element, but
while 'ought' statements can imply 'is' statements, the former cannot be deduced
from the latter. This is obviously of great significance because it means that a
positive science which is concerned purely with questions of fact has no
normative implications for practice whatsoever. It cannot be used scientifically
to defend or attack particular views about what ought to be the case. To be

sure, just as there are occasional attempts to invent perpetual motion machines, so there have been attempts to falsify this claim, but none of these refutations has won wide acceptance. (Incidentally, the historical significance of the non-deducibility of 'ought' from 'is' is considerable. It has been used to defend science's claims to autonomy from and neutrality towards political and moral interests. Although this autonomy will be disputed later, it cannot be denied that its assertion has sometimes had progressive effects, as in freeing science from religious dogma.)

Later, I shall criticize the non-deducibility claim by challenging its premises, but there are some common errors and paradoxes which occur within this framework and which require prior examination. First, the non-deducibility doctrine cannot, as is often thought, serve to protect science from normative judgement. For whereas we cannot say that a theory of ecosystems is morally wrong or right and we cannot deduce what we ought to do from statements about it, we can still evaluate the application of the knowledge, and we can also evaluate the practice of the scientists who researched it (Keat, 1979). (The choice of a natural science example is intentional: social science cases are more complex, as will be shown.) Precisely because the relation between 'ought' and 'is' is not deductive and not necessary, we are free to evaluate the positive theory in either of these ways, provided that we do not pretend that the evaluation follows deductively from that theory. Our evaluations might be derived by means other than by reference to (positive) science. We could only prohibit such normative judgements by showing that positive science is the only sound or proper knowledge.

Secondly, there is a common misconception about the associated dichotomy of means and ends, which is invoked to support the allegedly value-free nature of policy science. The idea is that all value-judgements are restricted to the determination of ends (e.g. 'we must decentralize population'), leaving the choice of means towards achieving these as a purely technical, value-free one. The validity of the dichotomy has been ably criticized by Streeten (in Myrdal, 1959), but even if it were valid, and even if we accepted the values contained in the ends, it would not protect the means from negative evaluation by reference to other criteria (Keat, 1979).

A popular but unsatisfactory solution to the problems of values is Myrdal's 'come clean' principle in which one is supposed to declare one's values as honestly and openly as possible at the beginning of any research report in order that others may not be misled by them (Myrdal, 1959). As many critics have noted, this is unhelpful because if our values are so obvious that they can be separated out from our analysis, then it is surely unnecessary to do so; and if they are inseparable or hidden or both then we cannot follow Myrdal's advice anyway. Yet it is precisely because so many recognize that values in social analysis are not easily separated out, and that they don't present themselves in the 'sore-thumb' manner in which philosophers like to idealize them ('it is wrong to kill'), that so many orthodox as well as radical social scientists reject the strict value-freedom thesis.

Now, as has probably already been noticed, a strange paradox—indeed a dilemma—is generated by the non-deducibility principle, for *as* a *principle*, it appears to have *normative force*, and yet it is asserted in a framework which denies that these can be deduced from knowledge which can be shown to be true or false. More generally, the questions are 'How can we justify the *values* of science and logic?' and 'Why ought we to be logical and honest?'. In Popper's system, for example, the principle that one ought fearlessly to expose one's theory to attempts at falsification cannot be deduced from statements about matters of fact, or 'conjectures' (Popper, 1959). The price science pays for trying to present itself as the *only* knowledge (which Popper was not trying to do, at least not ostensibly) and for denying any rational content to ethical questions is to make not just non-science but its own practice appear indefensible and irrational. If theoretical reasoning (about what is the case) cannot logically entail practical reasoning (about what we ought to do),[2] then how can the rules of logic which appear to govern how we ought to reason theoretically (which arguably can be considered a kind of 'doing') be defended? On this question positivists and Popper are forced simply to appeal to a pure (groundless) decision to do so, and upon this extraordinarily feeble foundation the whole weight of that most prestigious kind of knowledge—science—is admitted to rest. Accordingly, Habermas (1978), in his critique of the claims to neutrality and rationality of science, attacks the basis of this dilemma as 'decisionism'.

Thus the presuppositions of the fact-value dichotomy and its non-deducibility claims begin to crack, for the *practice* of science obviously *cannot* be reduced to a question of the logical properties of *statements*. But apart from these problems, particularly the last-mentioned one, the value-freedom thesis is, within its own terms, very compelling and indeed apparently logically-watertight. I have suggested but not yet demonstrated that matters look very different when one goes beyond these terms, beyond matters of the logical properties and relations of simple isolated statements to questions of communication in its wider context and in which science is just a part. Yet much of the debate about values in social science is in an uncomfortably ambiguous position here, for while the standpoint of communication in a practical context is rarely adopted explicitly and the narrower terms of reference outlined so far are generally accepted, the conclusions are often refused. Nowadays, it is common for social scientists to accept that no knowledge is value-free, or 'completely' (and much hangs on that word) value-free, and yet despite their apparent *unavoidability* values are still seen as a *problem*. A common response to this latter paradox is to say that although values will creep in somewhere, we should as least try to minimize their intrusion; after all, just because surgical operations can never be carried out in a completely sterile environment, it doesn't mean that they may as well be conducted in sewers. This sounds sensible enough, although on reflection it only begs more questions: 'why should values be seen as a form of 'contamination'?'—the analogy with infection is persuasive but is given no justification—and, more generally, 'what are values and what do we have against them?'. I shall argue that values need only constitute a problem if it turns out that they are indeed science-free, or beyond rational defence.

In this debate about minimizing value-intrusion, it is particularly clear that a partial break has been made with the limited framework within which the fact-value dichotomy and its implications are most usually discussed. The tensions that arise probably stem from the simultaneous acceptance of the restrictive orthodox framework for discussion of values as a philosophical issue and a practical experience both in everyday life and the substantive wider framework of ordinary communication. From the latter, there is a general awareness that values usually enter in very subtle, discreet and perhaps insidious ways—only relatively rarely (especially in academic research) do they intrude or obtrude in such obvious terms as 'ought', 'good', 'bad', 'better', bearing little flags marked values.

The problem about the present state of the debate is this: if the non-deducibility argument is *valid*, then we cannot both accept its premises and reject its conclusions as untrue.[3] The only way we can concede that the argument is valid and yet reject its conclusion is by rejecting the premises. Indeed, it is precisely because the value-freedom thesis is generally defended by means of formal, deductive arguments, and yet the truth of its conclusions is dubious, that we should suspect that the problems of values are created by the framework of premises itself in the shape of the fact-value family of dichotomies. These have the effect of rendering values science-free, hence making them a serious problem *for* science when they intrude.

VALUES IN THE CONTEXT OF COMMUNICATION
AND PRACTICE: NORMATIVE IMPLICATIONS
OF TRUTHS OF REASON

I have argued that the adoption of the fact-value dichotomy and allied distinctions prejudices the analysis of the role of values in social science. However, even if one starts from within this framework, it is possible in certain special cases to demonstrate the necessity for moving beyond it. Consider the following argument put forward by Edgley (1969, p. 49ff).
From statements:

    (1) 'p implies q', or
    (2) 'if p, then q';

it follows that:

    (3) the argument from p to q is *valid* and *sound*, a *good* argument, not an invalid, unsound, or bad argument;

(4) it is *inconsistent* to believe that p and (simultaneously) that *not-q*; and
(5) that fact that *p justifies* the belief that q.

In this, p and q may each be analytically true (true by definition) or statements about matters of fact which may be true or false.(1) and (2) are *truths of reason*; the logical verbs 'implies' and 'follows' concern relations between things that can be said. (3), (4), and (5) contain terms which are evaluative of actual or possible arguments, inferences or beliefs, such as 'inconsistent' and 'justifies'. This suggests that truths of reason about what is the case do have *normative* implications for doing or 'practice', if the latter are interpreted in a broad sense.

RESTRICTIVE ASPECTS OF THE ORTHODOX FRAMEWORK

Contemplative epistemology

It is important to appreciate the restrictiveness of the terms of the debate on the problem of values imposed by the orthodox, analytical framework. Most generally it prejudices the discovery of a connexion between theoretical reason (about what is or is not the case) and practical reason (about what ought to be done) by adopting a theory of knowledge which assumes a merely *contemplative* relationship between knowing subject and object of studying rather than an active, practical one. Practical reason is immediately given a handicap and marginalized as a purely instrumental application of reason which itself depends upon some extraneous value-judgements that knowledge or reason ought to be applied. This value-judgement is in turn made to appear beyond the scope of reason as a purely voluntaristic decision. The result is a dichotomization of cognitive powers into knowing what is the case—which is supposedly rationally-defensible—and deciding what to do, which is not. As has already been shown by means of Edgley's argument, this dichotomization is suspect even on its own terms. Yet what is more important is that it generates an extraordinarily alienated and restrictive view of human action.

A restrictive view of language

In analytical discussions of the problem of values, a highly restrictive view of language is normally assumed without any justification, although it gains implicit support through being compatible with a contemplative epistemology.

First it is considered acceptable to atomize language into simple building blocks, presumably on the grounds that nothing is lost in the process and that there is a pay-off in terms of ease of logical analysis. Yet this loads the questions asked in favour of value-freedom, for when considered in isolation, simple propositions such as 'the proportion of immigrants in Ealing is $X\%$' seem innocent enough, but when placed in a larger discourse, they could be central to a highly emotive, normatively-charged argument. (That no evaluative propositions follow deductively from that simple statement is not the point, as will be shown shortly.) Especially where symbols are used in place of actual statements or theories, in order to assist logical manipulation, there is a danger of underestimating the richness and subtlety of language and the ways in which evaluation may be communicated within the statements or theories concealed behind those innocuous symbols.

Secondly, language is often reduced to statements which are either analytically true or synthetic on the one hand (the factual, descriptive, positive side of the dichotomy) and, on the other, statements in which 'ought' or some cognate terms appears (the value side). But these by no means exhaust the range of functions of language; functions such as ordering, addressing, questioning, requesting or simply establishing a relationship are overlooked (cf. Gunnell, 1975, Chaps. 8 and 9; Edgley, 1969).

Thirdly, logic is reduced from the study of the structure and principles of reasoning to the study of deductive inference in particular. Deduction is certainly the most powerful mode of inference as a tool of logical analysis, because deductive relations hold necessarily; in a valid deductive argument, if the premises are accepted the conclusions must be too, unless we are guilty of contradiction. But this is by no means the only vehicle of thought, and indeed it cannot be. Deductive inference cannot itself provide information about the world which is not already present in some premise. The content of the latter has to be acquired by other means. Moreover—

(A)rgumentation differs from mere deduction by always subjecting the principles according to which it proceeds to discussion (Habermas, 1976b, p. 214; Cf. Habermas, 1976c, p. 106; and 1972, p. 137)

Therefore the practice of reasoning cannot possibly be reduced to deductive inference, although the latter may be useful in the (second-order) analysis of that reasoning.

Fourthly, the concentration on formal logical analysis of statements enables us to forget the nature of language as an active social process, as communication (cf. Williams, 1977, Chapter 2 and Habermas, 1972, p.193). To speak or write is to invite a relationship, and *how* we speak or write is influenced by our expectations of the pre-understandings, preferences, and prejudices of our audience. Meaning is always *for* someone; it is not simply reducible to a set of labels for objects. We find things out, make statements or ask questions in order to confirm or change existing knowledge. Facts are stated for a reason, to advance or counter an argument or belief, and it is the relation of these facts (which are used as reasons) to those received ideas which generates evaluative implications. Values are not simply intrinsic to words such as good or bad (the fetish of discourse), they concern evaluations *of* things *by* people. To refer to a value is to denote an active relationship and not simply a term. When the evaluative elements of knowledge are seen in this relative way, it becomes clear that fragments of discourse with identical logical structures may carry or secrete very different evaluative loadings according to their relative congruence with received knowledge (cf. Taylor, 1967). Indeed, such fragments only take on meaning against this background of pre-understanding. The evaluative implications of an injunction to "smash capitalism" simple cannot be understood and assessed until capitalism is understood. The evaluative implications of the title of a pamphlet 'Did 6 million Jews really die?' cannot be assessed by simple inference from that statement alone. The author of that pamphlet might welcome the protection from abuse and suspicion provided by the central claim of the value-freedom thesis that ought cannot be logically deduced from is. But that defence is inadequate because statements or questions only become meaningful in a wider (hidden) context of beliefs, values, received knowledge and social relations.

On the speaker's side of the communicative relationship, we must also recognise that to understand someone we must discover more than simply what the words that they use mean; we must interpret what the speaker meant or intended them to mean. Again, the author of that pamphlet might be happy to see apologists collapse the latter into the former, for he could be sure that most ordinary readers, unburdened by the value-freedom thesis, would pick up the intended but unstated meanings. Insisting that the words used were purely factual and therefore did not favour any particular belief is as naive as accepting that a National Front march through a black residential area of an English city in protest against economic policy is really about that: meaning does not have to be stated to communicated. Communication is by no means as clear and above board as the orthodox analytical framework would suggest, and this hidden, unspoken dimension is not an unfortunate element which can be purged. The difference between intended meaning and the meaning of the words used is inevitable, but it is by no means always deceitful. The distinction is, in fact, a condition of the possibility of communication: words, on their own, do not communicate, and to make sense an intended meaning has to be imputed. Some linguistic philosophers have recognised this and have looked beyond the immediate meaning of statements (Gunnell, 1975). (However, in this respect they have lagged far behind their continental European counterparts in the hermeneutical tradition. See, for example, Apel, 1972; Giddens, 1976; Connerton, 1976.) It has been considered important, for example, to study the effects *on* people produced by statements (e.g. embarrassment or irritation) and the way in which some kinds of utterances are simultaneously actions and not mere descriptions of action (e.g. 'I promise').

Constitutive meanings

In these ways language has been put back into the social process from which it was torn in orthodox analysis, but there is another aspect of its context which also challenges the assumption of a contemplative relationship between subject and object in social science. We are not indifferent to statements about the social world because, indirectly or directly, they concern and are about us; in social science there is a partial identity of subject and object, because in principle the object consists of ourselves and other subjects. Natural science studies objects which do not understand one another, which do not have intrinsic meaning; their nature is indifferent to scientists' theories. But a change in *social* theory amounts to an intervention (with)in, and argument with(in), society's self-understanding. That self-understanding—however confused, conflicting and informal—is part of what society *is*; it is constitutive. A fascist society depends in an important way upon fascist ideas, concepts and practices. The latter could not be what they were but for those constitutive meanings (Taylor, 1971). Often these meanings are not merely confused, but deceptive, mystifying and hypocritical. For example, the efficacy of the dominant usage of the concept of 'the national interest' depends upon the way its meaning deceives (Gellner, 1962). Therefore, the meaning and the practices which they inform can only be understood and explained *critically*. In such cases, the division between positive and either evaluative or normative study breaks down. That the concept of a simple unified national interest is hypocritical and a mystification is part of what it and the practices it informs *are*.

To understand constitutive meanings we must explain their function in the practices in which they are embedded and we cannot do this without evaluating them. Consider the following example: in British law double standards have often been exercised where a single set of standards has been declared; sanctions-busters have received rather different treatment from those arrested under the 'sus' laws (i.e. it is suspected that they intend to commit a crime). Now it would be impossible to explain this situation adequately without providing an account which differed from and indeed contradicted, or was critical of, the official account. And even if the double standards that existed in practice were not noticed, the explanation would not be indifferent to the official position but would be *compatible* with and *supportive* of it. There would be no use in appending a note saying that the report did not seek to judge the official interpretation and that it merely aimed at discovering 'the facts', for included in the facts themselves would be judgements and evaluations, and these would have to be *assessed* or interpreted in order for the researchers to make any sense of them at all.

Evaluative terms with descriptive content and rationally-defensible values

The extent of the interpenetration of explanation or understanding and evaluation goes even further than this because some terms are *simultaneously* evaluative and descriptive. Words such as terrorist and freedom-fighter, overpopulated and underdeveloped are both evaluative of human actions and capabilities and descriptive of them. Likewise, the statement 'Hitler was a cruel man' actually tells us more above an objective state of affairs than does 'Hitler was a man' because it is suggestive of actual things that he *did*. In other words, not all evaluative words are reducible to primitive emotive 'grunts'[4] which are beyond the bounds of rational discussion. Yet when the fact-value distinction is made into a rigid dichotomy, this emotivist conception of values is automatically generated.

In some cases, it may be possible to substitute less evaluative words without loss of meaning, but in many cases the evaluative and descriptive content are directly rather than inversely proportional. Compare the following statements about what happened in Germany under Nazi rule (the example is Isaiah Berlin's and is cited in Bhaskar, 1979, p. 75):

— the country was depopulated;
— millions of people died;
— millions of people were killed;
— millions of people were massacred.

Here it can be seen that the less value-laden the wording, the *less* informative are the statements factually.

We must be wary of a fetishism of discourse here, however, for if a thing is highly valued positively or negatively it makes little difference whether we denote it by a word which is obviously evaluative or non-evaluative. Through new associations, formerly 'neutral' words may become 'evaluatively-charged' (e.g., in 1979–80, 'nuclear', 'Ayatollah', 'monetarism'), and so any attempt to purge language of evaluative terms (by substitution of technical terms) will usually eventually produce a new set of value-laden terms. It is important to note the qualification 'usually eventually' for language is not a neutral medium, having no real effects of itself. On the contrary, the point of challenging conventional descriptions or names of familiar things is to provoke their re-evaluation and re-explanation. There are good reasons for refusing the convention of 'he' as a shorthand for 'he or she', for refusing to reserve the term 'dissident' for non-western societies, for experimenting with reversals of terms like freedom-fighter and terrorist. In this way, it is possible for language to be turned against the mystifications which it supports by setting up a dissonance where the circles of reciprocally-confirming actions and ideas or values are thought to be vicious. Drawing attention to the hidden implications of such terms is intended not merely to change the definition as such, but to provoke a change in the social practices which confirm those definitions.

It can be seen from these examples that, both in everyday practice and social science, how we describe and explain social phenomena affects our evaluations of them. Taylor (1967) takes this further and argues that evaluative influences are most substantially generated at the level of theories. Through their emphases, and particularly their exclusions of what is to be explained, theories secrete certain values. Harvey's (1974a) essay on the population debate can be interpreted as a substantive analysis of the way in which different evaluative implications are secreted by Malthusian, Ricardian, and Marxian theories and methods of analysis.

A rather philosophical example, which is not unrelated to the implicit epistemological assumptions of the present discussion, illustrates this point. Certain people (called radical behaviourists) have a theory of human behaviour which claims that all behaviour is reducible to physical responses to physical stimuli and that meaning and feeling are purely epiphenomenal. From this one would expect behaviourists to respond to human problems by recommending physical solutions; for example, electric shock treatment and not psychotherapy for mental illness, and totalitarian physical control rather than open discussion for political grievances. Behaviourists cannot *logically deduce* these normative proposals from their positive theory, and yet it would be surprising if a thoroughgoing Skinnerian proposed the alternatives of psychotherapy and open discussion. The non-existence of a deductive relationship between is and ought would not leave us content; we would presumably point out an inconsistency and ask for a *justification* for the refusal of the value secreted by the theory: 'If you regard meaning and understanding as epiphenomenal, how can you propose psychotherapy and open political discussion when these involve assumptions that negotiation of meanings has some real effect?'. Taylor (1967) argues (not through this example) that the aberrant response could only be justified either by arguments which *undermine* the objection (in the above example, by showing that pyschotherapy and political discussion can be accommodated within the stimulus–response model of behaviour) or by *overriding* arguments which accept the objection but appeal to some separate circumstances which override the imperatives secreted by this particular theory. (The latter might be used where electric shock treatment and political repression were banned, and if the behaviourist considered psychotherapy to be less bad than a third alternative, such as religion.) A simpler case of an overriding argument would be where a smoker who is aware of the dangers of lung-cancer prefers to die a young and happy smoker than an old and unhappy non-smoker. In such cases the argument would be unlikely to stop there, but the lack of a deductive relation between is and ought would not stop us demanding and offering rationally-defensible explanations. (Incidentally, the misfit behaviourists' overriding argument that society would not allow their preferred prescriptions is by no means far-fetched; where bilateral of multilateral social relations are concerned, *individuals* who want to change them commonly find that they have to compromise their prescriptions and live in bad faith because of the burden of the structure of existing society.)

In his attempt to reconstruct how we argue rationally over values and over prescriptions, Taylor (1967) suggests that implicit in value-judgements such as 'x is good (bad)' are wider claims that 'x is good (bad) because it is (in) compatible with fundamental human needs'. Although Taylor's point can be defended (see below), a persistent critic could perhaps claim to outflank it by asserting that what constitutes fundamental human needs is itself a matter of (ultimately indefensible) value-judgements.

In an interesting argument, Bhaskar (1979, p. 69ff) proposes that the values that must be chosen are those which are secreted by the theory which provides the most adequate explanation of the phenomena in question. If, for example, we are studying a system of racial discrimination which is based on, or informed and sustained by, a theory of racial differences which has subsequently been shown to be false, then we must judge that this particular social consciousness was false because we have explained its *referents* by means of a superior theory. Having made this rationally-defensible judgement of the (constitutive) theory as false, that negative evaluation is therefore also transferable to whatever practices (if any) necessitate this false consciousness (entrenched systems of exploitation of certain races) and whichever actions or practices or institutions are informed or sustained by it (Bhaskar, 1979, p. 80). If change is possible (i.e. if there are no overriding circumstances) and we are rational, then the imperative 'change it' follows. In some cases, the false consciousness may simply be an error of thought in society, but in others it may have sufficient practical adequacy to have enabled real practices and institutions to objectify it and be sustained by it (cf. Geras, 1972). In the latter case, though not always in the former, the material forces necessitating the illusory beliefs must themselves be changed if the beliefs are to be changed.

As a second example of this argument, take the informal theory about the nature of wages implicit in the notions of a 'fair day's pay for a fair day's work' and 'you're paid what your worth and worth what you're paid'. These ideas are both theoretical and evaluative (in a moral sense). Neoclassical economics supplies formalisations (and hence legitimations) of these in treating wages as a payment to a scarce factor of production which reflects its marginal product. Against these, marxism argues that for profit to be made, even where the owners of the means of production do no work, the value of what workers produce must be greater than that which they are paid, and that wages are paid to reproduce the worker's ability to work, not for the work done. If surplus labour (i.e. labour over and above that necessary to produce the workers' own subsistence) were not undertaken there would be no goods other than wage goods on which those in receipt of profits (or any income related to mere ownership) could spend their money. The mere fact of ownership and control of the means of production enables the capitalist to make workers produce surplus value as a condition of their being able to produce goods to the value of, and receive, a wage to reproduce themselves. If workers did receive back in wages value equal to that which they produced, there would be nothing left in profits. Therefore, the marxist theory *contradicts* popular (and neoclassical) ideas that wages are a payment for work done and in so doing is implicitly critical of the particular moral evaluations that these explanations secrete, such as that one is paid what one deserves, what one ought to be paid. Against these values, marxism secretes opposed values which suggest that the owners of the means of production are getting something for nothing or which they have done nothing to deserve. But the choice of these values does not depend upon political values, ideology or location in Eysenck's (1954) personality diagram, but upon the relative powers of the contending theories in explaining their objects; in this case, the origin of profit. Some readers may argue that the marxist theory is itself inadequate as an explanation. If they do, this would be entirely consistent with the *philosophical* point that it is the theory behind values and not the values in isolation that must be appraised.

In defence of rationally-defensible values

Critics in this field are unusually persistent and some anticipated objections must be faced. The usual tactic is to outflank the claim that values can be rationally-defended at every turn by positing an infinite regress of alternating value-judgements and factual or explanatory claims. In the case of the argument just advanced, the response might be to suggest that we cannot know (be certain of) which theory is superior in explanatory terms except by some ultimate recourse to value-judgements. (Actually, I think this response is disingenuous because in practice we are all perfectly capable of distinguishing and rationally defending some theoretical preferences, though admittedly not all. Moreover, I know of no one who has sufficient genuine scepticism (as opposed to the affected kind) consistently to make everyday theory-choices purely on random 'Dice Man' principles, or on either hedonistic or emotive grounds.) In answer to this, it must be understood that it is not denied that all knowledge is, in principle, fallible. The point of the argument is that we can establish *relative* superiority by reference to criteria of internal consistency and congruence with shared beliefs about the world. Precisely because absolute knowledge is unthinkable, it is inconsistent to cite failure to attain it as a criticism. In such situations, where the most fundamental bases of knowledge are in question, we cannot possibly expect to find 'bases of these bases' without generating an infinite regress. We are only able to doubt particular ideas by provisionally accepting others which are to be used as tools of sceptical thought: we cannot doubt everything simultaneously except by suspending thought. So the only way in which we can justify basic claims is by showing them to be *pre-supposed* by practices upon which all parties to the debate are agreed. The argument which Bhaskar proposes is that

> the possibility of coming to say to another or oneself 'now this is why you erroneously believe such and such' *is a presupposition of any rational discourse or authentic act of self-reflection at all* (Bhaskar, 1979, p. 82, emphasis added).

In the very act of arguing *against* the proposition that evaluative terms (such as 'erroneous') are rationally defensible, our persistent critic is guilty of a contradiction. And it makes no difference that the '(an)other' that we can criticize is not an easily-identifiable person but a set of meanings, ideas, or theories *in* society, for meaning can be constitutive of its object where social phenomena are concerned.

If the stubborn critic should retort with the charge that the assumption that we must be rational is an extraneous, indefensible value-judgement, this will only deepen his or her contradiction, for if this were so, it would threaten the factual discourse which was being defended from contamination as much as the value discourse (Bhaskar, 1979, p. 31). Moreover, more generally, as Winch (1960) and Habermas (1972) argue, a commitment to what we misleadingly call 'principles' or 'value-judgements' of 'truth-telling' and 'mutual recognition' is a condition of the possibility of communication. To be able to communicate or to interpret, we must assume that the speaker or writer is not using every term deceptively. The possibility of lying does not undermine this claim, for the functioning of certain statements in a deceptive way depends precisely on the pre-supposition that the listener assumes that the truth is, by and large, being told. By the same token, because speaking and writing invite social relationships, the latter must involve a substantial degree of mutual recognition and trust if communication takes place. Commitment to truth-telling need not be understood as some voluntaristic attachment to a lofty indefensible moral value, but as essential to our very nature as social beings, as beings who communicate.

A further common objection is more easily dealt with. This is the refusal of the assumption that social objects can in any sense be false, such that they can be criticized. The case for the opposition is perhaps most persuasively put by claiming our argument to be absurd because it is tantamount to advising social scientists to say that 'it's the world that is wrong, not our theories'! Applied to natural, science it *is* absurd, but the arguments raised above about constitutive meanings are sufficient to repudiate the charge in social science. It is perfectly possible to criticize beliefs in society as illusory *and* represent them authentically. (This is not to deny that sometimes disagreements or criticism can stem from misunderstanding, but again if this were *always* the case, rational discourse could not take place.) Another factor which explains our opponent's erroneous belief is a common *methodological individualism* which supports the belief that only individuals can be mistaken. It does so by collapsing everything that is irreducibly *social* and *inter*subjective—language, rules, social relations, institutions, etc.—back into voluntaristic productions of the isolated individual. Also there is usually a further reinforcing but erroneous presupposition which centres on a conflation of the distinctions real (existent)/unreal (nonexistent), and true/false, or rational/irrational. Since, as already shown, it is possible for false ideas such as witchcraft to have some practical adequacy, such that action may be informed by them, it is simply a (category) mistake to argue that social phenomena cannot be falsely-based if they exist. So there *are* often cases where we can say both that it is the social world that is wrong, not our theories, and that those theories understand that world *as it exists*. An important implication of this is that it is misleading to represent marxism (or any other critical theory) as either simply another positive theory, or (perhaps following a simplistic interpretation of the 11th Thesis on Feuerbach that 'the point is to change it') as *simply* a normative theory. And because '*non*critical' theory cannot avoid evaluating social phenomena in the very process of understanding them, it is also equally true to say that liberal or conservative theory cannot be adequately described as simply positive or normative.

THE NATURE OF VALUES

Not the least of the problems of conducting a debate on values is that there is not much agreement about what values or value-judgements are. Appeals to everyday usages for clarification (as in the method of linguistic philosophy) are hard to resist but risky because, like any other beliefs, they are possibly false.

Against everyday notions that moral principles are supra-historical or even supra-social, I would tentatively suggest the following reconstruction of their meaning and origin.[5] First, they are socially constructed, negotiated, and imposed. Appeals to supra-historical religious authority are a way of obscuring the origins of general moralities to the extent that they are imposed by ruling minorities with special interests. Moral principles are necessary conditions for the existence and maintenance of particular forms of association between people. Those principles which are grounded in the most enduring characteristics of human behaviour, such as communication and truth-telling, have a trans-historical character. But within the limits set by these, characteristic historically-specific forms of social organization are associated with similarly specific moral principles. In both cases the moral principles are one set among many necessary conditions for the existence of these types of social association: they are not independent of the latter but interdependent with, or internally related to, them. For example, it is not so much that rules against stealing are not followed in societies lacking private property, it is rather that such rules simply have no meaning in these contexts. Although moral principles are socially produced, they are rarely freely negotiated but usually imposed. As principles or rules, they can be broken, but because they involve social relations this invariably involves penalties. As Skillen suggests:

> Morality is a medium of social exchange, relations are mediated through it and for the specific rewards and punishments it represents; it rests on and enforces a break-down of directly motivated relations of cooperation and reciprocity. (Skillen, 1974, p. 14)

So far, this appears to be a rather cynical, functionalist and even amoral conception of morality because no mention has yet been made of the criterion of goodness, which is generally held to be essential to any conception of moral values. Before dealing with this, the dangers of trying to understand moral values by looking at notions of goodness in abstraction from their determinate historical conditions, thereby producing the de-rationalized or emotivist conception of values against which we have argued, must be realised. There is no contradiction between understanding morality to have intrinsic notions of goodness and accepting that the forms which they take are historically-specific. Moreover, there is nothing idealist in this claim, for as will be recalled, I have, following Habermas,[6] already grounded certain very basic moral principles in the material practice of communication. Both mutual recognition and, more specifically, truth-telling are also conditions of the possibility of our arriving at agreement on what is objective.

Often a distinction is made between logical evaluation and moral evaluation, along the same lines as the fact-value dichotomy; the former appraises the adequacy of reasoning about either matters of fact or analytic truths, while the latter appraises actions. At first sight there is an apparent contrast between the mandatory nature of logical appraisal, insofar as it recognizes only logical necessity, and the indeterminacy and voluntarism of moral appraisal. However, logical appraisal cannot itself justify its own basic principles of commitment to truth and consistency, but this does not mean that there are not rational grounds for either kind of appraisal. Both are grounded in our orientations towards nature through collective or cooperative production—which requires mutual agreement on what is objectively changed through production—and towards one-another in socialization through communicative interaction which provides the medium and means of that agreement.

Trying to suppress these necessary conditions of social existence only simultaneously constrains the exercise of our powers as social beings. In class societies, however, these conditions are repressed to a certain extent through power relations which are to the advantage of the few and at the expense of the many. They can never be repressed entirely without bringing an end to the production and socialization which maintains social life. An example of the repression of these basic orientations or principles is the treatment of meaningful action (e.g. expression of grievances) as mere (aberrant) physical behaviour. Presumably, radical behaviourists could not and would not want to relate to one another in this way. But whereas mutual recognition and allied orientations or interests can be universalized (and develop our powers in the process), universalization of their repression can only undermine our existence as 'a species that reproduces its life both through learning processes of socially organized labour and processes of mutual understanding in interactions mediated in ordinary language' (Habermas, 1972, p. 194). So even within a repressive society, a degree of mutual recognition is an essential condition of existence. This means that contradictions are set up between practices which repress and practices which develop mutual recognition. Since there is an asymmetric relation between these (repressive actions require mutual recognition in limited spheres in order to override it in others, but not *vice versa*), an emancipatory tension is set up. To take a more mundane and limited example: once it is recognized that boys and girls have equal intellectual potential, and once there is some recognition of this in the structure of education, it becomes more obvious that it is simply inconsistent to acknowledge this potential at one stage in life only to deny it in practice in adult life. In this way, there is an endless emancipatory pressure in every aspect of society which eventually develops what Wellmer (1972) terms a 'draft meaning' to higher levels. It will be noted that the so-called value-judgements involved in this emancipatory force are subject to the conditions of explanatory adequacy outlined earlier. To say that morality is *ultimately* based on notions of goodness that have no material basis is simply to reproduce morality's ignorance of its own origins.

The definition and enforcement of morality is itself an area of conflict in which ruling groups or classes try to establish, rationalize, and legitimize restricted interests based on exploitation as the general interests of society as a whole. But this stuggle is not *just* a matter of brute force; for insofar as it presupposes a degree of mutual recognition and understanding it cannot ignore completely the constraints of truth-telling or what Habermas terms 'discursively-redeemable validity claims' (Habermas, 1976c).

HARVEY'S CONCEPTION OF THE PROBLEM OF VALUES: FURTHER COMMENTS

Having offered this account of the nature of values and how they are, in principle, capable of rational defence, it may be useful to clarify agreements and dis-agreements with Harvey. The general argument of his essay on the population problem, that values are secreted by particular theories and approaches and that we should judge the former by reference to the explanatory adequacy of the latter, is acceptable. But on the question of practice as a solution to philosophical problems such as those of values, his arguments, especially those in *Social Justice and the City*, are less satisfactory. The idea that such problems are, or can be, solved through practice is all too easy; there is something curious about the coexistence of a belief in the pervasiveness of false consciousness in society's commonsense self-understanding of its everyday practice with a faith in the ability of practice to solve difficult problems. There is also a peculiar tension between the emphasis on the necessity of theory and the solution of practice, which is evident when it is acknowledged that theory is itself a practice. This is usually answered by an appeal to the concept of 'revolutionary praxis' in which practice is intimately informed by theory and in which the latter is tested by the former. This generates a danger of a circular argument in which revolutionary theory is that which survives practical test and that which does not, is not. Yet far more important than this objection is the problem of what constitutes a test in practice. The theories of false consciousness and commodity fetishism presuppose that false ideas may be objectified (successfully) in practice, and marxist ideas are by no means the only ones which can create social practices in their own image. So how is one to assess the relative merits of a successful marxist practice against that of a successful liberal or fascist practice?

The major problem is that values, and especially moral values, have been situated in their material social context in such a way as to *reduce* them to those contexts. The result is an implicit conception of (moral) values which is not only apparently functionalist and cynical but also non-moral and non-evaluative; values are specific to particular contexts but it is not evident that they have a rationale of appraisal which enables them to be used in making decisions. This silence in the account is typical of a positivist element in the interpretation of marxism. It constitutes a reading of marxism which might give rise to a 'scientific socialism'. As Keat (1979) argues, to object to scientific socialism is not to argue that marxist theory cannot be scientific but simply that it cannot be understood purely as science.

Harvey recognizes the limits to science when he notes that the principles of scienfific method cannot be justified by appeal to science's own methods (Harvey, 1974a); this is the same point made earlier in the discussion concerning decisionism. But Harvey does not fully demonstrate how this is to be avoided, and how a rationale for these and other normative principles can be given. Consider the following hypothetical interchanges in a debate between critical theory (C) and scientific socialism (S).

C. How is one to decide what is the right thing to do?
S. That always depends on the context.
C. Yes, that is conceded, but how is one to decide?
S. The answer will be decided upon by the people. It is not for us to make blueprints. The answer will be decided in practice.
C. But how? According to what standards and criteria of rationality and justifiable action?
S. You must remember that such standards are not ahistorical and do not float above society as eternal principles.
C. Granted, but nevertheless how are they decided?

This impasse produces an appeal by the scientific socialist to decisionism, though this time not on behalf of scientists as was the case with Popper, but on behalf of the people, the masses or the class. The question of the rationale which guides the formation and application of values cannot be answered because it is not amenable to a positivistic scientific practice which is concerned with the explanation and prediction of objective processes. The sharing of meaning and the principles of mutual recognition which is a precondition of communication (including communication about positivism) fall outside the conceptual space of the positivistic interpretation of scientific socialism. It is therefore able to situate values but not to understand their rationale or the nature of a 'draft meaning' in society. They are collapsed back into material social processes until they effectively disappear. This non-moral or a-rational interpretation of values in society is then rightly suspected of pre-figuring an authoritarian version of socialist practice in which party theoreticians determine needs as technical, quantitative ends, and look upon the means to their achievement in a purely instrumental way, in much the same fashion as in positivist science (cf. Wellmer, 1971). Harvey is presumably aware of this problem when he notes that a full discussion of ideology or values would require an analysis of the nature of rationality, but his decision to omit it exposes his account to these kinds of criticism.

In *Social Justice and the City*, Harvey asks the important question: 'Why these beliefs?'. This needs to be answered in *two* ways; in terms of the material contexts which give rise to the beliefs, and in terms of their rationale. Harvey gives answers of the first type, but tends rather hopefully to leave the latter to be answered by 'practice'. As I have shown, despite the fact that these normative principles cannot be theorised within science as it is normally understood, they can nevertheless be demonstrated as both rational and grounded in practice.

REASON AND COMMITMENT

We feel that even when all possible scientific questions have been answered, the problems of life remain completely untouched (Wittgenstein, 1922, 6.52)

It is widely believed that reason is and should be disinterested, and that *objectivity* requires *neutrality*. The latter is a curious view because it seems to suggest that objectivity has something to do with the distribution of (subjective) support for ideas. We presumably would not advise scientists to choose whether Einstein's theory was more objective than Newton's theory by taking a vote on it or choosing the modal point in the distribution of views, and yet this could be said to be implied by the assumed equivalence of objectivity and neutrality. The truth of a belief has nothing to do with its location in a distribution of attitudes, whether it is at the centre or an extreme. Even if a more charitable view of the meaning of this assumed equivalence is taken, in which neutral is construed as 'standing apart from' or 'indifferent towards' rather than as 'in the middle', this does not help the case. Trying to adopt such an attitude of indifference is not possible in the sense that we cannot avoid some standpoint, and in any case there is no reason, *a priori*, why that standpoint should be the most correct of the alternatives.

Far from being neutral, disinterested, and impartial, reason in pursuit of objectivity is always critical, committed, and partial, always *for* some ideas and *against* others. By committed, I don't mean a blind, dogmatic commitment: it need not exclude profound scepticism. Those marxists who describe and defend their position as being 'on the side of the working class' against ideas which are 'on the side of the ruling class' are over-simplifying matters, unless an argument is offered (and there are such arguments) that the former's interests embody the 'objective interest'. Since Marx's dictum was to 'doubt everything', he could not have advocated commitment *without* scepticism, *without self-criticism*. And as was argued in the preceding section on the nature of values, marxism can no more exclude normative questions or right and wrong, truth and falsity, than any other putative science of society.

Although it is not possible to suspend belief in all values simultaneously, one can suspend particular values and this may be fruitful insofar as it prompts a critical re-evaluation of the theories that secrete those values. The conclusion of this re-evaluation may confirm one's theories and values, but there will be a gain in terms of self-understanding from such attempts to suspend beliefs. Once again, acceptance of the inevitability of value-ladenness does not entail any dogmatic retreat from reason. So what I am proposing is a commitment to a rationally-defensible knowledge which includes values. And this norm is itself a condition of the possibility of rational discourse and the reproduction of the species through production and communicative interaction.

In contrast to this, the orthodox view takes reason to be a neutral tool—'a faculty of the correct handling of formal logic and methodological rules' (Habermas, 1976a, 147). The approach advocated here, which recognizes the role of reason in social science's own object, in the social life process as a 'draft meaning', establishes not an external relation between a separate theory and a society *upon* which reason operates, but an internal one; an interpenetration of frames of meaning within which both practical and theoretical reasoning is conducted. This is radically opposed to the combination of an emotivist conception of values, a purely contemplative epistemology and an instrumental view of reason which estranges either science or theory from practical life and which is so aptly described in the despairing quotation from Wittgenstein that heads this section.

This estrangement is particularly deeply engrained in positivism, even where those broadly within this tradition retract the point (which is often incorporated into definitions of positivism) that science is value-free. Even with this concession, positivism still reifies social action and hence expels reason from practical life. It still turns '*questions of validity* [about social action] into *questions of behaviour*' (Habermas, 1976c, p. 6) and it still converts the 'actual antagonisms [within society] into a pluralism of irrational value judgements' (Wellmer, 1971,

p. 21). The refusal to reason with social values in the status quo means that a positive theory of the status quo inadvertently takes a dogmatic stand upon the dominant system of values objectified in and sustained in society's existing power structure. And where it mistakenly assumes that the real cannot be irrational, any challenges to society's rationality are made to appear as objections to rationality itself. Yet it follows from our arguments about constitutive meanings and false consciousness that social science cannot avoid questions about what is right in attempting to find out what is the case.

Positivistic accounts of science which present normative questions as ultimately beyond rational defence cannot make sense of rational discourse in general, let alone of their own scientific discourse in particular. The orthodox position presents attacks upon the neutrality and autonomy of science as threats to reason and yet the converse is the case; for in being unable to comprehend its own values and rationale and in 'irrationalizing' non-science, it

> . . . . arbitrarily silences a more comprehensive rationalization and it converts the strength of reflection, in the name of precise distinction and sturdy empiricim, into sanctions against thought itself (Habermas, 1976, p. 143)

And from the opposed position of critical theory, knowledge is not limited to a 'science' estranged from practical life, but is concerned precisely with questions of 'how shall we live?'.

POSTSCRIPT

This has been a philosophical argument, not a substantive one. It has tried to establish the possibility and indeed the necessity of reasoning with values, but has not tackled substantive questions regarding particular values. The conclusions cannot be expected to be more than tentative: the paradox of values—that they are both thoroughly ordinary and yet mysterious—makes philosophical discussion of the subject more than usually contestable. Many of the arguments developed above are of the 'in principle' kind; in particular that in principle it is possible to assess values rationally by evaluating the explanatory power of the theories which secrete them. *In practice*, there are some areas of inquiry where explanatory theories are so weakly developed that the grounds for a possible rational evaluation are too insubstantial. The values we hold about the aesthetic quality of landscapes might be an example. Perhaps an argument could be developed to show that these values fall outside the range of what is rationally defensible in principle as well as in practice. In the absence of such a thesis, I would optimistically suggest that they simply lie in areas where explanatory theory is at present weakly developed, and ask that we do not use this absence as an excuse for the refusal of argument and inquiry implicit in the 'it all depends upon your value-judgement' answer. However *difficult* argument is about values, we are quite rightly dissatisfied by retreats from reasoning about them. Hegel summed it up rather well:

> 'Since the man of commonsense makes his appeal to feeling to an oracle within his breast, he is finished and has done with anyone who does not agree; he only has to find and feel the same as himself. In other words, he tramples underfoot the roots of humanity. For it is in the nature of humanity to press onward to agreement with others; human nature only really exists in an achieved community of conscious being. The anti-human, the merely animal, consists in staying within the sphere of feelings, and being able to communicate only at the level (Hegel, *Phenomenology of Spirit*)[7]

Perhaps the major implication of this paper is that work in geography, indeed right across the academic division of labour, should be 'committed' in the sense outlined above. This proposal has, of course, been made before (see for example, Gregory, 1978, 1979; Lewis and Melville, 1977; and Sayer, 1979) but this paper arrives at it from a slightly different route. The conventional pretence at exclusion of values from academic writing is not a safeguard to sound knowledge but a threat. It was argued that not even conservative or status-quo theory (Harvey, 1973) could avoid evaluating social phenomena. The problem is that it does so explicitly only in the most limited ways. Usually, the conscious evaluation is restricted to a tiny part of human practice which is curiously termed 'policy', while the vast majority of everyday practices which reproduce and transform the structures on which policy is supposed to act are taken as an inert background. It is as if policy were the only kind of human action directed by considered decisions and all other actions were a-rational and automatic and hence not susceptible to criticism. This characteristic kind of reification prevents criticism of ideas opening out into critique of practice for it never looks beyond particular false ideas to the social practices which sustain and are sustained by them. Therefore, although it can be argued that critical social science is already immanent in conventional approaches, the latter are a long way from a genuine form of committed inquiry which refuses arbitrary restrictions upon the scope of inquiry. One such restriction is that of confinement to one's discipline. If we cannot reject the constraint on critical thought posed by the insistence that we do not trespass outside geography, however it may be defined, there is no hope of achieving the 'more comprehensive rationalization' of practice that Habermas seeks.

Finally, having attacked some of the philosophical and professional inhibitions upon committed, critical inquiry, it is to be hoped that substantive questions regarding particular values and associated social practices, such as those involved in the population debate analysed by Harvey, can be tackled more effectively.

NOTES

1. This nice inversion is not my own but Bhaskar's (1979). Those sensitized against scientism by Habermas should note that in this context 'science' simply refers to rationally-assessable knowledge and not to restrictive positivist definitions.
2. This is one of the main problems tackled by Olsson in *Birds in Egg* (1979)
3. An argument that is valid is not necessarily true. For example: 'All animals with wings can fly. Geographers are animals and have wings. Geographers can therefore fly', is a valid but untrue argument!
4. This apt term was coined by E. P. Thompson (1978, p. 368) in his critique of (among other things) emotivist conceptions of values held by some marxists.
5. Some parts of my account have been influenced by Skillen (1974), but there is a more general dependence on the work of Habermas. The latter is as difficult as it is ambitious, and its discussion is in danger of becoming ghettoized. My account will therefore seem idiosyncratic in that I have deliberately tried to avoid reproducing Habermas's own terminology and have used, where possible, terms which 'tie it into' theories and philosophies that are more familiar and less abstruse. If there is a risk of 'bowdlerization' then it is worth taking as it is more likely to provoke clarification of the obscurities of his theory by his defenders than is faithful reproduction.
6. Here I think Bhaskar (1979, p. 71) is wrong in attributing to Habermas the idea that values are ultimate and independent.
7. I am indebted to Richard Gunn for this quotation.

REFERENCES

Adorno, T. W. *et al.* (1976). *The Positivist Dispute in German Sociology.* Heinemann, London.

Apel, K.-O. (1972). Communication and the foundations of the humanities. *Acta Sociologica*, **15**, 7–27.

Bhaskar, R. (1979). *The Possibility of Naturalism.* Harvester Press, Brighton.

Chisholm, M. (1975). *Human Geography: Evolution or Revolution.* Penguin Books, Harmondsworth

Connerton, P. (1976). *Critical Sociology,* Penguin Books, Harmondsworth

Cutler, T. *et al.* (1978). *Marx's Capital' and Capitalism Today,* Routledge and Kegan Paul, London.

Edgley, R. (1969). *Reason in Theory and Practice,* Hutchinson, London.

Eysenck, J. J. (1954). *The Psychology of Politics,* Routledge and Kegan Paul, London.

Gellner, E. (1962). Concepts and society. In R. Wilson (ed.) (1977) *Rationality,* Blackwell, Oxford.

Geras, N. (1972). Marx and the critique of political economy. In R. Blackburn, *Ideology and Social Science,* Fontana Books, London.

Giddens, A. (1976). *New Rules of Sociological Method,* Hutchinson, London.

Gregory, D. (1978). *Ideology, Science, and Human Geography,* Hutchinson, London.

Gregory, D. (1979). The ideology of control: systems analysis and geography. Paper presented to the Anglo-French Symposium on Ideology and Geography, University of Cambridge, March 1979 (published in Tijdschrift voer Economische en Sociale Geografie, **1981**, 71, 108).

Gunnell, J. G. (1975). *Philosophy, Science, and Political Inquiry,* General Learning Press, New Jersey.

Habermas, J. (1972). *Knowledge and Human Interests,* Heinemann, London.

Habermas, J. (1976a). The analytical theory of science and dialectics, in T. W. Adorno *et al. The Positivist Dispute in German Sociology* (translated by G. Adey and D. Frisby) Heinemann, London.

Habermas, J. (1976b). A positivistically bisected rationalism. In T. W. Adorno *et al., The Positivist Dispute in German Socialogy* (translated by G. Adey and D. Frisby) Heinemann, London.

Habermas, J. (1976c). *Legitimation Crisis,* Heinemann, London.

Haggett, P., Cliff, A. D., and Frey, A. (1977). *Locational Analysis in Human Geography,* London: Edward Arnold.

Harré, R. *The Philosophies of Science,* Oxford U.P., Oxford.

Harvey, D. (1973). *Social Justice and the City,* Edward Arnold, London.

Harvey, D. (1974a). Population, resources and the ideology of science, *Economic Geography,* **50,** (3), pp. 256–77 and reprinted in R. Peet (ed.) *Radical Geography,* Methuen, London.

Harvey, D. (1974b). What kind of Geography for what kind of public policy? *Trans. of the Institute of British Geographers,* **63,** 18–24.

Hay, A. M. (1979). Positivism in human geography: a response to critics. In D. T. Herbert and R. J. Johnston (eds.) *Geography and the Urban Environment,* Volume 2, Wiley, London, 1–26.

King, L. J., and Golledge, R. J. (1978), *Cities, Space, and Behavior: the elements of urban geography,* Prentice-Hall, Englewood Cliffs, New Jersey

Keat, R. (1979). Scientific socialism: a positivist delusion. *Radical Philosophy,* **23,** 21–23.

Myrdal, G. (1959). *Value in Social Theory,* Routledge and Kegan Paul, London.

Nagel, E. (1961). *The Structure of Science,* Routledge and Kegan Paul, London.

Olsson, G. (1979). *Birds in Egg,* Pion Ltd., London.

Popper, K. R. (1959). *The Logic of Scientific Discovery,* Hutchinson, London.

Sayer, R. A. (1979). Epistemology and conceptions of people and nature in geography. *Geoforum,* **10,** 19–43.

Skillen, T. (1974). Marxism and morality. *Radical Philosophy,* **8,** 11–15.

Taylor, C. (1967). Neutrality in political science. In *Philosophy, Politics and Society* III, P. Laslett and W. G. Runciman (eds.)

Taylor, C. (1971). Interpretation and the science of man. *Review of Metaphysics,* **25,** 3–51.

Thompson, E. P. (1978). *The Poverty of Theory,* Merlin Press, London.

Wellmer, A. (1971). *The Critical Theory of Society,* Herder and Herder, Berlin.

Williams, R. (1977). *Marxism and Literature,* Oxford U.P., Oxford.

Wilson, A. G. (1978). Book review of 'A Critique of Urban Modelling' by R. A. Sayer. *Environment and Planning A,* **10,** 1085–1086

Winch, P. (1960). 'Nature and convention' in R. Beehler and A. R. Drengson (eds.) *The Philosophy of Society,* Methuen, London.

Wittgenstein, L. (1922). *Tractatus Logico-Philosophicus,* Kegan Paul, London.

Geography and Urban Environment
Progress in Research and Applications, Volume IV
Edited by D. T. Herbert and R. J. Johnston
© 1981 John Wiley & Sons Ltd.

Chapter 3

Ideology and Urban Residential Theory in Latin America

Rod Burgess

INTRODUCTION

There is an apocryphal story from Australia about an aborigine who after acquiring a new boomerang then experienced great difficulty in throwing away the old one. This has been exactly the dilemma of the geographer in the 1970s. Eclecticism, characterized by the inability to discard old and no longer useful intellectual ideas, has reigned triumphant over this period. This form of shameless relativism, that sees no particular theoretical difficulty in the espousal of mutually contradictory theories, has been particularly evident in urban and development geography.

The study of urban slums and shanty-towns is necessarily multi-disciplinary, but from the geographical viewpoint it has been affected by some of the gravest problems in geographical theory. These include the failure to conceptualize the relationship between theory and reality, derived from the absence of a materialist epistemology; the failure to arrive at a satisfactory understanding of the relationship of theory to policy, derived from an inadequate concept of the state; the inability to reconstruct the relationship between the spatial and the social without falling into some form of spatial determinism or social idealism (i.e. the social production of space versus the spatial production of the social); and the failure to conceptualize adequately the relationship between social structures and individual behaviour.

A thorough critique of the role of ideology in Latin American urban residential theory would have to be based on a close examination of all these failures. In this essay however, there is only space to discuss two central issues: firstly, the general inability of Latin American urban geography to provide a satisfactory account of the relationship between the broader historical process of economic and social change and the process of change at an urban or intra-urban level (i.e. an inadequate articulation of the relationship between 'development' theory and 'urban' theory); secondly, the notable absence of any vigorous examination of the relationship between social and spatial processes on the one hand and social and spatial modes of explanation on the other. Of course the absence of conscious theoretical reflection on these issues, does not mean that some notion of these relationships does not lie embedded as an implicit pre-suppositional basis and ideological bedrock of the theory. One of the most urgent requirements for improving our understanding of Latin American cities is therefore to make explicit what has so often remained implicit. What in effect we are dealing with in the post-war literature on spatial issues in Latin American cities is a series of theoretical frameworks whose propositions and assumptions have been elaborated at different spatial levels. This creates a kind of division of labour amongst theories sharing the same propositions, that use a spatial criterion as grounds for the definition of their theoretical object, (e.g. global, national, regional, or urban).

In this way the framework offered by structural functionalist theory was elaborated into the modernization and diffusion theories of development at a national level which dominated Latin American studies until the late 1960s. At an urban level the same propositions were expressed in a variety of urban theories ranging from modified Chicago School land-use approaches to culture of poverty and marginality, formal or informal sector models, etc. dependency theory, which dominated the Latin American intellectual scene from the late 1960s to the mid-1970s, was largely unsuccessful in generating theory at an urban level outside of a few relatively isolated attempts (Leeds, 1969; Walton, 1976). The historical structural approach, based on the Althusserian reading of Marx, developed a body of theory at an urban level based somewhat uneasily on the theory of marginality, and more convincingly on concepts such as the articulation of modes and forms of production, the industrial reserve army of labour, surplus, and necessary social labour, urban social movements, and concepts derived from the marxist theory of social class.

This overall conceptual framework cannot be elaborated here in greater detail but some of its obvious difficulties can be stated. Firstly, there is the question of the intellectual status of these broader frameworks and the relationship among them. Are they paradigms for example and, if so, do paradigm shifts occur? Secondly, there is the obvious problem of boundaries; marginality theory, for example, seems to straddle both structural functionalism (e.g. Germani, 1972; Vekemans and Silva, 1969) and historical structural marxism (e.g. Quijano, 1973; Nun, 1969). Thirdly, there is the problem of how the different frameworks differentiate discrete spatial entities and explain spatial relationships both within and between spatial scales, such as the relationship between theories based on *urban or rural* differences and those based on *regional* differences, the problem of whether spatial relations at one scale are simply those of another scale writ large or small, etc.

It should be pointed out, however, that these theories stand in opposition to each other. The history of Latin American urban studies has been the history of the development of alternative theoretical frameworks which have vied for dominance. All of them have developed concepts of an analytical and critical character providing tools for the study and definition of urban problems and a critical framework for dealing with alternative treatments of these issues (e.g. Gunder–Frank's critique of modernization theory (1969); Laclau's critique of Frank (1977); Pradilla's critique of marginality theory (1976); Leeds' critique of culture of poverty theory (1971); Booth (1975) and so on).

The purpose of this essay is to provide an overview of current and past pre-occupations of research into Latin American slums and shanty-towns and to indicate from a critical marxist perspective where the ideological errors of this research lie. The fact that marxist categories are being used in a critical rather than analytical fashion should not be taken to mean that there are no problems arising from their analytical use. Indeed much of recent marxist research has been directed towards exposing the ideological content of purportedly marxist theories.

The scope of the critique has been narrowed down to three central preoccupations: the treatment of the relationship between spatial and social processes; the treatment of the process of the production, exchange and consumption of housing and settlement goods and services; and the treatment of the critical issue of social classes and class conflict. The area of the critique could quite easily be extended onto the political and cultural—ideological levels and related to the problem of the classification of settlements. Indeed an adequate analytical framework for the study of settlement processes would require an approach that integrated all of these considerations.

The ideological elements have been identified in the manner suggested by Stavenhagen (1968) as a series of erroneous propositions or departures as follows:

A. The treatment of the relationship between social and spatial processes.
  1. *The attempt to resolve the theoretical and methodological problem of the limits of urban and settlement analysis on the basis of a spatial criterion and a consequent tendency towards spatial determinism.*
  2. *The attempt to claim a universality for urban models and theories that are in fact the product of an historically and spatially specific social formation.*
B. The treatment of the process of the production, consumption, and exchange of housing and settlement goods and services.
  3. *The misunderstanding of the relationship between needs, exchange-values and use-values in the study of low-income housing and settlement processes and of the nature of land and housing as commodities.*
C. The treatment of social classes and class-conflict in the study of housing and urban settlement.
  4. *The tendency to shift the study of housing and settlement processes away from a class-based and structural framework onto a level of individual,*

family or household behaviour which is subsequently generalized for a settlement or social group.

5. *The tendency to treat the social structures of slums and shanty-towns as homogeneous and undifferentiated.*
6. *The tendency to construct housing and settlement models upon unproven assumptions about overall levels of social mobility of low-income groups.*

These propositions will now be examined, and in the final section a brief and critical review of recent marxist analysis of these three areas will be discussed.

THE TREATMENT OF THE RELATIONSHIP BETWEEN SOCIAL AND SPATIAL PROCESSES

The attempt to resolve the theoretical and methodological problem of the limits of urban and settlement analysis on the basis of a spatial criterion and a consequent tendency towards spatial determinism

The attempt to claim a universality for urban models and theories that are in fact the product of an historically and spatially specific social formation.

All of the problems that emerged out of the structural-fuctionalist formulation of the relationship between space and society at the international, national and regional levels have also manifested themselves at the urban and intra-urban levels. These include the problem of the pre-selection of discrete spatial entities as valid theoretical objects, the problem of the relative level of significance attached to spatial and social modes of explanation (in particular the over-determination of the social by the spatial), and the problem of the relationship between social and spatial phenomena within and between spatial scales. Moreover, the theories and models of urban structures and settlement processes that have been used to understand the Latin American city offer an explanation (or better still a description) of those historically-specific spatial forms that are appropriate to advanced capitalist societies of the West. At the urban level, a body of theory was presented (largely based on the work of the Chicago school of urban ecology) that attempted to explain the discrepancy between the Latin American urban reality and its own theoretical formulation of this reality in terms of a unilinear, dualistic, and irreversible transition to Western urban structures and processes.

In the late 1950s and early 1960s the capitalist development of agriculture and import-substitution industrialization of a capital intensive and monopoly nature began to have profound effects at the urban level. In the same way as western development theory had identified urbanization as an autonomous process, had established a dualism between the 'urban' and the 'rural', and had proposed that urban processes were governed by their own laws, so a body of theory was also developed from the same ideological tradition, that reproduced all of these errors at an urban level. The study of urbanization 'in and for itself' thus had its parallel in the study of the city 'in and for itself'. The city became a spatially de-limited 'microcosm within which different aspects of social ecology, culture and political organization are examined' (Portes and Browning, 1976, p. 4).

The principal influence on this endeavour was the Chicago School of Urban Ecology whose theoretical and methodological formulations were extensively applied to the analysis of Latin American cities (Amato, 1968; Turner, 1968; 1969; Harris, 1971; Schnore, 1965; Hoyt, 1963). Making allowance for some individual variations, the common theme of the writers of the Chicago school (Burgess, 1925; Park, 1925; McKenzie, 1925; Wirth, 1938) was the *production of culture by nature*, a thesis derived from the nineteenth century traditions of Social Darwinism and Human Ecology. In the Chicago school this structure of determination takes on a highly mediated form; the urban is essentially a cultural form which is ultimately produced by a particular ecological entity known as the city.

The influence of the Chicago school was immense and dominated Latin American urban studies throughout the 1950s and 1960s. The conception of the city as an 'organic entity' led to the attempt to understand urban changes in terms of the process of urbanization itself, while the adoption of the notion of 'urbanism' allowed urban processes to be seen as operating independently of modes of production. There was the elimination of the concept of social class from urban enquiry and its substitution by income-dominated categories; an *a priori* acceptance of urban-rural dualism; an over-determination of the social by the spatial; and an exclusion of the issues of scarcity and power that has led to an under-emphasis of the role of politics in urban processes. All of this has been carried out within a functionalist framework that has asserted social and spatial integration, stability and consensus at the expense of dysfunction, conflict, and disorganization which, where recognized, have been labelled as particularly *urban* problems (e.g. urban-induced conditions of pathology, anomie, criminality, and marginality).

The Latin American variant of this tradition did yield some valuable results through the measurement and description of urban and housing issues at an empirical level. Examples are found in the field of urban residential patterns, in the intra-city movement of migrants, and in the spatial preferences of low-income groups. The basic assumptions, however, prevented any effective analysis either of the constituent element of the urban problematic or of the general laws governing its transformation.

The question of 'urban'

The notion that urbanism is the product of a given ecological context, the city, is merely an attempt to resolve the urban question by adopting a concept of spatial determinism—the idea that natural, environmental, or spatial phenomena *in themselves* constitute a source of explanation for social phenomena.This whole conceptualization of the relationship between society and space has been effectively undermined (Lenin, 1972, pp. 202–217; Castells, 1977, pp. 115–128). It is hardly feasible, to say the least, to ground a theory of urban processes or indeed a theory of social change on the behaviour of certain 'natural' (demographic) variables. Any development in the dimensions and differentiation of a human group is itself the product and expression of a social structure and is subject to the laws of its transformation. In response to all of this, Castells (1976) has attempted to demonstrate on a more profound level the conceptual improbability of the urban 'theoretical' and urban 'real' object alike. The relationship between spatial structure and social structure, he argues, cannot be conceived of in terms of the spatial determination of the social, though this is not to deny all notions of spatial effects on human activity, but rather to emphasize 'the need to include this space in the web of social structures, not as a variable in itself, but as a real element to be retranslated each time in terms of social processes . . .' (Castells, 1971, p. 25).

The treatment of the city as an isolated unit with a separate and independent economic, social, and spatial structure governed by a largely autonomous history and dynamic was essentially an attempt to resolve the methodological problem of the limits of urban analysis on the basis of a spatial criterion. Moreover, this kind of approach, as Massey (1978) has pointed out for regional analysis, is ultimately based on a tautological mode of reasoning—it implies the prior definition of internally coherent spatial units which are then theoretically confirmed as a result of that analysis. The attempt to elaborate the dynamic of a 'modernization' process within a series of spatial levels was carried out at the expense of those relationships between spatial structures at different spatial levels and it thus fell into the trap of asserting that spatial relations at one scale were simply those of another scale writ large or small (Anderson, 1975). Moreover, the attempt to establish the urban instance as autonomous served an even more distinctly ideological purpose in that it interpreted a relationship between social phenomena (ultimately that between wage-labour and capital) as a relationship between spatial phenomena.

What the Chicago school and its Latin American imitators identified as 'urbanism' is nothing more or less than the mode of social organization that corresponds to the historically and spatially specific condition of advanced capitalist development. The discrepancies emerging from the attempt to apply this model to an entirely different social reality—that of a dependent, neo-colonial, capitalist, social formation—will be evaluated below, but in both cases the definition of the *urban* in opposition to the *rural* is entirely false. Urbanization is a function of the internal structure of a mode of production and a function of the specific organization of modes of production that are historically articulated in a dominant or subordinate relationship within a concrete social formation. The dualist, ahistorical and uni-linear conceptions of urban ecology that falsely polarize the urban and the rural are directly in conflict with objective reality. The urban and the rural are fully integrated in terms of the operation of a dependent social formation and what happens within and between them cannot be understood through the use of methodologically prescribed and spatially determined limits of enquiry, but only through a close examination of the laws that govern them both.

It is relatively easy to trace the weaknesses of this theoretical framework in terms of its empirical validity—much of what happens at an urban and intra-urban level is not distinctly 'urban' and can only be understood in terms of the national and international system of production into which it is inserted. Indeed this is a defining characteristic of industrialization and urbanization undertaken under conditions of dependent capitalist development.

Thus, the urban and housing problems of Latin American societies can best be understood as a problem of the general conditions of an historically specific process of capitalist development rather than as 'urban' or 'housing' problems *per se*, or as products of particular ecological, technical, or industrial conditions. These general conditions constitute the structural source of both the urban and the housing problem and have been adequately specified by Pradilla (1976a). In his prognosis, the spread of capitalist relations in the countryside leads to the expulsion of the peasantry to the city, and industrial development of a dependent, monopoly and capital-intensive nature, leads to the destruction of labour-intensive manufacturing. The outcomes include: the commodity status of land and housing and urban objects, the search for profits by the various 'fractions' of capital tied to urban and housing development, the distribution of income derived from the relationship between wage-labour and capital, the transmission of the principles and ideologies of private property and consumption; the high levels of dependency on foreign finance capital which, amongst other things, determines levels of interest, the size of urban and housing budgets, and subjects the provision of housing, services, and infrastructure to fluctuations in the national and global capitalist economy and, finally, the intervention of the state in the urban process at a national and local level in the interest of locally and nationally defined 'fractions' of capital in co-ordination with the requirements of foreign capital. Thus both the housing and the urban question can only be correctly understood at the level of the capitalist mode of production and at the level of the existing social formation.

Community-based studies

Not surprisingly, most of these problems are also identified in those studies that were carried out at the intra-urban level. In the 1950s and 1960s, the western social science tradition of community-based studies with a general functionalist ideological bias came to dominate research into Latin American urban processes, in the same way that modernization theory was imparting similar propositions in development studies. This led to the proliferation of work that used the *barrio* (neighbourhood) as a methodologically de-limited microcosm for the investigation of economic, social, cultural, and political phenomena. This tradition was spawned by precisely the same current in the social sciences that had identified urbanization as an autonomous process, had claimed that cities could be studied in and for themselves, and had failed to make a causal relationship between urban processes and the operation of modes of production. The *barrio* is not an effective point of departure for an understanding of intra-urban housing and settlement processes in the same way that 'urban' events cannot be divorced from societal contexts.

Though there can be little doubt that community has a much more significant presence in Latin American urban life than in advanced capitalist societies, it is also true that in relation to many aspects of housing and settlement processes, the *barrio* is not an effective unit of analysis. Thus Brett (1974) remarks that *barrio*-based studies have tended to rely on the assumption that the settlement constitutes a 'relatively homogeneous universe' with the consequence that the observer fails to identify elements of change within the settlement and underestimates the significance of residential mobility.

The methodological autonomy given to the settlement in studies of self-help building (Turner, 1972; 1976) has also led to a gross neglect or underestimation of those forces and elements that lie outside of the *barrio* and have influenced its course of development or regression.

It is relatively easy to identify the faults that are associated with the *barrio*-oriented survey approach. They include a tendency to generalize *barrio* life from individual data, to generate misunderstanding of the significance of internal social differentiation for the physical improvement of the settlement and the social and cultural life of the community, and to understate the effect of extra-*barrio* forces. All of this amounts to the theoretical and methodological re-ification of the *barrio* with the consequence that all major aspects of its life are understood as being primarily determined at local rather than at broader levels whether this is in terms of the urban system or of the social formation. In other words it represents a conceptual over-determination of the degree of autonomy of the neighbourhood within the broader urban and capitalist context.

Searching for the Chicago models

It is in the interpretation of the residential structure of the Latin American city that the work of the classical writers of the Chicago school, along with an associated body of concepts such as filter-down theory (Lowry, 1960) and urban rent models (Alonso, 1967; Muth, 1969) has been most widely used. Burgess and to a lesser extent Hoyt (1939) have been particularly popular. Burgess (1925) noted a drop in land-values and a rise in family-income with increasing distance from the centre, a distinct spatial separation of residential, industrial, and commercial functions, and a concentric pattern of land-uses around the

CBD. Hoyt (1939) identified a sectoral pattern of urban land-uses based on the communication axes that radiated out from the centre. Writers on Latin American structure have been quick to identify similar models. Turner (1969) for example identifies an urban residential structure in terms of Burgess's concentric rings and Amato (1970) maintains that Hoyt's reasoning is valid for 'elite' residence patterns in a selected group of Latin American cities.

However, even these urban ecologists could not fail to identify one major discrepancy between the residential structure of the Latin American city and the urban models of the Chicago school—the central location of high income groups, and the peripheral location of low-income groups. The fact that both land-values and family income dropped with increasing distance from the centre would seem to indicate different models than those provided by the Chicago writers. How was this discrepancy to be explained?

One way was simply to identify these discrepancies as variations in the basic structure proposed by the model. The Latin American urban structure merely provided new empirical variants of the original models whose basic structure remained intact (Alonso, 1964; Hoyt, 1964). Far more common, however, was the attempt to marry urban ecological theory with the assumptions and methods of modernization theories of development and particularly with the 'stages of growth' approach. Thus Schnore (1965) simultaneously stressed the need to embark on cross-cultural research and asserted the 'universal' significance of the process of urbanization. The differences between the residential structures of Latin American and North American cities could be interpreted in terms of different stages in a similar urbanization process, whose dynamic revealed the growing approximation of the former to the latter as an effect of economic growth, transport improvements and higher density low-income settlement of central areas abandoned by the outwardly-mobile 'elites'. Beyer (1967), whilst pointing out some of the differences between Latin American urban land-use patterns and the models of the Chicago school, also stressed that Latin American cities were beginning to develop similar urban structures to those of North American cities. Turner (1968) constructed an urban settlement model that situated residential patterns and processes within an historical context. It attempted to show through a staged model the changes in the settlement patterns that 'transitional' cities undergo in the process of migration, urbanization, and modernization.

Thus in the same way as traditional societies were transformed by the continuous, unilinear, and irreversible march of the universal-progressive forces of modernization, as exemplified in the experience of the advanced capitalist countries, so too is the Latin American urban structure progressively transformed by the processes of urbanization and modernization into the 'universal' urban structures proposed by Chicago urban ecological theory. The distance between the existing Latin American urban reality and the classical models can then be explained by situating them in a unilinear, evolutionary continuum or stages model. Moreover, the cities are identified as functional mechanisms that realize the stability and integration that accompanies modernization. Squatting will decrease as productivity and personal incomes rise and cities are mechanisms that guarantee economic and social mobility for the vast majority of newcomers (Stokes, 1962; Turner, 1968; Mangin, 1967). The current and appalling problems of Latin American cities can thus be identified as simply teething problems or temporary maladjustments in a continuous unilinear process of growing approximation to the Western urban model. The residential logic of peripheral squatter settlements is thus understood in terms of the implicit assumptions of modernization theory (economic and social mobility, stability, cumulative and progressive change, etc.). The settlements will show a tendency to gradual physical improvement and will ultimately arrive at complete legal and physical integration into the city as legitimate, working-class suburbs.

This type of analysis can be deeply discredited on empirical, methodological, and theoretical grounds. Quinn (1940), for example, in a review of Burgess's work has isolated many of the assumptions that underlie his model. These include social heterogeneity, a commercial-industrial city, the predominance of private property, an equally available transport network throughout the city, cheap land on the periphery and location governed only by the rules of the market. Not many of these assumptions hold for the Latin American city. Colonial urbanism and local topography are more important influences on the urban structure; there are greater inequalities in access to transport and a greater emphasis on collective rather than private transport, there is little heavy industry and a more footloose light manufacturing industry. There is no strict segregation of industrial, commercial, and residential functions with artisan, commercial and retail activities widely distributed throughout the urban fabric. There is an historically significant tradition of state intervention into private property rights and of state ownership of urban land. Collective decision-making (squatter invasion groups, the state and urban-landed capital) has greatly influenced the free-play of the land market and there have been faster rates of population growth and rural to urban migration. Income inequalities are much greater. There has been middle-class competition with squatters for peripheral land and a smaller middle and upper class has resulted in a much smaller stock of upper income housing available for filtering down with greater lags in the process and there has been a lack of international opportunities for migration. Other significant differences could be identified and the list is clearly formidable.

On a methodological level a series of major problems can be isolated. The transitional stages model of urban structure, like the modernization continuum or stages model, can be criticized as being a 'uni-directional process with a-pre-determined point of arrival' (Nun, 1969). It shares all of its dualistic, a-historical, and unilinear assumptions. At the same time as Latin American cities were manifesting a deterioration in living conditions, lower employment opportunities and an increase in income inequalities, it asserted the transitory nature of these conditions and the functional role of the city as a force for integration, economic, and social mobility, and stability. The methodological procedures display many of the general ideological flaws of structural-functionalist theory and, in particular, the systematic eradication of the historical dimension from the study of social facts. The assumption that the relationship between man and his habitat is mediated in terms of function is quite obviously partial and one-sided because it favours the integrative aspects of human activity and hence the conservative nature of social institutions and behaviour. It is dominated by the concept of social equilibrium and harmony. Moreover, these functions necessarily have to adapt a universal legitimacy that makes the method essentially ahistorical. Thus functionalist models constantly attempt to 'freeze' the dynamic process they are studying, analyse it, and *then* attempt to restart it by introducing a fuctional past and future as 'stages'. This method produces immense difficulties in its account of social change. Those elements that confront this integrative functional 'rationality' have to become negative 'dysfunctions' (e.g. class-conflicts over the ownership of land and the means of production), even though they may well be new functions in the crystallization of a new social order. The methodological denial of history on which functionalism thrives, leads to what Marcuse (1967) has called the study of 'social statics' in which concepts are subordinate to facts, the past is artificially isolated from the present, the future is conceived of as the linear projection of the present, and there is a proliferation of typologies which aggregate historically specific phenomena into quasi-scientific classifications.

This critique is weighty enough but it is in terms of theory and ideology that the attempt to apply Western urban land-use models to Latin American realities can be most severely criticized. The ideological nature of the Chicago school theories has already been demonstrated—'urban culture' or 'urbanization' are not as it suggests self-determining phenomena but are determined by the laws of a given mode of social organization. The 'models', rather than being universally valid for all countries at a certain stage in the urbanization process, are nothing more than the ideological representations of the North American city at a specific period in the process of advanced capitalist development.

It is argued here that the Burgess model rests on a false claim of universal applicability; its application to the Latin American case has taken this ideological claim at its face value and any attempt to understand urban processes occurring under very different conditions in terms of the model inevitably fail. Though a discrepancy between the classical formulation of the models and the urban structure of contemporary Latin American cities has often been recognized, the emphasis has been to show how the Latin American city is moving towards the model rather than to question its theoretical adequacy.

Debate has then centred around which of the models shows the least discrepancy with the Latin American reality or, alternatively, on their characterization as two stages in the same process. The mechanism that allows this to take place is based upon the precepts of modernization theory. The ideological significance of both the models and the theories thus becomes clear: they are to the examination of the process of dependent urbanization in Latin America as 'modernization' and 'stages of growth' theory is to the understanding of dependent neo-colonial capitalist development. The Latin American city derives all of its essential features from the structural characteristics of the dependent social formation in which it is located. Its key features include the absence of heavy industrialization, the creation of a massive 'army' of the unemployed and underemployed, a highly-skewed income distribution and a distinct class structure, early and pronounced state intervention, and the articulated relationship between petty-commodity forms of production and exchange.

The Chicago models say nothing of all this. Logically, Chicago will be the pre-determined point of arrival, the last 'stage' towards which the Latin American city is progressing, in the same way as the national economies and societies will eventually arrive at the experience of the Western 'modern' society. The universal model is that of the advanced capitalist city. Needless to say, it is exceedingly doubtful if the distortions in the urban structures of those countries that are the victims of imperialism can be understood in terms of the spatial distortions of those that are the victors!

Theories of spatial and social relations: marginality and dependency

The ideological nature of the treatment of the relationship between the 'spatial' and the 'social' contained within a body of loosely related theories that have been used in the study of Latin American urban structures must now be considered. These include spatial dualism, culture of poverty theory and ecological marginality theory.

For what are obviously historical reasons the theory of spatial dualism—the notion of two polarized forms of spatial orgazination, defined according to physical criteria—did not receive as much popularity in Latin America as in Africa or Asia (where there was much talk of the juxtaposition of 'native' and 'western' cities). The importance of Oscar Lewis's culture of poverty theory will be discussed fully later, but his work also contributed to the notion of a dualistic ecological structure to the city, where material conditions were responsible for a social and cultural dualism within the urban fabric.

The theory of marginality, however, was much more important in popularizing these concepts in the study of Latin American cities. Marginality theorists were largely concerned with a so-called 'lack of participation' of large numbers of the unemployed and underemployed and new migrants in the physical structure of the city and its social, cultural, and economic life. There was some dispute amongst 'marginalists' over the origins and nature of this condition. Some (Germani, 1972; Vekemans et al, 1969) held it to be a temporary and transitional maladjustment that occurred as a result of the fundamentally irreversible and progressive processes of urbanization and modernization. Marginality, according to this view, could be eradicated by enlightened planning and social welfare legislation (full employment, education and health facilities, better housing and services) and by encouraging policies that stimulated 'popular participation' (community development, 'self-help' programmes, etc.). Others (Quijano, 1973; Nun, 1969) held that marginality was a permanent condition that could only be resolved through a profound structural transformation of society.

The notion of ecological marginality, as Perlman (1976) has pointed out in her comprehensive review of marginality theory, was the version that 'most readily captured the allegiance of government officials in Latin American nations' (Perlman, 1976, p. 105). With the proliferation of makeshift shanty-towns on the peripheries of Latin American cities from the late 1950s onwards, the concept of their 'marginality' was constructed out of their location and the appalling physical conditions that differentiated them from other parts of the city. As Perlman put it: 'A marginal situation was clearly defined as a condition of inhabiting marginal neighbourhoods, i.e. favelas' (Perlman, 1976, p. 102). The policies that came out of this assessment were the physical eradication of slums and bad living conditions and the provision of low-cost public housing, the implementation of which would result in the disappearance of the 'psychotic, personality traits and 'anti-social' behaviour patterns typical of these settlements (another classical example of spatial determinism). The integration of the marginal population could be secured through enlightened state urban housing policies.

Many of the criticisms levied against the Chicago land-use models could also be maintained against ecological marginality theory. It can similarly be described as a study of social phenomena within a spatially-delimited and determined framework which restricts the search for causation to the level of the settlement and carries the associated false assumptions of that approach. Particularly important, however, is its lack of empirical validity; the so-called 'ecologically-marginal' settlements are far from marginal. Both the *inquilinatos* and the peripheral settlements are fully integrated (however imperfectly and illegally) into the urban structure in terms of their location, access to services and infrastructures. They are also integrated into the urban land market. Speculative and illegal markets for urban land for low-income groups are widespread throughout Latin American cities and in some countries, such as Colombia, they are the most common form of low-income access to land. Even where there has been invasion and self-improvement of land, new ground-rents are produced and these are subject to the operations of the state and the market. The capitalist development of urban land not only determines the appearance of invasions but also indirectly controls the process of land-valuation occurring within them. Illegal submarkets for land are often an important motive force behind many invasions ('professional invasions'). The peripheral shanty-towns fully participate in the processes governing the consumption of urban and housing objects as part of the reproduction of social labour-power and capital and are an integral element in the spatial organization of capitalist production, consumption and exchange. They are both governed by and are a manifestation of the process of income-command of space and are therefore integrated into the system of urban-social segregation. They are also integrated into the existing industrial and commercial structure of the city through petty-commodity forms of production and exchange.

Finally, a brief note on dependency theory. One of the most curious aspects of dependency theory has been its general inability to provide a suitable framework for explanation at the urban level. Apart from the pioneering work of Leeds, (1969), one article by Gunder-Frank (1969), and a recent collection of articles edited by Portes and Browning (1976) there has been no systematic attempt at elaborating the dependency argument at the urban level. Dependency theory has taken the social production of space as the critical starting-point for its theoretical elaboration of social and spatial relationships and has established the need to context urban and spatial phenomena in the dependent capitalist social formations, with all the characteristics that the accumulation process at a global level imposes. However, it has been less successful in elaborating historically and spatially specific structures and processes at an urban level than at the international, national, and regional spatial scales. Despite all of its efforts to avoid a spatial bias and to use phenomena merely as relational points of reference in common with structural-functionalism it has automatically imposed a prior definition of coherent spatial units as the starting point of analysis which was subsequently verified theoretically as a result of the analysis. Moreover, the call of writers like Walton (1976) for 'vertically-integrated' analysis has tended to create a mechanistic image in which relations of domination have been isomorphically reproduced at different spatial scales. In other words, there has been a conceptual over-determination of the significance of relations at the global and national scale in the shaping of the internal structure and dynamics of a lower spatial scale (e.g. the role of the city in the urban hierarchy is the most formative influence on intra-urban structures).

The principal reason for the absence of a significant body of dependency literature at an urban level has been the general confusion of spatial and social processes that is typical of the theory and especially of Frank's version. Thus two of Frank's three contradictions of capitalist under-development—surplus expropriation or appropriation, and metropolitan or satellite polarization—refer to two distinct aspects of reality—to spatial relations and to social relations. The conceptual relationship between these two 'contradictions' always remains confused in Frank's work. The collapsing of social and spatial relations, sometimes taken to show a lack of 'concreteness', can be achieved relatively easily in the rural context. The spatially-defined chain of metropolitan or satellite relations which ends up with a *latifundista* involves a shift from the spatial to the social which is relatively well-concealed, because of the position of land in the process of production. In the city, however, this shift cannot be made so easily because the production process does not have such a pronounced spatial component.

The treatment of the process of the production, consumption and exchange of housing and settlement goods and services

The misunderstanding of the relationship between needs, exchange-values and use-values in the study of low-income housing settlement processes and of the nature of land and housing as commodities.

Introduction: the misunderstandings

The misunderstanding of the relationship between needs, use-values and exchange-values is perhaps one of the greatest weaknesses in current theoretical efforts to understand low-income housing and settlement processes in the Latin American city. Although classical political-economy did make a distinction between exchange-value and use-values, it failed, as Marx pointed out, to identify the dialectical nature of their interpenetration in the commodity form and converted them into partial, one-sided, and falsely polarized categories that referred to two separate measurements of value. In this way use-value was equated with 'total utility' and exchange-value with the 'ratio of exchange'. The attempt was then made to reconstitute the reality (the commodity) in terms of these polarities by asserting a functional relationship between the two, but this inevitably led to the assertion of one polarity at the expense of the other. In urban land-use and housing literature this has led to division of labour in the realm of theory. On the one hand there exists a body of theory, which includes urban ecology and morphology, that has dealt with the commodity forms of land and housing merely in terms of their use-values and has dwelt on the quantification of 'utilities' asserting the primacy of use-values over exchange-values under certain circumstances (e.g. self-help housing). On the other hand, there is a body of theory that asserts exchange-value at the expense of use-value through the construction of utility-maximizing models which equate use-value with exchange-value at the margin, often through recourse to devices such as 'revealed preference'. Both kinds of theory have been applied to housing and settlement processes in Latin American cities.

All of these approaches have neglected the theory of 'need' for reasons which are not difficult to find. The assumption has been made that the market automatically indicates human needs and—given the indisputable rationality of the market—the social concept of need can therefore be equated with the economic concept of demand. Human needs, moreover, are held to be spontaneous and 'natural'; if needs can be satisfied then the market will see to it, if they cannot be satisfied the lack of availability of the means of their satisfaction on the market will either merely indicate this fact or will indicate that the market is not working 'correctly'. In this way the historical and social concept of 'need' has become the ahistorical and individualized concept of 'demand'. All of this of course is linked to the assumption of the hegemony of the market—a somewhat heroic assertion especially in relation to the 'housing problem' or to underdeveloped countries where resources are poorly allocated and incomes grossly maldistributed—in short where the vast majority of the population lack the resources to translate their housing needs into demand. The notion of 'effective' and 'ineffective' demand has been introduced to accommodate this problem without in any way challenging the fundamental assumption of the rationality of market-forces. In other words the misunderstanding is based on the capitalist reification of 'needs'. As Heller (1978: p. 25) points out:

> The analysis and assessment of need are developed from the viewpoint of capitalism and they are therefore purely economic: economic value is the only value, the highest of all values, and cannot be transcended from any other point of view. The needs of the worker appear as *limits* of wealth, and are analysed as such. At the same time, however, the need that appears in the form of effective demand is a motive force and a means of economic development.

Before going on to analyse the specific manifestation of these difficulties in studies of Latin American housing and settlement issues, it may be worth while stating Marx's analysis of relationships between use-value, exchange-value and need.

Marx (1887; 1889; 1977) proceeds by directly defining use-value in relation to needs. All commodities have to satisfy a need, otherwise they would not be produced. There can be no value (exchange-value) without the satisfaction of needs (use-value), but use-values can exist without value (exchange-value) in the satisfaction of a need. In other words, all commodities must have a use-value as well as an exchange-value, but not all use-values have to take on the commodity form. Exchange-values are not determined by the quantitative proportions by which use-values are exchanged, but rather their value is derived from the application of socially necessary labour-power to material objects in the production of commodities that satisfy needs. In the context of a commodity, use-value and exchange-value have no meaning in themselves but only in terms of their dialectical interaction.

In the commodity form then, use-values can only be realized as exchange-values. The consumption of a commodity is the process of the destruction or appropriation of its use-value in the satisfaction of a need. These needs, however, are not fixed, like those of an animal, they are human rather than 'natural' needs. They are not simply defined by biology but are variable, social and historical and ultimately determined by man himself according to the level of material development reached by society and the collection of values (i.e. ideology) that is attached to the process of consumption.

In a society dominated by a capitalist mode of production concerned with the deepening of the social division of labour and the generalization of commodity production, these needs become 'alienated' needs. The goal of commodity production is not the direct satisfaction of needs but rather the satisfaction of those needs that can fulfil the process of reproduction and expansion of the value of capital. In this form, the need appears only in the market in the form of 'effective' demand and human needs are transformed into the alienated needs of capitalist production: the need, for example, to reproduce and expand the value of capital, the need for the simple or expanded reproduction of social labour-power, the system of needs derived from the division of labour, ranked and structured according to the distribution of the social product amongst social classes, and so on. It follows from this that an adequate understanding of housing produced and exchanged within the capitalist mode of production can only be arrived at through the identification of the specific inter-penetration of use and exchange value within each of the wide range of housing objects that this mode of production can produce; all of these can assume the commodity form.

This is precisely what geographers, planners, sociologists, and economists have failed to do in the study of Latin American housing and urban processes. The exclusive concentration on use-values has been the basis for the examination of urban structures and land-use patterns and the reduction of housing *need* to effective housing *demand* has been the basis for the investigation of housing problems. There has been precious little work or explanation of ways in which these two aspects of the land and housing commodity can be brought together. These studies, therefore, are based on a misunderstanding of the historical and social determination of need; of the nature of exchange-value and upon the methodological separation of use-value from exchange-value *between* theories rather than an attempt to understand their inter-relationship *within* a theory.

Evidence of misunderstanding in studies of Latin American housing

It has already been noted that Chicago school land-use models were widely used in the study of Latin American housing and settlement processes in the 1950s and 1960s and were integrated with the assumptions of modernization theory. They continue to provide many of the implicit assumptions in contemporary empirical studies on a settlement and household level. Unfortunately the functionalist methodology, the use of empirical and quantitative techniques, and the exclusive concern with the use-values of housing and settlements has yielded nothing more than generalized *descriptions* of patterns of use in the urban space-economy. The collection of a huge mass of data, mainly in the form of monographs and case-studies on an individual settlement level, has preceded rather than followed conscious theoretical reflection. Consequently, it is hardly surprising that these data have reflected the implicit ideological assumptions that have been left unchallenged and have been constructed merely into *ad hoc* hypotheses or descriptions of particular situations.

Models based on consumers and 'rational' behaviour

In the late 1960s, however, again in close association with the optimistic and ideological assumptions of modernization theory, a whole range of studies, often openly linked to policy objectives, attempted to apply the more sophisticated utility-maximizing models to Latin American cities. These models retained the basic assumptions of their intellectual progenitors—a generalized *description* of the urban space-economy was presented as *theory* under the fundamental presumption of utility-maximizing behaviour on the part of individuals or households trading off quantity of housing (space), accessibility and the need for other goods and services within limits determined by income. This effort to explain the settlement patterns and processes of Latin American cities purely in terms of the use-values of the house for its consumer was also integrated with newly-collected data on the intra-urban movement of migrants to the city. As a result of these labours (Turner, 1968, 1969; Mangin, 1967) it became clear that the peripheral squatter areas, rather than being the rural enclaves identified in previous literature, were not so much the 'first port of call' but rather the 'last port of call' for rural migrants to the city. The origin of these settlements was then understood in terms of the life-history of the migrant in the city and settlement types were established and analysed exclusively in terms of their functional utility to their inhabitants. The residential structure of Latin American cities reflects housing and settlement priorities. Settlement patterns must be examined in relation to their functional role in the satisfaction of these priorities structured according to income and the settlement process must be seen in terms of the changing priorities of various groups of people who are economically, socially, and geographically mobile.

Perhaps the most systematic, integrated, and influential presentation of this argument is to be found in the work of J. F. C. Turner. All migrants look upon housing for the satisfaction of certain existential needs (identity, security, and opportunity) which are objectified in the use-values of different kinds of housing. Turner presents a model of the patterns of residential settlement that follows from the satisfaction of the changing needs of the migrant for location, tenure, and amenity. The basic components of this model involve the trade-off of housing (space-requirements and standards), accessibility (costs of transport to place of employment), and other essential goods and services (fuel and foods) within an overall budget constraint. Settlements can be classified according to the way in which these various priorities are fulfilled. One of the principal conclusions is that the inner-city slums and squatter settlements will *deteriorate* in their function as receptor areas with a high incidence of renting, whereas the peripheral consolidating squatter settlements will *improve* and eventually convert themselves into orthodox working class suburbs. In this way, according to Turner, the inner-city slum, the interstitial shanty-town and the peripheral squatter settlement 'all perform the principal functions demanded by their inhabitants' and 'in spite of their many and often severe drawbacks they often act as forward-moving vehicles of social and economic mobility' (Turner, 1969, p. 510). Housing and settlement-types are defined in terms of the functional relationship between their use-values and the social needs of low-income groups. These needs are spatially crystallized into a variety of settlement types, according to a set of priorities that changes with the domestic and economic cycle of the migrant as he adjusts on a permanent basis to urban life.

The basic weaknesses of these approaches to Latin American housing and settlement issues arise from their misunderstanding of the nature of housing and settlement needs, of use-values and exchange-values, and of their relationship within the commodity form. Though housing use-values are closely related to the satisfaction of certain basic needs, these are not determined merely at a fixed biological or existential level; they are variable, social, and historical. They thus will be defined according to the level of development of the social forces of production and the system of values (ideology) attached to the house. Though the individual can formulate these housing needs in terms of requirements for shelter, space, access to employment, services, status, etc., these needs are historically and socially determined and are not merely a function of some autonomous realm of individual rationality. Low-income housing and settlement types cannot be identified or explained through ways in which their use-values satisfy these individually-determined needs, but only through reference to the manner in which housing use-values are produced, exchanged, and consumed within a specific social formation. In a social formation dominated by the capitalist mode of production, for example, housing needs can only be satisfied in the market according to the dictates of capital—i.e. only inasmuch as they facilitate the reproduction and expansion of the value of capital (in the form of commodities), and permit the maintenance and expanded reproduction of social labour-power.

The idea that the residential structure of Latin American cities can be understood as the functionally rational expression of individually determined use-values is a distinctly ideological attempt to apply an equilibrium model derived from the experience of an advanced capitalist city to the urban conditions of a dependent social formation. However, all the evidence indicates that low-income groups are excluded from the private and state housing and land markets because their socially-determined income levels put them beyond 'effective demand'. In other words the transformation of need into use-values in a capitalist society has to be mediated by a money relationship. As Pradilla (1976a, p. 74) puts it:

> The housing-object is confronted by a 'solvent consumer' (that is to say by a person who has a sufficient quantity of money available to buy the object), and not by a consumer-in-need of a house, since if he only possesses his need, he would not be able to acquire the object on the market (translated by author).

It may seem particularly inept to apply equilibrium models to urban land-use systems that rarely if ever approach equilibrium even in advanced capitalist societies, but the attempt to postulate these conditions for cities where over 70 per cent of the urban population is beyond effective housing demand, is not only implausible but also leads to some highly disturbing interpretations of what is essentially the irrational allocation of resources to social needs characteristics of dependent capitalist urbanization. The attempt is made to reconstruct this equilibrium, by identifying the satisfaction of low-income housing needs in a variety of forms of 'popular' housing (shanty-towns and inner-city slums). By concentrating exclusively on the use-values of the house to the individual or household and by claiming that this relationship is a functional and rational expression of utility-maximizing behaviour, the most appalling housing and living conditions can be justified and mystified in an inversion process by which the housing 'problem' becomes the housing 'solution'. It can again produce spatial determinism, for given the assertion of the primacy of use-value in housing and the mobility of the migrant, it is hardly surprising that the slums are designated as functional—a sort of spatial constant. This represents a classical example of the reduction of an historical and social variable to an ahistorical and spatial constant. Once a system of individually determined existential needs is matched against an *ideological* set of material needs (priority for freehold tenure, modern material standards, etc.) through a set of housing priorities that are a function of *income*, the social segregation of the environment is designated as a rational allocation of use-values.

The capitalist mode of production is typified by generalized commodity production which has as its end the expansion and reproduction of the value of capital; all objects are either produced as commodities or have the potential of becoming commodities. As commodities they consist of the specific interpretation of use-value and exchange-value and it is no longer possible to analyse them merely in terms of their relations of consumption (relationship between the object and its consumer). The individual now not only has an interest in their existing and future use-value, but also in their actual or potential exchange-value. In other words they have to be looked upon in terms of the social process of being or becoming 'use-values' for others. Land, housing, and improvements can thus only be understood in terms of their commodity character which articulates the fundamentally *social* process of their production, consumption, and exchange and establishes the many class-based interests tied to the commodity cycle. Pradilla (1976a) has identified these social agents of production and exchange as owners of land, owners of productive capital in land and housing development, small and large depositors of money-capital and income in institutions that finance housing, bankers and financiers, intermediate technical agents (contractors, architects, engineers, planners etc.), skilled and unskilled workers, estate agents, owners and managers of credit capital for production and consumption, owner-occupiers, renters, landlords, illegal land, and housing developers, and many others.

A residential land-use theory for the Latin American city cannot be formulated purely in terms of the consumer's appropriation of the use-value of housing, land and improvements when quite obviously these relations are constrained, limited and determined by the interests of other groups. These exert a dominating influence over the total context in which housing and settlement decisions are made. Moreover recent research (Burgess, 1979; Valenzuela and Vernez, 1974) has pointed to the development of land and housing as commodities by the settlers themselves ('informal' or 'petty-commodity' housing). An adequate understanding of low-income settlement processes must take into consideration not only the use-values of the owner-possessors of land and housing, but also the interests of tenants and landlords (in the development of rental submarkets in squatter settlements), political intermediaries who can play the role of 'informal' estate agents, professional invaders ('informal' land developers), skilled or unskilled paid construction workers, contractors, loan-sharks advancing capital for construction and so on. These theories have a great deal of difficulty in accommodating these groups but their presence is universal.

Finally, outside their obvious ideological partiality, their essentially descriptive nature and the fact that they are based solely on the use-value of the house to the user, these models also display the fundamental weakness of the functionalist approach in that they are essentially static and cannot easily accommodate change. As Harvey (1973) has pointed out, the absence of equilibrium conditions in an urban land-use system can be traced to the peculiarities of land and housing as commodities (their high levels of physical immobility and the monopoly rights to location conferred by private property) and to the fact that their consumption in an urban context takes place sequentially rather than simultaneously. When the models attempt to introduce an historical dimension, they have generally followed the ideological assumptions of modernization theory, which often stand in open contradiction to the equilibrium conditions identified in the contemporary model. Thus Turner's historical model shows that the principal determinant of the trajectory of low-income settlements is not so much a function of the relationship between user and material housing object, but rather a function of the *context* in which these relationships operate. To interpret these settlements on the basis of the different weighting that a household puts on the variables of location, tenure, and amenity assumes the inner consistency of these variables, but the mere fact of urban growth, by its effects on access, density, land supply, etc., can change them outside of the determination of the household. This contradiction emerges at several levels but one of the most obvious examples of it, as Brett (1974) has pointed out, is that between 'choice determining location and location determining choice'.

Theories of dualism

The origins and survival of the notion that low-income housing and settlement processes can best be understood in terms of their use-values to their consumers can also be directly traced to the popularity of dualistic theories in the study of urban and development issues. In Latin America there has been a virtually uninterrupted sequence of variants of the dualistic model since the 1950s. These include the anthropological models of Redfield (1947) in the immediate post-war period, Lewis' 'Culture of Poverty' theory (1966) and the early versions of marginality theory (Germani, 1967) in the 1960s; and the formal and informal sector models (ILO, 1970; ILO, 1976: Tokman, 1979; Birkbeck, 1979) of the 1970s.

Dualist modes of explanation were first established as a sociological method of investigation by Max Weber whose approach involved the methodological abstraction of the 'ideal-typical' characteristics of an object of interest and their contrast with the ideal-typical features of their logical and polar opposite. Empirical instances were then matched against the ideal-type for 'fit', and subsequently ordered themselves in a continuum between these two logical extremes. It was not long before dualism was used as an analytical construct for studying the economic, social, cultural, and spatial structures of less developed countries. In all of its variants it established a basic dichotomy between the two polarities and a process of interaction between them which, it claimed, mirrored the distinction in the real world between two separate poles (urban or rural, modern or traditional) each of which had its own historical, dynamic, and productive system. However, it was not until the late 1950s and early 1960s that dualist models were used to analyse the internal structures of the Latin American city. The reason for their appearance at this juncture is clear: the urbanization and migration processes stimulated by the impetus of demographic growth, the capitalist development of agriculture and import-substitution industrialization were beginning to have a profound impact on the size and structure of Latin American cities as an ever-increasing number of migrants began to establish themselves in the city.

Culture of poverty

Oscar Lewis's work on the 'culture of poverty' clearly saw the shanty-towns and slums as culturally, socially (and implicitly spatially) opposed polarities of an ideal type variety. A rural-based 'culture of poverty' had been transferred to the city by the migration processes associated with modernization and over-urbanization. An inefficient, marginally employed, subsistence-based and parasitic mass was now firmly installed on the urban perimeter, largely isolated from city life and living in the most appalling conditions of anomie, social and cultural deprivation, violence, and social deviancy. Lewis's work, and the dominance of modernization theory at this time, was largely responsible for creating the highly popular view that the residential structure of the Latin American city was characterized by the juxtaposition of what was essentially a rural, peasant village economy reconstituted in the city alongside a modern industrial and capitalist urban economy. Housing and settlement activities were thus understood in terms of the co-existence of two distinct economies each with a separate system of production: the modern capitalist city in which land, housing, and improvements were provided through the laws of market (i.e. production of commodities and exchange-values), and the peripheral squatter settlements where housing and settlement activities were seen as being the result of subsistence production for the self-consumption of the user (production of use-values). In the same way as the virtues of the 'modern' had been affirmed as progressive, rational and inevitable by contrasting them with the conservative, irrational, and historically-transient values of the traditional, so too were the housing and settlement forms characteristic of the opposed economies viewed in the same light. A consequent interpretation was that progress and rationality could only come about by eradicating the slums and hovels of the shanty-towns, and replacing them with public and private housing that conformed to 'modern' (i.e. Western) minimum standards. The traditional *'bohios'* were to be replaced by the *superbloques* in the name of modernization and progress.

Marginality theory

In many ways the several versions of 'marginality' theory that came to supplant these approaches did not challenge the dualistic and unilinear nature of their analysis, but merely extended them to cover all aspects of production, consumption and exchange, and social, cultural, and political life. Thus the explanation for the unequal distribution of income, consumption, and employment opportunities was to be found (Germani, 1972) in the 'lack of participation' of the 'urban poor' or 'marginal masses' in the economic, political, and social life of the city and society. This lack of participation could ultimately be traced to the inability to exercise certain fundamental and formal human rights (e.g. equality). The condition of marginality was then derived from the survival of traditional attitudes such as the lack of access to education, employment, and health facilities, and inadequate levels of consumption. Though there was some debate as to whether marginality was a permanent or temporary condition, the earlier versions of the theory generally held that it was a temporary maladjust-ment in the process of increasing integration of society which accompanied modernization and industrialization. According to the early variants of marginality theory, the explanation for the instability, poor living conditions and lack of services in 'marginal' or 'popular' housing and settlements could be found in the marginality of their inhabitants. The production, consumption and exchange of 'marginal' housing took place outside the modern economy—the popular or marginal sector was isolated, autonomous, and obeyed its own laws of motion. Popular housing was characterized by the dominance of use-value over exchange-value: housing was self-produced and self-consumed and exchange occurred within its autonomous sector. According to this view the typical popular or marginal house had the consumer as the principal manager and builder, using progressive self-help building techniques, subsistence in-comes, rudimentary building materials, and family-based labour to construct a constantly improving dwelling on illegal and unserviced land.

In the classical Weberian fashion the ideal-typical features of marginal housing and settlements (the production of use-values outside the commodity form) were abstracted and contrasted with the equally ideal-typical features of their polar opposites produced by the 'public' and 'private' sectors (the production of housing for exchange value). In this way the Latin American housing and settlement process was seen to be dominated by a series of polarities: institutionalized and self-help building systems, popular and official housing, marginal and integrated settlements, and so on. This emphasis on the self-pro-duction and consumption of housing and settlement use-values led theorists into a different policy-direction from their predecessors. They had maintained that the transition from these types of housing conditions to those that occur-red elsewhere in the city could only occur through their removal and replacement by state or private sector housing built to modern standards. By the mid-1960s the sheer impossibility of fulfilling this task, given the high rates of rural-urban migration, became apparent along with the growing disquiet with the results of the implementation of these policies. Everywhere in Latin American cities there was massive resistance, vandalism in the *superbloques*, and widespread rent-defection. A close examination of the socio-economic role of housing centred around the questions: Why do squatters refuse to move into 'modern' housing and why do they prefer to live in the shanty-towns when con-fronted with the alternative? The fact emerged that the self-production or con-sumption of marginal housing was preferred because it satisfied the fundamental needs (use-values) of its inhabitants (who were the best judge of these needs) at the lowest possible cost (because it was produced and consumed in a popular sector outside of the workings of the urban land and housing markets). The one-sided concept of housing as use-value was generalized as a definition for all housing (Turner, 1972) and despite material inadequacies, marginal housing and settlements were seen as the manifestation of a range of functional utilities. Self-help building meant the consolidation of families and communities offering a series of psychological and material supports to the poor; it created employment, and opportunities for augmenting family budgets through the sub-letting of land and space; it offered proximity to kinsfolk; housing activities could be related to the changing requirements for space as the family cycle proceeded. Further, the settlements offered considerable labour opportunities as the house could be built on free land at half the cost of one built by a third party and use could be made of cheap goods and services in the popular sector.

Given all of these functional utilities and the assumption of the separate and autonomous nature of the popular sector, which led to the idea that there were no structural constraints to the expansion of its activities, then the solution to the housing and settlement problem could come from the state helping the poor to help themselves. This could be achieved by carrying out policies that removed existing obstacles to 'popular' construction (such as lowering of minimum standards, revising municipal codes, and granting legality) and by giving people access to technology and resources through programmes of popular participation and community development.

A variant of dualism: the formal/informal sectors

In the 1970s, the dualist mode of explanation reappeared in the guise of the formal/informal sector model, though this time largely in the debate on urban employment. Originally developed in a body of work based on the African experience, it was introduced into Latin America by the ILO Employment Mission to Colombia (1970) and the ILO/WEP city report on Sao Paulo (1976). Moser (1979), in reviewing the history of the concept, has shown that the formal/informal sector model has been somewhat indiscriminately applied to characterize a whole range of phenomena. The term 'informal' has also been used to characterize certain kinds of occupation and used, euphemistically, to describe the urban poor and squatter settlements in general. Most versions are concerned with the dualistic nature of the employment structure in the city and the ILO Kenya Report (1972) definition is perhaps the most widely accepted. In this, the informal sector is characterized by its ease of entry, its reliance on indigenous resources, family ownership of firms, the small-scale nature of its operations, its labour-intensive and adapted technology, its informally-acquired skills, and its unregulated and competitive markets. This was contrasted with its ideal–typical polar opposite, the formal sector, which was characterized by difficulties of entry, reliance on foreign resources, corporate ownership, large-scale operations, capital intensive and often imported technology, for-mally-acquired skills and protected markets.

Though more emphasis was placed on the inherent characteristics of the two polar opposites rather than on the nature and dynamic of the relationship between them, it was generally maintained that their activities were mutually beneficial and complementary. The informal sector complements formal sector activities by catering for those markets which the latter find too small or too risky for profit-making. It provides cheap consumer goods for low-income groups, its workshops are a source of indigenous capital goods, and the formal sector can expand output quickly in response to increases in demand with low-capital outlays by sub-contracting arrangements and so on. One of the new elements that was introduced into the dualistic framework by the model was the notion that the informal sector had an inherent capacity for self-sustaining growth, as opposed to an eventual complete transformation into its polar opposite (e.g. the inevitable transformation of the traditional into the modern in modernization theory). The principal obstacle to further growth of the informal sector was the negative attitude of government.

In the area of housing and settlement activities attention was focused on informal systems for developing and exchanging land and informal housing produced, consumed, and exchanged within the sector. A lot of interest was shown in the construction sector which was dominated by informal systems of production, consumption and exchange. It was argued that opportunities for expanding the informal construction sector were restricted by policies and regulation that included: the removal of slums and shanty-towns, the refusal to grant legality of tenure to long-established squatters, the imposition of restrictive legal codes concerning densities, levels of services, zoning of land-uses and minimum building standards and the prohibition of credit facilities to illegal occupiers. Government, it was argued, should either revise or rescind these restrictions in order to allow informal construction activities to increase. It should extend credit and technical assistance through its various agencies to self-help building and neighbourhood improvement schemes, it should help to establish and finance co-operatives producing building materials and it should implement urban policies that encourage the expansion of services and infrastructure programmes utilizing labour-intensive employment. These programmes, according to a widely adopted World Bank scheme should be 'integrated' with educational, health, employment, training, and cultural programmes targetted at the lowest-income groups.

The general dualistic framework: a critique

Let us now deal briefly with some criticisms of the dualist framework as it has been applied to housing and settlement processes. This critique can focus on three inter-related areas:

1. The establishment of partial, one-sided and falsely polarized dualities.

2. The nature of the criteria by which housing and settlement dualities are established.
3. The relationship and linkages that exist between these two polarities.

The false polarities

Proponents of the ideal typical method have justified its use on the basis of its ability to produce testable hypotheses about the phenomena under study. The testing of these hypotheses immediately presents the 'problem of fit' and the impossibility of matching empirically-defined phenomena with the logical dualities that have been established. A defence against this accusation is that the ideal-type is simply a mental construct that cannot be attacked for its failure to approximate reality; it points the way to the issues which should be studied. This argument, however, assumes that the mental constructs are 'value-free' and scientifically distinct from the object of study, and is implausible. Once these conceptual frameworks have been situated in the context of a materialist epistemology, their true ideological quality emerges; the definition of the problem, the choice of a subject, and the selection of a method all embody the values and experiences of the western bourgeois sociological tradition. The notion that housing and settlement processes can be represented as the relationship between two polarized ideal-types can be described in similar terms. Theory is separated from reality; partial, one-sided and falsely polarized categories are evolved to explain an integrated totality which is subsequently reconstituted in terms of these false polarities. In this way the specific inter-penetration of use-value and exchange-value in a range of housing commodities is understood on a *theoretical* level as a false opposition between use-value and exchange-value and on a *practical* level as a false opposition between 'institutionalized' and 'self-help' housing; 'popular' and 'private' construction sectors; 'formal' and 'informal' housing, etc. The same problem emerges at the level of the settlement types which are identified according to the domination of exchange-values or use-values.

In other words, this approach is entirely inadequate for understanding the nature of land, housing, and improvements as commodities, because it is based on the methodological separation of use-value and exchange-value rather than an understanding of their inter-relationship within a theory that is adequate to their inter-relationship in real life. These dualities are to the bourgeois treatment of the housing and urban questions what the dualities of rural and urban, and modern and traditional are to the bourgeois treatment of the development question.

Criteria for dualism

Although there may be some clarity and unanimity over the need to *establish* logically abstract ideal types, there is little consensus over the nature and precise *definition* of the phenomena under study. Ideal type dualities seem to shift randomly from people to activities, from social processes to spatial processes and from individuals to households. As Bromley (1979) has pointed out some people may work in both the informal and formal sectors at different stages in the life-cycle or at different times of year or day, and some activities can be ascribed to both. On top of all this, different forms of dualism have tended to concentrate on discrete aspects of what are essentially inter-related phenomena; *culture of poverty* on the cultural values appropriate to a condition of material deprivation, *marginality* on the lack of participation in the economic, cultural, and social life of the city, and the *formal/informal sector model* on distinctly economic phenomena (systems of production, circuits, sectors, etc. but especially on employment).

Housing and settlement issues have therefore not been studied in a consistent fashion and many of the ideas of the dualist tradition on these issues have remained implicit and unstated. Certainly, an attempt to found a dualistic system on the basis of a concept of rights, values and norms rather than on the actual working of society would be immediately suspect because these already contain an ideological representation of what are the workings of this society. As Pradilla (1976b) has pointed out, the attempts of writers like Germani to define marginality in terms of the inability to exercise certain fundamental human rights are based on the acceptance of an ideological concept of what these rights are (liberty, equality, fraternity). They thus end up claiming a false universality for the norms and values dominating society and identify what is ultimately the capital–wage labour relationship as an equal rather than unequal relationship. Pradilla goes on to identify the real and basically unequal nature of this relationship in its urban dimension which it is characterized by the highly concentrated nature of private property in urban land; the character and magnitude of urban ground rents; anarchy in capitalist production; the concentration of productive capital in land; the commodity nature of architectural objects; the ranking of the spheres of consumption governed by the unequal distribution of the social product; segregation of the habitat according to social class, the urban policies of the state that guarantee the class interests of bourgeois and landowner; and the role of the city as a means of reproducing bourgeois ideology.

What these theories have in common, however, is an inordinate degree of emphasis on the consumption side of housing and settlement processes. Indeed, insofar as consumption is the destructive appropriation of the use-value of an object, this merely restates our basic proposition in a new form: that in the study of Latin American slums and shanty-towns there is an excessive degree of emphasis placed on the use-value of land, housing, and improvements and consequently a misunderstanding of the nature of land and housing as commodities. This emphasis on consumption is clearly untenable. First, because consumption is merely one moment in the total and integrated process of housing production, exchange and consumption. Second, because consumption is by no means the dominant moment of the commodity cycle, this position being held by production. Third, because this consumption is seen as an individual utility-maximizing relationship between object and consumer as revealed in housing priorities and preferences. The act of appropriation of use-value is thus understood *outside* its fundamentally *social* determination without regard for its acquisition as a function of income (and hence as a function of the user's place in the division of labour), the ideological values governing housing consumption and its role in the reproduction of social labour-power and capital accumulation. Thus even from the narrow and one-sided viewpoint of consumption, housing and settlement processes must still be defined inside the determinant social form of the capitalist mode of production and a dependent capitalist social formation.

Once it is recognized that all objects produced in a society dominated by a capitalist mode of production acquire a commodity character then it becomes meaningless to speak of housing and settlement dualities established on the basis of a separation of use-values and exchange-values and it becomes imperative to identify the specific commodity forms that housing and settlement activities can assume.

Relationship between ideal types

The third area of criticism is the treatment of the relationship and linkages that exist between polar ideal types. All of the dualistic models that have been examined have been more concerned with form than with process and all have been more interested in establishing the mutually exclusive characteristics of polar ideal-types than with the relationships between them. The result has been a static framework that fails to offer any meaningful analysis of the origins and future direction of the phenomena under study, other than a reiteration of the ethnocentric and ideological assumptions of modernization theory on linear evolutionary progress. The counterposing of what is essentially a capitalist economy, society, and culture to an isolated, subsistence, pre-capitalist informal, or marginal form within a dualistic framework is an entirely illusory representation of a reality which has already been penetrated by the modern capitalist mode of production. Any dualistic model of the urban housing and settlement process has immediately to confront the problem of the relationship between the two poles and this relationship has to be situated within a structural and historical context. The key to this problem lies in an understanding of commodity processes and the laws of capitalist development. As Marx suggested: 'capitalist production first makes the production of commodities general and then by degrees transforms all commodity production into capitalist production' (Marx, 1972, p. 36). The historical pre-condition for this process has been the destruction of small-scale inefficient, pre-capitalist forms of production dedicated to the production of use-values and their replacement by the large-scale and efficient production of commodities for the purpose of reproducing and expanding the value of capital. In the process of deepening the social division of labour and generalizing commodity production, the capitalist mode of production will exercise its *dominant* and *determinant* position in a social formation by *articulating* all pre-existing forms and modes of production to a *subordinate* relationship. In this way, for example, the capitalist mode of production in housing subordinates the petty-commodity forms of housing production to its laws of development. The most important questions that can be asked about this process then become: How far has the capitalist mode of production deepened the social division of labour and generalized commodity production for the purposes of reproducing and expanding the value of capital? What are the specific problems and characteristics of the development of this process in a *dependent* social formation?

The explanation for the unequal distribution of income, consumption, employment, appalling housing conditions and the absence of all manner of services available to the urban 'poor' does not lie in their 'culture of poverty' or 'marginality' nor in the degree of 'informality' of their economic activities, but rather in the nature and level of development of the capitalist mode of production. No matter how these activities are described they are all articulated to the dominant capitalist mode of production and exchange, as well as to its broader ideological and political structures. This articulation takes place at all levels of production, consumption and exchange. It is the capitalist development of agriculture that expels large numbers of the peasantry from the countryside to the city, it is the destruction of artisan and manufactured production under the impact of capital-intensive and monopoly industry and the limited size of the labour force necessary for capitalist development that determines the size of the unemployed and underemployed population and the type and scale of subordinate activities that produce subsistence incomes. Consumption is also a social process insofar as needs, prices, and consumption levels are socially and ideologically determined. Exchange activities are similarly determined by the laws of the capitalist market and for all of these reasons it is impossible to regard the situation of the 'urban poor', the 'marginal population' or the 'informal sector' as the result of autonomous and self-generating conditions. If anything a 'marginal' population is 'marginal' precisely because it is integrated. As Pradilla (1976a, p. 100) has put it: 'It is a curious theory of knowledge that leads the social scientist to exclude from society those who are the fundamental basis of its existence as a society'.

The commodity process will embrace all forms of production of land, housing and improvements and because of this simple fact it becomes meaningless to contrast these forms with their polar opposites. In effect, large numbers of wage-workers, the unemployed and the underemployed are initially excluded from access to the housing commodities produced directly by the capitalist mode of production because they have insufficient incomes to constitute themselves into 'effective' demand for a commodity the price of which incorporates the profits of the large number of the different factions of capital that have contributed to its production and exchange. They are therefore forced to undertake their own housing solution, but *not* under conditions of their own choosing; their situation can best be described as 'necessity' to build rather than 'freedom' to build. These housing 'solutions' can take a wide variety of forms ranging from the self-produced and consumed rudimentary shack on invaded land to the purchase of a 'manufactured' house to order in a subdivision where land has been bought and sold albeit illegally. But all of these forms are articulated by the capitalist mode of housing production and find themselves subordinate to it in the realm of production, consumption, and exchange. First, the forms of capitalist development of land, housing, and improvements, by control over availability, costs, and services, determine the appearance of the slum and the shanty-town. Subsequently, the houses and settlements do not remain outside of the process of creation of ground rents and land values are dominated by the mechanisms of the urban land market. All housing incorporates some quantity of commercially-purchased and industrially-produced commodities and will thus be influenced by the development of the capitalist, building-materials sector. The vast majority of these houses are produced with high levels of wage-labour and even the value of the free, kin-related labour will have a price on the market if the house is put up for sale or rent. Interest rates indirectly determined by the operations of finance capital will come into play if capital (no matter how small) has been advanced for construction. The exchange process will be dominated by market mechanisms, as will the speculative use of land and space within the house and settlement; rent levels in the shanty-towns for example will ultimately be determined by rent levels elsewhere in the city. The consumption of these housing objects is a social process taking place according to the ideological norms of society and as a function of income-levels and is ultimately a part of the process of the reproduction of labour-power and capital.

Policy outcomes of dualistic misconceptions

It can be seen that the establishment of housing and settlement dualities is a patent misunderstanding of the structurally and historically determined relationship of domination and subordination between the capitalist mode of production and the petty commodity form of production. The inability of dualist models to identify the nature of this articulation and its historical dynamic, together with the failure to identify the commodity nature of housing produced in a social formation dominated by the capitalist mode of production, has led to a series of policy recommendations of a somewhat alarming nature. These policies are often put forward not only as a method for solving the housing problems but also as means of generating employment opportunities and economic growth. They have suggested an autonomous capacity for growth in the construction sector that can be realized by removing restrictions on land, housing and construction activities, by extending credit and technical facilities for self-help housing, by providing urban services and infrastructure through community development and other similar measures. All of these analyses postulate an autonomous and self-generating capacity for growth of the marginal, small-scale, and informal activities and fail to explain how capitalism can reverse the whole basis of its historical development, a process which has, as its pre-condition, the destruction of these activities and forms of production. Moreover, the refusal of dualistic theories to understand the housing and settlement processes of low-income groups in terms of the *structural* framework of commodity relations and the *historical* framework of the laws of development of the capitalist mode of production, has led to their inability to recognize the essentially backward and exploitative nature of those very forms of housing production whose virtues they extol. The attempt to characterize 'self-help' housing purely in terms of its functional utility to the user has resulted in the acceptance of the most appalling living conditions as 'adequate', the celebration of the extension of the working day in the form of unpaid labour, the mystification of the institution of private property in land—which is in effect a major element contributing to the continuation of the housing problem—the sanctification of the exploitative and speculative relationships governing the use of space and housing goods and services, and the multiplication of inefficient and backward forms of construction activities that often involve the highest levels of exploitation such as collection of sand from rivers, use of below minimum-wage labour and the employment of women and children in the most deplorable working conditions. Recently, for example, state-assisted self-help policies have been suggested that allow for the encouragement of landlord–tenant relations in the new settlements and the sale and rental of plots to other settlers as a means of financing housing development—in other words, a housing solution at your neighbour's expense. It is in schemes such as these that the true ideological quality of the self-help argument shows itself very clearly. A petty-bourgeois concept of capitalist development is presented and its protagonists become the mouthpieces of petty commodity producers against the increasing monopolization of the productive process which the bourgeoisie represents as 'modernization' and 'progress'. This indeed is a far cry from the early days of the self-help movement in the mid-1960s when the self-help argument was justified with the most liberal of intentions—the state would intervene in the general interest 'to help people to help themselves' and in the process of building homes, families would be brought together, and community relations cemented. Fifteen years or so later, the shabby concept that the poor must continue and indeed must be encouraged to exploit the poorest emerges as the most tangible outcome of these lofty ideals.

The treatment of social classes and class-conflict in the study of housing and urban settlement

> *The tendency to shift the study of housing and settlement processes away from a class-based and structural framework onto a level of individual, family, or household behaviour which is subsequently generalized for a settlement or social group.*

> *The tendency to treat the social structure of slums and shanty-towns as homogeneous and undifferentiated.*

> *The tendency to construct housing and settlement models upon unproven assumptions about overall levels of social mobility of low-income groups.*

The 'behavioural' dimension: explanations at the individual scale

The attempt to build an individualistic psychology into an explanatory mechanism for interpreting values, meaning and action has a solid tradition in bourgeois social science. The twin idea that the meaning of society can be found in its values and norms and that deviance can be traced to the role of individual behavioural and personality attributes, can be traced back to the work of Weber, Durkheim, and Schumpeter. In the 1930s these themes were developed by Parsonian social science and the school of structural functionalism into the more sophisticated versions of role theory and approaches built around attitude measurement. The Chicago school of urban ecology, for example, was apt to characterize and explain urbanism in terms of the individuality of decision-making, personal anonymity, and the multiplicity of roles that the individual could play, rather than look for explanation at a more structured level. Park identified the characteristics of marginality at the level of individual psychology and Burgess' urban model explained settlement patterns ultimately in terms of the utility-maximizing behaviour of firms, families, and individuals.

In the 1960s modernization theory developed these pre-occupations in the discussion of the development, industrialization, and urbanization of less developed countries. Hoselitz (1960), McClelland (1964) and others tried to combine Parson's pattern variables (universalism, achievement-orientation, and functional specificity) with Weber's ideal-typical method and found the mechanism for the transformation of the one into the other, following Schumpeter, in the causative psychological state of the individual. Modernization involved the assimilation of urban-industrial values by individuals in a process of transition. The inhabitants of the slums and the shanty-towns were not integrated into urban life because they *lacked* the 'modern' attitudinal behaviour syndrome. The modernization process could be explained in terms of the attitudinal changes of the individual and obstacles to this process could be traced to the persistence of a traditional mentality. This notion was therefore closely linked to the idea of shanty-towns as rural enclaves in the city.

Oscar Lewis (1966) subsequently developed the idea that the social organization of these settlements could best be understood in terms of the rise of certain
personality traits in response to a situation of deprivation, rather than in terms
of the laws of social structure. These personality traits which made up a
subculture of poverty were transmitted through the process of socialization to
future generations. In the 1960s, marginality theory similarly tried to identify
the origins of social conditions within shanty-towns. Earlier concepts, such as
that of 'marginal man' characterized by a dual personality structure (Park,
1928; Stonequist, 1935), were developed in the attempt to characterize a 'modern
man' personality type (Inkeles, 1966) and to construct marginal personality
scales (Merton, 1957). Indeed in the work of the 'DESAL' (Centro para el
Desarrollo Económico y Social de América Latina) school the argument was
even developed to the point where the 'marginal masses' were specifically
considered to be beyond any discussion of class-analysis: 'it can be said of
them (marginal masses) that they are not socially and economically integrated
into a society, in a class system, because they do not belong to the economic
system' (Vekemans and Silva, 1966, p. 44).

The whole idea that the social structure of low-income settlements could best
be explained in terms of the decisions, attitudes, roles, and values of individuals,
families and households received an extra fillip in the 1960s with the populariza-
tion of role theory, decision-making theory, pluralism, game theory and general
systems analysis. In all of these approaches the individual is the *ultimate* source
of explanation of social phenomena: class and power relationships are measured
in terms of the behaviour of *actors* and their preference patterns and the
structural framework of class relations is lost in the multiplicity of roles,
decision-making capacities and personal characteristics of the individual. More
recently Lloyd (1979) has attempted to integrate decision-making theory, the
individual's perceptions of opportunities, and certain behavioural techniques,
into a theoretical framework for the study of the social organization of slums
and shanty-towns. Arguing very strongly against the use of concepts such as
class, he identifies the world of slums and shanty-towns as being peopled by
actors, each of whom carries two cognitive maps in his head that represent
his perception of his role in the social structure. The 'ego-oriented map' stresses
the achievement of individual and immediate goals and the 'externalized map'
deals with the perception of constraints upon actions which are inherent in the
structure of society. Settlements can be classified into 'slums of hope' and 'slums
of despair' on the basis of this structure of perception.

Lucien Goldmann has remarked that a 'consciousness that does not get
beyond the I is a consciousness for which history cannot exist' (Goldmann,
1969, p. 29). Although man is by *definition* a species-being, his nature is
inherently social, and this social nature is expressed in interactions with habitat
and fellow men. All attempts to build an individualistic psychology into an
explanatory mechanism for interpreting values, meanings, and actions must

lead to a radical elimination of social and historical elements from the study of man's relationships with his habitat. In effect this social and historical reality is reduced to the universal repetition and accumulation of individual actions and motives. Lloyd (1979, p. 72), for example, is quite explicit in this purpose: 'from the individual images of countless members of society, each image expressed partially, in numberless situations, we try to present for the subjects of our study a coherent generalized picture'. Goldmann (1969, pp. 74–75) sums up the inherent weaknesses of these approaches admirably:

> Thus psychologistic and micro-sociological theories, sub-relativism, ideological distortions and descriptive methods all end by misrepresenting human reality in the same way. They obscure the historical character of this reality and convert the real problems, the problem of the laws of evolution and that of the significance of the individual fact in the spatio-temporal whole, into the description of a particular without a context, a particular seen as part of a totality which is implicitly regarded as rigid and susceptible at best only to imperceptible changes.

It is also clear that Lloyd and other writers profoundly misunderstand the relationship between individual and class, often to the point of denying both the relevance of class-analysis and the existence of social classes in the slums and shanty-towns. They are incapable of identifying social classes as *objective* structures and individuals as agents or bearers of this structure ('träger' as Marx put it). Social classes are on the contrary reduced to a system of inter-personal relationships between individuals and these individuals are seen to be 'the generic principle of the social whole' (Laclau, 1977, p. 53). The functionalist theory of society proceeds to build this assumption into its models of social structures and compounds the confusion by insisting that society is an integrated system defined by a shared set of values, in which the explanation for class relationships and class power is ultimately to be found in the behaviour of individual 'actors'. The way is then open for the introduction of equilibrium models from economics, systems analysis and game theory that identify structural positions and relationships in terms of the preference patterns of individual actors or of individual utility-maximizing behaviour.

What this leads to is clearly ideological and untenable. The relationship between actors is defined empirically, without being situated within the structural framework of class interests and a great deal of difficulty is encountered in the attempt to establish an adequate relationship between 'causative' psychological syndromes and 'derivative' social structures. Structural positions and relationships are taken out of the discussion and the concept of class is either denied or reduced to a 'contentless' inventory of social roles and shared attributes and values. In this way, for example, 'poverty' is identified as a consequence of the individual characteristics of the poor, rather than as a structural condition within society; class-based positions and relationships are lost in the emphasis on individual decision-making and individual perception; the origins of social and economic inequality are sought in a multitude of individual or household based attributes, such as personality, stage in the life-cycle, family-size, migrant wealth brought to the city, and so on. The explanation for social change is found at the level of values and consciousness rather than at the level of the mode of production or social formation. It is sought in the change from ascriptive particularism to universalistic achievement that accompanies urbanization and industrialization (Hoselitz, 1960; Parsons, 1951) in the transformation of a rural-value system into an urban one, or in terms of individual pathology, cultural maladjustment, anomie (Park, 1928; Lewis, 1966; Vekemans and Silva, 1969).

The elimination of class is also achieved through the eradication of notions of power and the domination or exploitation of one class by another. Functional models, social role and game theory are all based on the common acceptance by the actors of the political and ideological frame of reference (or 'rules') of society. If all conflicts of interest are carried out within the rules of the game, then quite obviously the idea of class struggle has become irrelevant. Writers such as Lloyd (1979) go as far as to deny the concept of class altogether in discussing the social structure of the slums and shanty-towns, but this implies the inapplicability of the concept of class, and the existence of social classes. Such a denial at the existing conjuncture in Latin America is to deny the existence of capitalism. Are we to conclude from this that Latin America is not capitalist?

The idea that housing and settlement processes can be understood as the functional expression of the decisions, choices or priorities of atomistically defined individuals is the idea that the satisfaction of human needs occurs under conditions of social equilibrium and harmony, a concept which ignores the contradictions of the capitalist system and constitutes a methodological denial of the reality of class struggle and conflict over the provision of local and urban resources. It identifies choice rather than its constriction, accessibility rather than the 'tax' of distance, the exercise of existential preference rather than the low level of income command over space, as explanations for the urban structure. Clearly, individuals do express choices, preferences and values, often through a system of priorities, but the structurally determined inequalities in access to urban resources all conspire to limit the ability of individuals to make self-determined choices. The critical control remains that of the positions and relationships of individuals within the social structure.

The idea of an individual, family, or household-based consumer sovereignty that is autonomous and spontaneous and which operates on the basis of utility-maximizing behaviour cannot be constructed into anything more than an *ideological* understanding of settlement and housing processes. The reasons for this are clear: it represents the methodological and theoretical subordination of class-based options in housing to the different options necessary in the family or individual life-cycle. It necessarily standardizes for these class-based options—they are taken as given, and so too is the social segregation they give rise to. The settlement process and the social segregation of the urban environment are then understood in terms of a banal, descriptive, and fundamentally tautological mode of reasoning—location determines choice and choice determines location, similar people like to and do live close to each other, people behave in the way they behave, and so on. The concept of social conflict over the local allocation of resources is removed and the individual's struggle in the course of his life-history is put in its place. It allows urban studies to exclude the issues of power, scarcity and redistribution. It identifies the contradictions of class society and the class struggles in the housing and settlement processes at the phenomenological level-as the irrationalities of local bureaucracies, the particularisms of local politicians, and the special circumstances of the local provision of community services. In other words, it offers a Latin American version of Pahl's gatekeeper thesis (Pahl, 1975). Above all else, by reducing housing and settlement processes to the individual, family or household level it shifts the discussion of housing away from its determinant instances—the social process of housing *production*—to discussions of housing utility and consumption. It thus conceptually side-steps the analysis of the critical role of housing and settlement in the process of the reproduction of labour-power and the accumulation of capital.

As the behaviour of individuals is not understood as an expression of the objective contradictions of class society, the door is thus left open to discussions of housing solutions outside considerations of class. As existing housing and settlement processes are regarded as 'functional', their reproduction by the state is then suggested as a housing 'solution'. In this way the most appalling conditions of social deprivation are regarded as functional; the failure of a specific formation to satisfy fundamental human needs is seen as a rational process; the continued existence of horrifying inner-city slums is theoretically sanctified; and the survival and encouragement of pre-capitalist housing solutions which involve conditions of real hardship is regarded as 'solution'.

Finally, although the barrio may not provide a satisfactory scale of reference for housing and settlement issues, it is even less certain that the family or household level constitutes a more effective point of reference. The principal determinants of individual, family and household behaviour are governed by their relationship to the production process which is inserted into a national and global economy. Indeed many of these analyses, particularly those of the behavioural school, deliberately choose to remain at the phenomenological level: they accept the consciousness of the housing situation of those who experience it, as being the *real* housing situation even though these very people may have very little knowledge, for example, of the influence of broader forces on their housing situation. It is hardly surprising, therefore, that they merely

reproduce in a generalized, descriptive form the ideological frame of reference
of those whom they purport to explain.

The tendency to treat the social structure of shanty-towns and slums as homogeneous and undifferentiated

The tendency to treat the social structure of shanty-towns and slums as
an homogeneous and undifferentiated mass has its roots in several theoretical
traditions that have been deeply penetrated by bourgeois ideology. As Perlman
(1976) has noted, the immediate post-war period in Latin America was
dominated by anthropological explanations for the social phenomena of
shanty-towns and slums. The anthropologist accompanied the migrant into the
city and explanations of social and cultural changes were heavily influenced
by ethnographic traditions. The search for explanation at the level of culture,
values and institutions was combined with a notion of 'peasant' societies as
homogeneous, functional, and integrated. The social characteristics of shanty-
towns and slums could thus be analysed in terms of the preservation or
destruction of 'peasant' attitudes and institutions, and their adequacy for the
process of adaptation. In other words, the concept of 'mass versus class' was
introduced into the Latin American urban literature—a peasant 'mass' with a
distinct cultural and social identity was counterposed to an urban 'class-based'
society in a dualistic fashion. The social structure of the settlements was thus
interpreted from the socially undifferentiated viewpoint expressed in images
like the 'peasant in the city', and the 'migrant in the city'.

This interpretation dovetailed with the central pre-occupation of modernization theory—the assimilation of modern urban-industrial values on the part of
individuals in a process of transition. The social dynamics of the settlements
could then be understood in terms of the functional and unilinear process of
social integration of migrants of rural origins to the urban culture of modern
society. Oscar Lewis took this concept of culturally-defined, polar-opposite,
ideal types within the city a step further. The idea of the population of the
slums and shanty-towns as an undifferentiated social 'mass' was retained, as
indeed was the overall perspective of explaining social differentiation on the
basis of culture, values, and norms. In this view a culture of poverty arose
amongst groups having no strong class or ethnic basis for identity in response
to a situation of material deprivation ('poverty'). The populations of the slums
and shanty-towns could be differentiated from the rest of the urban population
because they had accumulated certain shared personality traits in response to a
common condition of poverty. This sub-culture of poverty was reproduced
through the socialization process by subsequent generations and a cycle of
poverty was established in which poverty itself generated those attitudes that
would lead to its continuation.

Marginality theory added to this interpretation in the 1960s. The **DESAL** school saw Latin American cities as being characterized by two juxtaposed social systems (European–Indian) in which the marginals lacked social differentiation and lay outside the productive system. Other writers talked about their common identity as 'cultural hybrids' or of their shared position in the 'anomic gap' (Germani, 1972) on the boundaries of two conflicting cultures. This idea, that the population of slums and shanty-towns constituted an undifferentiated 'mass' defined by a shared condition of generalized poverty, proved extremely resilient in Latin American urban studies where the notion of the 'urban poor' has retained considerable allegiance. It should be noted in passing that ideas such as 'marginal population' and 'urban poor' have been closely associated in Latin American with 'populist' political positions. Undoubtedly there is a similar politico-ideological relationship between theoretical concepts such as 'popular housing' (Turner, 1976; Valenzuela and Vernez, 1974) and current attempts by government and international agencies to stimulate intermediate technology, 'informal sector' activities and 'self-help' building programmes.

The principal criticism that can be levelled against these attempts to homogenize the social organization of the slums and shanty-towns is their failure to identify at a structural level, the sources and fundamental elements of social differentiation that stratify not only the settlement populations but also the 'peasant' masses from which they are drawn. Thus whilst these writers have recognized different aspects of social heterogeneity within the settlements, these aspects have largely been identified at the (determined) level of individual or family experience, or even as the qualities of different settlement characterstics. Thus length of residence in the city, different stages in the personal and family life cycle, variations in educational experience, amounts of capital brought to the city by the migrant, and the age, size and location of settlements are all identified as sources of heterogeneity.

This failure to recognize significant class differentiation amongst the population of the slums and shanty-towns can be criticized for its lack of theoretical, methodological, and empirical validity. On a theoretical level, the class problem, like the whole discussion of urbanization, migration, and industrialization, has to be situated at the level of the capitalist mode of production and of a dependent, capitalist, social formation before an adequate explanation can be found. The crucial element in understanding the objective social situation of these populations is to understand their relationship, whether direct or indirect, with the structures of the dominant capitalist mode of production.

The social structure of the Latin American city and countryside has been the subject of a profound transformation that has come about as a result of the historical advance of the capitalist mode of production and the related developments of social classes and class conflicts. As Lenin (1977) remarked, 'the home market for capitalism is created by the parallel development of capitalism in agriculture and industry, and by the formation of a class of rural and industrial wage-earners on the other'. The capitalist development of agriculture, the decomposition of the peasantry, the development of new class antagonisms, the creation of the labour-power commodity, the development of monopoly and capital–intensive industry, the destruction of manufacturing and artisan production, and the articulated reproduction of petty-commodity forms of production and exchange have all resulted in the creation of a complex and interlinked class structure in urban and rural areas alike. In other words, the objective social situation of the settlement population can only be revealed by an examination of the social relations of production which fix individuals in the system of production and social structure characteristic of a dependent capitalist social formation.

The recognition of social classes can only be arrived at through the use of concepts that adequately reflect the real relationship between the individual and broader social structures such as class. Poulantzas (1972. p. 34) provides us with a clear statement of this relationship: 'social class is a concept that indicates the effects of the totality of structures in the matrix of a mode of production or a social formation on the agents that constitute its supports; this concept then indicates the effects of the global structure on the realm of social relations'.

The population of the slums and shanty-towns is in fact dedicated to activities that are directly or indirectly articulated to the capitalist mode of production. This population is partly made up of all those social classes that are directly defined by their relations of production to the capitalist mode of production— an industrial proletariat and a white-collar working class (the majority of which lie beyond effective housing demand), a petty bourgeoisie, and occasionally a rural proletariat. It is also partly made up of all those who are dedicated to petty commodity forms of production and exchange which are indirectly articulated to the capitalist mode of production (artisans, street traders, subcontractors, journeymen, etc.) It is also in quantitative terms largely made up of what has been variously called a 'lumpen-proletariat' (Marx), a sub-proletariat (Grupode Estudios Jose Raimundo Russi, 1975) or a proto-proletariat (McGee, 1974), largely comprising a mass of unemployed and under-employed who constitute a surplus population. However, it would be a mistake to identify this large group as being outside the laws of capitalist development—rather the opposite. It is a product of capitalist development, subject to its laws. The development of the capitalist mode of production means the development of the productive forces in all branches of production and the destruction of pre-capitalist forms. As the social forces of production increase, the relationship between socially necessary labour and surplus labour changes. The smaller amount of necessary labour required leaves the surplus labour as an industrial reserve army of labour that provides a reserve of labour power for periods of industrial expansion and which generally keeps wages low (see, however, Quijano (1973) and Nun (1969)). This reserve army is almost exclusively housed in the slums and shanty-towns. Nor should that social differentiation which derives from the speculative use of land, space, and services within the settlements, the development of tenurial relations in housing and land, and the relations associated with private property in land and housing, be forgotten.

In other words, all of the productive activities of the slums and shanty-towns are located in or are articulated by the capitalist mode of production; they are linked both to the processes of commodity production and exchange and to the legal-political and ideological structures of capitalism. It is this intricate web of relationships that is responsible for the complex class stratification of these settlements. The attempt to identify an undifferentiated mass, outside class considerations in terms of its marginality, lack of integration, or shared poverty, is an ideological distortion with serious political, social and economic consequences.

The belief that 'poverty' is a product of individual personality or attitudinal defects is as ideological as it is elitist. This assumes that the 'poor' are isolated and powerless, denies the active integration of the population into the productive process and sees all possibilities for change as originating from above or without. It is also clearly untenable for theoretical reasons as it obscures the fundamentally different class positions and interests that structure the population according to their specific form of participation in the productive process. As production is the determining moment of the overall condition of poverty, all attempts to give conceptual priority to 'poverty' analysis over class analysis must be doomed to failure. Marginality theory further compounded the difficulty by postulating an integration or equilibrium model when marginal groups are already integrated into society, albeit in a way that is highly prejudicial to their interests. In other words the basically ideological nature of its 'integrationist' propositions prevents it from identifying the capital or wage labour relationship as an unequal one, resting on exploitation and class domination. Pradilla (1976b) has pointed out the ideological nature of notions such as a 'popular mode of production' (Turner), a 'popular sector' (Valenzuela and Vernez) and 'popular classes'—none of which refers to an objective relationship at the economic, political or ideological level. If anything, they are based on nothing more substantial than the identification of the individual's position in the social structure through a position occupied in the system of income distribution already determined by position in relation to the system of production. Pradilla exposes the petty bourgeois, populist background to these concepts which eliminates discussion on social classes and conflicting class interests in the notion of the 'people'.

Contrary to all these ideas about 'marginal' and 'popular' groups and sectors, notion of the 'urban poor' and so on, a complex class structure does exist in the settlement populations. The recognition of these specific class differences is of vital importance. The class composition of the slums and shanty-towns is a crucial influence on the levels of political co-optation open to government, political parties, and local *caciques*; it is a vital factor in determining the success or failure of different technical systems of self-help building and it influences the potentialities for revolutionary mobilization on issues of collective consumption.

The tendency to construct housing and settlement models upon unproven assumptions about the overall levels of social mobility of 'low-income' groups

Research in the 1950s and 1960s generally conveyed the image of the shanty-towns and slums as the permanent homes of a socially and geographically immobile population which perpetuated its appalling economic, social, and cultural living conditions from generation to generation. The low income residential structure of the Latin American city was thus identified as an inner ring of slums and peripheral ring of 'semi-rural' shanty-towns, both of which were the home of an undifferentiated mass of newcomers from rural areas.

In the mid 1960s this image began to change under the ideological impact of the assumptions of modernization theory. Cities were recognized as mechanisms that guaranteed economic and social mobility for the vast majority of newcomers who realized the stability and integration that the modernization process implied. These assumptions were integrated with empirical data on the intra-urban residential mobility of migrants in the city. Early accounts identified 'slums of hope' and 'slums of despair' (Stokes, 1962)—a theme recently taken up by Lloyd (1979). The former were peopled by the upwardly social and economically mobile, showed a tendency to gradual physical improvement, and ultimately were integrated into the city as legitimate working class suburbs. The 'slums of despair'—the inner-city *inquilinato* zones—were peopled by the socially and geographically immobile and would stagnate and deteriorate as areas of individual, social, and cultural breakdown. Turner, Mangin, and others identified the urban settlement process in terms of the changing housing priorities of mobile low-income groups. These housing priorities changed with the domestic and economic cycle of the migrant and with low-income household under a basic presumption of social and economic mobility with longer residence in the city. This model of the inner-city slums as receptor areas for new migrants, and of the peripheral shanty-towns as the last point of residence for established migrants, dominated Latin American urban studies in the 1960s and 1970s. It is based on certain assumptions: that the overwhelming majority of migrants are eventually upwardly socially mobile; that residential mobility is an outcome of this mobility; and that *within* the shanty-towns further economic and social mobility may express itself in the residential stability of the population. Its 'explanation' of the low-income urban residential structure has proved increasingly difficult to square with the accumulating empirical evidence of limited or restricted social mobility, of widening income inequalities, of static or worsening unemployment and of a growing discrepancy between rate of population growth and job creation.

While it is indisputable that the rates of economic growth achieved in some Latin American countries, particularly in the 1950s and 1960s, were sufficient to guarantee some degree of upward social and economic mobility for urban newcomers, there is considerable controversy over the scale of this phenomenon. Even if Turner, Mangin, and others offer an effective description of the residential process in the 1960s when limited rates of economic growth gave mobility sufficient for people to move out of the *inquilinatos* but not to come within the 'effective demand' for capitalist housing solutions, it is extremely doubtful if this is the general situation in the late 1970s and early 1980s. Thus Perlman (1976) remarks of her favela studies in Rio that: 'If the data are correct migration simply amounts to changing membership from the lower sector of rural society to the lower sector of urban society with no appreciable increase in income. This conclusion would have to be discounted if there were avenues of escape from the favela to high sectors of society, but it is our impression that this kind of mobility is practically non-existent'. Roberts (1978, p. 110) believes that this is the general situation for all Latin American cities: 'In the early period of industrialization in Latin America the existence of extensive opportunities for social mobility was one factor that reduced the class militancy of urban low income workers. The present situation is in most cities a very different one: urban incomes are becoming more unevenly distributed, and the opportunities for good jobs are expanding less fast than is the urban economically active population'. A series of empirical studies on Monterrey (Balan, Browning, Jelin, 1973), a city with an exceptionally high rate of industrial growth for Latin America, showed that some socio-economic mobility had occurred but factors such as access to educational qualifications may act as a future block to migrant social mobility. Berlinck and Cohen's study of occupational mobility in Sao Paulo (1979) showed a general tendency for downward mobility amongst the working population in comparison with their parents. Moreover, there is a substantial body of empirical evidence to show a widening of income inequalities, particularly in periods of economic growth. Fishlow's (1973) study of Brazil showed that whereas in 1960 the top 5.8 per cent of the employed received 29.8 per cent of the monetary income, in 1970 they received 37.9 per cent. Income inequalities were not only widening between those employed directly in the capitalist sector and those engaged in petty-commodity activities, but also amongst those employed within the capitalist sector. Though there is some confusion over whether rates of unemployment and under-employment have been increasing or not, they have certainly not diminished on anything like the scale required to postulate a general improvement in rates of socio-economic mobility. Moreover the figures for the rate of creation of new jobs indicate that industrial growth is progressively generating less employment. Lloyd (1979) quotes studies that show that in the 1940s a 1 per cent growth in industry resulted in 0.6 per cent more jobs, and in the 1950s only 0.26 per cent more jobs. There is little to indicate that this trend was not continued in Latin America in the 1960s and 1970s, given the high rate of organic composition of capital characterstic of industrial developments during this period.

The significance of this evidence for Latin American settlement models has yet to be fully appreciated. If the rate of social and economic mobility is decreasing, if income disparties are widening, if unemployment and under-employment are either remaining static or increasing, and if employment opportunities are diminishing in relation to population growth, then the following questions can be quite fairly asked: What priorities for housing and settlement emerge when there is no or little social and economic mobility? What precisely is the relationship between the variability of these priorities and the processes of economic growth? How do considerations of the relationship between social mobility and economic growth affect our understanding of the urban settlement pattern and process? Before examining these questions, it is worthwhile re-iterating Pradilla's critique (1976c) of Turner's work in this area. The inherent assumption of an absolute and relative increase in the income of the 'popular' sector in Turner's work is based on nothing more substantial than the assumption that housing consolidation over time indicates an increase in income levels, i.e. an improvement in the housing situation equals an improve-ment in the income situation. This is an obvious error.

For the Turner–Mangin model to work there must be a balance between the rate of urban population growth, the rate of supply of land and housing, and the structure of demand according to income, age and type of family. These are, of course, highly volatile variables which certainly in most cases lie beyond the level of household choice. They constitute a distinctly *ideological* basis for the urban model, however. Also implied is equilibrium between housing supply and demand, a constant or diminishing rate of migration, and the notion that residential mobility follows on socio-economic mobility up to the moment of residence in the shanty-towns. After this, mobility is expressed in the form of geographical stability, housing consolidation and settlement improvement. The overall levels of social mobility are challenged, as are these ideological and essentially optimistic assumptions about the functionality of slums and the self-improving nature of peripheral shanty-towns. One idea is that the *inquilinato* population can be stabilized through the introduction of rent controls which under conditions of a high rate of inflation can make continued residence there more attractive. There is in fact often a diminishing supply of *inquilinato* housing as a result of the expansion of the CBD and urban renewal, which can lead to the development of usurious *inquilinato* relationships in the shanty-towns; direct first residence by the newly-arrived migrant in the shanty-town may be increasing as a result of the cumulative nature of the migration process. Moreover, residential mobility can be the very vehicle whereby social mobility out of a shanty-towns is achieved (e.g. speculative use of land and housing in shanty-towns to facilitate access to the 'official' housing markets).

Certainly the widespread development of sub-markets of land and housing in shanty-towns appears to indicate that the sharp geographical division of settlements based on rented accommodation and owner occupation is an increasingly inadequate characterization of the residential structure of the Latin American city.

CONCLUSION

Each proposition has now been discussed in some detail and further summary is not necessary. It is preferred, by way of conclusion, to review some of the problems associated with current marxist research into the slums and shanty-towns of Latin American cities.

Treatment of the relationship between spatial and social processes

The question of the relationship between social and spatial processes has in recent years become a matter of serious debate in marxist circles, largely a result of the Althusserian-influenced work of the French school of urban sociology (Castells, 1976; 1977). There is an urgent need to re-examine the central proposition of this relationship contained in that work (the social production of space) in line with the critique of the Althusserian account of Marxism as a form of idealism (Thompson, 1978), the account of nature of space offered in certain classical marxist texts, and particularly in Lenin's philosophical works (Lenin, 1972). The notion of the social production of space used by Castells and others from this perspective can be understood as a form of idealism counterposed to its vulgar materialist opposite—the spatial determination of the social. In this sense there is an inadequate treatment of specificity of the spatial in these accounts. What exactly is the theoretical status of the spatial and what is the relationship between the spatial and historical specificity of a social formation? This ties in with the well-established debate in geography on the relationship between nature, space, and place. If, for example, it is argued that the relationship between time and space, and nature and place is a relationship involving the specification of the abstract in the concrete (place is time–space specified), then a different conception of the subordinate position given to space in Castell's formulation must be posited. This would also involve a re-examination of the importance of 'space' in the specification of a social formation that does not fall into the trap of either idealism or vulgar materialism.

The treatment of the process of the production, consumption, and exchange of housing and settlement goods and services

The relationship between needs, exchange-values and use-values in the study of low-income housing and settlement processes has been approached in recent Marxist work through the use of two inter-related conceptual frameworks: firstly, the study of land, housing and improvements in terms of their commodity character (Pradilla, 1976a; 1976b; 1976c; and Burgess, 1977; 1979); and, secondly, the concept of the articulation of the capitalist mode of production with pre-capitalist modes and petty-commodity forms of production within a specific social formation (Burgess, 1979). Some of the difficulties in the use of these concepts can be catalogued.

First, there is a set of difficulties that revolves around the distinction between a 'potential housing commodity' and a 'real housing commodity' (Pradilla, 1976a)—self-help housing as a commodity differs from other housing commodities insofar as it is constructed immediately for the use of the producer rather than being produced for exchange by agents different to the consumer. The difficulties centre around the question: when does an object acquire commodity status? Is it in the actual act of exchange or when it is perceived as a commodity? An object of human labour can only acquire the status of a commodity under the social conditions of private property, division of labour, and exchange. The obvious difficulty with self-help housing is that although it can be built for immediate use and not exchange, it can later enter into the exchange process and its constituent elements (land, materials, and labour) have generally already entered into this process. The consumer of the self-help house in general is not the only producer of the house and some Marxist accounts tend to underestimate the quantity of wage-labour involved in the production of so-called 'self-built' housing and to overestimate the non-existence of capital–wage labour relationships in this process.

Second, there is a series of problems that revolves around the definition of forms and modes of production and their inter-relationship within a social formation. The suggestion that the relationship between the petty commodity form of production and the capitalist mode of production is essentially a dualistic one can immediately be discounted. This relationship is as much social and historical as it is logical in nature, but it is also one of *articulation* involving conditions of domination, subordination, and determination rather than an association of dualistically-counterposed opposition in a unilinear and dichotomous framework. Again, the general criticism can be made that there has been an inadequate discussion of the precise nature and the mechanisms of articulation that exist between modes and forms of production co-existing within a social formation. The fact that the laws and mechanisms of this articulation are also part of a general historical dynamic, also creates problems which in the structuralist reading of Marx identify themselves as problems of limits or boundaries. The general tendency of structural analysis has been to 'freeze' reality—to assert structures at the expense of the dialectical processes that create and transform them. Structural Marxism has attempted to 'resolve' this difficulty by creating higher level structures that subsume these specific difficulties at lower levels (e.g. from the 'concept' of mode of production to the 'reality' of social formation). In effect this means not the resolution but rather the shifting of many of the problems onto an abstract-formal plane. It often degenerates into heated and laborious discussions on the degree of relevance of structures, and into quasi-metaphysical analyses of boundaries (Hindness and Hirst, 1975).

Related to all this is the problem of the conceptual status of the petty-commodity form of production and its relationship with the capitalist mode of production. The issue centres on the relevance of Marx's analysis of the transitional role of petty-commodity production in the development of capitalism in nineteenth century Europe to existing conditions in the less-developed countries. It focuses specifically on the historical inability of the petty-commodity form of production to reproduce itself developmentally and independently of the various different modes of production. On the other hand, the dynamics of petty-commodity production are such that it is increasingly being penetrated and transformed by the capitalist mode of production as an essential part of the relationship of articulation. This transition is characterized by an increase in the organic composition of capital and the proletarianization of the work force. This is precisely the boundary between the artisan (self-help) and manufactured forms of housing production (Pradilla, 1976a). In this sense the intermediary position of the manufactured form between the industrialized and the artisan forms tends to make static what is essentially a dynamic movement between production for use-value and production for exchange-value. This is a grave conceptual problem because what is obviously lacking is a set of dialectical categories that adequately reflects the historical dynamic of the transition from a production for use-value to a production for exchange-value which constitutes the process of the deepening of the capitalist division of labour. The framework presented in Lenin's *Development of Capitalism in Russia* (1977) is extremely instructive in this respect but its analysis of artisan production has a limited applicability to urban phenomena because of the association of the production of use-values with subsistence agriculture and the absence of foreign capital and foreign markets in the process of capitalist development which limits the effectiveness of the analysis in a situation where the process of transition can be distorted through the imposition of the manufactured and industrial forms from without, rather than their evolution from within.

Finally, there exists a series of problems associated with the theory of fractions of captial. Recently Clarke (1978) has demonstrated the need for caution in the use of the concept of fractions of capital. He condemns the wide range of criteria that has been used to define a fraction of capital (e.g. *branch of production*—agricultural, mining, industrial; *nationality*—imperial, national, local; *size*, etc.), and insists that fractions of capital must be identified according to their historically specific function in the circuit of capital (e.g. productive capital, bank capital, commercial capital, landed capital). Moreover, the

Poulantzian notion that fractions of captial can only exist as such through their representation in the political process has also been attacked (Clarke, 1978). The reduction of class relations to the relationship between political organizations, it is maintained, merely generates an account of pressure group activities interpreted in terms of a theory of social class.

The treatment of social class and class conflict in the study of urban and settlement processes

Marxist class analysis starts from the position that the foundations of the class structure are based on the relations of production—a class structure cannot be considered as based on the distribution of the social product and the organization of consumption, because both of these are determined by the position of the individual in the productive system. The class problem then has to be situated inside the conceptual framework of the capitalist mode of production. In a capitalist mode of production, the system of social classes is based on capitalist relations of production—the specific relation of wage-labour and capital—which involves the conversion of the means of production into capital and of labour-power into a commodity. However, the existence of a capitalist mode of production in a dominant position in a social formation in effect means that this conversion has been only partially generalized and as there are only partially generalized capitalist relations of production, there is only partially generalized capitalist class structure. As classes exist *in* and *through* their relationships with each other, this means that effective class analysis can only be undertaken in terms of the specific constellation of class relations characteristic of a dependent capitalist social formation.

This simple fact has been the source of many of the problems in the application of marxist concepts of class in Latin America. In the dependent capitalist social formations of Latin America the process of polarization of a bourgeoisie and proletariat is far from complete and there is a highly complicated class structure based on the relations of production inherited from pre-capitalist modes and forms of production in addition to a variety of transitional forms *at any one time*. The principal problem of marxist class analysis has been to identify the specificity of class structures in relation to dependent social formations and to preserve the concept of totality without losing that of movement; to preserve conceptually the inherent dynamic of the protracted or accelerated transformation of pre-capitalist to capitalist relations of production. This recent insistence on the need to analyse the specificity of class structures in terms of dependent social formations and to situate the class structures of both the advanced and underdeveloped countries in terms of their mutually-determined insertion to the process of global accumulation has done much to dispel the 'Eurocentricity' of previous attempts to apply Marx's class analysis of nineteenth century Europe to existing conditions in less developed countries. The emphasis has shifted to the exploration of the limits of these categories, to the evolution of new concepts that correspond to the specificity of social formations, and to the recognition of the global significance of the process of capital accumulation.

The vast majority of the population who live in shanty-towns and slums carry out activities that are either directly or indirectly articulated to the capitalist mode of production. Though it is relatively easy to identify the class location of those who are directly involved in the capital–wage labour relationship (bourgeoisie–petty bourgeoisie–proletariat) it is those who are indirectly and variously articulated to the capitalist mode who provide the greatest difficulty for effective class analysis. For this reason we shall concentrate on this population, who constitute a large majority in the slums and shanty-towns of Latin American cities. However, this should not be taken to mean that there are no problems associated with the definition and identification of the other social classes who live in these settlements (manual and non-manual proletariat, petty bourgeoisie). There is, for example, the problem of multiple employment and the distinction between the 'new' and 'traditional' petty bourgeoisie. The activities of all those who live in the settlements are either located in the capitalist mode of production of articulated to it. Thus the accelerated expulsion of the peasantry from the land under the impact of the capitalist development of agriculture and the low rate of growth of urban employment has determined the size of the unemployed and underemployed population and has reproduced and partially transformed a range of activities carried out under a variety of capitalist relations of production. How does this population defined by a highly complex range of relations of production fit into the class structure?

Defining a 'class' structure

First, there has been an attempt to categorize this population as a *sub-proletariat* (Castells, 1971; Grupo Russi, 1975). This sub-proletariat consists of three groups not quite belonging to the proletariat and yet not strictly classified as a lumpen-proletariat. The first group comprises all those who, although they do not generate surplus-value, contribute to the general process of production. They suffer from the greatest degree of exploitation through the extraction of absolute surplus value (extension of the working day, job insecurity, low price for labour, etc.) and encompass a wide range of occu-pational employment (e.g. tertiary sector, industrial, commercial, and artisan establishments, commerce and transport, lower levels of bureaucracy, etc.). The second group consists of a *permanent army of the unemployed* which does not have the opportunity to sell its labour-power because of the limited job-creating possibilities offered by changes in the organic composition of capital. However, a third group can be recruited from this army of the unemployed in periods of expansion of capitalist production and therefore functions as an *industrial reserve army of labour*. The consciousness of this class is ridden with contradictions; it can be deeply penetrated by bourgeoise ideology, particularly through paternalism, but it can also arrive at a revolutionary consciousness during local struggles as long as these are under the direction of a revolutionary working-class party. Supporters of the concept of the sub-proletariat are anxious to distance themselves from Marx's concept of the lumpen-proletariat—the sub-proletariat is a class characteristic and is specific to a dependent capitalist social formation. By so doing they have also moved a considerable distance away from Marx's unfavourable comments on the lumpen-proletariat, and have moved more to a Fanon–Maoist assessment of the revolutionary rather than reactionary potential of this sub-proletariat.

Some doubt can be expressed about the telescoping of the unemployed, the industrial reserve army and the mass of petty commodity producers into one class, however; in general the concept does not effectively conceal its catch-all and residual nature. The precise differences between a proletariat, a sub-proletariat, and a petty bourgeoisie are not adequately dealt with, the problem of contradictory class locations is not discussed, and serious doubt can be expressed about the inability of a large part of this class to produce surplus-value.

The industrial reserve army

Much of recent debate about the class position of the population of slums and shanty-towns has centred around the discussion of the origins, nature, and role of the 'industrial reserve army' in Latin America. In classical marxist analysis the size of necessary and surplus labour is determined by the laws governing the process of reproduction and expansion of the value of capital. The size of the necessary population is determined by the level of development of the social forces of production and the specific form the process of capital accumulation takes; the size of the surplus population depends on the degree of destruction of pre-capitalist forms of production and the class structures tied to them. As the social forces of production increase, the quantity of socially necessary labour decreases. The growing surplus labour then becomes part of the industrial reserve army which survives at the margin and provides reserves of labour-power for phases of industrial expansion; it also serves to keep wage-levels low.

The debate on the industrial reserve army has centred either on the degree of significance attached to explanations of its nature and role that are based on the process of the deepening of the capitalist division of labour and the generalization of capitalist relations of production in the development of an internal market or on explanations relating to the insertion of an economy in a dependent fashion into the global economy; in other words between those explanations which see it as being primarily determined by the nature of the relations of production in a specific social formation and those which see it as being primarily derived from the specificity of a condition of dependency. Thus

Pradilla (1976b) is clear that the size of the industrial reserve army in Latin America is determined by an increase in the rate of demographic growth, by the decomposition of pre-capitalist forms of agricultural production under the impact of capitalist development and the migration of the surplus population to the cities, by the decomposition of urban – artisan and manufacturing forms under the impact of capitalist industry, the slowness and discontinuity in the process of capital accumulation in industry and by the limited incorporation of a mass of labour power because of the monopoly and capital intensive nature of industrial production with a high organic composition of capital. On the other hand, the question of the role of the industrial reserve army also relates to the wages–productivity debate between Emmanuel (1972) and Bettleheim (1972). Mandel (1978) agrees with Bettleheim in stressing the critical determination of wages by the productivity of labour, but also situates the origins and role of the industrial reserve army in the context of global capitalist development. The accumulation of capital in the advanced capitalist countries proceeded by disrupting pre-capitalist modes and forms of production and the social classes tied to them in the process of the creation of the domestic market; this led to the destruction of more jobs than were being created, the growth of an industrial reserve army and falling wage-rates. However, as soon as the accumulation of capital ceased to rely primarily on the domestic displacement of pre-capitalist relations: 'it started to create more jobs than it destroyed in the metropolitan countries because the jobs it destroyed were henceforth located in the underdeveloped countries' (Mandel, 1978, p. 363). Thus the origins of the industrial reserve army in Latin America, according to Mandel, lie primarily in the changing nature of the process of global accumulation of capital. He goes on to argue that the secular trend of the industrial reserve army is increasing in less-developed countries because the rate of capital-intensive industrial growth cannot keep pace with the displacement of the peasantry from the land under the impact of capitalist development. The switch of foreign capital to finished goods re-inforces this trend, replacing the high number of labour-intensive jobs with a low number of capital-intensive jobs. On the other hand, the specific mixture of pre-capitalist and capitalist relations of production in an under-developed economy can prevent the universalization of the capitalist mode of production because low wages, the size of the subsistence economy, and the army of the unemployed and underemployed all limit the further expansion of the domestic market and the process of accumulation.

Attempts to incorporate marginality theory

Similar difficulties have emerged out of the attempts to marry marginality theory with historical structural marxism. Quijano (1974), for example, argues that a marginalized labour force is created as an irreversible and permanent phenomenon because of the inability of capital-intensive industry to create an adequate number of jobs in relation to population growth, the destruction of labour-intensive, artisan production by capital-intensive industry, and the displacement of the existing workforce from productive activity, by capital-intensive industry. This creates a large surplus population that does *not* play the role of an industrial reserve army, which does *not* have a significant role to play in the process of capital accumulation, and which is forced to work in the urban tertiary sector in activities that do not provide full-time employment but generate low profits and incomes and are highly unstable. As those so 'marginalized' do not play the role of an industrial reserve army and do not play a significant role in the process of capital accumulation, they constitute themselves into a precarious and unstable class that is highly dependent on the state. Nun (1969), on the other hand, identifies marginality that is functional ('industrial reserve army') from that which is not ('marginal mass'). Marx's category of relative surplus population takes the form of an industrial reserve army only where this population acts to depress wages or to affect the capitalist control of the labour process. This is not the case for the 'marginal mass', who do not compete for jobs in the capital-intensive sector as these jobs demand high levels of skill and qualification, and wage rates within it are more influenced by the high productivity character of capital-intensive production. The marginal mass is therefore 'a-functional'.

The Quijano–Nun concept sees marginality as a permanent and irreversible phenomenon (in opposition to earlier theories of marginality), and sees economic growth in Latin America as inherently limited by the capital-intensive nature of this development. It concludes that a large, mostly powerless, mass has been installed in the cities. This position has been widely challenged on both theoretical (Cardoso, 1971) and empirical grounds (Faria, 1976; Oliveira, 1972). Empirical evidence from Peru and Brazil does not indicate an increasing marginalization of the urban population with capital-intensive industrialization and those sectors closely linked with the capital-intensive sector seem to be the most dynamic in creating jobs. Although there had been an overall decline in artisan employment, this decline has been largely concentrated in rural areas and urban artisan employment may well have increased considerably (Roberts, 1978). Similarly both authors are ambiguous about the relations between the working class and the marginalized mass. On a more general level Pradilla's (1976b) critique of these efforts is apposite; the attempt is made to rescue the concept of marginality by informing it with a new content and the ideological constraints of this exercise are the origin of many of its difficulties.

The same could be said perhaps of the CEBRAP school argued by Faria, Oliveria, Cardoso, and others, who have come to different conclusions on the class position of this urban population, whilst retaining the framework of marginality theory. Those who Quijano sees as 'afunctional' to capitalism, CEBRAP see as necessary for the expansion of capitalist production under conditions of underdevelopment. Capitalist development depends more on the development of the internal market and internal capitalist relations of production than on the external conditions involved in a dependency relationship. This process involves a slow and uneven transformation of local class structures. In a situation where capital is relatively scarce, bottlenecks in economic growth can be resolved by creating production possibilities within the labour-intensive tertiary sector. This can facilitate the distribution of the industrial product, enable capital to be reserved for activities directly related to high profit sectors, and reduce the reproduction costs of labour-power in the capital-intensive sector by providing cheap consumer goods. The marginal population is thus employed in a productive sector with a variety of linkages (e.g. domestic subcontracting) to the capitalist sector, that determine its whole character and dynamic. Though there is no classical reserve army in Latin America, in the sense that Marx employed the term (amongst other things because of the role of the state), this sector does play the role of an industrial reserve army by reducing the labour costs of capital-intensive production (Roberts, 1978). This entails a different view of the class structure than that proposed from the Quijano–Nun position. Because of these linkages, the relationship between the proletariat and the marginals is closer and their interests in the production process are more in accord. Moreover, the increasing dependence of contract work and these linkages leads to their increasing 'proletarianization'. Marginality is thus for CEBRAP a method of facilitating the early industrial stages of capitalist development, the expansion of the internal market and the deepening of capitalist development, albeit unevenly and slowly.

Class and the petty commodity producers

Finally, the discussion of the class position of petty commodity producers has been taken up in recent years through the use of structural marxist categories such as 'class-in-formation' and 'contradictory class locations'. This position starts from what is seen as a fundamental characteristic of contemporary capitalist development—the dissolution of the pure ownership of the means of production into the separate but clearly related functions of 'possession' and 'control' (Olin Wright, 1976; 1978), and the existence of more complex technical relations of production (foremen, supervisors, and managers). This results in situations where an individual combines the classical bourgeois and proletarian roles in the production process. Olin Wright identifies three such positions—managers, small employers, and semi-autonomous wage-earners, all of whom occupy (contradictory class locations'. Gerry and Birkbeck (1979) have extended this analysis to cover those previously classified as a 'traditional petite bourgeoisie', and those involved in petty commodity forms of production and exchange that are linked in a highly complex and differentiated manner to activities in the capitalist sector. There exist three strata amongst petty commodity producers who are differentiated according to their degree of insertion and type of subordination to capitalist relations of production. There are 'lumpen-capitalists'—one-person, market-orientated, and low-level operators who own their own means of production; 'disguised wage-workers' who though they can exert some degree of control over their own labour process, and even own some of their means of production, in reality have very little control over the labour process or their level of remuneration (e.g. outworkers); and 'incipient bootstrap capitalists' who are progressively introducing capitalist methods and relations of production into their enterprises. The lumpen-capitalist and the disguised wage-earner occupy contradictory class positions, both being integrated into capitalist relations of production—the one into the sphere of production, and the other into the sphere of circulation. To these contradictory class positions there corresponds a contradictory ideological position (a volatile class consciousness oscillating between bourgeois and proletarian positions).

Though there is much of merit in this line of argument, particularly the importance given to a close examination of the relations of production, it suffers from the basic flaw of the structuralist reading of Marx—asserting totality at the expense of movement and therefore providing a static and somewhat mechanistic account of class structures 'frozen' at a moment of time. Movement, the inherent and historical dynamic of capitalist development involving the constant process of the destruction and formation of social classes, is lost in the proliferation of ever more detailed substructures that structuralize historically transient conditions.

This essay is not an exhaustive enquiry into the ideological nature of urban residential theory in Latin America. It attempts merely to indicate the inability of Latin American urban studies to provide a satisfactory account of the relationship between the broader historical process of economic and social change and the processes and forces shaping phenomena at an urban level. It also tries to indicate some of the difficulties involved in a treatment of the relationship between spatial and social processes. A full account of the ideological nature of the relationship between theoretical developments and changes in the Latin American reality at all spatial levels has still to be elaborated. Moreover, this critique has dwelt little on the relationship between theory and policy; it has not dealt with the profound penetration of ideology into the understanding of urban phenomena at the political and ideological–cultural levels and it has not examined the ideological nature of the various attempts to classify settlements on the basis of some criterion of consumption. The critique could quite easily be extended to cover all these topics at all spatial levels.

REFERENCES

Alonso, W. A. (1964). The form of cities in developing countries, *Papers Regional Science Association,* **13**, 165–173.

Alonso, W. A. (1967). Reformulation of classical location theory and its relation to rent theory. *Papers of the Regional Science Association*, **19**, 23–44.

Amato, P. W. (1968). *An Analysis of Changing Patterns of Elite Residential Locations in Bogota, Colombia*. Latin American Studies Program Dissertation. Ithaca.

Amato, P. W. (1970). A comparison population densities, land values, and socioeconomic class in 4 Latin American Cities. *Land Economics*, **46**, 447–55.

Anderson, J. (1975). *The Political Economy of Urbanism: An Introduction and Bibliography*. Department of Urban and Regional Planning, Architectural Association London; unpublished discussion paper.

Balan, J., Browing, H. and Jelin, E. (1973). *Men in a Developing Society: Geographic and Social Mobility in Monterrey, Mexico*, University of Texas Press, Austine.

Berlinck, M. T., and Cohen, Y. (1979). Desenvolvimento economico, crescimento economico e modernizacao na cidade de Sao Paulo, *Revista de Administraçâo de Empresas*, **10**, 1, 45–64 Rio de Janeiro.

Betteheim, C. A. (1972). In Emmanuel, A. (ed.), *Unequal Exchange*, New Left Books, London.

Beyer, G. H. (ed.) (1967). *The Urban Explosion in Latin America: A Continent in the Process of Modernization*, Cornell University Press, Ithaca, New York.

Birkbeck, C. (1979). Self-employed proletarians in an informal factory: The case of Cali's garbage dump. In Bromley, R. (ed.) *The Urban Informal Sector*, Pergamon, Oxford, pp. 1173–1186.

Booth, D. (1975). A. G. Frank: an introduction. In Oxaal I., Barnett, T., and Booth, D. (eds.). *Beyond the Sociology of Development*. Routledge and Kegan Paul, London, pp. 50–85.

Brett, S. (1974). Low-income urban settlements in Latin America: the Turner model. In de Kadt, E., and Williams, G. (eds.). *Sociology and Development*, Tavistock, London, pp. 171–96.

Bromley, R. (ed.) (1979). The Urban Informal Sector: Critical Perspectives on Employment and Housing Policies, Pergamon Press, Oxford.

Burgess, E. W. (1925). The growth of the city. In Park, R. E., Burgess, E. W. and McKenzie, R. D. (eds.) *The City*, University of Chicago Press, Chicago, pp. 47–62.

Burgess, R. (1977). Self Help Housing: A New Imperialist Strategy? *Antipode*, **9**, 50–59.

Burgess, R. (1979). Petty commodity housing or dweller control? A Critique of J. F. C. Turner's views on housing policy. In Bromley, R. (ed.), *The Urban Informal Sector*, Pergamon, Oxford. pp. 1105–1133.

Cardoso, F. H. (1971). Comentarios Sobre os Conceitos de Superpopulacâo Relativa e Marginalidade, *Estudos Centro Brasileiro de Análise e Planejamento*, Sâo Paulo **1**, 99–130.

Castells, M. (1971). Problemas de investigacion en sociologia urbana, Madrid, Siglo XX1. Quoted in Yujnovsky, O: Urban Spatial Configurations and Land Use Policies in Latin America in Portes, A., and Browning, H. L., (eds.) *Current Perspectives in Latin American Urban Research*. ILAS, Austin, pp. 23–4.

Castells, M. (1976). Theory and Ideology. In Pickvance, C. G. *Urban Sociology*, Tavistock, London, pp. 60–84.

Castells, M. (1977). *The Urban Question*, Edward Arnold, London.

Clarke, S. (1978). Capital, fractions of capital and the State: neo-marxist analyses of the South African state. *Capital and Class*, Vol. **5**, 32–77.

Emmanuel, A. (1972). *Unequal Exchange*, New Left Books, London.

Faria, V. E. (1976). *Occupational Marginality, Employment and Poverty in Urban Brazil;* unpublished Ph.D. disseration, Harvard University.

Fishlow, A. (1973). Some reflections on post-1964 Brazilian economic policy. In Stepan, A. (ed.) (1973) *Authoritarian Brazil;* New Haven and London, Yale University Press, 69–118.

Germani, G. (1967). The city as an integrating mechanism: The concept of social integration. In Beyer, G. H. (ed.) *The Urban Explosion in Latin America,* Cornell University Press, Ithaca, New York, pp. 175–214.

Germani, G. (1972). Aspectos teoricos de la marginalidad. *Revista Paraquaya de Sociologia,* No. 9, No. 30.

Gerry, C., and Birkbeck, C. (1979). *The Petty Commodity Pioneer in Third World Countries: Petit Bourgeois or 'Disguised' Proletarian.* Mimeo, Centre for Development Studies, University College of Swansea, Wales.

Goldmann, L. (1969). *The Human Sciences and Philosophy,* Cape Editions, London.

Grupo de Estudios 'Jose Raimundo Russi (1975). *Lucha de Clases Por el Derecho a la Ciudad,* Edit. 8 de Junio, Bogota.

Gunder–Frank A. (1969) The sociology of development and the underdevelopment of sociology in Latin America. In *Underdevelopment or Revolution,* Monthly Review Press, New York, 21–94.

Harris, W. D. (1971). *The Growth of Latin American Cities,* Ohio University Press.

Harvey, D. (1973). *Social Justice and the City,* Edward Arnold. London.

Heller, A. (1978). *The Theory of Need in Marx,* Allison and Busby, London.

Hindness, B. and Hirst, P. Q. (1975). *Precapitalist Modes of Production,* Routledge and Kegan Paul, London.

Hoselitz, B. (1960). *Sociological Factors in Economic Development,* Glencoe, The Free Press.

Hoyt, H. (1939). *The Structure and Growth of Residential Neighbourhoods in American Cities,* Washington, D. C., Federal Housing Administration.

Hoyt, H. (1963). Residential and retail patterns of leading Latin American cities. *Land Economics,* **39**, 164.

Hoyt, H. (1964). Recent distortions of the classical models of urban structure. *Land Economics,* **40**, 199–212.

Inkeles, A. (1966). The modernization of man. In Weiner, M. (ed.) *Modernization: The Dynamics of Growth,* Basic Books, New York: pp. 138–50.

International Labour office (ILO) (1970). *Towards Full Employment: A Programme for Colombia,* ILO, Geneva.

International Labour office (ILO) (1972). *Employment, Incomes, and Equality: A Strategy for Increasing Productive Employment in Kenya,* ILO, Geneva.

International Labour office (ILO) (1976). *Urban Development and Employment in Sao Paulo,* ILO, Geneva.

Laclau, E. (1977). *Politics and Ideology in Marxist Theory.* New Left Books, London.

Leeds, A. (1969). The significant variables determining the characteristics of squatter settlements, *America Latina,* **12**, No. 3, 44–86.

Leeds, A. (1971). The concept of the 'Culture of Poverty' conceptual, logical, and empirical problems with perspectives from Brazil and Peru. In Leacock, E. B. (ed.) *The Culture of Poverty,* Simon and Schuster, New York, 226–84.

Lenin, V. I. (1972). *Materialism and Empirio-Criticism,* Foreign Languages Press, Peking.

Lenin, V. I. (1977). *The Development of Capitalism in Russia,* Progress Publishers, Moscow.

Lewis, O. (1966). The Culture of Poverty, *Scientific American,* **215**, No. 4, 19–25.

Lloyd, P. (1979). *Slums of Hope?* Penguin Harmondsworth.

Lojkine, J. (1976). Contribution to a Marxist Theory of Capitalist Urbanization. In Pickvance C. G. *Urban Sociology: Critical Essays,* Tavistock, London, pp. 119–146.

Lowry, I. (1960). Filtering and housing standards, *Land Economics,* **36**, 362–70.

McClelland, D. (1964). A Psychological Approach to Economic Development. *Economic Development and Cultural Change,* **12**, No. 3 (April 1964).

McGee, T. G. (1974). *The Persistence of a Protoproletariat: Occupational Structures and Planning for the Future of Third World Cities*. University of California School of Architecture and Urban Planning, Los Angeles.

McKenzie, R. D. (1925). The ecological approach to the study of human community. In Park, R., Burgess, E., and McKenzie, R. '*The City*', pp. 63–79.

Mandel, E. (1978). *Late Capitalism*, Verbe, New Left Editions, London.

Mangin, W. (1967). Latin American Squatter Settlements: A Problem and Solution. *Latin American Research Review*, **2**, 3, pp. 67–98.

Marcuse, H. (1967). *Reason and Revolution*, Routledge and Kegan Paul, London.

Marx, K. (1887) (1970). *Capital Vol. I*, Lawrence and Wishart, London.

Marx, K. (1972). *Capital: Vol. II*, Lawrence and Wishart, London.

Marx, K. (1977). (1889) *A Contribution to a Critique of Political Economy*, Progress Publishers, Moscow.

Massey, D. (1978). Regionalism: Some Current Issues. *Capital and Class*, **6** Autumn 106–125.

Merton, R. (ed.) (1957). *Social Theory and Social Structure*, New York, The Free Press.

Moser, C. (1979). Informal Sector or Petty Commodity Production: Dualism or Dependence in Urban Development? In Bromley, R. (ed.), *The Urban Informal Sector*, Pergamon, Oxford, pp. 1041–1065.

Muth, R. (1969). *Cities and Housing*, University of Chicago Press, Chicago.

Nun, Jose (1969). Sobrepoblacion Relativa, Ejercito Industrial de Reserva y Masa Marginal. *Revista Latinoamericana de Sociologia*, **5**, 2 July, 174–236.

Olin Wright, E. (1976). Class boundaries in advanced capitalist societies. *New Left Review*, **98**, 3–41.

Olin Wright, E. (1978). *Class, Crisis, and the State*, New Left Books, London.

Oliveira, F. de (1972). A economia Brasileira: critica a razao dualista. *Estudos CEBRAP*, **2** (Oct), 5–82.

Pahl, R. E. (1975). *Whose City?* Penguin Harmondsworth.

Park, R. E. (1925). The city: suggestions for the investigation of human behaviour in the urban environment. In Park, R. E., Burgess, E. W., and McKenzie, R. D., *The City*, University of Chicago Press, Chicago, pp. 1–46.

Park, R. E. (1928). Human migration and the marginal man. *American Journal of Sociology*, **33**, No. 6, 881–893.

Parsons, Talcott (1951). *The Social System*, The Free Press, Glencoe, Illinois.

Perlman, J. E. (1976). *The Myth of Marginality*, University of California Press, Berkeley, Los Angeles.

Portes, A. and Browning, H. L. (1976). Introduction in *Current Perspectives in Latin American Urban Research*, ILAS, Austin, pp. 3–16.

Poulantzas, Nicos (1972). *Poder Politico y Clases Sociales en el Estado Capitalista*, Siglo XXI Espana. Quoted Pradilla, E. (1976). **6**, 34.

Pradilla, E. (1976a). Notas Acerca del Problema de la Vivienda; *Ideologia y Sociedad*, No. 16 Jan/Mar, pp. 70–107. Bogota.

Pradilla, E. (1976b). Notas acerca de las politicas de vivienda de los Estados Latinoamericanos. *Revista de Material Didactico* Jul/Aug 1977 Escuela Nacional de Arquitectura–Autogobierno UNAM 7. Mexico City.

Pradilla, E. (1976c). La Ideologia Burguesa y el Problema de la Vivienda Critica de dos teorias. *Ideologia y Sociedad*, No. 19, Oct-Dec Bogotá.

Quijano, A. (1973). *La Formación de Un Universo Marginal en las Ciudades de América Latina*. In M. Castells, ed. '*Imperialismo y Urbanización en America Latina.*' Gustavo Gill, Barcelona.

Quijano, A. (1974). The marginal pole of the economy and the marginalized labour force. *Economy and Society*, **3**, November 393–428.

Quinn, J. A. (1940). The Burgess zonal hypothesis and its critics. *American Sociological Review*, **5**, 210–218.

Redfield, R. (1947). The Folk Society. *American Journal of Sociology*, **52**, 293–308.

Roberts, B. (1978). *Cities of Peasants*, Edward Arnold, London.

Schnore, L. F. (1965). On the spatial structure of cities in the two Americas. In Hauser, P. M., and Schnore, L. F. (eds.), *The Study of Urbanization*, Wiley, New York, 347–99.

Stavenhagen, R. (1968). Seven Fallacies about Latin America. In Petras, J., and Zeitlin, M. (eds.), Latin America. *Reform or Revolution*, Fawcett, Greenwich.

Stonequist, E. V. (1935). The problem of the marginal man, *American Journal of Sociology*, **41**, No. 1, 1–12.

Stokes, C. (1962). A theory of slums. *Land Economics*, **38**, 23, 187–197.

Thompson, E. P. (1978). *The Poverty of Theory and Other Essays*, Merlin Press, London.

Tokman, V. E. (1978). Competition between the informal and formal sectors in retailing: the case of Santiago. In Bromley, R., (ed.) *The Urban Informal Sector*, Pergamon, Oxford, pp. 1187–1198.

Tolosa, H. (1979). Causes of urban poverty in Brazil. In Bromley, R. (ed.), *The Urban Informal Sector*, Pergamon, Oxford, pp. 1087–1103.

Turner, J. F. C. (1968). Housing priorities, settlement patterns and urban development in modernizing countries. *Journal of the American Institute of Planners*, **34**, No. 6, 54–63.

Turner, J. F. C. (1969). Uncontrolled urban settlements: problems and policies. In Breese, G. (ed.), *The City in Newly Developing Countries*, Prentice Hall, Englewood Cliffs, N. J., pp. 507–534.

Turner, J. F. C. (1972). Housing as a verb. In Turner, J. F. C., and Fichter, R. (ed.), *Freedom to Build*, Macmillan, New York pp. 148–75.

Turner, J. F. C. and Fichter, R. (1972). *Freedom to Build: Dweller Control of the Housing Process*, Macmillan, New York.

Turner, J. F. C. (1976). *Housing by People*, Marion Boyars, London.

Valenzuela, J., and Vernez, G. (1974). Construcción popular y estructura del mercado de la vivienda: el caso de Bogota. *Revista SIAP* No. 31, Sept. Bogota, Colombia.

Vekemans, R., and Silva, F. (1969). *Marginalidad en America Latina: un ensayo diagnostico*, Helder: Barcelona.

Walton, J. (1976). Urban hierarchies and patterns of dependence in Latin America: theoretical bases for a new research agenda. In Portes, A., and Browning, H. L. (eds.), *Current Perspectives in Latin American Urban Research*, ILAS, Austin, pp. 43–69.

Wirth, L. (1938). Urbanism as a way of life. *American Journal of Sociology*, **44**, July, pp. 1–24.

Geography and the Urban Environment
Progress in Research and Applications, Volume IV
Edited by D. T. Herbert and R. J. Johnston
© 1981 John Wiley & Sons Ltd.

Chapter 4

The Politics of Redevelopment: Covent Garden

Terry Christensen

The decline of the inner city has been a serious urban problem in recent decades. The centres of many large cities have deteriorated as middle-class residents, industry, and commerce moved to the suburbs. For people who could afford the move, the suburbs offered the fulfilment of their dream of a single-family or semi-detached home. For industry, the suburbs offered cheap land, lower taxes, and lower construction costs. Shopping centres followed and drained the inner city of department stores and retail trade. Left behind in the decaying housing of the inner city were racial minorities, the poor and the aged.

The decline was most precipitous in American cities, where affluence and the automobile accelerated the pace of suburbanization. But by the 1950s and 1960s, inner city decline had become a problem in London and other European cities as well. Declining areas were dangerous, depressing, and uneconomic—for business, landowners, government, and residents. Until recently, such areas usually stabilized at some point as working class or lower class neighbourhoods or revived themselves gradually and on a small scale through workings of the private economy. But in the 1950s, there was a fear that this private renewal would not occur. The process of suburbanization had drained away too much too fast. It appeared it would be necessary for government to act to stem the tide.

Changes in the scale of private redevelopment added impetus to the demand for government intervention. Instead of a house here and a house there, contemporary corporate developers operated on a grand scale, making huge investments in major projects for great profit. To operate on this scale, developers needed governmental assistance. In many older areas, large-scale redevelopment was hindered by fragmented ownership of small parcels of land. Resistance from just one owner of one small shop could bring an entire project to a halt. Private developers had no legal power over the recalcitrant small property holder, but government did. Through the power of eminent domain (in the United States) or compulsory purchase (in Britain), government could acquire land at market value, though the threat of compulsory purchase was usually sufficient to force resistant landowners to give in.

Thus the developers needed governmental assistance and they lobbied for it vigorously, supported by major financial interests. Aside from pleasing these forces, government was persuaded that public redevelopment programmes were needed to revive cities and bring in new tax revenues. Planners also gained a chance to plan and politicians got an opportunity to act on a grand scale.

The result of these pressures was government-assisted, urban renewal programmes. Through the actual or threatened use of the power of compulsory purchase, government could acquire inner city land, assembling sites for large-scale redevelopment and becoming, in effect, a land speculator. Once assembled, the sites were cleared, improved as needed, and sold to developers. The purchasers gained a subsidy in that much of their work was already done for them and paid for with tax money. Government justified the subsidy by pointing to the benefits expected to follow redevelopment: inner city revival, jobs, and tax revenues.

The 1960s saw considerable redevelopment in cities around the world. The typical process was to target a declining area, demolish most of it and redevelop on a grand scale, with high-rise office buildings and often some public facilities. In the process the neighbourhoods that existed before redevelopment were destroyed. Usually lower-income areas, such neighbourhoods were unorganized and lacking in the political skills to combat redevelopment. When they did organize, it was often too late and they lost to the more powerful developers. By the 1970s, some of the negative externalities of redevelopment were becoming apparent. The destruction of inner city neighbourhoods weakened the social fabric of the city as a whole, breaking the fragile social bonds that integrate people in urban areas, making more people dependent on government assistance and destroying small businesses as well as reducing the availability of low cost housing.

The slow awakening to the complex effects of urban renewal led to increasing questioning and resistance. Though the developers and the pro-development mentality of government almost always triumphed over the neighbourhoods targeted for redevelopment, Covent Garden, a neighbourhood in central London, was an exception to the rule.

COVENT GARDEN

Covent Garden has been the site of a pitched battle between residents, businessmen, developers, planners, and politicians for 15 years. These lucrative 90 acres in central London were the home of the famous produce market for 300 years, but redevelopment planning began with the government's 1964 decision to move the market to modern facilities south of the Thames. (see Figure 4.1) The vacuum left by the move gave the developers and planners their opportunity.

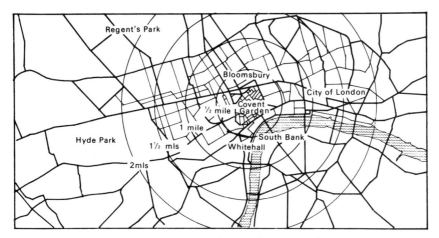

FIGURE 4.1. Covent Garden in its urban-regional context

Covent Garden was originally developed in the 17th Century. The Piazza, designed by Inigo Jones for the Earl of Bedford, was laid out in 1630 as London's first residential square. The burgeoning fruit and vegetable market soon pushed the gentry out, however, and for three centuries, the principal economic function of the area was produce wholesaling.

For almost as long, the area has been an artistic and cultural centre, with many publishers and theatres. The combination of the market, theatres, printers, craftsmen and coffee houses gave the area an around-the-clock vitality, but Covent Garden has always been a residential area as well. Beginning with the gentry living on the piazza, the neighbourhood gradually changed to a predominantly working class population, mixed with artisans and theatre people. Covent Garden's population declined steadily in this century, from 8,917 in 1901 to 3,000 in 1971.

Most of the remaining residents are working class. Thirty per cent are older than 65. Most live in single-person households and 99 per cent renters, mostly in local authority and housing trust facilities. Most of the people have lived in Covent Garden for a long time and most of them want to stay. This stable residential population is what makes Covent Garden a community. There is a strong feeling of neighbourliness and a high degree of social contact on the streets and in the pubs.

When the decision to move the market was made, the planners and developers saw a classic example of an area ready for renewal: a declining population of workers, elderly people and renters; buildings 100–200 years old; a 17th Century maze of streets; and one of the most lucrative locations in London. In the boom years of the 1960s, new developments were rising all around Covent

Garden. Not surprisingly, developers and speculators had been casting their eyes on Covent Garden even before the Market Authority determined to relocate.

PLANNING

London is governed by a two-tiered system with the Greater London Council (GLC) in charge of regional policies and 32 boroughs responsible for more local concerns. The GLC deals with public transport, major roads, sewerage, water, refuse disposal, industrial development, general planning and special redevelopment projects while the boroughs provide welfare services, parks, libraries, local streets, refuse collection, and specific planning for their areas.

Covent Garden is governed by the GLC and both the boroughs of Westminster and Camden, but the GLC took charge of planning when Covent Garden was designated a major redevelopment area, thus resolving potential conflict between the boroughs. The GLC then proceeded to plan in the usual way. The politicians gave the planners guidelines and the planners came up with proposals for review after consulting interested parties, in this case almost exclusively property owners and developers. At the end of the planning process, the Council must approve and the plan may be appealed to the Secretary of State for the Environment who has veto power.

In 1965, the GLC announced plans to redevelop Covent Garden on a grandiose scale (see Figure 4.2). During 1966 and 1967, the GLC planners gathered data. Aside from a sample survey of public attitudes, there was no attempt to gain public input. There was, however, substantial consultation with major landowners and developers. In 1968, the planning team published their proposals. They stressed the need for GLC intervention to manage inevitable redevelopment, arguing that public control was preferable to private exploitation. Government intervention was also said to be necessary to assemble sites for developers, thus overcoming the pattern of fragmented land ownership and providing incentives for private developers.

The planners recommended the demolition of 60 per cent of the area (including 82 per cent of the housing) to be replaced by carefully differentiated 'bands' of commercial, entertainment, and residential developments connected by pedestrain walkways. Major new roadways, hotels, office buildings, a conference centre and parking facilities would also be included. The old Central Market Building and some other structures in the centre of the area were to be preserved as a 'line of character'. Though massively destructive, the plan was relatively innovative for its time in that it attempted to retain a mixture of uses and some of the older buildings. GLC Planner Geoffrey Holland says 'we got a lot of flack in 1968 for retaining old buildings. We were considered very backward'.

In order to carry out their plan, the GLC needed to have Covent Garden designated a Comprehensive Development Area (CDA) by the Secretary of

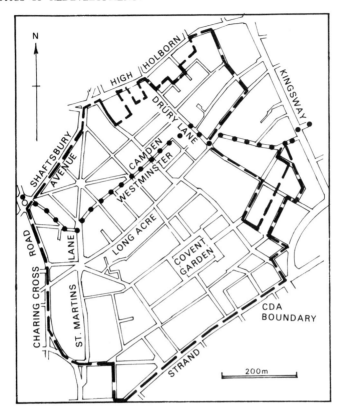

FIGURE 4.2. Covent Garden showing the boundary for the
Comprehensive Development Area

State for the Environment. They submitted their plan for this purpose in 1971
and a public inquiry was held. The inquiry is a public hearing presided over
by a supposedly neutral 'inspector' designated by the Department of the
Environment who makes recommendations to the Secretary of State for the
Environment.

The court-like format of the public inquiry is not conducive to public
participation. A case is made by the barrister for the proponents (the GLC)
and an opposing case is made by barristers for the registered objectors to the
plan. Nevertheless, the GLC plan was subject to a barrage of criticism at the
1971 inquiry. There were 128 registered objectors to the plan, including the
Town and Country Planning Association, the Society for the Preservation of
Ancient Buildings, the Georgian Group, and the Civic Trust.

The objectors were led by the Covent Garden Community Association
(CGCA), a group that had been formed by residents with the assistance of a
renegade planner and some radical young architecture students. The CGCA

had held a series of press conferences and protest rallies which were lavishly covered by a national media suddenly interested in conservation in general and in the colourful neighbourhood of Covent Garden in particular.

After 42 days of hearings, the inquiry concluded. In January, 1973, Secretary of State for the Environment Geoffrey Rippon made his ruling. The Secretary approved the CDA but rejected the road proposals essential to massive redevelopment and recommended more emphasis on conservation and public participation. To ensure more conservation, the Secretary added 250 buildings to the protected list. Rippon's decision was cautious, a compromise decision that accepted the main goal (a CDA) but recommended revision and review. With GLC elections coming up in the spring of 1973, Rippon may have wanted to avoid embarrassing the then Conservative GLC majority. Nevertheless, the Conservatives were defeated in the April 1973 GLC elections and the relatively pro-neighbourhood Labour Party took charge of the planning of Covent Garden. In December the Labour Covent Garden Committee set forth its new guidelines for the area, rejecting skyscrapers, new roads, and additional offices and emphasizing conservation and housing.

A CONSERVATION PLAN

To comply with Rippon's request for more public participation in the next round of planning, the GLC created the Covent Garden Forum of Representatives. The Forum is comprised of 9 residents, 9 business people, 9 service workers, and 3 property owners elected by people who live, work or own property in Covent Garden. In 1974 4,374 persons registered for the Forum election and about one third of them voted, choosing from among 78 candidates.

Since 1974, the Forum has met on a regular basis, reviewing planning policy as well as specific planning applications. The power of the Forum is strictly advisory. Two representatives of the Forum attend meetings of the GLC Covent Garden Committee and may voice the Forum's views there.

Originally, the CGCA participated heavily in the Forum, but in 1975 a split developed. The Forum's style of operation was parliamentary and reactive, frustrating the more action-oriented CGCA leadership. The Forum *reacted* to proposals of planners and developers; it was passive, unable to take the initiative. With such a diversity of interests represented, consensus was difficult to attain and without consensus, initiative was impossible. This passive, reactive position is not unusual in formalized public participation structured by government and most of the Forum representatives were educated, middle class people who adapted well to the structure and style of their organization.

Such was not the style of the CGCA, which was active and radical and preferred initiative to reaction. The CGCA had been building membership and strength since 1971, partly by providing tangible services to the neighbourhood. They opened a social centre, established a food co-operative and community theatre, published a newsletter, rehabilitated buildings, organized neighbour-hood festivals, did their own planning studies and continued their political action. The CGCA defined its goal as protection of the existing residential community and showed little concern for the fate of property owners. They had reached internal consensus and so were able to take the initiative and they were willing to use the full spectrum of political tactics available, from lobbying to protest marches.

Though the Forum and CGCA split in 1975, the groups agreed on broad objectives and worked together on an *ad hoc* basis during the development of the new plan.

In 1976, the planners presented a new draft plan, including alternatives. They proposed a substantial reduction in the scale of redevelopment, though 25 per cent of the area was still to be demolished. The new plan emphasized retention of the existing community, with residential use a top priority but with a continuation of mixed uses in the area. There was to be no new office space and the grandiose road scheme, hotels and conference centre had disappeared. An exhaustive series of public meetings was held through 1976. The Forum and the CGCA hammered away at the plan. The Forum, in its moderate way, criticized and debated the planners' proposals. The CGCA took more initiative, developing and publishing a plan of their own and making alternative site recommendations to those of the planners. The essential conflict was over the degree of redevelopment versus the degree of rehabilitation. The CGCA opted for maximum rehabilitation. The Forum was willing to accept slightly more redevelopment.

The CGCA and to a lesser extent the Forum challenged the planners on their own grounds. For a change, the planners found themselves confronted with an expertise rivalling their own and by virtue of greater familiarity with the area, more fervour of belief, better consultation with residents and cheaper end-products, the community proposals were often superior to those of the planners. In October, 1976, the GLC Covent Garden Committee approved a revised plan which as GLC Planner Geoffrey Holland conceded, represented a substantial victory for the CGCA and the Forum. After another public inquiry, the plan was given final approval by the full GLC in June, 1977—despite the Conservative victory in the May GLC elections.

The thrust of the plan as a whole was one of sensitive renewal, emphasizing rehabilitation and maximizing housing, maintenance of the existing community, mixed uses and small scale. Office development was to be restrained and there were to be no new roads or hotels. As to the specific site proposals, the emphasis was on rehabilitation with only very selective in-fill redevelopment. The plan was the diametric opposite of the 1968–1971 plan and a substantial scaling down of the June 1976 proposals. It can only be viewed as a triumph for the defenders of the community, a major reversal for property speculators and developers and a major concession by the planners and the GLC.

A very rare event in the international history of urban renewal had occurred: a neighbourhood survived. The residents will be able to stay; their community will be protected. Community resistance—especially that of the CGCA—was crucial to this victory. But no single force changed the plan. The community activists were a necessary element, not sufficient in and of themselves. They operated within the broader context of local and national politics, public opinion, and the economy.

THE PLANNERS

The case of Covent Garden illustrates a major change in the planning process in Britain—a change that has also occurred in other societies where the power of bureaucracies and experts has been challenged by citizen involvement.

Planning is an esoteric business, with a language of its own and an elaborately evolved professionalism. Lay-persons such as politicians and citizens can easily be daunted by this professionalism. The professionals know this and may willingly cloak themselves in the authority of their purported expertise because it is a primary source of power for them. This is not as it should be, but it is a natural tendency in all professions—unless the professionals are brought down to earth by the people who comprise their clientele. The business of planning is figuring out what to do with the houses and streets where we live. But planners usually prefer to think and speak in 'strategic' or 'structural' terms—with a long range view of the city as a whole. Such conceptual terms are grasped by the lay-person only with great difficulty, precisely because they are concepts—abstractions without a physical reality—whereas our homes, our streets and our neighbourhoods do have a reality for all of us. If planning could be done in such concrete specifics, we could all be participants. Planning was not, however, done in this way in the 1960s and only occurs now in circumstances such as in Covent Garden, where this sort of micro-planning was forced on local government and the planners by the people who are affected.

Until the 1970s, local planning authorities were free to work in relatively isolated and insulated conditions of low visibility. Planning decisions were made public only after they had been made and discussion was rare. Geoffrey Holland, the GLC Planning Team Leader for Covent Garden, said alternative plans were considered but not presented to the public. 'In those days, one was expected to do a plan with the technical ability one had got and present it after you had considered the alternatives. This is the fundamental change that took place with the involvement of more people in planning.'

On those rare occasions when public discussion was permitted, it was done on the planners' grounds, with their forms, procedures and language and under quasi-judicial circumstances such as legislative hearings or public inquiries. All of these obscure the planning process, making it more intimidating to people who aren't planners and discouraging citizen involvement. The process is further complicated by the fact that the roles of the boroughs, the Greater London Council and the national government overlap and under certain conditions, one level of government can over-rule the other(s). It is a system that is difficult to understand and more difficult to manipulate and this too adds to citizen difficulties.

Corporations with an interest in development can solve such difficulties quite simply. They do it with money. They can hire the expertise they need, rather than relying on volunteers and good will as citizen groups must. Trained planners are quite willing to work for employers other than public bodies. Architects and engineers and barristers can all participate in the politics of planning with professional ease. The ability to hire the necessary technical and procedural experts is one very simple reason why the corporate developers have so often had their way in the past.

Another factor which has operated to the disadvantage of citizens has been the apolitical image of planning, an image which has been carefully cultivated by the planners. Planning is presented as a technical process, not a political one. Therefore politics, politicians, political parties and citizen groups must stay out of planning and leave decisions to the professionals. Keeping politics out of planning retains power for the planners. Many politicians willingly go along with this because they get enough heat on other issues and prefer to avoid the pressures that more open, political decisions might involve. Major economic interests such as developers and landowners also prefer this professional, apolitical approach because it keeps issues out of the public forum, where they would fare less well.

But of course the idea that planning is apolitical is absurd. Politics is simply the making of choices. Some one has to make them and if they affect the public, the public should have the right to hold that person accountable or to participate in the decision-making itself. Planning choices have technical aspects and for these, the professionals are essential—but as advisers, not as the final authorities. As public interest in the planning process grew, it became apparent that choices were being made and that they were not always the preferences of the people affected. Gradually, the losers began to see just how political the planning process was—and they entered the battle over the resistance of the planners, the politicians, and the developers, all of whom preferred the safe cocoon of insulated decision making. The issue was who should decide. The issue was power.

But in the 1960s, the planners were more or less on their own. Their decisions were permeated with what Harvey Cox has called the ideology of planning (Cox, 1976). The components of this ideology were apparent in the planning of Covent Garden and many planners still function under these assumptions.

First, planners generally accept the capitalist use of land and the rights of private property. There has been an erosion of this value in Britain and most industrial nations, but it is still an accepted and influential assumption in planning. This produces a commitment to the 'highest and best' use of land, which of course is in limited supply. It is in the interest of local government as well as the landowner that land be put to its highest (and most profitable) uses, whether the local government is the landlord, collecting rents, or merely collecting property taxes which, of course, are higher on highly valued property. So prime property, like Covent Garden in central London, must be developed to its maximum potential, which is usually not working class housing or homely shops:

> One result of the general conservatism which pervades the planners' thinking is that their view of the appropriate configuration of land uses in the city tends to rationalize the view held by operators of the private land market. Thus land near the centre of the city is tacitly assumed to be appropriate for 'central area uses' which is actually an official category on land use maps. (Ambrose and Colenutt, 1975, p. 149).

A second, related, component of the ideology of planning is the clear differentiation of communities with land uses carefully defined and segregated. The planners are encouraged in this by the corporate developers, who are interested in massive, single purpose development. Planners and developers disdain congestion, chaos, and disorder; they see mixed land uses in these terms. Planners and developers prefer land uses to be clearly defined as industrial, commercial, or residential. Another word for this is segregation, not only of land uses but of social classes. The planners' penchant for differentiation was apparent in the initial plans for Covent Garden with their elaborate zones and bands and with the elimination of many traditional and contemporary uses of buildings and land in the area.

A third component of the ideology of planning is that the planners are primarily concerned with the built environment—with buildings and architecture, with streets and traffic flow—rather than with the social ecology of an area or with human life. Again, the initial plans for Covent Garden showed this lack of concern for the people who lived and worked there.

A fourth tendency among planners is to think and plan in terms of the city as a whole, rather than in terms of its parts. This holistic perception of the city is a valid one and surely the good of all the residents of the city is important. But most of us tend to think of our own good. In planning, we start from our own homes, streets, and neighbourhoods and once these are taken care of, we may think of the good of the city as a whole. Planners start from the other end—the top—and work down to the neighbourhoods. In the case of Covent Garden, they looked at a strategically located central area and how it could fit into their overall scheme for Greater London. They looked at it as a neighbourhood with people only when they were forced to.

One more factor needs to be added to the 'mind-set' of planners: bureaucratic inertia or resistance to change. Like all bureaucrats everywhere, once planners have made their proposals, change becomes unthinkable. The planners defend themselves, resisting revision and innovation. Jean Merriton, Labour Chairman of the GLC Covent Garden Committee says that on more than one occasion, the

> officers fought a real rear-guard action, accepting the principle but making no effort to implement it. During consultation . . . I felt as if I was standing between Covent Garden and the GLC (planners) and that I didn't belong to either of them. What I hope I did was to get the officers (planners) to accept decisions which they hadn't promoted without them feeling that they had lost face.

This, then, is the professional ideological context in which the planning of Covent Garden occurred. It explains much about the plans that were produced in 1968 and 1971. What happened next reflects the change in public interest, politics and planning itself. The public grew interested and assertive. The process was opened up by a suddenly interested press. The politicians reacted. The process was changed by the introduction of more public information and participation. The planners adapted reluctantly, hoping that the public interest was only a passing fancy.

Lest all this be taken as a barrage of cheap shots at the planners, unjustly blaming them for all problems, let it be remembered that they are here being discussed for their independent contributions. In mild defence of the planners, it should be pointed out that they are like other professionals in that all of us are defensive about our own areas of expertise. Teachers prefer to think that they are the only ones who know how to teach; butchers prefer to think that they are the only ones who know how to cut meat. Some of us rise above such pettiness to accept criticism and suggestions from those we serve, but all professions have their dogmas and their vulnerabilities. Perhaps we are right to ask more openness of the planners because they are public employees and because they affect our lives more than many other professionals through their power to destroy, alter or preserve whole communities. Their training should prepare them for this responsibility, but until recently, there is little to suggest that this has been the case.

Planners do not plan alone. They are servants of the local authorities and so work with some direction, particularly from elected officials. Again they aim to please, if only to keep their jobs. From 1966 to 1971 the Covent Garden planners had proceeded in an orthodox way, developing what they thought their employers wanted. By the time they produced their plan, however, the employers had changed their minds. In fact, the employers had changed. In 1973, Labour replaced the Tories as the GLC majority and just as the revised plan was completed in 1977, the Tories returned to power and the planners found themselves with new employers once again—and scrambled to please them. 'It's just a matter of what the democratically elected people at the time want,' says Planner Geoffrey Holland.

THE POLITICIANS

Though the politicians gave directions to the planners, an heroic view of the politicians involved is not justified by a close look at events. The politicians were responding to forces swirling around them—the community, public opinion, the press, the planners, the developers, and the economy. It cannot be said that they performed a leadership function in the revision of the Covent Garden plan, though some were attentive and responsive to their constituencies.

In 1971, some Labour members of the GLC and the Labour majority of the Camden Borough Council had shown support for the Covent Garden community. As part of their 1973 campaign platform, the GLC Labour Party came out in opposition to the plan, which was on its last legs anyway. Jean Merriton said Labour switched because 'it became clear that it was possible to modernize and, you know, we had all been told it was not'. This rather lame reason illustrates the dependence of elected officials on their expert staff—and the power of the planners. All of these actions came late in the planning process.

At the local level, the only Tory recognition of public concern was the appointment of Lady Dartmouth, a leading conservationist, to chair the GLC Covent Garden Committee. This was undoubtedly an attempt by the Conservative GLC majority to assuage preservationist opposition to the plan, but it failed when she resigned in disillusionment in 1973 and came out against the plan.

In 1973, Labour replaced the Tories as a majority on the GLC. An overview of the events of 1968–1977 might suggest that party politics played a significant part in the reversal of the plan, since it was a Conservative majority that proposed the original plan to demolish and redevelop and a Labour majority that developed the conservationist plan. The change in plan very tidily coincided with the reversal in party fortunes. In fact, the Conservatives were pro-development and the Labour party was antagonistic to developers, office buildings, hotels, roads, and parking.

This is, however, a simplistic view. By the time of the Labour takeover in 1973, opposition to the plan had been running strong for over two years. The conservationist movement was at its national crest. The economy was beginning a severe contraction. And, in January, 1973, before the Labour electoral victory, a Conservative Minister of the Environment had sent the plan back for revision.

So while the change in plan coincided with the change in electoral fortunes, the role of the political parties was not crucial. Though GLC barrister John Taylor sees 'Labour political overtones' in the new plan Geoffrey Holland says 'party politics never really came much into Covent Garden anyway' and suggests that there has been 'consensus between parties' in the Covent Garden planning process which has been 'remarkably free of party politics'. Simon Jenkins more forthrightly states that 'party politics might not have been invented' with regard to Covent Garden. 'The political leadership was confused and inarticulate' and 'party politicians were conspicuous absentees' in the debate and inquiries on Covent Garden (Jenkins, 1973a p. 54).

The politicians did not lead, they followed public opinion and economic developments. Some of them, particularly those who chaired the GLC Covent Garden Committee, did make an effort. Conservatives Alan Greengross and Lady Dartmouth and Labourites Tom Ponsonby and Jean Merriton, in their own ways and from their differing personal styles and politics, tried to lead. Lady Dartmouth entered the fray with vigour and attempted an energetic persuasion for the plan in which she soon no longer believed. Merriton was a somewhat less visible chairman, but spent more time in Covent Garden than any of her predecessors and made sure that the reversal in direction was made clear to the planners and through them to the public. She was annoyed at allegations of a lack of leadership, and said:

We published . . . a manifesto for Covent Garden in 1973. It was just a page and a half of foolscap. One of the proudest claims that I can make is that though it is a crude, unsophisticated statement of principle, it is the bones of the plan. So we were right, weren't we? And isn't that leadership? When the press got on to me about (leadership) a good deal as of course they did, I said that Rippon told us to draw up a plan in the light of consultation. And that's what we've done.

At the national level, Conservative Secretary of State for the Environment Rippon might be considered the hero of Covent Garden. It was he who refused to accept the 1971 proposals. His decision was the major turning point for the plan and for Conservative policy. But it was a compromise decision designed to assuage public opinion and the conservation lobby without embarrassing the Tory GLC too much. He accepted the need for a Comprehensive Development Area (CDA), but rejected the road system, required more open space and public participation and capped it all by listing 250 buildings in the area. The Tories got their CDA, but the possibility of massive redevelopment was eliminated by rejection of the roadways and more especially by the listing of so many more buildings.

Geoffrey Holland calls the decision 'a supreme, face-saving compromise' with 'tremendous inconsistencies' which was 'the only way (Rippon) could see at that time'. John Taylor agrees, suggesting that Rippon's decision also represented a triumph for the bureaucrats of the historic buildings branch of the Department of Environment in an internal struggle among the Mandarins. Rippon was caught between two forces—the rapidly rising public interest in conservation and the redevelopment interests of the GLCs Conservative majority. Elections were coming up for the GLC in 1973 and for Parliament in 1974. Rippon attempted to steer a cautious course between the two forces and produced his compromise decision. It was not hailed at the time as great leadership, though Rippon's public comments subsequent to the announcement of the decision indicate that he thought the time had come for a reversal in redevelopment policy.

Again, the politicians followed rather than led public opinion. This gap between the political 'leaders' and their constituencies is illustrative of a major change that was occuring in British local politics. The traditional hierarchical, elitist structure was breaking down as more people and pressure groups grew sufficiently concerned about the well being of their communities to enter the political process. The British have traditionally had more faith in their rulers than Americans or citizens of some other Western democracies. The spirit of public service, the high quality of civil servants, and the mundane nature of local politics have contributed to this elitism. Decisions have been left to the officials who are are supposed to make them. Elected officials operated without major constraints from their constituents—either out of faith, trust, or ignorance.

This is reinforced by party politics. The principal division in British politics at the national and local levels is the party division, Conservative and Labour, and this is fundamentally a division based on social class. This division manifests itself with great consistency in local as well as national politics. Unfortunately, national politics often seems to overshadow local politics in local elections. The Conservative victory in the 1977 GLC election was generally thought to reflect dissatisfaction with the national Labour Party and the state of the economy rather than the local party which had been in control of the GLC. As for the politicians, their primary loyalty is often to their party rather than their constituency.

So in the past, elected officials have enjoyed a double insulation, elitism and partisanship, isolating them from their constituencies. They were protected by party structure, by the acquiescence of those they ruled, by apathy and by the hierarchical structure of local government. All that changed in the 1970s as the public grew more assertive and class and party lines were blurred as neighbourhood and conservation groups organized and extraordinary coalitions between left and right were formed to protect communities.

On the whole, however, local government has not adapted particularly well to the change. Increased citizen interest has been greeted with fear and loathing. The ponderous, hierarchical structure with two local authorities (the GLC and the boroughs) sharing planning powers, the powerful and secretive legislative committee system, the massive bureaucracy, the formalistic and quasi-judicial decision-making process, and the traditions of partisanship and elitism make citizen involvement difficult and give government innumerable escape or veto mechanisms.

As a consequence, citizen pressure frequently shifted to the next higher level of government and appeals to the Secretary of State for the Environment increased spectacularly in the 1970s. National government was somewhat more responsive to neighbourhood and conservationist concerns than local governments, perhaps because they are less susceptible to the pressures of developers and less concerned about property tax base, but they too followed rather than led public opinion.

Clearly, some better mechanisms for the involvement of the public in the planning process are necessary. Recognizing this, in 1968, the national government established a committee to consider how greater participation might be obtained. The result of the committee's work was the Skeffington Report (1969), which made many recommendations for broader participation, including more public information and the creation of advisory groups like the Covent Garden Forum of Representatives. Though not all of the recommendations were implemented, the fact that the study was done and the direction in which it pointed gave legitimacy and impetus to demands for more public involvement.

Revisions in planning procedures can open up the process, inform the public and give them a better chance to express their views to those who make decisions. But the public is still trapped in the formalistic process and it will still be the elected officials who make the final decision. Unless they become more responsive to their constituents, changes in the planning process will be futile. Even if the politicians are responsive, the community must bear the burden of organizing and pressurizing with minimal resources.

COMMUNITY RESISTANCE

The illusions of the planners and politicians were shattered in Covent Garden by the resistance of the people for whom they were planning. Such neighbourhood resistance has rarely succeeded in redevelopment politics, not only in Britain, but in cities all over the world. Neighbourhood politics is usually defensive—people respond to specific threats to their own interests. This was the case in Covent Garden, which is why community interest was minimal until 1971. It was not until that year that the plan was well publicized in the community and the reality of threat was perceived. When it was, reaction was strong.

By 1971, leaders were emerging. a former market porter with an interest in community-organizing, a Camden Borough Councillor, the Vicar of the Church of St. Martin's-in-the-Fields, a businesswoman, a former GLC planner and an architecture student. Though these leaders lived or worked in Covent Garden, the community association also depended on the assistance of many young volunteers who often did not live in the area but who joined in its defence as a matter of principle. Such idealists provided much needed skills and energies to an organisation, but their presence may also have discouraged the emergence of indigenous leadership and the development of political skills among permanent residents, creating a dependence on outsiders that can be debilitating when they depart.

Be that as it may, the local leaders and their outside reinforcements tapped a widespread concern and gave it focus in the Covent Garden Community Association, which began as a relatively broad-based mass membership organization. Many of Covent Garden's working class and elderly residents supported it, along with theatre people, small businessmen, and people from outside the neighbourhood. Once underway, the resistance built up a momentum of its own, stimulated by the central event of the long 1971 public inquiry. That inquiry gave the organizers an event on which to focus and provided an education vehicle for the community, the press and London public opinion.

But the generation of leadership, the community support, and the dramatic public inquiry might have ended in failure, as has usually been the case in community resistance to redevelopment, had it not been for the extraordinary organizational skills of the CGCA—skills in organizing block by block, skills in using the media, skills in using the public inquiry as a forum. The CGCA found ways to make their resistance more than reactive. They moved from the defence to the offense, taking the initiative to propose solutions, being positive rather than exclusively negative. They worked from a base of a community united by the threat of demolition. They brought in the professional skills of architects, valuers, and planners with which to confront the professional skills of the GLC planners and the development interests. They effectively exploited the growing interest of the press in conservation and planning politics, holding their own press conferences, attending those of the GLC and staging media events such as rallies and marches. They forced the issue of Covent Garden into Greater London politics and gained national attention.

They effectively exploited the merits of the area. Covent Garden is exceptionally rich in history and romantic nostalgia was easily evoked. The Market and the Royal Opera House have given Covent Garden international fame. Nell Gwynne, Samuel Pepys, Samuel Johnson, Hogarth, and Voltaire were among the hundreds or renowned people who trod the streets of the Garden. Rules' Restaurant, favoured by Dickens and Thackeray and a rendezvous for the Prince of Wales and Lily Langtry had been scheduled for demolition in the 1971 plan. The house where David Garrick lived, the bank where T. S. Eliot worked—the list is endless, all images to be evoked to express the merits of the neighbourhood. The shades of the famous were joined by present day craftsmen working in ramshackle buildings and struggling new businesses in renovated buildings to strike a responsive chord with the press and the public. The elderly and working-class population were further reasons for sympathy. The neighbourhood had more to preserve than most and the merits of what they were trying to protect were more easily communicated to an increasingly sympathetic press and public. And this interest was skilfully manipulated by the CGCA.

Additionally, the Covent Garden community found powerful allies. The press was interested because Covent Garden was a colourful story. The public grew interested as conservation became the ascendant urban issue. An unusual coalition of conservationist pressure groups took shape, allying radical community activists with conservative, aristocratic, elitist preservationist groups. The National Trust, the Society for the Protection of Ancient Buildings, the Georgian Group and the Victorian Society all gave testimony at the 1971 public inquiry, as did Sir John Betjeman, Britain's poet laureate and a leading spokesman for conservation. At the other extreme were community organizations like the CGCA and Street Aid (for transient young people). These groups were joined by the Town and Country Planning Association, which has substantial national prestige and influence and which has long been opposed to high-rise urbanism as expressed in the 1971 plan. All of these groups shared an interest in resisting the sort of change the GLC had proposed. Beyond this shared interest, after 1971, the coalition had no strength because there was no agreement on what should be done with Covent Garden other than that it should not be destroyed. Nonetheless, the informal coalition was effective in 1971.

Further support for the Covent Garden community came from their successful lobbying efforts with the Camden Borough Council and Labour Councillors on the GLC. To a degree, the plan became a partisan political issue and the Labour Party lined up with the community. When Labour won the 1973 GLC elections, the outlook for Covent Garden improved considerably. But the Labour majority on the GLC was not entirely trusted by the community and tended to follow rather than to lead. It is much to the credit of the CGCA that they were able to operate effectively in the corridors of power as lobbyists and to establish rapport with the GLC Covent Garden Committee and with the Camden Borough Council. To do so constituted a radical revision in their initial tactics of protest politics.

Politics in Covent Garden itself became more complicated after the GLC's creation of the Forum of Representatives in 1974. The Forum came about in response to Rippon's mandate for greater public participation in the renewed planning process and also reflected recommendations for greater public involvement in the Skeffington Report (1969). Within a year, the community had split over the question of the most suitable form of public participation. The CGCA felt the Forum was too conservative, bureaucratic and passive and that it was dominated by property owners. In 1975, the CGCA went its' own way. In the following years, both organisations spoke for the community. The Forum, a structured mixture of all interests in Covent Garden with an electoral base, came to represent the more moderate and middle class elements of the neighbourhood. It had the advantage of GLC recognized legitimacy and direct involvement in the process. The CGCA probably had more genuine popular support, especially from the working class and radical elements of the neighbourhood. Unlike the Forum, which related to its constituency only through its annual election, the CGCA was in constant contact through community meetings, rallies, festivals, and a newsletter.

Though the two organizations have often been at odds with one another, in the final analysis it must be recognized that both played important parts in the survival of Covent Garden. The CGCA took the offensive: they made extreme demands, they got publicity, they applied the pressure. The Forum took similar, though more moderate, positions, presenting them humbly and politely and making them more palatable to the GLC than they might have seemed had they come from the CGCA alone. The Forum legitimized many neighbourhood demands, demonstrating that concern for neighbourhood survival was not limited to radicals and working-class residents but included business people, property owners, and middle-class residents.

Members of both groups worked long, hard hours over the plan and both deserve credit for the survival of their community. Without the CGCA the 1971 plan would not have been rejected. Without the CGCA and the Forum, the 1977 plan to protect and enhance the neighbourhood might never have been written. But they might not have triumphed alone. The planners and politicians responded, if belatedly. And two major external factors were also essential to the success of community resistance.

PUBLIC OPINION

The 1970s witnessed a great awakening of public interest in planning, conservation and neighbourhood politics. People began to perceive a threat to something they valued—and the things they valued were not merely buildings of architectrual or historical significance but the neighbourhoods where they lived. When external forces threatened destruction of their neighbourhoods, a political reaction was in turn produced: resistance. And the people of London and Britain often rallied to each others' defence, recognizing the importance of maintaining whole cities on a human scale.

GLC Covent Garden Committee Chairman Jean Merriton said:

Suddenly Londoners woke up to the idea that modernness, convenience and this and that weren't a good enough substitute for what is familiar—and familiar didn't just mean buildings, it meant activities. And they were beginning to find themselves in a world which didn't feel like home. There was a complete revolution which by the time Rippon came to make his decision made it inevitable that he couldn't accept the . . . curiously old fashioned . . . plan. So I don't think the community association could fairly claim to have chopped out the first plan.

People looked, disliked what they saw, and the public consciousness grew. This same process, this same reaction, was underway in virtually every major city in England and the United States. The late 1960s and early 1970s saw an unprecedented rise in neighbourhood groups or amenities societies dedicated to protecting and enhancing places where people lived.

Public interest in planning was encouraged by the press, which had caught on to a good story. There were folk heroes to be made. There were easy villains: nasty developers, haughty architects, insensitive bureaucrats, sleazy politicians. Many community groups learned to manipulate the press and established sympathetic contact with reporters and editors. A bit of press can make a local item such as the Covent Garden plan, into a national issue. Covent Garden is not the only area of London that has been given this treatment. Piccadilly, Soho and Bloomsbury were saved from the bulldozers on the strength of public opinion combined with the interest of the press, the activity of local organizations and the preliminary victory in Covent Garden.

The public became interested in planning, assisted by the press. The weight of public opinion turned the planners and politicians around and forced the developers to beat a hasty if temporary, retreat. Geoffrey Holland said there was

a national nervous breakdown . . . The whole of Great Britain was involved in saving something. In the 1960s, change was considered a good thing because it improved the city, provided new facilities, open space, new housing, all the kinds of things people wanted and the profits could be made to pay for these things. Almost overnight this became a bad thing. From insensitive development to don't touch a thing. The fact that we were even looking at a site was practically enough to have a march down king Street (to the GLC Planning Team offices). If some one was standing in front of a building with a piece of paper, the building was threatened and a petition was got up. The whole country went lunatic.

Holland and virtually everyone involved in the planning of Covent Garden agree that this development in public opinion—in Covent Garden, in London, and in Britain—was a major factor in changing the plan. Holland goes so far as to refer to 'national and international' public opinion as influencing the planning of Covent Garden.

Plans to redevelop Covent Garden were not the only ones to go down to defeat. Neighbourhoods throughout London were stimulated to organization and opposition of redevelopment or other projects for their areas. A period of stalemate in urban development began. 'Appeal planning' by public inquiry and ministerial adjudication' became the norm. (Taylor, 1973 p. 432) Simon Jenkins wrote 'we may have accidentally evolved . . . a system of negative control which responds to the public's dislike of the many recent upheavals in their surroundings,' (Jenkins, 1973b, p. 269).

The end result was a major change in the thrust of national urban development policy. By 1975, government ministers were announcing a 'new emphasis . . . on renewal and rehabilitation . . . rather than the vast demolition and rebuilding programs that have dominated council policy in the past 20 years . . . The involvement of residents will be vital'. (*The Times*, January 30, 1975). Anthony Crosland, Secretary of State for the Environment, announced 'the end of grandiose and gigantic plans for the wholesale demolition and comprehensive redevelopment of historic metropolitan sites.' (*The Sunday Times*, February 23, 1975). Conservation became the theme. The listing of buildings and designation of conservation areas proceeded apace. Public participation became an increasingly frequent factor in planning.

A variety of forces had contributed to the change in public opinion. Foremost among these forces of change was the simple fact that the intervention of the planners was becoming more substantial. There was *more* planning being done and *more* people were being affected. And because of the activists in the community, a more vigilant press and legal notification requirements, more people knew about what was being planned before it was implemented. The 1960s also saw a shift to planning and redevelopment in existing neighbourhoods. Before that time, major redevelopment in Britain was largely confined to areas destroyed by bombing in World War II—areas where there were no real neighbourhoods to destroy. In the 1960s and 1970s redevelopment threatened things that already existed: housing, workplaces, narrow streets and communities, some of which were architecturally interesting while others were valued as social entities. The roadways, offices and tower block housing that were proposed were not acceptable to many Londowners.

Additionally, the 1970s have seen something of an international urban renaissance, bringing a modest revival of central city neighbourhoods. Slowly, people have been returning to the city. They liked the old houses and made renovation stylish. They liked the nearness of things; the urban revival coincided with the reaction against the automobile and the increasing concern with ecology. The wave of nostalgia that swept western civilization in the mid-1970s may have been an added stimulant. The economic recession made it more expensive to live in the suburbs—to buy a house and commute. The city could be economical as well as exciting and ecological. More and more people began to recognize the neighbourhood as an important part of urban living. The isolation and loneliness of the city is partially assuaged by the familiarity we may develop with the area where we live and our identification with the place, our sense of belonging. Delicate neighbourhood social networks of friends and acquaintances came to be highly valued.

In summary, the assertion of public concern that changed British planning came about from the public's negative experience with the urban development of the 1960s, from increasing threats of intervention in existing neighbourhoods and from urban revival and neighbourhood movement of the 1970s, aided by community organizers and the press. But forces at work in the economy also played a significant role in changing national urban policy and the plan for Covent Garden.

THE ECONOMY

The early 1970s saw a major contraction in the national economy and a subsequent reduction of public spending, leading to a considerable scaling down of commitments by both government and private developers. John Taylor, the barrister who represented the GLC in the Covent Garden inquiries, says the initial plan was 'conceived in a completely different climate. It was a plan of the 1960s' which was 'almost inevitably replaced by a plan of the 1970s, a conservation plan' because of changes in the economy.

The developers had been major participants in the initial 1968—1971 plans. Jim Monahan states that during the 'planning process' the planning team held countless meetings with private developers, most of whom had no connection with the area whatsoever. The result was that the 100 acres was carved up into four to five 'twenty-million pound lots' for individual developers (Monahan, 1976).

Such involvement was not apparent in the development of the 1976 conservation plan. The expected showdown between the developers and the community did not occur because for the most part, the developers withdrew from the field of battle. A few remained interested; some gained development rights to the edges of Covent Garden (which was of greatest interest to them anyway); a few shifted their plans to rehabilitation of property they already owned; one filed an objection to the 1976 plan, but the objection was over-ruled.

Perhaps the developers withdrew because the strength of public opinion intimidated them. More realistically, it was the collapse of the property and development boom that caused them to withdraw. The property owners and the GLC may have been fortunate that their 1971 plan was defeated. Jean Merriton said that if they had approved the original plan, 'we would have gotten as far as demolition and we probably wouldn't have gotten further' because of the economic decline. As the British economy went into deep recession, there was less money available to borrow and to spend on development. This was compounded by the excessive speculation that preceded it and by the probable exhaustion of the market for office blocks due to over-building up to 1973. Meanwhile, government had become a very undependable partner in property development. It had withdrawn its subsidy to hotel builders, removing this stimulant. It had introduced the Community Land Act, threatening to rake off developmental profits for local government. John Taylor said that 'low trust for the Greater London Council as a redeveloper' may have led developers to lay low, 'waiting to see what would happen'. 'People decided to invest elsewhere', said Jean Merriton, 'as the planning dragged on so long'. All of these forces pointed to a vague future for the property market and made the period from 1973 to 1977 a bad one for making major commitments to big projects. So the developers beat a timely retreat.

The recession also meant that local government had less money to spend. Geoffrey Holland points out that the 'switchover conveniently coincided with running out of money. I think if money was available now, one would get a reversion to ideas of grandeur, as still operate in France, for example'. The recession gave local government added encouragement to heed the cries of the community. And then the developers lost interest, the GLC did not even have to make a choice between them and the community.

It should be remembered that this may only be a strategic and temporary retreat on the part of the developers. When the economy recovers and when local revenues are greater, the old schemes for office towers, conference centres and new roads may be revived. The developers and major property owners have the wherewithal to play a waiting game, holding onto their property and even profiting by renovating it in the short run. In ten or fifteen years, perhaps the public will lose interest and the economy will be strong and the developers can again seek to maximize their profits. Covent Garden will remain 'a distant plum, one day there for the picking', says John Taylor.

EPILOGUE

The case of Covent Garden illustrates a single situation in which a plan for massive demolition and redevelopment was converted to a plan for conservation and community protection. The survival of the neighbourhood resulted from a fortuitous interplay of local and more general forces of which community resistance, public opinion and a recession economy were the most important. Without each of the three, Covent Garden might not have survived.

The planners and politicians, those nominally in charge, reacted to these forces rather than leading them. To their credit and somewhat to the surprise of the community, some of the planners and elected officials managed to react responsively, changing not only the plan for Covent Garden, but the planning process as well.

The community appears to have won. Without the interest and effort of the residents of Covent Garden and the activists that led them, the plan would have been approved in 1971. But they were there and they forced reconsideration. Supported by the flow of national public opinion in the direction of conservation and by a neighbourhood revolution that was occurring not only in Britain but in the United States, they won their victory. However, this case does not test the strength of public opinion and community activism against the economic forces of the developers, because by 1973 the developers had virtually withdrawn from the contest. This may be taken as an admission of defeat but, more likely, it is a consequence of the economic recession. It may also be a tactical retreat until the time is right politically and economically to return to reap their profits.

Covent Garden may have been a turning point in the history of urban renewal in Britain. It was a major victory for neighbourhood and conservation interests over planners and developers. It was a crucial experiment in public participation in the planning process. But the battle is not over. The conservation plan brought with it 'gentrification'. Much of the renovation that has been done is for chic boutiques and posh restaurants of little use to working class residents. Neighbourhood shops and light industry are being driven out by rising rents. They cannot compete for leases with offices or smart shops. So despite the apparent victory of the residents, their neighbourhood inexorably changes.

The irony of all this is that it was the very forces behind gentrification that helped save Covent Garden from the bulldozers. It was middle-class idealists who rallied to the aid of the CGCA. It was middle class public opinion that put conservation on the agenda for the 1970s. It was a revived middle class desire to live, shop, and work in the inner city that made conservation economic. Those who were once allies are now a threat to the continued existence of Covent Garden as a working class neighbourhood.

The CGCA and to a lesser extent the Forum are attempting to combat gentrification, but the GLC became less sympathetic when the Conservative Party won control in 1977. Though the Conservatives approved the conservation plan, residents of Covent Garden have questioned the degree to which they have followed it. Tory Councillor Alan Greengross says the plan is only a set of guidelines 'allowing you to realize your aspirations'. He hopes to 'liberate enough whealth' through commercial development 'to subsidize community facilities' and sees gentrification as a positive sign of the area's revival. Wherever possible, the GLC has maximized commercial development over housing, thus detracting from the residential orientation of the plan.

REFERENCES

Ambrose, Peter, and Colenutt, Bob (1975). *The Property Machine,* Penguin, London.
Cox, Harvey (1976). *Cities: The Public Dimension,* Pelican, London.
Jenkins, Simon (1973a). The press in local planning. *Political Quarterly,* **144**, 1, 54.
Jenkins Simon (1973b). The politics of London motorways. *Political Quarterly,* **144**, 3, 269.
Monahan, Jim (1976). Up against the planners in Covent Garden. In *Community Politics,* Peter Hain (ed.), John Calder, London.
Skeffington, A. (1969). *Report of the Committee on Public Participation in Planning: People and Planning,* HMSO. London.
Taylor, Athol (1973). Piecemeal tokenism, *Built Environment,* Volume 2, Number 8, p. 432.

Geography and the Urban Environment
Progress in Research and Applications,Volume IV
Edited by D. T. Herbert and R. J. Johnston

Chapter 5

The Rate Support Grant in England and Wales 1967–8 to 1980–1: A Review of Changing Emphases and Objectives

Robert J. Bennett

INTRODUCTION

The rate support grant (RSG) is a major intergovernmental grant—in 1979–80 it involved the transfer of £7,000 m from central to local government in England and Wales. It is a general grant programme aimed at providing access to the national tax base for the local authorities. As such it is typical of many intergovernmental grants in the western world: for example, in the United States, Revenue-sharing, Community Development Block Grant, Counter-cyclical Revenue-sharing, Public Service Employment, and Health Education and Welfare Grants are similar programmes. Indeed most countries in the western world employ a method of grant allocation to local authorities and various forms of such grants account for high proportions of local spending in most countries: 40 per cent in Australia, 32 per cent in Canada, 19 per cent in the USA, and 11 per cent in West Germany (percentage of State or Province expenditure financed by central government: Bennett, 1980).

The allocation of intergovernmental grants has important geographical, economic, and political implications. Clearly the allocation of grants from national to either State or local governments has profound spatial implications. As a result explicit geographical differences between local authorities are normally the major aspects taken into account in allocating grants. For example, spatial differences in the size of the tax base, tax rate (or tax effort), expenditure level, expenditure need, and other factors form part of the allocation rules used in most countries. US Revenue-Sharing, for example, uses a mixture of tax base, tax effort and expenditure need, and the Rate Support Grant employs a complex formula incorporating tax base, tax rate, expenditure level, expenditure need, plus safety nets, damping, and other provisions. An important aspect of such grants, therefore, is the extent to which their allocation accords in some way with principles of geographical equity. Indeed it is equalisation of differences of tax base and expenditure need which is the explicit aim of most of these grants.

At an economic level the allocation of intergovernmental grants also has profound implications as a major manifestation of the role of the state. As such, grants are an important aspect of the division of the economic resources of a nation between various functions. First, they may have important implications for prices and economic efficiency in the economy as a whole and will affect production through indirect externalities and direct incentives and subsidies. Second, grants will affect the distribution between groups of people; they will affect the tax burdens and consumption of benefits received as a 'social wage'. Third, grants will affect the overall stability and economic growth of an economy as a whole, and are frequently used in counter-cyclical policy and regional policy. Each of these aspects has, in addition to its macroeconomic effects, profound geographical consequences in effecting spatial price differences, spatial differences in tax burden and social benefits, and in modifying the geographical differences in regional cyclical stability and economic growth. Despite their importance, however, they have been relatively neglected aspects of the geography of the state until a growth of interest by such writers as Johnston (1979), Bennett (1980), and Dear and Clark (1978).

At a political level intergovernmental grants have two main effects: first, on the structure of central-local government relations; and second, through interaction with elections and voting patterns. With respect to the structure of the relations between central and local government, intergovernmental grants are important controls of the extent to which there is relative autonomy or centralization of public spending; the extent to which there is geographical variation in services provided and in their qualities of provision; the extent to which there are horizontal subsidies arising from spillovers of tax burdens and expenditure benefits between local administrative units; and the extent to which central policies on tax burden or service distribution are frustrated by local actions, or vice versa. With respect to the interaction of intergovernmental grants and elections and voting patterns, there is a controversial literature for Britain (see the survey in Johnston, 1979). This literature has sought to examine the relation between local party control and both aggregate spending level and division of relative expenditure levels between different services. For example, it is usually hypothesized that Labour-controlled councils in Britain will both spend more in aggregate and more proportionally on housing and education. Such political hypotheses find considerable support in U.S. literature. Results for Britain, however, demonstrate that, whilst there are some detectable patterns, the pattern is extremely complex because of the strong inter-correlation of party control and socio-economic factors which dictate different spending needs. Similarly, British research on the relation of central government grant allocation to local party control is again very weak. Whilst there is a general relationship hypothesized that Labour governments at Westminster favour allocation to the cities and Conservative governments favour allocation to more rural areas, this hypothesis has been far from easily or convincingly confirmed (see Johnston, 1979; Bennett, 1980; Alt, 1971; Nicholson and Topham, 1971; Oliver and Stanyer, 1969; Boaden, 1971). Nevertheless, intergovernmental grant allocation has profound political as well as economic implications, and this in turn possesses important geographical features for the balance of central-local power, the extent of variety of public service provision, and the possible implications for party control and electoral response.

The rate support grant (RSG) in England and Wales possesses features relating to each of the foci of attention discussed above. However, it is an exceedingly complex programme which has evolved over a long period to encompass objectives which differ from those explicitly stated at its inception. Similarly, like most public policy programmes, it has encompassed an 'inherited' pattern of allocation deriving from previous methods of allocating grants to local governments (see for example, Boyle, 1966; Foster et al., 1980). A general block grant in the form of the RSG was initiated in Britain in 1929 (the so-called General Exchequer Contribution). This was aimed at reducing the burdens of local taxation and making available the large tax resources of the national government. This grant was replaced in 1948 by the Exchequer Equalization Grant, which was in turn replaced in 1958 by two grants: the Rate Deficiency Grant and the General Grant. Each of these grants encompassed the same aims: tax-base sharing and reducing local tax burdens. But the 1948 grant saw the introduction of explicit equalization criteria based on differences in local tax bases. The 1929 grant had seen the introduction of a form of need equalization (mainly in terms of local populations and the number of school children), and this was further refined in the 1948 and 1958 grants. For the 1967–8 financial year the RSG was initiated, but this derived from combining the preceding General Grant with a large number of previously separate specific grants (to become the needs element of the RSG), and also modifying the preceding Rate Deficiency Grant (to become the resources element of the RSG)

In addition to its inheritance from the previous grant arrangements, the RSG has also been rendered even more complex by considerable modifications since its inception. Indeed since 1974–5 modifications have been introduced at least once a year, and these have often affected final outcomes very severely. As a consequence of the instability introduced by these rapid changes, and of other wide-ranging criticisms directed against it, the Conservative Government has severely modified the method of grant allocation for 1981–2, with transition arrangements for the intervening 1980–1 year. Potentially this is the most radical rethinking since 1966, and perhaps in some ways since 1929.

Because of the radical changes to be introduced to the RSG from 1981–2, it is appropriate to review the form of allocation of the grant up to this time. With this end in view, this chapter reviews the manner in which the RSG in England and Wales has evolved over the period since its inception in 1967–8,

up to 1980–1. It then attempts to determine the extent to which its evolution
has modified the objectives which it has sought to satisfy. The rest of the chapter
is divided into four parts. The first examines various objectives which have
been used, explicitly or implicitly, in making decisions on the RSG. Second,
a review is presented of the points in the RSG procedure where changes have
been introduced. Third, an assessment is made of how far these changes have
resulted in the objectives of the grant being modified over time. Fourth, a
conclusion is drawn as to the form of modification to the grant structure that
might be considered in the future.

THE OBJECTIVES OF THE RATE SUPPORT GRANT

The RSG is a general grant, or block grant, given by central to local
government at the level of both counties and their constituent districts. It is
composed of three elements. First, there is a *domestic* element which is a form
of specific grant acting á a subsidy to domestic as opposed to non-domestic
(commercial and industrial) local taxpayers. Second, there is a *resources* element,
paid directly to districts, which seeks to achieve an equalisation in the ability
of local governments to raise taxation at a given tax rate, i.e. it seeks equalization
of tax bases. Third, there is a *needs* element which seeks to provide support to
local governments (also termed local authorities) with relatively high expenditure
requirements arising, for example, from the sparsity of their population, the
age of their infrastructure, and the demographic, social and economic character
of their population. Hence, three major explicit objectives of the RSG (as stated
by GB Government 1966, 1974) have been: first, shifting fiscal incidence from
domestic towards non-domestic taxpayers; second, achieving resource equalization; and third, providing for needs equalization. In addition to these major
objectives, however, the RSG has also included, at various times, emphasis
upon other explicit and implicit objectives. The eleven objectives underlying
grant distribution, which are either explicit or implicit, can each be briefly
summarized as follows:

(i) *Equalization*   This is the major explicit aim of the RSG over the entire
    period 1967–8 to 1980–1 and involves consideration of both resource and
    need equalization. Also, up to 1973–4 and since 1977–8 a form of explicit
    cost equalization has also been included (see Table 9). The aim is to place
    each local authority in an equal position to provide a given quantity of
    services at a given quality, at the same tax rate, by providing comparable
    tax bases. Because of the effects of equalisation on tax rates, this aim relates
    closely to the second objective.

(ii) *Neutrality to income distribution*   The aim of grants to local governments
    is to ensure a similar pattern of services in each local authority. Some of
    these services are orientated specifically to client groups of need (the old,

the young, the disabled, those needing public transport, and so forth). Such services are clearly redistributional in intent. Hence, the expenditure side of local finance has an intentional income effect. However, on the revenue side, it has usually been taken as an explicit aim of local taxation and grant programmes that they should be relatively neutral in their income effects. This is important for two reasons. First, it is usually deemed preferable to solve the income distribution issue of taxation at a national level; people should not bear different tax burdens merely because they live in different areas (see Musgrave and Musgrave, 1976; Oates, 1972; 1977; Hunter, 1973; Bennett, 1980). Second, marked differences in tax burdens for income groups between areas provides an important stimulus to migration, generating so-called fiscal migration (Tiebout, 1956; Oates, 1969). Such migration presents important difficulties since it frequently allows the rich to escape their 'just' tax burden and hence induces regressivity into the tax system. Hence a major aim of RSG, like grant programmes in most countries, has been to reduce, as far as possible, differences in tax rates and burdens on similar groups living in different areas.

(iii) *Fiscal balance and adequacy*   Deriving from the objectives of equalization and neutrality to income distribution, a third main objective has been to maintain fiscal balance between levels of government. Many public services can be efficiently organized only at local levels, but most of the high yielding revenue sources are usually best reserved to central governments (especially personal and corporate income tax). In addition most revenue sources which can be used at local level are relatively regressive; major examples are the property tax and many forms of sales tax. Hence it is necessary to employ some mechanism for reallocating revenues between levels of government in order to achieve fiscal balance: both to ensure the adequacy of local revenues and to limit the extent to which regressive tax bases are used. This is a primary motive in the RSG, but methods of revenue-sharing and systems of tax credits and deductions can also be used to achieve fiscal balance (see Bennett, 1980).

(iv) *Neutrality to local behaviour*   A primary aim of the RSG is that, after achieving equalization and fiscal balance, the grant distribution should be free from effects of manipulation by local governments which might increase their allocations unfairly. Hence, the grants should be neutral to local authority choice to provide a particular form or quality of service. This requires the distinction of discretionary from non-discretionary spending, and this in turn usually requires the definition of both 'standard' or 'minimum' service levels and 'standard' tax rates.

(v) *Feasibility*   Grant programmes can be implemented only with data which it is feasible to collect and the accuracy of which is beyond question; it must be possible to implement distribution in practice. This often leads to rather cruder formulae for grant distribution than would be desired in an ideal world. In particular it is often impossible to implement grants requiring detailed costing of local services or, in Britain, grants which use data on personal incomes for local areas.

(vi) *Facilitating local discretion*   Related to the previous aims, grants may seek to encourage or suppress local discretion in providing given services. It is usually considered that local governments are important agents of democracy. As a result, grant programmes should aim to facilitate that degree of local discretion in taxing and service provision which is consistent with encouraging the democratic process at local level. This aim requires the differentiation of responsibilities for different expenditure functions between levels of government: central government is responsible for national 'merit' goods, local governments for 'local' goods, intermediate governments for 'regional' or State goods, and so forth. For example, to achieve 'minimum standards' in national goods at local level, matched non-need-related forms of grants are usually employed (see Musgrave and Musgrave, 1976). With large variations in local fiscal capacity, however, the local matching requirement cannot be employed to achieve 'minimum standards', and this is the case of the Rate Support Grant.

(vii) *Accountability*   Related to the issue of differentiating local from central (and intermediate-level) government decisions on taxing and spending is the aim of making local decisions clearly accountable to the local electorate. This also relates to maintaining the democratic process. Accountability requires clear lines of responsibility for local financial decisions to be visible to the local voter. This means that local taxation and other charges (the local 'costs' of local services) represent a significant proportion of local spending and clearly reflect local expenditure decisions, an issue emphasized in the Layfield report (GB Committee of Enquiry, 1976). This in turn requires that grants should be kept below a certain level as a proportion of local spending or else local services will become markedly underpriced relative to their costs, and this will affect demand, efficiency (q.v. below) and hence accountability.

(viii) *Intelligibility*   A major aim of grant programmes should be that they are readily comprehensible both to the voters and to the elected representatives at each level of government concerned. This aim relates to the accountability objective and ensures that the role of political and professional judgements is laid bare.

(ix) *Encouragement to efficiency or productivity*   Grants should not subsidize profligate local spending or unjustifiably high labour–output ratios. This requires that grants allow as close as possible a relation between services provided and their 'cost' through taxation. Clearly this aim is often severely limited by that of equalization such that the question is usually one of the appropriate fiscal balance. Efficiency also requires that grants should aim to have a minimal impact on the price rules in the private sector, thus maintaining efficient allocation of resources in the economy as a whole. This leads to favouring of grants incorporating a measure of cost comparison between local authorities and 'standard' costs for given levels of service provision. A common form of such grants is the 'unit cost' approach.

(x) *Compensation for cost and benefit spillover*   Grants can also provide a primary means for overcoming either local cost spillovers (one jurisdiction pays a part of the costs of another jurisdiction and receives no benefits) or benefit spillovers (one jurisdiction receives benefits from another jurisdiction at no cost—the 'free-rider' problem). The use of grants in such cases derives from Pigou (1947) and is usually referred to as the *compensation principle*. Where compensation for benefit spillover is sought, selective and matching grants can be used. Where it is sought to equalise differences in the local tax rates required to give equal levels of local service benefits, general unmatched grants such as the RSG are employed.

(xi) *Stability and certainty*   Grants should as far as possible maintain a stable pattern of distribution from one time period to another, with certainty as to the magnitude of the total sum available. This encourages efficiency in local authorities and aids their expenditure planning. Changes in grant distribution procedures should be introduced only as a result of objective changes in circumstances, either (a) changes in the local need to spend and ability to raise revenues, or (b) changes in national priorities resulting either from national political shifts (such as the party colour of central government) or from the effects of overall economic management criteria which modify the total sums available.

Each of these criteria plays a role, relatively major or minor, in the design and practical implementation of any grant programme and each has certainly affected the RSG. Hence, although the major explicit aim of the RSG has been equalization, any evaluation of this grant programme must incorporate other criteria. For the Rate Support Grant, the issues which are particularly important in addition to that of equalization are the degree of local discretion, adequacy, neutrality, encouragement of efficiency, stability, certainty, and data feasibility. As a result, these criteria emerge at many stages to restrict the form of equalization grant that might be implemented in an ideal world. Moreover, as will be seen in the following discussion the extent to which one objective has been used or publicized rather than another has varied a great deal over time.

THE RATE SUPPORT GRANT AND ITS EVOLUTION
1967–8 TO 1980–1

The allocation of the Rate Support Grant over the period from 1967–8 to 1980–1 has been governed by the *Local Government Act* (1966) which initiated the grant system, and the *Local Government Act* (1974) which modified some of the distribution arrangements and re-established the grant for the period following the 1974 reorganization of local government (GB Government; 1966, 1974). In addition, modifications in detail, often very significant in their distributional impacts, are decided on an annual basis by the Secretary of State for the Environment and specified in *Statutory Instruments* (GB Government, *Statutory Instruments*, various dates), issued usually in November or December of each year. Further modifications in detail are introduced via Department

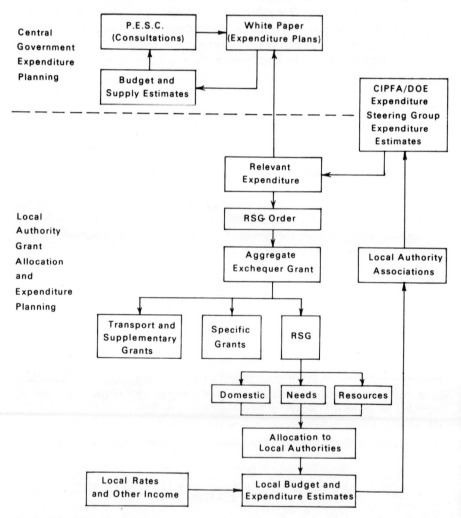

FIGURE 5.1. Stages in decision making in allocation of the Rate Support Grant showing the interactions between central and local government and the local authority associations

of the Environment *Circulars* (GB Government: DOE, MHLG, various dates).

There are five main interrelated stages in allocation of the grant as shown in Figure 5.1. First, forecasts are made of local government expenditure. Second, a decision on the level of Aggregate Exchequer grant is made. This is derived from the estimates of total local authority expenditure by deciding what proportion will be accepted as 'relevant expenditure' by central government for grant purposes. Third, a decision is made as to the proportion of relevant expenditure which will be met by rate support and other grants. Fourth, there is a decision on how the grant should be distributed between its three elements (of domestic, resources, and needs). Fifth, there is the most complex decision of all; how these elements should be distributed between the local authorities. Each of these five stages of decision is discussed in turn below.

Forecasts of local expenditure

Forecasts of total local expenditure derive from the integration of local authority expenditure forecasting with central government expenditure planning. The present system of central government expenditure planning derives from the Plowden Committee's report which concluded that 'regular surveys should be made of public expenditure as a whole, over a period of years ahead, and in relation to prospective resources' (GB Government, 1961, para. 12). This resulted in the setting up of the *Public Expenditure Survey Committees* (PESC). From 1968–9 onwards the procedure was amplified by the introduction of the annual Public Expenditure *White Paper* which 'would set out the figures for the whole public sector for a number of years, and in a new form which would help to show the likely claims on resources entailed by those public outlays' (GB Government, 1969, para. 5). The *White Papers* give firm government plans, amplify PESC, introduce new tables including current year expenditure provisional out-turns, forecast planned expenditure for years 2 to 5 into the future, and provide constant pricing, estimates for the nationalized industries, and estimates of tax receipts and transfers to local authorities. In 1972, and subsequently, these procedures have been modified progressively, with the most significant change being the introduction of tables of past expenditures data for the preceding five years (GB Government, 1972). In addition to the *White Papers* published in December or January, the *Supply Estimates* and *Budget*, normally debated in Parliament in March, April, or May, are also significant in introducing changes and more detailed planning of specific programmes.

Up to 1975 little attempt was made to integrate local authority expenditure estimates with central fiscal planning; the estimates, in effect, acted as forecasts which were implemented without very close scrutiny. Since 1975–6, however, the RSG and PESC procedures have been more closely linked through the central government's *White Paper* for England and Wales this integrates the estimates of local expenditures deriving from the RSG *Order* of November into the *White Paper* in December to January. For Scotland, however, the negoti-ations on RSG are not usually completed early enough, and provisional estimates of local expenditure have to be employed instead. Since 1975–6 the forecasts of local expenditure are derived by combining estimates of future expenditure needs generated by local authorities for each of their spending departments with the central Government forecasts made by an Expenditure Steering Group within the Department of the Environment. This group scrutinises local expenditure forecasts and makes decisions as to what is acceptable. It then produces the final forecasts which incorporate those features which the Secretary of State for the Environment is required to take into account in making RSG decisions (GB Government, 1966; 1974):

    (i) The latest available information on local relevant expenditure;
   (ii) any probable fluctuation in the demand for relevant services (as far as this can be attributed to national circumstances outside local authority control);
  (iii) the need to develop and increase services in the light of general economic conditions; and
  (iv) the current level of prices, costs, and remuneration of wages; and any future variation which is likely to result from decisions already taken which will affect prices, costs and remunerations.

These factors, in general terms, incorporate the costs of maintaining past expenditure patterns, changes in demand, changes in priorities, and changes in prices, costs and wages. Past expenditure patterns are largely determined. Changes in demand are estimated from national economic forecasts of economic fluctuations, plus the estimated effect of local changes in demographic structure and similar factors (affecting the number of schoolchildren, old peoples' services, etc.). Changes in priorities derive from the central government's legislation over the past year, and usually include no allowance for changes in local government policies. Changes in prices, costs and wages are estimated from national economic forecasts combined with the PESC estimates and their *allowed* effects for cost changes, especially in wage levels when central government is pursuing a policy on either or both of pay and prices.

    Although the procedure for central expenditure planning is now fairly satisfactory, its integration with local authority expenditure planning is still somewhat loose. First, the estimates of local expenditure derive from discussion between the DOE and the local authority associations and at the early stages do not involve or consider PESC, Treasury or other central departments. Second, the *price basis* of the RSG *Order* and the *White Paper* differs: the White Paper refers to prices of November of the previous year whilst the RSG *Order* refers to prices in November of the present year. This was severely criticised by the Layfield report (GB Committee of Enquiry, 1976). Third, the *coverage* of the *Order* and *White Paper* differs: rate subsidies to the Housing Revenue Account are excluded from the *Order* but are included in the *White Paper*, whilst loans and some charges met from revenues are included in the *Order* but excluded from the *White Paper*. This has also been severely criticised by the Layfield report and elsewhere, but has been overcome by changing the form of the White Paper since 1977–8. Fourth, the RSG *Order* settling local relevant expenditure (q.v. below) is too close to the *White Paper* stage: most local expenditure is already committed for the following year by November of the preceding year and so is not amenable to easy modification. This introduces great uncertainty into local expenditure planning and rating decisions. Fifth, parliamentary debate has been clouded by the poor relation of the *Supply Estimates* to the *White Paper,* in particular the exclusion from the *White Paper* of transfers from and within central government, and some items of revenue and borrowing (see GB Government, 1972). A sixth problem, recognized by Nield and Ward (1976), is that central forecasts of local expenditure have often been affected by central aims of keeping local expenditures under control and rate increases down. However, they produced evidence that over the period 1968–9 to 1973–4 local expenditure was no more out of control than central government expenditure. As a result, they concluded that considerable errors in expenditure forecasting have been derived from central rather than local government.

Aggregate exchequer grant, cash limits, and relevant expenditure

The Aggregate Exchequer Grant includes *all* specific, supplementary, transport, and other central grants in addition to RSG. This is determined by the central government very largely in terms of criteria of national economic management. Hence, the grant derives from the forecasts of local expenditure. Once this level of total local expenditure had been agreed, up to 1975–6 this directly determined grant totals. However, since 1976–7 increases in grant have been subject to an additional control of *cash limits*. These provide a ceiling amount which will be paid as increased grant (through subsequent *Increase Orders*) in respect of increases in local expenditure. Howevers, the cash limit has not usually compensated fully for cost increases, a major proportion of which have often been passed on to the local rates. Hence, the cash limits have been used in various ways as instruments of national economic management. In both 1976–7 and 1977– 8, for example, final cash limits were reduced as part of general public expenditure policy. However, in 1976–7 final cash limits were not reduced by the £ 73.1m originally intended, an additional supplement of £ 38m (both in 1978 prices) being eventually allowed (compare *House of Commons Paper* HC–28 (1976) with HC–58 (1977)). Similarly with a change of the party of central government in 1979 the cash limits were again used as major instruments of central economic control. In addition specific grants have not been subject to cash limits, but increases in service costs leading to increases in specific grants have been subtracted from the cash limit or the RSG and supplementary grants. Thus, in total impact, cash limits have presented potential for central government to regulate pay and price increases.

The forecasts of total local expenditures are not carried through without modification in the determination of the level of Aggregate Exchequer Grant. An intervening stage is a decision as to what proportion of total local estimated expenditure is accepted by central government as 'relevant expenditure' for grant purposes. The proportion of expenditure accepted as relevant is a function of two criteria, one objective and one political. The objective criterion for defining relevant expenditure derives from estimating that proportion of total local expenditure which results from local undertaking of services, as devolved agents of central government, which places a burden directly on local taxpayers as opposed to central taxpayers (see GB Government, 1966; GB MHLG Circular 12/67). As a result of this definition, an attempt is made to differentiate non-discretionary devolved spending from that which is discretionary (undertaken by local authorities in response to local preferences or political priorities). Expenditures which are supported directly by user charges are also excluded, such as receipts derived from local bus fares, legal fees, and public sector housing rents. In addition attempts are made to differentiate expenditures supported by different forms of grant; for example, expenditures deriving from specific and supplementary grants and mandatory payments (such as rate rebates and student grants) are excluded from the expenditure accepted as relevant for RSG purposes. The political criterion for defining relevant expenditure derives from the central government's choice of which are and which are not devolved services, the extent to which it will allow increases in wages and other costs to be borne by central grants, the estimate of increases in costs, wages, and other inflationary factors which will be accepted at Westminster, the level of resulting local rate bills which can be tolerated at both local and central level, and other factors. For example, from 1971–2 to 1974–5 a term was introduced to reduce relevant expenditure as a result of improved local efficiency: no actuarial or statistical estimate of either the existence or magnitude of this term was made. In 1974–5, following local government reorganization, a modified allocation was necessary to take account of the transfer of debts and reallocation of sewerage and health services. From 1968–9 school milk and meal charges were introduced as offsets to relevant expenditure, and this was modified again in 1980–1. Again in 1980–1 a reduction in relevant expenditure was introduced to allow for charges for local school buses. Although it was planned that local authorities should be able to make such charges, the government were defeated in the House of Lords on this point, and this effect on relevant expenditure could not be reintroduced until the RSG *Increase Order* stage.

Table 5.1 demonstrates that the total level of local expenditure accepted by central government as relevant rose rapidly in the 1960s and early 1970s but

TABLE 5.1. Local authority total and relevant expenditure in England and Wales Public Expenditure Survey basis (Sources: Public Expenditure *White Papers*; House of Commons *Papers*; CIPFA *Local Government Trends, 1979; Local Government Financial Statistics*)

Financial year	Total local authority current expenditure £m (1978 prices)	Relevant expenditure for RSG purposes (PES basis) £m (1978 prices)				Relevant expenditure as percentage of total
		Current	capital to be met from revenue	Loans	total	
1966–7	10674	N/A			5665	53.1
1967–8	11319	N/A			8485	74.9
1968–9	11728				9049	77.2
1969–70	11959				9618	80.4
1970–1	12483	N/A			10995	88.1
1971–2	12573				11319	90.0
1972–3	13684	9187	256	867	10310	75.3
1973–4	14544	9457	328	1216	11001	75.6
1974–5	16175	10442	305	1299	12046	74.5
1975–6	15979	10910	516	1203	12629	79.0
1976–7	15211	10891	541	1282	12714	83.6
1977–8	14343	10691	564	1145	12400	86.4
1978–9	14650	10982	505	1232	12719	86.8
1979–80	14760	11335	589	1068	12992	88.0
1980–1[a]	13833	10920	559	909	12389	89.6

[a] Planned.

Dashed lines show where data are not directly comparable due to changes in local government responsibility for services and changes in the rendering of statistics.

has levelled off since about 1977–8. This is usually accounted for by the influence of three factors. First, the desire to give a greater proportion of central support in a form which is unhypotheticated to local use (i.e. as general rather than specific grants). Second, and related to this first factor, is the question of fiscal balance. The rapid and accelerating rate of inflation in the economy as a whole, particularly marked in the high proportion of labour-intensive local services, has outstripped the capacity of the local tax base. The only major source of locally-raised revenue in Britain is the property tax of the 'rates' and is relatively non-bouyant to income and inflation changes. Third, the rates are relatively regressive, and since the introduction of rate rebates (in 1967–8) are proportional in the burden they place on different income groups of local taxpayers. Hence, most central governments have thought it undesirable that too great a proportion of local revenue is derived from this property tax. As a result they have sought to achieve fiscal balance by supporting local finances to an increasing extent from the more progressive central tax base. This policy has meant that, with the very rapid inflation in the British economy over the period since 1967, central government has supported an increasing proportion of local service costs up to 1978–9.

The levelling off and decline in central government support since 1978–9 is a result of a changed view as to the extent to which local services should be supported by central government. For example, the Layfield report (GB Committee of Enquiry, 1976) suggested that by 1976 the proportion of central support had reached a level at which local accountabilty and price-efficiency was undermined. The changing pattern of central support also results from a change in philosophy, most clearly represented by the Conservative government since 1979, indicating that the steady increase in the proportion of public spending deriving from local government could no longer be supported and that shift to a greater proportion of local burdens placed on local taxpayers will result in better control of public expenditure as a whole. Also important has been the recent increased desire to make local authorities 'toe the line' on wage controls.

In the decisions on the size of the Aggregate Exchequer Grant, on cash limits, and on the proportion of local expenditure which will be supported as 'relevant', therefore, there are four important lines of changing emphasis. First there has been an annual and rather *ad hoc* response of central government to national economic and political conditions, especially the level of public sector wages and the general underlying rate of inflation. Second, the proportion of these cost increases which central government deems should be passed on from local to central taxpayers has changed. Third, the changing climate regarding general as opposed to specific grants first favoured fiscal balance by tax-base sharing through general grants, but now places a greater emphasis on fostering accountability through local taxation. Fourth, there has been a changing view as to the role local government should play in supporting central government policies. This has affected the decisions on relevant expenditure as to the extent to which local governments are devolved agencies of the national government, but it has also affected the degree to which central government has sought the backing of local government in controlling salaries and inflation.

The size of RSG and other grants

Having made decisions as to the total size of the Aggregate Exchequer Grant, cash limits, and the level of allowed relevant expenditure, the next and interrelated stage of decision is the determination of the division of the Aggregate Exchequer Grant between its components of RSG, specific, supplementary, transport, and other grants, which are all included within the Aggregate Exchequer Grant. The relative share of these grants is shown in

TABLE 5.2. Local authority expenditure, current account spending and central government grants 1967–1981 at 1978 prices (Source: *House of Commons Papers*)

Note the RSG results are modified by outturn figures: up to 1975–6 the grant was paid on outturns, from 1976–7 it was subject to cash limits

	Aggregate Exchequer Grant final order (£m)	Relevant expenditure final order (£m)	Aggregate Exchequer as percentage of relevant expenditure (%)	RSG. (£m)	RSG as percentage of Aggregate Exchequer Grant (%)	Specific grants as percentage of Aggregate Exchequer Grant (%)	Transport and supplementary grants as percentage of Aggregate Exchequer Grant (%)
General Grant 66–7	4548	5665	80.3	3094	68.1	31.9	—
67–8	4587	8485	54	4162	90.7	9.3	—
68–9	4983	9049	55	4525	90.8	9.2	—
69–70	5396	9618	56	4956	91.8	8.0	—
70–1	6269	10995	57	5755	91.8	8.2	—
71–2	5609	11319	57.5	5977	91.8	8.2	—
72–3	7551	13021	58	6952	92.1	7.9	—
73–4	7736	12914	60	6989	90.3	8.1	—
74–5	9978	15294	60.5	9198	92.1	9.9	0.04
75–6	11914	17877	66.5	10384	87.1	8.4	4.5
76–7	10659	16711	65.5	9203	86.3	9.0	4.7
77–8	9334	15326	61	8009	85.7	10.5	3.8
78–9	9186	15157	61	7844	85.4	11.0	3.6
79–80[a]	9269	16004	61	7751	83.6	12.6	3.8
80–81[a]	8466	11738	61	7051	83.3	13.0	3.7

[a]Estimated

Table 5.2. From this table it is clear that although there has been a steady rise in the total level of Westminster support to local authorities up to 1975–6, followed by a levelling-off to the present, the total proportion RSG has steadily declined (except for 1974–5) since 1971–2. This has been as a result of the growth in significance of specific grants, which have increased by 40 per cent since the initiation of the RSG in 1967–8, (mainly as a result of rises in the police and transport grants). However, despite this change of emphasis, the RSG still represents by far the greatest proportion of central government support. The pattern shown in Table 5.2 results from two main features: first, the changing expenditure levels of different local services and the degree to which central government has deemed the expenditure 'relevant'; and second, the variable

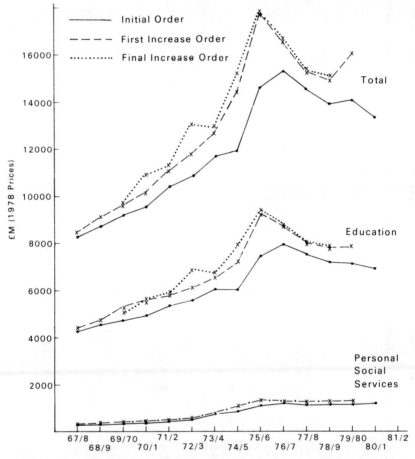

FIGURE 5.2. Relevant expenditure for RSG purposes at constant 1978 prices. The graphs show the expenditures as assessed at initial, first increase and final increase *Order*. (Source: House of Commons *Papers*)

incidence of inflation on different services and the allowances permitted by central government towards increased costs.

The expenditure level supported by the RSG under each of the main service categories is shown in Figures 5.2 and 5.3 at constant 1978 prices. From these it can be seen that total relevant expenditure increased steadily and rapidly up to 1976–7, but has decreased since that date except for a small rise in 1979–80. However, the pattern varies considerably between service categories. Police and fire services have shown the least effects of cutbacks since 1976–7; education has been affected by the severest cutbacks. Of course, no account is taken in these figures of changing levels of need (such as the changing size of the school population). However, the figures do display aggregate responses of combined central and local policies to changing circumstances which have resulted in shifts in the relative magnitude of expenditure in various service categories.

These features are further emphasized in Table 5.3, which also introduces the variable degree to which cost inflation has been taken into account. It displays the annual rate of increase in expenditures for each of the main local services over three periods in relation to the rate of general price changes. In the period up to 1973–4 expenditure on personal social services, police, local environmental services and planning all expanded relatively rapidly, and only the administration of justice expanded less rapidly than the rate of price increase in the economy as a whole. In this period, therefore, considerable expansion of service quality, manning levels, and service quantities was possible. In the period since 1973–4, in contrast, only personal social service expenditures have expanded more rapidly in costs than general price increases, and education in particular suffered very marked contraction in cost terms. After 1979–80 all service expenditures have increased much less rapidly than general price increases, and only three main service categories (police, justice, and fire) have not suffered absolute contractions of relevant expenditure levels.

A major source of changing central support in the RSG is introduced by changes in grant levels allowed at the *Increase Order* and at second and subsequent *Increase Order* stages. These usually occur in the respective November of the current year, and in the November of the following financial year. As shown in Table 5.4 many services, especially education, local transport, and fire protection, have tended to have consistently high rates of increase in expenditures from the *Order* to *Increase Order* stages. In contrast, services such as personal social services, police and housing have tended to have consistently lower rates of increase in expenditures from the *Order* to *Increase Order* stage. Although these differences reflect differential changes in the objective costs of providing the different services, the subsequent *Increase Orders* have also given central governments opportunities to respond to changes in local service needs, and to encourage shifts of spending between service sectors. Closer examination of these effects, as shown in Table 5.4, brings out two further features of the incremental effects of modifications induced by the use

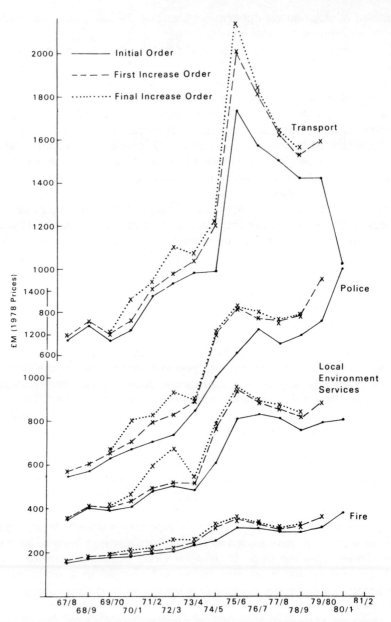

FIGURE 5.3. Relevant expenditure for RSG purposes at constant 1978 prices. The graphs show the expenditures as assessed at initial, first increase and final increase *Order*. (Source: House of Commons *Papers*)

TABLE 5.3. Change in level of relevant expenditure allowed in RSG calculations: increase of first *Order* over final *Order*. The 'other services' category is omitted because of lack of comparability arising from changes in local responsibilities (Source: *House of Commons Papers*: General prices: *Economic Trends*)

Service Category	Average Annual Percentage change at 1978 prices		
	1967–8 to 73–4	1973–4 to 79–80	1979–80 to 80–81
Education	10.1	1.5	−11.9
Personal Social Services	20.1	23.3	−9.9
Police	13.0	9.3	3.3
Admin. of Justice	1.0	8.1	1.6
Local Transport	11.9	7.5	−29.5
Fire	11.1	6.8	6.2
Local Environ. Services	17.5	5.4	−9.9
Town Planning	13.8	16.6	−9.9
Housing	—	13.4	−9.9
Total	10.7	3.8	−16.8
Average annual increase in general prices	8.0	20.9	13.4

of *Increase Orders*. First, *Increase Orders* have usually allowed a lesser rate of increase in local expenditures than the general rate of price inflation. This seems to be a particularly marked feature of the period after 1975–6. For the period up to 1972–3, the RSG was settled for two-year periods at *Initial Order* Stage and the second year's *Increase Order* was used to make good any deficit in the first year's allocation. This effect is clearly noticeable by the alternately high and low annual rate of difference from general rates of price increase over the period up to 1972–3. It could be argued that local government services, which are more labour-intensive than the national average, justify a higher rate of price increase than average prices, but Table 5.4 shows the opposite to be the case, especially for the period since 1975–6. A second feature of Table 5.4 is the extent to which increases in total local expenditures can be ascribed to particular services. Changes in education costs are most important for all periods whilst police, fire, and local environmental services have been important in the periods 1970–73 and 1978–80. If education costs alone could be more accurately estimated then considerably less change would be necessary in subsequent *Increase Orders*.

These tables show that, as noted earlier, central (rather than local) forecasting and control of local expenditure has been a major source of variation in local expenditure levels. In fact, it has been frequently recognized that the RSG and other components of the Aggregate Exchequer Grant have been used as much as a means of central control as of central support (see evidence by Treasury

TABLE 5.4. Percentage changes in relevant expenditure allowed in *RSG Increase Orders* in relation to changes in general prices. (Sources: *House of Commons Papers*; *Economic Trends*)

Service Category	Relevant Expenditure increase of Final Increase Order over initial Order at constant 1978 prices.													Average annual increase
	67–8	68–9	69–70	70–1	71–2	72–3	73–4	74–5	75–6	76–7	77–8	78–9	79–80[a]	
Education	2.4	3.0	5.8	12.9	10.2	21.8	12.8	31.7	26.3	10.3	6.5	9.4	9.8	16.8
Personal social services	5.5	4.3	4.7	22.8	6.5	14.7	11.2	27.4	17.2	9.5	6.6	9.4	13.3	13.0
Police	4.0	4.9	4.7	18.1	15.9	27.5	6.2	18.7	17.9	6.5	9.8	8.4	16.7	13.4
Justice	3.2	2.3	4.7	8.1	0.0	−14.6	6.7	19.8	16.0	7.2	6.0	6.5	11.0	6.0
Transport	1.9	2.1	6.0	20.7	8.1	17.6	9.5	25.9	23.9	17.1	8.9	8.9	12.0	14.7
Fire	3.6	7.2	9.0	18.9	15.4	29.8	7.6	26.2	12.0	6.0	6.4	14.4	15.0	14.6
Local Environment	1.7	1.5	5.6	14.9	23.5	33.2	8.5	28.2	16.9	7.8	7.8	10.3	12.1	15.7
Town Planning	—	—	—	—	2.2	14.6	14.9	28.9	16.9	7.5	3.3	4.7	9.1	11.6
Housing	—	—	—	—	—	—	—	27.9	−6.4	11.4	−33.9	−50.9	36.9	−10.4
Total	2.4	2.5	5.6	14.9	8.5	19.3	9.6	28.4	22.2	9.4	5.5	9.0	13.9	11.62
Date basis of costs: initial year	1966	1968	1968	1968	1970	1970	1972	1973	1974	1975	1976	1977	1978	—
Date basis of costs: final year	1967	1969	1970	1971	1972	1973	1974	1975	1976	1977	1978	1979	1979	—
Average annual rate of increase in general prices initial to final year	2.7	3.7	5.7	7.8	10.9	10.4	12.9	24.5	22.4	13.6	11.9	12.8	13.4	11.75
Difference in increase of relevant expenditure and general prices	−0.3	−1.2	−0.1	7.1	−2.4	8.9	−3.3	3.9	−0.2	−4.2	−6.4	−3.8	0.5	−0.13

[a]Estimate based on first *Increase Order* only.

and GB Department of Environment in Appendix to GB Committee of Enquiry, 1976). In addition, Neild and Ward (1976) have suggested that the use of the RSG as a means of control has been a major cause of steady increases in local expenditure levels: the central government has been reluctant to sacrifice its influence on the level of rates set by driving a hard bargain in the RSG settlement. However, additional control will be available under the unitary grant proposed to operate from 1981–2 onwards (GB Government, 1980).

The distribution of RSG between domestic, resources, and needs

The RSG, although transferred to local governments as a single sum of money, is not a single block grant, but is composed of three separate elements—*needs, resources,* and *domestic*—each of which has different aims and characteristics.

(i) *The needs element* seeks to allocate to each local authority a grant equal to its expenditure requirement. This is assessed according to a number of needs criteria which seek to take account of three factors: first, variation in the number of people who consume each service (the size of client group of e.g. the old, those in education at various levels, etc.); secondly, variation in the quantity of inputs required to provide services in each local authority (e.g. variations in pupil–teacher ratios between urban and rural areas); thirdly variation in costs of inputs in different local authorities (e.g. salary weightings in London and the South East).

From 1967–8 to 1973–4 (inclusive) the needs indicators were defined *a priori* and were relatively small in number. Since 1974–5 needs allocation has been based on regression analysis. This method attempts to 'explain' total local authority expenditure for each local authority in terms of 'needs' indicators by use of multiple regression. The dependent variable in this procedure is the total expenditure per head of each needs authority. The independent variables vary from year to year, but are consistent in including measures of population size, population characteristics, and size and density variation of local authorities. The regression formula is used for allocation by entering the current values of the independent variables as need indicators and then scaling the resulting allocation by the total sum of needs grant set aside by central government for all authorities.

(ii) *The resources element* is designed to compensate local authorities for their deficiency in tax base below a national standard. This element seeks, therefore, to overcome differences in local authority ability to raise revenue. A grant is paid to each local authority which falls below the 'standard' per capita rateable value per head set by central government for England and Wales as a whole. The size of the grant G_i is determined by the difference in the size of local tax base B_i from the standard $\bar{B}$, and the local tax rate t_i, and is given by the formula:

$$G_i = t_i(\bar{B} - B_i)$$

In effect, therefore, the central government acts as a local ratepayer on each local authority's deficit in tax base. Local authorities above the standard tax base are not penalized, but receive no grant. There are two problems with this method. First, it is not equalizing with respect to local authorities above the standard. Second, the size of grant is determined, in part, by local government in setting its tax rate t_i; this is the so-called 'feedback' effect.

(iii) *The domestic element* is a direct subsidy to domestic as opposed to commercial and industrial taxpayers. The domestic element is hypothecated in that local authorities are obliged to use this grant to reduce the tax rate to domestic ratepayers. Hence, it differs from both the needs and resources elements which are block grants, and as such is an incongruity in the RSG as a whole. As a result, it has often been suggested that it should be removed to become a specific grant and most of the discussion in this paper ignores this rather specific grant category.

The distribution of the RSG is also complicated by the fact that London Boroughs have been given separate treatment. Prior to 1974–5 London's grant was determined by a separate formula altogether. In 1974–5 and 1975–6 London was not included in the needs formula calculations, but it did receive needs grant using the non-London formula, although there were arbitrary supplements of 3 per cent in 1974–5 and 8 per cent in 1975–6. Since 1976–7 London Boroughs have been included in the general needs formula calculation (except for the City of London). However, a special adjustment, the 'resources adjustment' or 'clawback' is made to the needs entitlement to allow for the fact that the rateable values in London are, on average, two-thirds higher than in the rest of England and Wales. There is also a scheme of horizontal transfers, the London equalization scheme between London Boroughs, which is excluded from the rest of the RSG calculations.

The distribution of the RSG between its three elements is shown in Table 5.5, from which it is readily apparent that the grant was subject to a major policy change during the 1974–5 fiscal year. This has had the result of diminishing the level of the needs element from about 80 per cent to approximately 60 per cent of the total with the contrasting effect of increasing the resources element from approximately 15 to 30 per cent of the total, and increasing the domestic element from about 5 to 10 per cent of the total. Small scale changes between the three elements also produce year to year variations.

Since 1975–6 the 'expected ratio' of needs and resources elements has been kept at 67.5 and 32.5 per cent respectively, such that the variations in Table 5.5 arise from the general decrease in level of domestic rate relief granted. Prior

TABLE 5.5. Distribution of Rate Support Grant between its three elements. (Source: GB Government, Statutory Instruments, *Rate Support Grant Orders*)

Fiscal Year	RSG at final order						
	£m 1978 prices				Percentage		
	Total	Needs	Resources	Domestic	Needs	Resources	Domestic
General grant 1966–7	2628	—	—	—	—	—	—
1967–8	4162	3409	678	75	81.9	16.3	1.8
1968–9	4525	3653	720	152	80.7	15.9	3.4
1969–70	4956	4007	725	223	80.8	14.6	4.6
1970–1	5755	4631	817	306	80.5	14.2	5.3
1971–2	5975	4834	819	322	80.9	13.7	5.4
1972–3	6952	5654	935	363	81.3	13.5	5.2
1973–4	6989	5622	932	435	80.4	13.4	6.2
1974–5	9198	5990	2272	936	65.0	24.7	10.3
1975–6	10384	6259	3014	1110	60.3	29.0	10.7
1976–7	9203	5580	2687	936	60.6	29.2	10.2
1977–8	8010	4857	2340	813	60.6	29.2	10.2
1978–9	7810	4767	2297	746	61.0	29.4	9.6
1979–80[a]	7258	4434	2137	687	61.1	29.4	9.5
1980–1[a]	7051	4342	2092	606	61.6	29.7	8.8

[a] Provisional at Order or first Increase Order.

to 1974–5 the 'expected ratio' of needs and resources varied by $\pm 2\%$, but this effect is modied in Table 5.5 by the general increase in domestic rate relief then offered. For example, Table 5.6 shows the differing levels of rate relief offered to domestic ratepayers and residents of mixed hereditaments by the RSG domestic element. It is clear from this table that changes in government policy as to the level and distribution of domestic rate relief are major sources of changes. The period up to 1972–3 saw a steady rise in such relief, which was continued from 1974–5 onwards. However, 1973–4 saw a marked reduction in relief offered. The most marked changes, however, have affected the spatial distribution of domestic rate relief. Although uniform for England and Wales up to 1973–4, after that date a major differentiation was introduced to give Wales almost double the subsidy available in England. This was justified on the ground that with the reorganization of local government, Welsh ratepayers had to bear a greater burden of the costs of water supply. The uniform domestic element subsidy within England was maintained by the Labour government in 1974–5, replacing the variable domestic element which was planned by the

TABLE 5.6. Rate of domestic rate subsidy and subsidy to mixed domestic plus commercial hereditaments. (Source: GB Government, *Statutory Instruments, Rate Support Grant Orders*)

Subsidy p in £	Fiscal year													
	67–8	68–9	69–70	70–1	71–2	72–3	73–4	74–5	75–6	76–7	77–8	78–9	79–80	80–81
Domestic Rate subsidy														
England	2.1	4.2	6.3	8.3	9.5	10.5	6.0	13.0	18.5	18.5	18.5	18.5	18.5	18.5
Wales	2.1	4.2	6.3	8.3	9.5	10.5	6.0	33.5	36.0	36.0	36.0	36.0	36.0	36.0
London Boroughs (if differing)														
City	—	—	—	—	—	—	—	23.9	23.9	23.9	22.9	23.9	26.4	25.4
Camden	—	—	—	—	—	—	—	19.9	19.9	19.9	19.7	19.9	20.2	20.1
Kensington and Chelsea	—	—	—	—	—	—	—	18.7	18.7	18.7	18.5	18.7	18.6	18.8
Westminster	—	—	—	—	—	—	—	22.4	22.4	22.4	21.7	22.4	24.1	23.5
Mixed hereditaments														
England	0.8	2.1	2.9	4.2	4.5	5.0	3.0	6.5	9.0	9.0	9.0	9.0	9.0	9.0
Wales	0.8	2.1	2.9	4.2	4.5	5.0	3.0	16.5	18.0	18.0	18.0	18.0	18.0	18.0

outgoing Conservative government for introduction following local government reorganization. This had the effect of benefiting the metropolitan areas in comparison to the Non-Metropolitan Counties. In addition, 1974–5 also saw the introduction of variations in the levels of rate subsidy within London, the highest levels of subsidy going to the four boroughs with the largest rateable value tax bases. This London differential rate subsidy has been justified in terms of the need to provide additional support to domestic ratepayers in those boroughs with unusually high commercial rateable values who would otherwise be penalized by the low level of support deriving from the resources and needs elements.

The changing weight of emphasis on the three elements of RSG shown in Table 5.5 has a number of important distributional consequenees. First, the increasing share of RSG occupied by the domestic elements has increased the extent to which the grant is a per capita subsidy distributed irrespective of the income, rateable values or expenditure need of different areas. Second, the decline in the importance of the needs element, although still by far the largest element, has reduced the extent to which variation in expenditure is taken into account. Finally, however, the growth in size of the resources element has resulted in increased emphasis being placed on differences in the property tax base of local authorities. Hence, in comparison with the pre-1974–5 period, the RSG is now distributed with greater attention directed to resource equalisation, with important but less attention directed to expenditure need equalisation and with much greater emphasis on subsidizing domestic rate bills. This has had the effect of shifting support preferentially to London compared with earlier periods.

The distribution of RSG between local authorities

The previous three subsections have discussed the broad framework within which the RSG is allocated. Most controversy in any fiscal year, however, has been directed to the most complex decision of all: how each element of RSG should be distributed between local authorities. The domestic element is subject to very little spatial variation, as shown in Table 5.6, hence most attention has been concentrated on the distribution of the resources and needs elements and the discussion below is limited to these. Both elements have been subject to a considerable degree of modification and ad hocery which has been introduced in successive years.

(i) Resources element

The resources element is subject to annual *ad hoc* decisions in six ways: by decisions on the standard rate poundage; by the allocation of resource equalisation independent of need equalization; by the methods of precepting between authorities employed; by the treatment of London's 'excess' resources through 'clawback'; by the special treatment of London; and by the relief given to various classes of property. Each of these difficulties is discussed in turn below.

The standard rate poundage chosen in each year is shown in Table 5.7. Up to the 1974–5 year the England and Wales average rateable value per head was used as the standard. The raising of the level of the standard above the average from 1974–5 has resulted in a much larger number of local authorities receiving resources grants. This has been particularly important for many London Boroughs and some Nonmetropolitan Counties in the South-East. The resulting grant distribution became much more fully equalising between local authorities with different tax bases since resource differences can be compensated almost up to the maximum difference between the richest and poorest local authorities. However, this is at the expense of giving resource grants to relatively rich areas which prior to 1974–5 would have received *no* such grant. Since 1974–5 ad hoc choices of standard rateable value have resulted in two London Boroughs coming in or out of the resources distribution in successive years. In detail, the

TABLE 5.7. Standard rateable value per head used in allocation the RSG resources element. (Source: GB Government Statutory Instruments, *Rate Support Grant Orders*; GB Dept. of the Environment: *Rates and Rate Poundages*). (N.B. The number of local authorities above the standard is not directly comparable before and after the reorganization of local government in 1974)

Fiscal Year	Standard Rateable rateable head	Number of local authorities above standard				
		Post 1974 local authorities	Counties	Counties and county boroughs	Counties and county boroughs which would be Metropolitan Districts	Column (4) plus London Boroughs
		(1)	(2)	(3)	(4)	(5)
Rate deficiency grant 66/7	44	—	6	28	8	41
1967/8	45	—	6	28	10	43
68/9	46	—	6	30	11	44
69/70	48	—	6	30	12	45
70/1	49	—	6	30	11	44
71/2	50	—	7	32	12	45
72/3	51	—	6	31	14	46
Revaluation						
73/4	133	—	6	27	14	46
Reorganization						
74/5	154	48	—	—	—	—
75/6	170	31	—	—	—	—
76/7	176	28	—	—	—	—
77/8	173	34	—	—	—	—
78/9	177	28	—	—	—	—
79/80	175	35	—	—	—	—
80/81	178	36	—	—	—	—

setting of the standard rateable value derives from finding the right level which, when subtracted from local rateable value and multiplied by local tax rates, gives the total resources element planned in the Aggregate Exchequer Grant. However, it does seem that this procedure has the effect of inducing considerable instability into the size of grant allocations to be expected by local authorities.

The undertaking of resource equalization independent of need equalization is a second problem which has the effect that differences in tax base between local authorities are compensated irrespective of the levels of expenditures they need to undertake: no advantage is taken of the coincidence of high needs with high resources or low needs with low resources. Hence the *separate* treatment of needs and resources up to 1980/81 prevents full equalization. As a result GB Government (1980) have instituted a unitary grant which combines the needs and resources elements. This should have the benefits of taking advantage of coincidences of high needs and high resources on the one hand, and low needs and low resources on the other hand; arising from such coincidences, tax-rich low-need authorities can be penalized by exacting negative payments from the resources element by the device of reducing their needs element. As a result full equalization can be achieved, but at a lower total grant level.

The method of precepting employed introduces a third difficulty which concerns the relation between those authorities that levy the rates (since 1974 the Districts) and those which make various levels of expenditure. The Nonmetropolitan and Metropolitan Counties and the GLC each make important precepts on the District (the London Boroughs in the GLC area) rates in order to support the services provided by the larger government units. In addition police authorities and other bodies also make small precepts. The pattern of precepting is largely a matter for agreement between the local governments concerned. Precepting does affect the resources element since it provides resource equalization independent of expenditure need. At the small scale of Districts a considerable degree of variation leads to differential payments of resources elements. However, these payments are given irrespective of whether expenditure need at the local level warrants such a level of support. This feature leads to a substantial degree of support going to Districts which do not require it, hence either reducing local tax bills or leading to a supply expansion of local services. Hence, whilst separate resource equalization independent of need equalization is a source of inequity, resource equalization at District level and need equalization at County level induces still greater inequity. Moreover, the precepting of some of the resources element back to the County level blurs the lines of accountability for local taxes. A District levies taxes partly to provide County expenditure, and the resources element in part reflects the tax rate a District must levy to provide County expenditure. As a result, precepts induce a degree of divorce of the tax rates set by Districts from the expenditure decisions they make. This is both confusing to the taxpayer and reduces the meaning of local electoral issues.

The phenomenon of 'clawback' represents a fourth element of ad hoc decision-making introduced into the resources element. Clawback is a special adjustment to the needs entitlement of London Boroughs to allow for the fact that they have extremely rich resource bases and hence, in effect, are overcompensated by the needs element. The rateable values in London are on average two-thirds higher than the rest of England and Wales, so that a much lower tax rate can produce the same revenue yield as in the poorer authorities outside London. To compensate for this feature, the 'resources adjustment' of clawback has been subtracted from the needs grant entitlements of those London Boroughs which have a rateable value per head above the national average. The size of reduction for each of these Boroughs is calculated by determining the difference in rate poundage required to finance local relevant expenditure from the local tax

TABLE 5.8. Needs indicators used in the damped formula for the Rate Support Grant in England and Wales (excluding London). Some simplifications have been made and the dates to which variables refer have been omitted. (Source: GB Government, Statutory Instruments, *Rate Support Grant Orders: Rate Support Grant Regulation*)

Indicator	Fiscal year								
	General grant up to 1966–7	RSG 1967–8 –1973–4	1974–5	1975–6	1976–7	1977–8	1978–9	1979–80	1980–1
1. *Population*									
Population total	×	×	×	×	×	×	×	×	×
Population decline	×	×	×	×	×	×	×	×	×
2. *Area and Density*									
High density population[d]	×	×		×		×	×	×	×
Low density population[d]	×	×	×	×	×	×	×	×	×
Road mileage		×							
3. *Education Needs*									
Children under 5	×	×							
Number of pupils total[e]	×	×							
Education units[b]			×	×					
School meals served									
Nursery school pupils					×				
Primary school pupils					×	×	×	×	×
Secondary school pupils					×	×	×	×	×
Special school pupils					×	×	×	×	×
Direct grant pupils paid by Council					×	×	×	×	×
Further Education students					×	×	×	×	×

	C1	C2	C3	C4	C5	C6	C7	C8
4. *Social Service Needs*								
Persons over 65				×	×	×	×	×
Children in care	×				×	×	×	×
Pensionable age living alone		×				×	×	×
Personal Social Service Units^c		×			×	×	×	×
High density dwellings			×	×	×	×	×	×
Lack of exclusive amenities				×	×	×	×	×
Lone parent families					×	×	×	×
Shared households						×	×	×
5. *Area Weights*								
High cost Metropolitan^a	×					×	×	×
Nonmetropolitan sparsity		×					×	×
Special area weights^a						×	×	×
6. *Miscellaneous*								
Previous year's need entitlement			×	×				
Numbers employed				×	×	×	×	×
Dwelling starts				×	×			
Labour cost differential^a				×	×	×	×	×

Notes:

[a] Special area weights and high cost areas are absorbed into the labour cost differential from 1977–8 onwards.

[b] Education units include the bracketed variables for 1974–5 and 1975–6.

[c] Personal social service units include the bracketed variables for 1974–5.

[d] Density includes various definitions of acreages and thresholds.

[e] Total number of pupils includes most of other education need variables.

base, and the rate poundage required to raise the same expenditure on the national standard rateable value per head. The total size of the 'clawback' is £200–300 m annually and this contributes to the needs grants of the rest of the country.

In addition to clawback, London has also been subject to completely separate treatment of education and non-education services plus an internal equalisation scheme. This latter provides horizontal transfers between London Boroughs and is organized largely independent of Central Government. It has taken a number of different forms (see Jenkins and Rose, 1976). However, since the London equalization scheme utilizes the considerable tax bases of, in particular, the City of London together with Westminster, Camden, Kensington and Chelsea, it is not independent of the fact that the exceedingly high rateable values of these areas provide insufficient assistance to the rest of the England and Wales authorities outside London (i.e. clawback should absorb these internal London payments for full equalization to occur). Thus, because of the deficiency payments principle of the resources element, which ignores those resource rich areas (since 1974/5 all in London) which are above the standard rateable value per head, London as a whole is permitted to partake in higher service levels or reduced tax rates in comparison to the rest of the country.

The resources element is also affected, in a more minor way, by special relief given by the national government to various classes of property. In Scotland, industrial and commercial properties have been subject to special forms of relief dating from 1928. In England and Wales, industrial property was rerated in 1962, but special rating reliefs have been given to charities and other special organizations. From 1979–80 the rateable values of local authorities have been adjusted to allow for 50 per cent of the rate relief to charities. This, and similar *national* policies on rate relief, have small but important effects on local finances which intoduce rather ad hoc effects into the resources element entitlements.

(ii) Needs element

Perhaps no component of the RSG has been subject to a greater impact of changed priorities and ad hoc decisions than the needs element. The major source of 'ad hocery', and the one which has stimulated most controversy, has been that concerned with the choice of needs indicators adopted. Table 5.8 summarizes the main groups of indicators of need used from 1967 to 1981. Four periods can be recognized in this table. For the first period, up to 1973–4, needs indicators were defined a priori although their definitions were adjusted slightly and most derived from the earlier General Grant. A second period, covering 1974–5 and 1975–6, is one of ad hoc changes and experimentation in which new methods of defining 'units' of education and social service need were tried. A third period covers 1976–7, and 1977–8, when a shift was made to using census variables for measuring social service needs and other new variables were introduced. The fourth period covers 1978–9 up to 1980–81 and represents a relatively stable pattern as far as need variables are concerned, but with ad hoc decisions introduced into special area weights which have sought to achieve a balancing of need allocations unachieveable by use of the needs indicators alone.

These changes have introduced eight main components of instability and uncertainty into local finances; through the decisions on which indicators of expenditure need are adopted; through decisions as to the weighting to be placed on different needs indicators; the degree to which area bias has been introduced; the extent of damping employed; the extent to which updating of data has been permitted; the degree to which full needs equalisation has been employed; the method of distributing needs element between different precepting authorities in Nonmetropolitan areas; and the degree to which needs data can ever be rendered independent of local authority discretion as to whether a service is provided. Each of these difficulties is discussed in turn below.

The needs indicators defined *a priori* in the RSG up to 1973/4 comprised two components; a 'basic payment' per head of population, and a set of 'supplementary payments' which derived from the General Grant employed up to 1966. Each of the indicators (for young and old people, education units, high and low density, declining population and high cost Metropolitan Districts) was used in a similar form in the General Grant; only 'miles of road' was added as a new variable for the period 1967–8 to 1973–4. However, even before 1974–5 changes in definition of variables occurred, for example in the calculation of education units (see GB MHLG Circulars 11/69; 56/70). From 1974–5 onwards, considerable changes each year became possible and a new approach was adopted which, instead of employing needs indicators defined *a priori*, used past levels and patterns of expenditure to indicate need. It was assumed therefore 'that the best available indicator of spending need is the pattern of recent past expenditure' (GB Government DOE Circular 19/74, 1974, p4). The needs indicators were derived as a weighted average of past expenditures by categories of local authorities with the same characteristics, using the method of multiple regression analysis. The *a priori* definition of needs, therefore, was replaced by one which was essentially *a posteriori*. Over two transition years 1974–5 and 1975–6 the variables in the regression analysis were determined *a priori* but the weights were calculated *a posteriori* by regression analysis. The direct result of this change in methodology has been the search each year, since 1976–7, for the best regression equation based upon that set of explanatory variables which provides the closest relationship with past levels and patterns of expenditure. This methodology lends itself directly to instability and political influence since the variables that enter in any year, which give the best statistical explanation, and the weights placed upon them, will usually differ greatly from other years. Moreover, the choice of variables is not purely a statistical exercise.

TABLE 5.9.   Independent variables analysed in step-wise regression procedure 1975–6 to 1980–1. (Source: GB Government, *House of Commons Papers* HC-63 1978)

Variable	Year included in undamped needs assessment					
	1975–76	1976–7	1977–8	1978–9	1979–80	1980–1
Over 50 persons per hectare	S	—	—	NT	NT	NT
Persons per acre	NT	NT	NT	S	—	—
Acres over 1.5 per head	S	S	S	NT	NT	NT
Acres over 3.0 per head	S	—	—	NT	NT	NT
Acres per person	NT	NT	NT	S	S	S
Housing starts	—	S	—	—	S	S
Population decline over 10 years	S	—	—	NT	NT	NT
Population decline over 5 years	—	S	—	NT	NT	NT
Elderly living alone	S	S	S	—	—	—
Persons lacking basic amenities	NT	S	S	S	S	S
Overcrowding	NT	S	S	NT	NT	NT
Shared households	NT	NT	S	NT	NT	NT
Lone parent families	NT	S	S	S	S	S
Unemployment	NT	NT	S	—	S	S
Labour cost	NT	NT	S	S	S	S
Primary school pupils	S	S	S ⎫	S ⎫	S ⎫	S ⎫
Secondary school pupils under 16	S	S	S ⎬	S ⎬	S ⎬	S ⎬
Direct grant pupils under 16	S	S	S ⎭	S ⎭	S ⎭	S ⎭
Secondary school pupils over 16	S	S	— ⎫	— ⎫	— ⎫	— ⎫
Direct grant pupils over 16	S	S	— ⎬	— ⎬	— ⎬	— ⎬
Full-time further education students	S	S	—	—	—	—

Notes: S = Selected variable.
       NT = Variable not tested in that year.
       — = Variable tested in that year but not selected.
    Brackets indicate a combined factor.
    1980–1 is identical to 1979–80 except for a rolling forward of damping levels.

Since each definition of a regression equation results in differing patterns of grant payments, the choice of final equation is very much a political decision. As such, the decision on which variables and equation will be used has been a subject of liaison and discussions between the local authority associations and the central government, (see ACC *et al.* 1979). Thus although the weights applied in the needs formula are bound by statute, the list of tested and included variables is negotiable. Table 5.9 shows the independent variables chosen for inclusion in the regression equation since 1975–6 and those which were tested but not selected because they gave unacceptable allocation formulae for grant distribution. The result of this exercise has tended to stabilize grant distribution from year to year, but has made the needs formula used very unstable.

The weights placed on the various need indicators also vary significantly from one year to the next. Table 5.10 summarizes the weights applied to some of the major variables entering the regression equation since 1974–5. Although

TABLE 5.10. Variation in Non-London weights (in £ at 1978 prices) placed on major needs equation variables 1974–5 to 1980–81 (Source: GB Government, *Statutory Instruments*)

Need Variable	Fiscal Year (£)						
	74–5	75–6	76–7	77–8	78–9	79–80	80–81
Old people living alone	—	356.5	258.8	629.4	444.5	355.6	349.9
Lone-parent families	—	—	775.0	2384.1	3520.8	4262.2	4194.0
Persons in densely occupied buildings	—	—	99.1	209.7	147.2	117.6	116.2
Persons without basic facilities	—	—	21.5	70.6	80.1	86.9	85.6
Persons in shared h/holds	—	—	—	66.3	46.6	37.3	36.9
Primary school pupils	17.4	24.0	15.8	559.6	507.1	512.8	504.4
Secondary school pupils < 16 ⎫		38.9	26.8	838.1	703.9	670.4	659.2
⎬	83.7						
Secondary school pupils > 16 ⎭		60.3	41.7	1068.4	755.7	604.8	594.2
Full time students	65.2	87.4	60.2	1187.1	839.7	672.0	660.1
Unemployed	—	—	—	241.2	169.1	305.5	301.8
No. of people at 750 persons per acre	—	8.0	—	6.2	4.4	3.5	3.4
Dwelling starts	—	—	531.0	163.0	114.6	285.8	281.7
Population decline	93.8	39.6	0.054	31.0	21.8	17.4	17.1
	(10yr)	(10yr)	(5yr/ 1000)	(10 & 5 yr)	(10 & 5 yr)	(10 & 5 yr)	(10& 5 yr)

For 1974–5 education weights are obtained by allocating the percentage of the education unit to the £ weight given.

there are some general patterns, such as the steady increase in weight for lone-parent families, most of the weights vary a great deal from year to year. This makes the grant far from intelligible, makes it difficult to determine how much grant supports which service, induces instability, diffuses lines of accountability, and modifies the criteria used for equalisation from one year to the next.

Area bias (apart from the separate treatment of London) was first introduced explicitly into the needs formula in 1974–5 when a special weighting for both the South East and the West Midlands was employed. Since then various special weights have been introduced and the equivalent grant per head that these generate is displayed in Table 5.11. As can be seen, the two types of area favoured are the high-cost authorities of the South East and some of the sparsely populated rural areas. In later years, 1978–9 and 1979–80, an explicit bias to favour inner cities was introduced by the Westminster Labour Government. This has been entered into the RSG needs element not as an explicit variable but instead by choice of population density thresholds and other need factors which favour city areas. In practice, however, this method of introducing area

TABLE 5.11. Grants per head in £ for special areas outside London. Note that the 'labour cost differential' (*underlined*) used since 1977–8 has been reduced to per capita terms for each area. (Source: GB Government, Statutory Instruments, *Rate Support Grant Orders*)

Area	Weight applied to population of area in fiscal year (£ per head)						
	74–5	75–6	76–7	77–8	78–9	79–80	80–81
Berks		—	—	0.534	7.834	5.344	6.434
Bucks		—	—	0.534	2.542	—	—
Essex	5.99	—	—	0.512	2.805 / 0.627	7.931	9.119 / 2.677
Herts		—	—	0.979	3.242 / 9.297	16.594	14.387 / 0.358
Kent		—	—	0.334	1.575 / 0.418	3.375	0.963
Surrey		—	—	0.689	5.293	8.887	12.665
Beds		—	—	0.156	2.333	2.981	7.954
Hants		—	—	0.578	3.586	—	2.736
Oxon	1.04	—	—	0.133	2.333	8.100	8.156
E. Sussex		—	—	—	—	—	—
W. Sussex		—	—	—	0.498	—	—
I. of Wight		—	—	—	—	—	—
Hereford and Worcester		—	—	—	—	—	—
Salop	1.44	—	—	—	—	—	—
Staffs		—	—	—	—	—	—
Warwicks		—	—	—	—	—	—
Gwynedd	—	—	—	—	0.167	—	—
Powys	—	—	—	—	0.298	9.121	7.575
Districts							
Kirkless	—	—	—	—	0.164	—	—
Knowsley	—	—	—	—	0.387	—	—
Sheffield	—	—	—	—	1.762	—	—
Sunderland	—	—	—	—	0.238	—	—
Wigan	—	—	—	—	1.980	—	—
Manchester	—	—	—	—	—	—	0.267

bias has been much less effective than specific weights since the aid is often diffused to other areas in addition to those intended to receive it.

Damping is employed to limit the extent of variation in one year's entitlement from the next, and hence gives greater stability to each local authority's grant. No damping was necessary up to 1974–5 when the same needs indicators were employed each year, but after that date the annual search for a new regression

TABLE 5.12. Values of damping employed in RSG needs determination outside London

Year	Damping (Percentage of needs allocated on present year's formula).	Value placed on previous year's formulae (percentage of)			
		1 year previous	2 years previous	3 years previous	4 years previous
1973–4	N/A				
1974–5	N/A				
1975–6	50[a]	50			
1976–7	33.33[b]	66.66			
1977–8[c]	33.33	33.33	33.33		
1978–9[c]	25	25	25	25	
1979–80[d]	20	20	20	20	20
1980–81[d]	20	20	20	20	20

Notes:
[a] Includes a needs indicator of 71.3% of 1974–5 allocation.
[b] Includes a needs indicator of 83.86% of 1975–6 allocation.
[c] Requires averaging where old formulae do not contain new indicators.
[d] No new formula employed, data updated only.
  Source: GB Government, *House of Commons Papers*.

equation has led to a need to prevent allocations varying too much from one year to the next. The levels of damping employed are shown in Table 5.12. The effect of damping has been, on the one hand, to limit the destabilizing effect of annual 'ad hocery' in definition of needs indicators but, on the other hand, to introduce a new dimension to 'ad hocery' which permits year-on-year ad hoc decisions of the past to be summed and weighted together. The result of damping is therefore a more certain and stable distribution of RSG, but at the expense of using an almost indecipherably complex weighted sum of ad hoc decisions.

Updating of the variables used in the needs formula, like the decisions on which variables to include and how to weight them, has also been undertaken in an ad hoc way. It seems, in fact, that decisions on updating, weighting and inclusion of variables are all interdependent since the overall effect of these three sets of decisions is to achieve a level and distribution of grant which is acceptable to both central and local government.

A particular problem enters as a result of the infrequent updating of decennial census variables with the consequence that many of the variables used in 1981 are ten years out of date. This problem applies especially to data on personal social services but it has been accepted as the only method of obtaining objective measures of need for social services independent of local authority discretion to provide such services. However, two further characteristics also induce difficulties. First, there is the decision as to when to update a particular variable. Table 5.13 shows the range of dates at which particular variables have been updated since 1974–5. Clearly the information on social service needs is

TABLE 5.13. Variations in dates of non-London variables used in needs assessment 1974–5 to 1980–81 (Source: GB Government, *Statutory Instruments*)

Need variable	Fiscal Year						
	1974–5	75–6	76–7	77–8	78–9	79–80	80–81
Old people living alone	—	1971	1971	1971–76	1971–76	1971–77	1971–78
Lone-parent families	—	—	1971	1971	1971	1971	1971
Persons in densely populated buildings	—	—	1971	1971	1971	1971	1971
Persons without basic facilities	—	—	1971	1971	1971	1971	1971
Persons in shared households	—	—	—	1971	1971	1971	1971
Primary school pupils	1972	1974	1975	1977	1977	1978	1979
Secondary school Pupils < 16	1972	1974	1975	1977	1977	1978	1979
Secondary school Pupils > 16	1972	1974	1975	1977	1977	1978	1979
Full-time students	1972	1974	1975	1976	1976	1977	1977
				Oct	Oct	Oct	Oct
Unemployed	—	—	—	1977	1977	1977	1978
Persons at > 50 people per acre	—	1971	—	1971	1971–76	1971–77	1971–78
Dwelling starts	—	—	1975–6	1974–7	1974–7	1975–7	1976–8
Population decline	1962–72	1964–74	1970–5	{1966–76 / 1971–76}	{1966–76 / 1971–76}	{1967–77 / 1972–77}	{1968–78 / 1973–78}
Labour cost differential	—	—	—	—	1975–76	1976–77	1977–78

particularly out of date and has effectively been frozen since the 1971 census for each variable except old people living alone. Other variables have been updated as new information has become available, but in some cases considerable delays are present. Especially important is the considerable delay in updating unemployment data. Clearly a degree of ad hoc and political variation can be introduced at this level. A second difficulty has been induced by the way in which data relating to particular local authorities have been updated. Frequently local authorities have claimed that statistics for their areas are markedly incorrect. This has particularly characterized the population and social service variables. In addition many data are directly or indirectly provided by local authorities, such as the Registrar General's *Population Estimates*, and school pupils. As a result, a considerable number of protracted negotiations often characterize grant distribution with special adjustments being made for individual authorities in a rather ad hoc fashion. Because of this feature, since 1978–9 the RSG has included a provision to 'freeze' data after a particular date, usually one year from publication of the Order, to prevent negotiations and adjustments carrying on indefinitely.

A major issue of controversy over the form of the RSG has been the treatment of areas with differing needs positions. Full need equalization requires full compensation of differences in expenditure need of local authorities above the authority with the lowest need, except insofar as different levels of need can be supported by different levels of local tax base. Since the General Grant, such a form of full equalization, taking account of resource differences through the resources element, has been implemented. However, for that part of the needs element termed the supplementary payments or needs equalization component no such explicit equalization affects the population-based part of the needs element which has formed a considerable proportion of the total. The consequence of basing so much of the need distribution on per capita terms has been that low need authorities have been compensated through the needs element as well as high need authorities, thus undermining full equalization and setting off 'vicious circles' of enriched or impoverished service levels.

The distribution of the needs element between the different precepting authorities in Nonmetropolitan areas has introduced difficulties and arbitrariness since needs are assessed at the scale of the larger unit of the Nonmetropolitan County, whilst it is at the District level that taxes are raised and many expenditures are made. Between 1966 and 1978–9 the needs grant has been allocated directly to Nonmetropolitan Counties and Metropolitan Districts, with no reallocation to the other level. Since 1979–80, however, the needs grant has been divided between the Districts of the Metropolitan Counties by a complex sub-formula which has introduced a further level of arbitrariness. Three-quarters of the needs element is allocated to Districts using their share of the closest mid-year population estimates. The remaining quarter is allocated to the Districts using a three-step procedure to assess District need within the County. The first step measures each District's share of the previous three years County expenditures, revalued at constant prices. The second step scales the grant to each District in accordance with the difference of each District from that with the smallest expenditures per head in the County, thus seeking to achieve full needs equalisation. The third step involves paying the District needs grant in full if it amounts to less than the remaining quarter of total County needs grant. However, if the sum of the District needs grants is greater than one quarter of total County needs, the 25 per cent of needs grant can be distributed only in *proportion* to differences in the expenditure needs of the Districts. In addition in 1979–80 there was a safety net or damping to limit the poundage value by which the needs element falls short from the extra precept Counties will make. This safety net, which stood at 2p, was implemented only in 1979–80, as it was deemed necessary to limit the effects on ratepayers of the once-and-for-all shift of grant from Counties to Districts. Clearly the variable method of precepting, although improved since 1979–80, has considerably blurred lines of accountability and added additional complexity to grant distribution. For example, a Nonmetropolitan County received a grant reflecting not only its own needs, but also those of the Districts contained within it. As a result, the precepts that the County levied do not reflect just its own expenditure, and nor do the rates levied by the Districts reflect their expenditure.

The fact that much needs data is dependent upon local discretion to provide a service introduces a further major difficulty into needs assessment. Since total expenditure data of a local authority depend on the size and range of local services offered, the choices by local authorities to provide services at different levels reduce or increase their total expenditures per head. Hence total local expenditure imperfectly reflects local need. Similarly, for any given service category, the identification of the size of client groups is affected by local discretion. This affects most particularly special schools, provision of private and direct grant school places at local authority cost, the size of most personal social services, and the level of local transport spending. The number of children in schools for the handicapped, the number of home helps and of old people in homes, and the level of road maintenance depend to a large extent on the choice by local authorities to provide such services. Hence, the present size of client groups is not an objective measure of need and it is mainly for this reason that census and other 'objective' indicators of social living conditions have been introduced through the regression formula since 1975–6. However, the extent to which these discretionary effects are important depends upon the aims of the RSG and upon the attitude of central to local government autonomy. If central government perceives that the aim of grant support is to achieve either total equality of service provision everywhere or equal total rate bills, then local discretion is a major difficulty in needs assessment. If, however, central government perceives that grants are aimed at increasing the general revenue base and supporting whatever standard of service local authorities choose to provide, then the effects of discretion are unimportant. Over the period since 1967–8 it is clear that the view of central government has shifted from one favouring local autonomy and discretion to one seeking, first, to emphasise equalization and, second, to standardize services, with any differences above national minimum standards supported by local ratepayers.

CHANGING OBJECTIVES AND THE RATE SUPPORT GRANT

It is clear from the preceding discussion that the evolution of the RSG over the fourteen years since 1967–8 has been exceedingly complex and at various stages has sought to satisfy different objectives. Hence, it should not be expected that the pattern of changes reviewed above can be accounted for by redirection of the grant towards any *one* objective. The objectives which the RSG has been directed towards have been both explicit and implicit and it is clear that whilst major explicit objectives may have been claimed and publicised, other features of grant distribution have frequently been induced, often inadvertently.

The major *explicit* aims of the RSG have always concerned equalization, but it is clear that the precise concept of equalization employed has varied over time. In early years equalisation tended to favour needs more than resources, but more recently resource equalisation and per capita allocations have been favoured to a greater extent. For example, the needs element has reduced from 82 to 61 per cent of the Aggregate Exchequer Grant, whilst the resources element has increased from 16 to 30 per cent (see Table 5.5). In addition to equalization, however, other major explicit aims of the RSG have favoured the objectives of fostering fiscal balance through tax base sharing, and by improving local efficiency and productivity. Moreover, it is clear from the preceding discussion that the emphasis on these aims has shifted a good deal.

At its outset in 1967–8 a major aim of the RSG, in addition to equalizing the ability of local authorities to provide services at similar tax rates, was to overcome deficiences in the total magnitude of the local tax base. This is clearly stated by the GB Government (1966, p. 6) White Paper on local finance, which set up the initial RSG: 'the paramount need is not so much to encourage or assist the development of particular services as to ensure that the total cost of all services does not place an impossible burden on ratepayers and in particular on households'. Even for the 1974–5 settlement of the RSG it was still stated as a major aim of the grant that 'where under the new distribution formula authorities receive more grant . . . it is intended that rate-payers should benefit and that whenever possible rates should be reduced' (GB Government DOE Circular 19/74, 1974, p. 6). By the end of the 1970s, however, the emphasis had shifted to one in which the RSG could be used as a means of encouraging greater efficiency in local spending. Thus, a major aim of the new form of RSG to be introduced in 1981–2 is 'to deal with the problems of the major over-spending authorities and the pre-emption of grant that flows from high spending . . . It is critically important to provide a grant system which encourages economy and efficient management of resources by all authorities and which provides them with an incentive to keep their expenditure within reasonable limits' (M. Heseltine, Secretary of State for the Environment; reported in *The Financial Times*, 13 March 1980).

In addition to encouraging efficiency in local government, the explicit emphasis of RSG has also shifted towards gaining greater central control of local public spending. This has been seen as a major aspect of gaining greater control of public expenditure as a whole, which has been a particularly important aim of the Conservative government holding office since 1979. In 1980, for example, it was stated that the RSG represented the 'main means of influencing local authorities' rating and spending decisions' and that the 1980–81 RSG 'settlement was based on a logical extension of [national] economic policy . . . [requiring] careful planning and the co-operation of local government'

(M. Heseltine, Secretary of State for the Environment; reported in '*The Times*', 17 Jan. 1980).

Hence, over the period from the inception of the RSG to the proposed setting up of the unitary grant in 1981–2, there has been a steady drift away from using central support as a means of tax-base sharing, and towards the employment of central support as a means of both encouraging local efficiency and of gaining greater central control of both the level, and to some extent, the distribution of local expenditures. In addition to these more explicitly stated aims, however, each of the eleven objectives discussed in the second section of this paper has also been pursued explicitly or implicitly to a varying extent. Each of these is discussed below.

Equalization

The aim of equalization has been explicitly pursued throughout the period since 1967–8, but the form of equalization used has been subject to a number of changes. The gradual shift from need equalization towards resource equalization itself has, to a large extent, resulted from an implicit effect of raising the standard rateable value per head, which had the explicit aim of obtaining more adequate resource equalization. Moreover, increased emphasis on the domestic element plus the role of population as a variable in the needs element have made the grant more of a direct per capita subsidy and hence have reduced the need-equalizing effect of transfers. Moreover, the effect of damping of the needs element, the variable priorities of area-biased needs, and the lack of full needs equalization payments until 1979–80 have also reduced the equalizing effect of needs compensation. On the resources side, the level of 'clawback' from London and the immunity of the London equalization scheme to national redistribution have also reduced the degree of equalization possible. It is clear, therefore, that although need and resource equalization have been major explicit aims, subsidiary factors have considerably diminished the equalization that has been achieved, and produced a number of effects which are largely perverse to the original stated goals of the RSG programme.

The effect of these changes has been a tendency to favour the rural Counties in the early years of the RSG and the cities in later years. As shown in Table 5.14, the emphasis up to 1973–4 on need equalization and, in particular, the use of need variables such as miles of road, population totals and population sparsity, tended to give the greatest share of the needs grant to the Counties, especially those in sparsely populated Wales. Since 1974–5, however, the greater emphasis on resource equalization has brought many high-rateable-value metropolitan areas into receipt of resources element. This, combined with a shift to need indicators (as shown in Table 5.8) based on indices of social deprivation deriving from the 1971 census (shared, overcrowded and low amenity house-holds, lone parent families, etc.), has shifted the RSG as a whole in favour of

TABLE 5.14. Mean and standard deviation (in brackets) of level of per capita RSG need and resources elements in different administrative areas at constant 1978 prices, for selected years

Fiscal year		English Counties	Welsh Counties	Metropoliton Districts or CB	Inner London	Outer London
1965–6 Rate deficiency grant		12.0 (7.6)	35.7 (23.5)	14.4 (16.7)	0.4 (1.4)	—
Resources Elements	67–8	51.4 (106.7)	91.0 (53.2)	12.3 (15.2)	0.5 (2.0)	
	73–4	12.9 (8.3)	40.7 (22.6)	18.6 (18.2)	0.9 (3.1)	0.5 (0.2)
	74–5	38.8 (18.7)	81.4 (21.9)	57.5 (28.2)	5.1 (10.4)	4.2 (8.1)
	76–7	46.8 (15.7)	86.2 (18.4)	61.4 (23.3)	7.1 (13.2)	11.2 (13.2)
	79–80	43.4 (14.9)	76.6 (16.3)	56.8 (21.3)	6.4 (11.8)	9.3 (11.4)
General grant	65–6	49.1 (4.4)	60.9 (6.8)	45.8 (7.4)	43.3 (3.0)	40.4 (5.6)
Needs Elements	67–8	70.5 (7.0)	97.9 (22.3)	62.3 (5.4)	62.4 (3.5)	60.4 (3.6)
	73–4	98.9 (9.3)	123.2 (22.3)	93.0 (11.4)	54.5 (4.0)	87.7 (6.5)
	74–5	98.6 (21.3)	116.9 (34.4)	105.3 (16.9)	152.7 (28.4)	113.4 (14.8)
	76–7	87.1 (20.1)	107.5 (29.2)	102.3 (16.1)	148.3 (26.7)	118.7 (18.9)
	79–80	81.3 (13.9)	105.0 (26.1)	106.2 (21.9)	173.6 (27.6)	138.7 (22.9)
Total grant	65–6	61.1 (10.4)	96.7 (29.6)	60.2 (20.1)	43.7 (3.1)	40.3 (5.6)
	67–8	121.9 (111.3)	189.0 (74.7)	74.6 (18.0)	63.0 (3.4)	60.4 (3.6)
	73–4	111.8 (14.6)	163.9 (41.9)	111.7 (25.1)	55.5 (4.7)	87.8 (6.5)
	74–5	152.4 (24.4)	223.5 (40.2)	175.6 (27.6)	182.9 (20.9)	139.6 (13.9)
	76–7	149.2 (23.3)	213.1 (29.9)	176.9 (24.0)	181.4 (19.5)	152.0 (22.3)
	79–80	124.5 (24.3)	181.7 (27.3)	163.0 (29.1)	179.9 (25.3)	147.9 (26.9)

the cities. As shown in Table 5.14, this has particularly favoured London in terms of both resources and needs elements, but the allocation to the Welsh Counties has remained the highest overall.

Thus although equalization has been a continuous aim of grant allocation procedures, equalization has meant different things at different time periods. The relative favouring of the rural counties in the period 1967–8 to 1973–4 corresponds to three years of Labour control and four years of Conservative control at Westminster, whilst the relative favouring of the cities from 1974–5 until 1979–80 corresponds to a period of Labour government at Westminster.

This gives some grounds for believing that shifts in equalization criteria have been stimulated by the party ideology and priorities of the central government, but the results are far from conclusive regarding party influence and certainly require more detailed analysis (see Foster *et al.*, 1980; Bennett, 1980).

Neutrality to income distribution

With respect to the goal of making the allocation of the RSG neutral in its effects on income distribution, the RSG has again had variable and perverse effects over time. It is clear that, although neutrality to income distribution should only be achieved with respect to local taxation, the benefit or expenditure side of local budgets cannot be held independent of the tax rates required. A major feature of the RSG which has had perverse income effects has been its inability simultaneously to assess local expenditure and taxation effects. Thus, for example, individuals living in areas with large tax bases in relation to need, and also in areas with low tax bases and low need, have received much larger allocations of RSG than required for equalization, and this often has been passed on in reduced local tax bills. Conversely, people living in areas with small tax bases and large need have been penalized by the deficiency payments effect of the resources element, and people living in London Boroughs with large tax base but high needs have been penalized by 'clawback'. Since these effects have been a direct result of maintaining separate resource and need elements, the unitary grant introduced to operate from 1981–2 should reduce this effect (q.v. below). In addition, the shifting emphasis towards per capita allocation of RSG through the domestic and needs elements has also undermined the neutrality of rate bills with income. Moreover, where specific aid through the RSG has been directed towards low income or high cost areas, the effects of this aid have often been diffused to other areas by using need indicators which prevent specific targetting to areas of highest need. The deleterious effects of the RSG on income distribution are minimized at the lower end of the income profile by the effect of rate rebates. However, rate rebates do not guarantee equity between areas such that, over the lower-middle and upper income levels, considerable inequities in rate bills between local governments has resulted.

Fiscal balance

Fiscal balance between the tax-raising capacity of different levels of government has been a major explicit aim of the RSG, especially in its early years. However, incremental changes in the grant have produced a number of subsidiary effects. The rise in general level of RSG as a percentage of relevant expenditure over the period as a whole, from 54 to 61 per cent, but peaking in 1975–6 at 66.5 per cent, has allowed a better fiscal balance deriving from a higher degree of use of the central tax base. Fiscal balance has also been facilitated by a general rise in the proportion relevant expenditure represents of total expenditure, from 70 to 86 per cent. However, much of the improved fiscal balance since 1975–6 has been obtained by reducing the total level of services funded (in real terms), and reductions have been particularly significant in the capital account. Hence, the achievement of better fiscal balance has to some extent been at the expense of greater central control and diminished total service level.

Neutrality to local behaviour

With respect to neutrality to local behaviour, the RSG has been deficient in three main respects. First, the resources element has been subject to the feedback effect by which local authorities can, in part, determine their grant allocation by setting their tax rates. Second, the size of the needs element is affected by variables which to some extent reflect local discretion to spend. This was particularly true of the 1974–5 needs formula which included much personal social service data. Third, the data provided to central government in the needs formula are to some extent affected by the local authorities (for example, the population estimates). Thus the RSG, in important respects, has fallen far short of neutrality to local decisions and this has further undermined the objective of equalization.

Feasibility

The feasibility of implementing the RSG from existing data sources is a major problem. What has been sought since 1967–8, and will be sought even in the new grant structure after 1981–2, is a full equalization of the tax rates required in the face of unequal service costs per unit of need. To obtain data that allow such a perfect equalization would require a full 'unit-cost' approach, which would entail measurement of, for each local government, the factor inputs, the number of clients in each service group, the production functions, and the service quality provided (see Bennett, 1980). The feasibility of such an approach is greatly limited in Britain at present by having only a decennial census and the lack of sufficient alternative data. The central government (GB Government, 1979) have proposed a method of obtaining a larger proportion of data directly from local authorities, but this runs into the problem that much of such data is insufficiently neutral to local authority behaviour, as discussed above.

Facilitating local discretion.

The degree to which the RSG has facilitated local discretion has varied since 1967–8. The role of spending guidelines expressed through departmental circulars has increased greatly over this period (see GB Government, *MHLG* and *DOE Circulars*, various dates). In addition, the original aim of tax-base sharing which facilitates local discretion has been somewhat replaced by greater central control, as discussed above, and the Aggregate Exchequer Grant has been increasingly hypothecated. Specific grants, for example, have increased from 8 to 13 per cent of the total grants over the period since 1967/8, whilst the domestic element has increased from 2 to 9 per cent (see Tables 5.3 and 5.6). Clearly equalisation and neutrality to local behaviour are to some extent in conflict with the aim of facilitating local discretion such that it has been found difficult for the RSG to satisfy simultaneously these two goals.

Accountability

This requires, as noted by the Layfield Report, that local tax rates are clearly related to local expenditures undertaken. In the RSG system obtaining since 1967 accountability has been undermined in three important respects. First, the pattern of precepting used up to 1978–9 has made it very difficult for voters to determine who is responsible for given tax levels. Second, the total level of financial support of local government by RSG and other grants, rising to 61 per cent of relevent expenditure, has undermined local accountability, since local services have become heavily underpriced relative to taxes paid. Third, the whole complexity and arbitrariness of the process of deciding on the distribution of the RSG has undermined the ability of local taxes to relate directly to expenditures from one year to the next. Clearly, again, accountability conflicts to some extent with other objectives, such as equalisation, fiscal balance and economic efficiency; it seems that the form of RSG over the period since 1967–8 may not have resolved this conflict in the most appropriate way. However, further major difficulty with local accountability in Britain arises from the degree of relation of local tax rates to voters' decisions. A considerable body of evidence now suggests that there is only a small degree of relationship of local voting patterns to taxing and spending decisions (see e.g. Oliver and Stanyer, 1969; Nicholson and Topham, 1971; Newton and Sharpe, 1976). This seems to arise from three features; first, the dominance of national and party concerns over local issues in British local elections; second, the little regard that local councils of any party show to the tax consequences of their expenditure decisions; and third, the pressure of the general social climate of the period since 1945 which has produced (until the mid-1970s) general acceptance of an ever-expanding public sector at both national and local levels. As a consequence of these features, central government has often shown more concern with the level of local rates rather than the range of local services, as expressed for example in the assessment of relevant expenditure and the level of the RSG settlement, and this has made it more difficult to foster local accountability, whatever the form of RSG adopted.

Intelligibility

This is closely related to accountability as an aim, since the more simple and intelligible a programme is, the better the chance that it can display direct relationship of taxes to expenditure. However, intelligibility in the RSG, by any standards, is extremely low. As stated by one MP in a Parliamentary debate, 'it is a programme which defies comprehension'. The relation of the total size of the RSG to the *Public Expenditure White Paper*, the Budget, and PESC is extremely obscure and arbitrary; the form of domestic rate subsidy, 'clawback', and tax relief to certain classes of property are very complex; and the form of the needs element, apart from the statistical complexity of the stepwise multiple regression analysis, has switched needs data, variables, dates of data, methods of determining weights, and area biases in a manner such that the total consequences for grant distribution have become largely indecipherable.

Encouragement of economic efficiency in local government

This has been an increasingly important explicit aim of the RSG in the later 1970s. Certainly there are major problems for achieving efficiency which result from the various forms of RSG allocation which have been adopted. The regression analysis of RSG expenditure on needs indicators and the influence of various forms of damping has often been claimed to reward 'overspending' local authorities and penalize the more frugal. In addition, the total and increasing level of central grant support markedly underprices local services in terms of the effect on local tax rates; this can stimulate demand and supply expansion; and is further reinforced by the 'feedback' effect in the resources element. The pattern of precepting also tends to encourage supply expansion in the richer Districts within a County. However, it is also clear that a large share of the 'blame' for the 'overexpansion' of local spending must also fall on the central government's methods of expenditure planning. The relation of local spending and the RSG to PESC is extremely diffuse, and the forecasts of service levels, costs, prices and wages produced in the determination of relevant expenditure have often been greatly in error. These errors have been particularly marked for education and in total have overestimated the level of expenditure required at both the *Increase Order* stage and in the setting of cash limits (see Tables 5.3 and 5.4).

With respect to the stimulus high grant support may give to overspending and hence inefficiency, it has been argued, for example by the Department of the Environment (Appendix 1, GB Committee of Enquiry, 1976, pp. 91–3), that a high grant percentage in itself does not act as an incentive for local authorities to increase expenditure, and, moreover, marginal expenditure above grant settlement has greater impact on the rates the higher is the grant. But it is usually conceded that large increases in grant percentages may stimulate expenditure due to three factors. First, historic patterns of service supply and demand affect the levels of need that can be recognised in many service categories with the consequence that previously high expenditures attract high grants, and this is reinforced by both the regression formula for needs and damping. Second, neither central nor local forecasts of future price changes in local authorities are independent of local behaviour, especially in setting pay and manning levels, and such changes have often been passed on in grant *Increase Orders*. Third, the Rate Support Grant has not equalized perfectly between spending needs and tax base resources but has been subject to relatively volatile annual shifts, to feedback and deficiency payments of the resources element, and other difficulties (see GB Committee of Enquiry, 1976) which may have encouraged some local authorities to 'overspend'. Certainly by the late 1970s the Rate Support Grant system was seen as 'stimulative of overspending' to the extent that its reform to encourage greater control seemed essential (GB Government, 1980).

Compensation for spillover

The aim of compensating local authorities for spillovers of benefits and costs along the lines of Pigovian theory has not been a major feature of the RSG. Special arrangements were made with the reorganisation of local government in 1974, and these were especially important in their effect on the transfer of debt between old and new authorities. Spillover effects are to some extent catered for in the mixed County-District level of organization and in the pattern of precepting. However, it is clear that, at least since 1974, the size of local government in Britain has been large enough that spillover effects are a relatively minor feature in most areas.

Certainty and stability

The aim of providing certainty and stability in grant levels is mainly important to the local authorities in their expenditure planning. Whilst this has been aimed at in the RSG certainty and stability have seldom been achieved. In the period up to 1974–5 certainty was increased by providing RSG allocation for two years at a time; since 1974–5, however, one year allocations, frequently modified, have been the norm. Damping and data freezing of the needs element have also aimed at generating greater stability in grant allocation, and have indeed achieved improved stability; but since this stability has often been at the expense of poorer equalization it might seem to be a somewhat dubious achievement to provide more stable needs allocation against the wrong criteria! In general however the RSG has been subject to a rather high degree of uncertainty and instability, especially since 1974–5. The January Public Expenditure *White Paper* sets national economic pointers which affect the rate levies set in March of the same year. The RSG *Order* of November in the preceding year also affects the rate levies required; further modifications may be induced in the March–April *Budget*, after rate levies have been made; and yet further modifications are induced by *Increase Orders* in November of the current and following years, both after rate calls have been fixed. In addition, changes in central government (as occurred in 1970, 1974, and 1979) can produce radical changes to previous agreements with the local authorities on the RSG. Similarly, changes in overall economic conditions have induced important changes in cash limits and *Increase Oders* at relatively short notice, which have usually been introduced through departmental circulars (see GB Government, *MHLG* and *DOE Circulars* various dates); these short term economic fluctuations have often induced central government to impose much of the rigour of a central pay and prices policy on the local authority public sector. In addition, more explicit political effects have been introduced with changes of government in terms of the relevant expenditure accepted. This has affected especially the allowances for school milk, direct grant school fees, local efficiency assessment, town planning expenditure, and, most significant in cash terms, housing expenditure. As a result, the RSG has been a highly unstable and uncertain programme for individual local authorities. Whilst long term aggregate changes have been relatively slow and 'evolutionary', short term changes have severely affected the distribution between areas. This feature is also supported by information given by ACC *et al.* (1979) and Jackman and Sellars (1977).

From this discussion it can be concluded that although the major explicit aims of equalisation, fiscal balance and encouragement of efficiency have been pursued with reasonable vigour over the period since 1967–8, the extent to which they have been achieved has varied a good deal, and has been frustrated in many important respects. In addition, with respect to other more implicit aims of the RSG, it can be concluded that the grant has often had perverse effects on income distribution: it has not been neutral to local behaviour; it has not been supported by collection of adequate data with the result that it is probably too complicated and sophisticated; it has probably progressively suppressed local discretion, undermined local accountability, and has been largely unintelligible to both the public and to the politicians; it has tended to encourage inefficiency and the over-supply of services; and it has been extremely uncertain in total amount and relatively unstable in local distribution.

A number of these problems can be overcome by a transition to a unitary grant structure. In particular, equalization should be more fully achieved, neutrality improved, and accountability, intelligibility, and efficiency fostered. However, a unitary grant will probably not improve fiscal balance, may be no more feasible to implement with existing data, is likely to be just as uncertain although it should be more stable, and it is likely severely to undermine local discretion. Whether the Conservative Government changes for 1981–2 will achieve these improvements, and what their other effects will be is, as yet, uncertain.

CONCLUSION

This paper has reviewed the methods of allocating the RSG over the fourteen year period from its inception in 1967–8 until the major restructuring undertaken by the Conservative Government in 1981–2. This review will help to give a synoptic view of what has been one of the most important and complex intergovernmental transfer programmes to be developed in the Western world. The paper has also sought to compare the methods applied to allocating the RSG each year against the explicit and implicit objectives which characterize grant programmes. From this discussion, two main conclusions can be drawn.

First, the methods of allocation employed since 1967–8 have achieved a significant improvement in the balance of revenue sources available to local government; in the effects of local finances on income distribution; and in the degree of equalization which can be achieved between local governments in both the service levels provided and the local tax bills exacted. However, the methods of RSG allocation employed are still inadequate in a number of important respects. Most important of these are its unintelligible complexity, its encouragement of inefficiency, its lack of neutrality to local decisions, as reflected in its inability to differentiate discretionary from nondiscretionary spending, and its high degree of uncertainty and instability. As a result, the RSG is, for many local authorities, inflated in level beyond that which might reasonably be judged to be required, whilst for others it is inadequate to achieve appropriate equalisation and fiscal balance.

A second conclusion, deriving from the inadequacies of the methods of RSG allocation employed, is that reform is required. Minor reforms could have been based upon modifying each element as follows. The domestic element could become a specific grant category separate from the rest of the RSG and subject to a greater degree of standardization with respect to rate bills rather than the arbitrary spatial differentiation of subsidy now employed (see Table 5.7). The resources element could be made more fully equalising by incorporating either equalization up to the local authority with the highest rateable value per head, or (more efficiently) by exacting payments from the high tax base areas. In effect this would require elimination of the separate treatment of London, abolition of the 'clawback', and the participation of all local authorities in central responsibility. This in turn requires a clear distinction to be drawn between local expenditure undertaken as devolved agents of central government and local expenditure resulting from local political priorities, preferences and discretion; it requires differentiation of local discretionary from non-discretionary spending. This further requires greatly improved data on local service provision.

However, because of the difficulty of obtaining detailed data, and because of the impediments in the way of differentiating need, as measured by past expenditure, and 'latent' need, it has been concluded by central governments of both parties that reform should take the more radical form of a unitary grant. This combines needs and resources elements, to be called the *Block Grant* of the RSG from 1981–2. Such a reform does allow many of the criticisms of the RSG obtaining up to 1979–80 to be overcome. But it has been combined with provisions to penalize individual 'overspending' authorities. This particular development has met the resistance of all local authority organizations of all political parties and seeks radically to change the balance of relations between the central and local state. As such it seems likely that the RSG will prove an important area for research in the geography of public policy for many years to come. Particularly important in this research will be assessments of the extent to which administrative changes modify geographical outcomes, especially the effect on inner city problems, regional development, city-suburb disparities, and regional economic disparities.

REFERENCES

ACC *et al.* (1979). *Rate Support Grant 1979–80*, London, Association of County Councils, Association of Metropolitan Councils, Association of District Councils, London Boroughs Association, Greater London Council.

Alt, J. (1971). Some political correlates of County Borough expenditures, *British J. Political Science*, **1**, 49–62.

Bennett, R. J. (1980). *The Geography of Public Finance*, Methuen, London.

Boaden, N. (1971). *Urban policy making*, CUP, Cambridge.

Dear, M., and Clark, G. (1978). The State and geographic process: a critical review. *Environment and Planning*, **A**, 10, 173–83.

Foster, C. D., Jackman, R., and Pearlman, D. (1980). *Local finance in a unitary state*, George Allen and Unwin, London.

G. B. Government (1961). *The Control of Public Expenditure*, Cmnd 1432, London, HMSO, Report of Plowden Committee.

G. B. Government (1966). *Local Government Finance England and Wales*, Cmnd 2923, London, HMSO.

G. B. Government (1969). *Public Expenditure: a new presentation*, Cmnd 4017, London, HMSO. Green Paper.

G. B. Government (1972). *Public Expenditure White Papers—a handbook on methodology* London, HMSO.

G. B. Government (1974). *Local Government Act*. London, HMSO.

G. B. Government (1979). *Publication of Financial and other Information by Local Authorities,* London, Department of the Environment.

G. B. Government (1980). *Local Government Act*, London, HMSO.

G. B. Government, various dates. *DOE Circulars* Department of the Environment circulars, London, HMSO, see Appendix.

G. B. Government, various dates. *House of Commons Papers*, London, HMSO, see Appendix.

G. B. Government, various dates. *MHLG Circulars*, Ministry of Housing and Local Government Circulars, London, HMSO, see Appendix.

G. B. Government, various dates. *Statutory Instruments*, London, HMSO, see Appendix.
G. B. Government Committee of Enquiry, (1976). *Local Government Finance*, Report of Committee of Enquiry, Chairman F. A. Layfield, London, HMSO, with 10 Appendices.
Harrison, A. and Jackman, R. (1980). Changing the incentive to spend: A critical look at the new block grant. *CES Review*, **9**, 22–4.
Hunter, J. S. M. (1977). *Federalism and fiscal balance: A comparative study*. Australian National University, Canberra.
Jackman, R. A., and Sellars, M. B. (1977). The distribution of Rate Support Grant: The hows and whys of the new needs formula, *CES Review*, **1**, 19–30.
Jenkins, J., and Rose, M. (1976). Rate Support Grants and their application to London. *GLC Intelligence Quarterly*, **35**, 9–26.
Johnston, R. J. (1979). *Political, Electoral, and Spatial Systems*, OUP, London.
Musgrave, R. A., and Musgrave, P. B. (1976). *Public Finance in Theory and Practice*, New York, McGraw Hill.
Newton, K., and Sharpe, L. J. (1976). *Service Outputs in Local Government: some Reflections and Proposals*, Oxford.
Nicholson, R. J., and Topham, N. (1971). The determinants of investments in Housing by local authorities: an econometric approach. *J. Royal Statistical Society A*, **134**, 273–303.
Neild, R., and Ward, T. (1976). Evidence to G. B. *Committee of Enquiry*, Appendix 6, pp. 81–97, London, HMSO.
Oates, W. E. (1969). The effects of property taxes and local public spending on property values: An empirical study of tax capitalization and the Tiebout hypothesis. *J. Political Economy*, **77**, 957–71.
Oates, W. E. (1972). *Fiscal Federalism*, New York, Harcourt, Brace Jovanovich.
Oates, W. E. (1977). *The Political Economy of Fiscal Federalism*, (Lexington, Mass., Heath).
Oliver, F. R., and Stanyer, J. (1969). Some aspects of the financial behaviour of County Boroughs, *Public Administration*, **47**, 169–84.
Pigou, A. C. (1947). *A Study in Public Finance*, 3rd edn., London, Macmillan.
Tiebout, C. M. (1956). A pure theory of local Expenditures. *J. Political Economy*, **64**, 416–24.

APPENDIX: PUBLICATIONS OF GB GOVERNMENT RELEVANT TO RATE SUPPORT GRANT

1.   Public Expenditure white papers

Session	Date	Title
1967–68	1968	Public Expenditure in 1968–69 and 1969–70, Cmnd 3515
1968–69	1969	Public Expenditure in 1968–69 to 1970–71, Cmnd 3936
1968–69		Public Expenditure: a new presentation Cmnd 4017
1969–70		Public Expenditure in 1968–69 to 1973–74, Cmnd 4234
1970–71	1971	Public Expenditure to 1974–5, Cmnd 4578
1971–72		Public Expenditure to 1975–76, Cmnd 4829
1972–73	1972	Public Expenditure to 1976–77, Cmnd 5178
1973–74	1973	Public Expenditure to 1977–78, Cmnd 5519
1974–75	1975	Public Expenditure to 1978–79, Cmnd 5879
1975–76	1976	Public Expenditure to 1979–80, Cmnd 6393

1976–77   1977   The Government's Expenditure Plans, 2 volumes
                   Cmnd 6721-I, 6721-II
1977–78   1978   The Government's Expenditure Plans, 2 volumes
                   Cmnd 7049-I, 7049-II
1978–79   1979   The Government's Expenditure Plans, Cmnd 7439
1979–80   1980   The Government's Expenditure Plans, Cmnd 7841

2. House of Commons papers

Session	Paper	Title
1966–67	HC-252	Rate Support Grant Order 1966
1967–68	HC-19	Rate Support Grant (Increase) Order 1967
1968–69	HC-24	Rate Support Grant Order 1968
1969–70	HC-21	Rate Support Grant (Increase) Order 1969
1970–71	HC-172	Rate Support Grant Order 1970
	HC-173	Rate Support Grant (Increase) Order 1970
1971–72	HC-21	Rate Support Grant (Increase) (No. 1) Order 1971
	HC-22	Rate Support Grant (Increase) (No. 2) Order 1971
1972–73	HC-26	Rate Support Grant (Increase) Order 1972
	HC-27	Rate Support Grant Order 1972
1973–74	HC-47	Rate Support Grant (Increase) (No. 1) Order 1973
	HC-48	Rate Support Grant (Increase) (No. 2) Order 1973
		The Rate Support Grant 1974-75, 5532
1974–75	HC-74	Rate Support Grant (Increase) Order 1974
	HC-75	Rate Support Grant (Increase) Order 1975
	HC-460	Rate Support Grant (No. 2) Order 1974
1975–76	HC-31	Rate Support Grant Order 1975
	HC-32	Rate Support Grant (Increase) (No. 2) Order 1975
1976–77	HC-26	Rate Support Grant Order 1976
	HC-27	Rate Support Grant (Increase) Order 1976
	HC-28	Rate Support Grant (Increase) (No. 2) Order 1976
1977–78	HC-57	Rate Support Grant
	HC-58	Rate Support Grant (Increase) order 1977
	HC-59	Rate Support Grant (Increase) (No. 2) Order 1977
1978–79	HC-63	Rate Support Grant
	HC-64	Rate Support Grant (Increase) Order 1978
	HC-65	Rate Support Grant (Increase) (No. 2) Order 1978
1979–80	HC-280	Rate Support Grant
	HC-281	Rate Support Grant (Increase) Order 1979
	HC-282	Rate Support Grant (Increase) (No. 2) Order 1979

3. Departmental circulars

(a) *Ministry of Housing and Local Government (MHLG)*

Year	No.	Title
1966	42/66	Public Expenditure 1966.
1967	9/67	International obligation and local authority purchasing.
	12/67	Local Government Act 1966. Financial Provisions.
	18/67	Rate demands 1967–68. Information about reductions in poundage under section 6 of the Local Government Act 1966.
	21/67	The Rate Support Grant Regulations.
	26/67	General Rate Act 1967.
	28/67	The Rate Product (Amendment of Enactments) Regulations 1967.

1968	6/68	General Rate Act 1967. Rate Demands and Rate Rebates.
	7/68	International Obligations and Local Authority Purchasing.
	9/68	Local Expenditure.
	21/68	General Rate Act 1967. The Rate Product Rule 1968.
	39/68	Rate Rebates from Autumn 1968.
1969	11/69	Local Government Act 1966. The Rate Support Grant (Amendment) Regulations 1969.
	18/69	Part 1. Loan consent for small amounts. Part 2. Loan period for all loans.
1970	43/70	Local Government Statistics and Central Forecasting for Rate Support Grant.
	56/70	The Rate Support Grant (Amendment) Regulations 1970.

(b) *Department of the Environment*

Year	No.	Title
1970	2/70	Capital programmes.
1971	65/71	Capital programmes : Classification of detail of Circular 2/70
	66/71	Capital programmes : Arrangements for 1972–73
1973	77/73	Public Expenditure in 1974–75
	157/73	Public Expenditure in 1974–75
1974	19/74	Rate Fund expenditure and rate calls in 1974–75
	171/74	Rate Fund expenditure and rate calls in 1975–76
1975	51/75	Local Authority expenditure
	88/75	Local Authority expenditure in 1976–77—Formal planning.
	129/75	Rate Support Grant settlement 1976–77
1976	45/76	Local Authority current expenditure 1976–77
	84/76	Local Authority expenditure 1976–78
	120/76	Rate Support Grant settlement 1977–78
	123/76	Reductions in Public Expenditure in 1977–78 and 1978–79
1977	37/77	The Government's expenditure plans (Cmnd 6721): Implications for Local Authority expenditure 1976–79
1978	8/78	Rate Support Grant settlement 1978–79
	28/78	The Government's expenditure plans (Cmnd 7049): Implications for Local Authority expenditure 1978–82
	68/78	Inner Urban Areas Act 1978
1979	6/79	Rate Support Grant settlement 1979–80
	15/79	The Government's expenditure plans (Cmnd 7439): Implications for Local Authority expenditure 1979–83
	21/79	Local Authority expenditure in 1979–80

4. Statutory instruments

(a) *Orders and increase orders*

Year	No.	Title	Volume
1966	1612	Rate Support Grant Order	1966 III, p. 5053
1967	1877	Rate Support Grant (Licence) Order	1967 III, p. 5098
1968	1956	Rate Support Grant Order	1968 III, p. 5356
1969	1806	Rate Support Grant (Increase) Order	1969 III, p. 5618
1970	1875	Rate Support Grant (Increase) Order	1970 III, p. 6159

1970	1876	Rate Suprort Grant Order	1970 III, p. 6163
1971	2031	Rate Support Grant (Increase) (No. 1) Order	1971 III, p. 5821
1971	2032	Rate Support Grant (Increase) (No. 2) Order	1971 III, p. 5825
1972	2033	Rate Support Grant (Increase) Order	1972 III, p. 6016
1972	2034	Rate Support Grant Order	1972 III, p. 6020
1973	2180	Rate Support Grant (Increase) (No. 1) Order	1973 III, p. 7714
1973	2187	Rate Support Grant (Increase) (No. 2) Order	1973 III, p. 7734
1974	550	Rate Support Grant Order	1974 I, p. 2251
1974	2108	Rate Support Grant (Increase) Order	1974 III, p. 8192
1974	2109	Rate Support Grant (No. 2) Order	1974 III, p. 8198
1975	1248	Rate Support Grant (Increase) Order	1975 II, p. 4259
1975	2149	Rate Support Grant Order	1975 III, p. 7976
1975	2150	Rate Support Grant (Increase) (No. 2) Order	1975 III, p. 7983
1976	2201	Rate Support Grant (Increase) Order	
1976	2202	Rate Support Grant (Increase) (No. 2) Order	
1976	2203	Rate Support Grant Order	
1977	2113	Rate Support Grant Order	
1977	2114	Rate Support Grant (Increase) Order	
1977	2115	Rate Support Grant (Increase) (No. 2) Order	
1978	1867	Rate Support Grant Order	
1978	1868	Rate Support Grant (Increase) Order	
1978	1869	Rate Support Grant (Increase) (No. 2) Order	
1980	57	Rate Support Grant Order	
1980	58	Rate Support Grant (Increase) Order	
1980	59	Rate Support Grant (Increase) (No. 2) Order	

(b) *Regulations*

Year	No.	Title	Volume
1974	428	Rate Support Grant Regulations	1974 I, p. 1384
1974	788	Rate Support Grant (Specified Bodies) Regulations	1974 II, p. 3036
1974	1987	Rate Support Grant (No. 2) Regulations	1974 III, p. 6964
1975	5	Rate Support Grant (Specified Bodies) Regulations	1975 I, p. 4
1975	1950	Rate Support Grant Regulations	1975 III, p. 7246
1976	214	Rate Support Grant (Specified Bodies) Regulations	
1976	1939	Rate Support Grant (Adjustment of Needs Element) Regulations	
1976	2071	Rate Support Grants Regulations	
1977	1342	Rate Support Grants (Adjustment of Needs Element) (Amdt.) Regulations	
1977	1941	Rate Support Grant Regulations	
1977	2002	Rate Support Grants (Adjustment of Needs Element) (Amdt. No. 2) Regulations	
1978		Rate Support Grant (Adjustment of Needs Element) (Amdt.) Regulations	
1978	1701	Rate Support Grant Regulations	
1979	337	Rate Support Grant (Adjustment of Needs Element) (Amdt.) Regulations	
1979	1514	Rate Support Grant Regulations	

Geography and the Urban Environment
Progress in Research and Applications, Volume IV
Edited by D. T. Herbert and R. J. Johnston
© 1981 John Wiley & Sons Ltd.

Chapter 6

Towards a Geography of Urban Children and Youth

Frederick Hill and *Willliam Michelson*

This essay develops a geography of urban children and youth through an integration and expansion of existing research and writings and with support from original research (the Toronto Whole City Catalogue Project) in which we are engaged. Many scholars, from a range of disciplines, have undertaken the analysis of children in their urban milieu. By and large, they have either focused on specific components of the urban environment or taken particular perspectives. Some, for example, have focused on *formal institutions* such as schools, noting the implications of basic design or dimensions on children (e.g. Barker and Gump, 1964; Sharonov, 1980; Durlak, Layman, and McClain, 1973). Others turn to the environments encountered by children in more *naturalistic* settings (e.g. Hart, 1979; Medrich, 1977). Some observers have investigated the *perception* by children of their urban environments (e.g. Lynch *et al.*, 1977; Siegel, Kirasic, and Kail, 1978), whereas others study explicit behaviours considered related to environment (e.g. Becker, 1976; Chombart de Lauwe *et al.*, 1976; Farely, 1977). Still others focus on the Gestalt of *cultural* meanings and understood behaviours felt to be *learned* by growing up in a particular setting (Barker, 1968).

The intellectual focus of writers on children and environment varies from concern with abstract concepts like privacy (Wolfe, 1978; Parke and Sawin, 1979), to concrete design solutions such as adventure playgrounds (Cooper Marcus, 1970; Moore, 1980), and to pathologies thought to occur in unfavourable environments (e.g. Rapoport, 1979a; Sandels, 1974). Psychologists, who have dealt with children more often and in greater depth than other social scientists, have been reluctant until recently to advance beyond perspectives of the environment that are social or psycho-dynamic (Bronfenbrenner, 1977). although some (particularly those identifying with the field of environmental psychology) have recognized the need for balanced consideration of the physical and social environments in which all human beings realistically live (Altman and Wohlwill, 1978).

There is certainly no lack of interest in or work on children, and recognition of this fruitful cohort for research is increasing. *What is argued here, however, is that coordinated and explicit attention should be given children within the many realms of geography.* Most generalizations espoused by geographers pertain to the adult world. Children come in different sizes and shapes and with differing capabilities, but it is theoretically, empirically, and practically useful to consider the environments that concern children, quite apart from the assumptions made and conclusions drawn from adult behaviour and experience.

Children and youth, for example, differ from adults in a number of ways which have specific relevance to geography:

1. Children and youth differ from adults in terms of their behaviour. While certainly heterogeneous, such behaviour on the part of young people is partly channelled into various forms of education and partly into great amounts of play. Both are considered the 'work' of childhood in which the intellectual, physical, and social development of young people occurs (Bruner, 1976). What actually goes on during the day of the average child is different in content and in other concrete manifestations from that of adults.

2. The land uses and facilities which involve children are often different from those of adults. Hence, children's 'places' (Moore and Young, 1978) form a context for behaviour which in many ways differs from the context of adult behaviour. Furthermore, even when children and youth share the same settings as adults, such as at home or in the community, what they expect to do there is likely to differ and there may be variations in ways in which children and adults experience the same environment.

3. The sizes and types of territory which enter into the daily lives of adults and children tend to differ. As adults posses, on the average, greater degrees of personal strength, experience, and autonomy than children, they range through far larger daily territories. Most adults have access to a wider range of modes of transportation, and the demands placed on them as they fulfill a variety of domestic and work-related responsibilities contribute to a larger, more diverse daily round. Conversely, the more specific and restricted territory of children of specific ages takes on a more overriding importance in their daily lives: it is their effective environment, from which they are less able to escape.

4. Specific environmental entities are threats to people of some ages and not to others. The dangers to children from potential poison ingestion, low-lying pollutants, and discarded refrigerators, for example, are not normally hazards for adults.

5. Economics plays a major role in the establishment and distribution of land uses, but children are largely outside the economic system and are certainly outside the classical adult economic system. Therefore, the land uses of

central importance to children are determined in ways which are outside the experience and consumer preferences of those affected. Although arguments may be made that the same is true for many segments of adult society, the difference in degree is major, inasmuch as *all* children are outside the property market, notwithstanding the importance of children and youth to certain industries.

6. In terms of the political structuring of the environmental system, children are again formally excluded. They have no vote, no direct representation, and no explicit roles in the electoral and political system. Again, although children's interests are at stake, research into processes forming the environment have only dealt with the adult world. Pursuing the environmental interests of children requires unconventional contributions.

7. Finally, even when the same environments pertain both to children and adults, the interpretation and meanings of these places are not likely to be the same. Perception and cognition are functions of development and experience as well as the ways in which places are used and controlled.

Thus, many of the basic premises and ingredients of geographical studies which rest upon assumptions of the normative behaviour of adults, are undercut by the existence of a cohort in the population whose relationship to the environment is fundamentally different to that of all others. In this essay, the components of a geography relevant to urban children and youth will be explored. Following some basic considerations concerning the treatment of children and youth in this context and the relationship of young people to their environment, a number of areas of geography where special considerations about children could produce data of explanatory value regarding families, children, and the environment will be discussed. This will lead to an assessment of the new perspectives and information which may be required, the relevant units of analysis, and questions of measurement. Where appropriate, examples from work on the Toronto project will be used.

BASIC CONSIDERATIONS

The Dutch masters painted children to look like smaller adults. They had facial expressions, clothing, and activities which were unmistakably adult; only their body size tended to differentiate adults from children above infancy. Such depiction of children may not have been unrepresentative of how children were considered at that time. At present, however, thinking about children has veered to the other extreme. More recent research into human development, changed attitudes towards education and labour, and increasing social and cultural differentiation of age groups have all led to a greater awareness of general differences between children and adults, notwithstanding the various subcategories within each main group. Despite progress of this kind, adults responsible for decision-making and policies do not commonly recognize a wide enough range of distinction, let alone apply them sensitively in environmental management.

In this section, therefore, some aspects of child development which are pertinent to the urban environment and its study by geographers will be enumerated. The concept of child development is outlined first because it is the cornerstone to understanding what children do in the urban environment and how they react to it. In Boocock's (1978) carefully designed study of children and environmental influences, for example, the single most crucial factor explaining behavioural differences in the environment was developmental stage. Moreover, regardless of how adult scientists conceptualize and explain children and their behaviour, young people segregate themselves by age for their activities, indicating a *de facto* practice which exists regardless of adult approval (see Dahlen, 1977).

Specialists in child development have devised many different schemes to characterize the relevant stages of that process. While consensus may never be achieved in detail, there is nonetheless substantial agreement over typical stages of development, reflecting age, maturity, stimulation, support, nutrition, and other factors. The very youngest infants, for example, differ in many ways from toddlers, who in turn evolve into pre-schoolers (about three to five years of age). Researchers generally agree that children from about six to eleven or twelve years old have generally shared capabilities and needs, while adolescents enter a differnt world of experiences again. In recent years, further categories of older teenagers and, indeed, young adults have emerged, to fit cohorts within the population which have been increasingly influenced by popular culture and by ever-delayed entrance into the regular labour force (Rapoport and Rapoport, 1975). Development is thus a complex phenomenon involving a variety of processes, which are neither simultaneous not linear. Pollowy (1977) represents a broad consensus in differentiating between (1) intellectual and perceptual development, (2) physical growth, and (3) personal and social development. Each of these components deserves some individual discussion.

Piaget is justly known for his illuminating experiments on the learning processes of children of different ages (Piaget, 1952; Piaget and Inhelder, 1956). Various types of reasoning only come into play once children have reached particular levels of mental growth and functioning. Such reasoning applies also to cognitive and perceptual processes involving the physical environment. What children perceive, for example, is in large part a function of the nature of their territory, of the activities they may perform, and of culturally learned cues. Thus the child's perception will differ in many respects from adult views of the same object. Younger children, for example, are more likely to regard a given area as a *place* rather than as a way to get somewhere else; they pay much more attention and attach more value to minutiae such as ground surfaces and aspects of the natural environment than do adults (Lynch, 1978). Indeed, as children they 'respond more immediately to environmental conditions, freer of the overlay of symbolic, cultural, and past experiences that may obscure or distort adult reactions' (Altman and Wohlwill, 1978, p. 2).

Children's perception also reflects interests which diverge from those of adults. Keller (1979), for example, points to the common perception of adventure playgrounds by children as exciting locations, while adults view them as eyesores. What, on the other hand, may seem to an adult to be a safe, pleasant enclosure for a child may be a boring lifeless space. Moreover, the perception of danger, or lack of it, by children should be of considerable interest and concern to adult observers.

How children function in space reflects the development of cognitive processes. Siegel et al., (1978), for example, point out that finding one's way around a neighbourhood or city requires a degree of cognitive capacity that is only acquired in stages. Young children, for example, are extremely egocentric, paying attention mostly to themselves and rather less to that which is out in the world, excluding all but the most significant persons. They successively learn to recognize and pay attention to landmarks followed by the learning of typical routes, and finally by the internalization of environmental configurations (see the essay by Piché in this volume). Adults may still run into unfamiliar settings and get lost; but the cognitive process of understanding a new environmental context is one of which most adults are capable without delay. Children, on the other hand can achieve this only to the extent that their general cognitive development has progressed.

A second and obvious aspect of development is physical growth. Children have different degrees of agility and strength at different stages of development and these have a major influence on what they do in the environment and how they deal with such vital elements as doors, vehicles, and other people. According to Chombart de Lauwe, children come to terms with their bodies at the age of six and use their environment to exercise and demonstrate their emerging talents and strengths. Children at this age thus have 'a corporal view of space', differing significantly from the instrumental or aesthetic view or both held by most adults (Chombart de Lauwe et al., 1976, p. 34).

The implications of both mental and physical development focus interest on the six to twelve year-old group. The physical and mental capacities are available to go beyond the immediate vicinity of the home to engage in neighbourhood or playground activity and increasing energies demand other outlets and facilities. Some observers suggest that this particular age cohort has the most meaningful experiences with the natural environment (e.g. Tuan, 1978; Moore and Young, 1978) and the neighbourhood may offer a range of new and varied experiences.

A third type of development concerns relationships with other people, including personality development insofar as this results from experiences with others. Some observers feel that such moral and social development of children occurs at later ages than the other forms of development (Chombart de Lauwe *et al.*, 1976). The meaning of companionship varies greatly from the very early years (when children largely play side-by-side without significant interaction), through the pre-adolescent years (when they join in active pursuits together though without deeply personal involvement), to the adolescent years (when interaction begins to centre somewhat less on activity and more on capability and human relationships).

The physical environment is related to such personal and social development to the extent that it facilitates or hinders the kinds of interaction appropriate to the various stages of development, including the transition from one to the next. There are characteristic problems, for example, among teenagers who seldom have publicly-sanctioned locations at which to meet each other and to socialize under conditions which facilitate personal interaction. Schools and formal activities under the supervision of adults frequently serve this purpose, but the structuring and timing of such activities, with control in the hands of adults, hinder socializing in its own right. Interpersonal contact usually occurs only to the extent permitted, and as long as it conveniently fits with activities of quite a different nature. Many youths show disdain for organized youth activities but typical urban contexts provide very limited alternatives, with obvious counter-cultures appearing in reaction. As Lynch (1978) points out, young people are denied legal opportunity to own or control buildings and land of their own, and adults are loth to share many facilities, even with those adolescents who could afford them.

Privacy is an example of how personal and social development are treated environmentally. Studies indicate that environmental means of assuming and conferring privacy, such as closing or knocking on doors, increase as children grow older. Adolescents, although granted more privacy than younger children, still fail to gain the degree of privacy, both at home and in the community, accorded to adults (Parke and Sawin, 1979; Wolf, 1978).

Specific aspects of the environment can be highlighted for their relationship to child development. The environments relevant to children's lives may be understood according to at least three different perspectives: (1) functions; (2) physical dimensions; and (3) degrees of formality.

(1) Sensitivity to developmental stages provides a basis for understanding children's emphases at different ages; however, some brief discussion is needed of the range of active and passive *functions* which children demand of their environment. Such functions then serve to highlight the nature and diversity of environments to be understood with specific reference to children.

(a) Environments serve to *support or endanger survival*. Specific characteristics of the air, housing design, street layout, neighbourhood land use pattern and other entities carrying dangers or enhancing security are vital to the immediate wellbeing of the child.

(b) The nature of environment tends to enhance or hinder how well children *cope with the basic activities* of everyday life. External noises, access to bathroom facilities, land use texture, and other properties of the environment make differences in how well the satisfaction of sleep and cognitive development, toilet training, and diet, for example, are fulfilled.

(c) Children's play takes different forms depending upon the *opportunities available* in the local environment.What skills are developed, the extent to which crucial internal feelings of competence may emerge, and how well proprietary feelings about home, neighbourhood, and city become fostered are in part a function of environmental opportunities.

(d) One particular function served by the environment, which takes different forms according to the developmental stage of children and youth, is the *provision of access*. Children, like adults, must be able to get from A to B to do what they want at point B. As children become adolescents, their interests become more specialized, and the range of territory on which they draw becomes necessarily larger. Yet, the basic consideration as to whether young persons of any age have appropriate ways and means of access to what they need and want is a matter of considerable practical concern, requiring analysis and understanding independent of how adults view and plan transportation and land-use systems for their own purposes.

(e) The environment serves as the *locus for contact* with other persons. If there is no place at all to meet or if none exists which is safe, socialization is inhibited. We typically concentrate on provisions for children (including social contact) with regard to family and school; yet, as Chombart de Lauwe (1976, p. 39) points out, outside space for informal though intensive and influential contact forms a 'third milieu' which, though the least studied of children's areas, plays 'an essential role in socialization'. We typically ignore *interstitial* areas of neighbourhoods which are in fact used and are influential on children's wellbeing (Churchman, 1980; Verwer, 1980).

(2) There are many aspects of environment which acquire significance in children's daily activities and development; several of these have *physical expression*.

One crucial physical dimension is '*place*', the qualitative meaning and potential for activity of a given site. The nature of a place to some extent reflects the intrinsic implications of its design and intentions; but how it is used can be explained even more fully with reference to what people learn in their local milieux and how well the nature of the place ties in with the developmental needs and abilities of the children involved (see Barker, 1968; Gump, 1975). A number of researchers have investigated the kinds of places that are most relevant to children (Moore and Young, 1978). The relevance to them of a wide range of places is not surprising, but adults still place an oversimplified emphasis on home, school, and the traditional playground (see Becker, 1976; Moore, 1980). While young people do spend a great deal of their time in and around their homes, large amounts of time are also spent in areas defined by the types of vegetation on the site and its arrangement over space, and by the kind of people likely to be found there. Lynch *et al.* (1977), for example, lists a series of physical characteristics of places children typically adopt as their own. Gray and Brower (1977) took tours given by children of their favourite places in Baltimore's inner city; in this case, in an older central city, people and activity were crucial defining characteristics of children's haunts. There is some general evidence that the range of places which children use is broader than most adults realize, even in the pre-adolescent years.

The individual places which children use aggregate into *territories*, the size and relevance of which in the life of any given child is a function of age. The older the child, the larger the potentially relevant daily territory. Sex-role distinctions also explain the amount of territory customarily utilized; boys have larger territories than girls who are subject to more restrictions. (Moore and Young, 1978). Different sizes of area are also evident when considering those territories used every day for the bulk of activity, those used regularly but only for specific purposes, and those used only for occasional visits. Children's relationship to territory is surely coloured by habitual use, though occasional exposure is not without value.

When viewing territory from a pragmatic point of view, the researcher must consider how well those who plan for children recognize the relevant territories for given ages of children and youth. How do they ensure that appropriate opportunities within such relevant areas are available and accessible? If neighbourhoods and larger areas are important for pre-adolescents and adolescents, are the public resources of the city distributed equally? Do all children have access to accepted public goods? It is important to recognize significance of the way in which places of a size and character relevant to the various stages of development of the child are organized in space. (Andrews, 1973; Rapoport, 1979b).

A third physical dimension concerns the use of space as a *pathway*. Access is accomplished by means of pathways which have spatial and mechanical aspects. When concerned with very young children, the emphasis is often on *safe* passage. Can children obtain optimal opportunities without running grave risks? In established cities, it is easier to institute regulated crossings, with personnel like crossing guards, than to change the environments to provide protected access pathways. In newly planned communities, more initial effort has been placed on separating pedestrians from automobile traffic. Nonetheless, pathways and resultant access should be studied in order to cope directly with the kinds of situations which children face. The pathway situation is much more complex with older children and youth who are more likely to use public than private transportation systems on their own. Potential for behavior and activity is closely related to how well young people (and others, too) can take advantage of the overall transportation system. Few if any public transportation systems have been organized to optimize the needs of young people nor should they be organized on that basis alone. But the consequences of any given movement system are crucial to the understanding of what young people can and cannot do. Indeed, what many teenagers end up doing may be closely related to what opportunities they cannot reach with reasonable effort or cost.

3. A final aspect of urban environment, highlighted by the special situation of children and youth, is its degree of *formality*. Some places and parts of territories, in addition to pathways, are consciously provided by formal authorities. These frequently reflect planning activity and the expenditure of public money. Researchers have found, to public chagrin, that young people often use other places and sometimes even ignore those which are formally provided (e.g. Churchman, 1980).

This is not an argument for formal or informally provided space *per se*. What is critical to a relevant geography, however, is the inclusion of an understanding of all kinds of space used, together with the conditions of its use. So-called hidden spaces are real if their usage is real. A comprehensive geographic inventory of relevant places for children must also include all the informal and unintended areas as a baseline for realistic assessment and planning for children in the future.

To this point, some basic considerations underlying a geography of urban children and youth, touching both upon child development and environment, have been examined. Before proceeding to an analysis of how such considerations can be applied to ongoing research within geography, however, brief mention should be made of the dynamics linking children to these aspects of environment. There is no single dynamic linking independent and dependent variables in the contexts so far discussed. There are at least three patterns involved (Michelson and Roberts, 1979). The first set of influences comes directly form the environment. Such deterministic effects are important to recognize, but are not characteristic of most of the potential relationships. Nonetheless, the effects of many environmental stimuli such as pollution, noise, traffic dangers, and extreme housing conditions (such as bitter cold or exposure to rodents or dampness) can be direct causative factors affecting the wellbeing of children. A second set of influences is more indirect. Housing, neighbourhood, and city environments, for example, may provide or withhold opportunities for activity and socializing with others. These influences are not deterministic, but the environment serves as a neccessary, though not a sufficient, support for particular types of behaviour. A third set of influences comes through the mediation of adults. Adults' wellbeing affects the wellbeing of children, not least when children are dependent on the ability of adults to provide for them and to regulate their daily lives. Therefore, to the extent that the environment is supportive of parents' activities this will have an effect on children. Such considerations are now particularly relevant as greater numbers of single-parent and two-career families with major and difficult daily responsibilities become more typical of Western societies (Michelson, 1980). Parents also assess the supportive roles of environment in terms of their children's activities and impose constraints accordingly. Therefore, a geography of children cannot view children in a vacuum; adult actions mediate the relationship between children and environment in many circumstances. Furthermore, adults are ultimately responsible for forming the environments which influence children and adults' positions in the social and power structures can be highly relevant to children and the environments they command. Generally, only adults contribute to the design, allocation, and use of land. Increased knowledge of both structure and process is needed for improvements to take place.

COMPONENTS OF A GEOGRAPHY OF URBAN CHILDREN AND YOUTH

What would a geography of urban children and youth, recognizing the basic considerations already discussed, consist of? Some of its major components are discussed in this section and incorporate a few preliminary results from the Whole City Catalogue project underway at the Child in the City Programme. The project was an attempt to involve Toronto's teenagers in the collection of information on opportunities for children which exist in the city's various neighbourhoods, the equity of their distribution and the effect which their distribution has on teenagers' behaviour, activities, and attitudes about their neighbourhood. An objective of the project was to feed this information into the planning process and thus contribute towards better informed decisions about the planning and management of urban space in the interests of children and youth.

Where children live

A geography of urban children and youth inevitably includes a discussion of where children of various characteristics live within cities. Such basic information is required for an understanding of all the areas of inquiry discussed below. The spatial scale at which information on children's place of residence is required would depend on the particular problem being investigated. For some purposes a crude central city-suburbs distinction may be adequate, but much more commonly information will be required at the district, census tract, micro-neighbourhood or even block level. Because of the progressively larger territorial ranges which are relevant as children grow, the scale at which information on the location of children's homes is required also changes with age.

At whatever geographical level is appropriate, a range of questions may be asked about the child population of a given area: how many children of various ages live there, what percentage of the area's population are children of various ages, and what proportion of the city's population of various ages lives there? Other demographic data would commonly be required as well: the racial, ethnic, cultural or religious composition (or all four) of the child population; the socio-economic status of their parents (as measured by their education, income and occupation); family size, type, and composition; the labour force participation rates of their parents; their residential mobility; and so on. For many of these characteristics, summary measures of residential mix (such as an ethnic diversity index) would be a useful supplement to data on the actual breakdown of the population according to a characteristic such as ethnic origin, since one may wish to know whether children in the area are likely to come into frequent contact with a number of different ethnic groups or social classes in their neighbourhood, as well as what specific groups live in the area. Finally, data on the structural types of dwellings occupied by children in an area and the amount of space occupied by these dwellings—in other words, the net residential density of the area—are essential for a basic data set describing where children live in cities.

Most of these variables are the familiar ingredients of social area analysis and factorial ecologies. What distinguishes the data required for a geography of urban children and youth, however, is that only the population under a certain age must be included. This often poses a problem. Frequently data on the characteristics of the population, dwellings, and households are not available separately for children and adults, especially for small geographical areas. To assume that the data for the entire population in terms of socio-economic status, ethnic origin, or dwelling types, for example, adequately describe the child population of the area could lead to major errors. Childless couples, the elderly, and single people living in an area may well have quite different characteristics (status, dwellings, ethnicity) than children and their parents. This is not to say that adults who are not parents are totally irrelevant to children living in an area. In fact, there are instances when their presence has a substantial impact on the quality of children's lives, especially if their characteristics and life style lead to conflict with parents and children. Groups of transients, alcoholics, or mentally handicapped, for example, may exert considerable influence on parents' and children's assessment of a neighbourhood as a desirable place for family living. This does not detract, however, from the importance of looking at the child and parent population separately from both the population as a whole and childless households.

Although factorial ecologies have been performed for population sub-groups, such as the black population of certain American cities (Pettyjohn, 1976; Meyer, 1971), no-one has apparently used this technique to describe the social geography of a city's child population. Lack of neighbourhood or census tract data for children and youth, over a sufficiently wide range of variables, may be part of the reason although special tabulations of census data could be prepared. An untapped potential certainly exists in the census for this type of analysis. Traditional factorial ecologies and social area analyses admittedly provide some information relevant to where children live—a familism factor is invariably revealed in the analysis of Western cities (Timms, 1971; Johnston, 1971)—but descriptions based on the entire population are a poor substitute for a social geography of urban children and youth.

Such basic demographic information, whether subjected to factor analysis or presented in the form of simpler measures, would be of great benefit to those involved in making decisions on the location of facilities or services required by children of various ages and characteristics, to those researchers interested in sampling environments for more intensive study, and to investigations of the incidence and correlates of various types of pathologies.

The process whereby children of various ages, cultures, and family circumstances come to live in certain locations is considered implicitly in the various models of residential location, which include those based on neoclassical economics, the more realistic behavioural approaches, and the institutional approaches which deal with the behaviour of all the various actors in the property industry (speculators, developers, lending institutions, private and public landlords, real estate agents, planning agencies, etc., as well as consumers of housing)—most commonly from an anti-capitalist stance (Johnston, 1977). From the housing consumer's point of view, family size and composition (especially the numbers, age, and sex of the children) is the primary determinant of housing need, in terms of both dwelling size and outdoor space. In fact, among families with children the search for a better environment for the children and the need for more or less space as family size changes are among the most important factors in the decision to move and in the choice of location (Rossi, 1955; Michelson, 1977; though see also Morgan, 1973). These decisions are constrained by factors such as the family's financial circumstances, knowledge of housing opportunities, the location of available suitable housing, discriminatory practices, the rules under which public housing authorities allocate dwellings, and the desire to live among one's own ethnic group. The common spatial outcome of families' decisions to live where they do, however, is that children in Western societies are found in disproportionate numbers in suburban areas, in ethnic neighbourhoods in the inner city, and in neighbourhoods with large public housing projects for families.

The Whole City Catalogue project has not included a factorial ecology of Toronto's children. The Canadian census includes much information relevant to children at the census tract level, but essential measures of the socio-economic status of their parents, the characteristics of dwellings inhabited by children, and residential mobility are not currently available, although maps of certain characteristics relating to children from 1976 census data have already been published as part of other research efforts (Social Planning Council of Metropolitan Toronto, 1979). For the Whole City Catalogue project, therefore, an alternative source of information on where children live was used. A population tape of the number of children of various ages living in each *block* according to the 1978 municipal assessment rolls was obtained. With additional

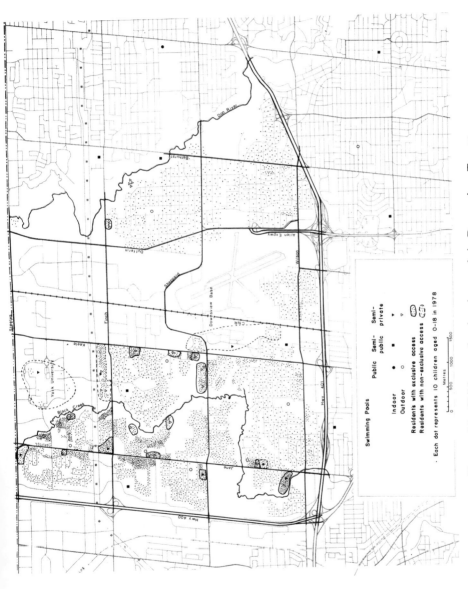

FIGURE 6.1. Children and swimming pools in Downsview, Toronto

information from land use maps and the city directory it was then possible to prepare accurate dot maps showing the distribution of children.

Figures 6.1 and 6.2 show where children live in two areas of Toronto. The immediate and striking impression is one of enormous differences in child density from one area to another. The density maps are partly but by no means entirely explained by dwelling types and the location of non-residential land uses. Some apartment buildings are for adults only, some have few children, and some have many; the apartment buildings and row housing owned by the public housing agency, Ontario Housing Corporation (OHC), account for the densest clusters of children, and the population in blocks with OHC housing commonly consists of as much as 45 per cent children. These important small-scale differences in density would not be apparent from census tract level

FIGURE 6.2. Children and swimming pools in the Parkdale–High Park area, Toronto

data or from maps which ignore the distribution of dwelling types, buildings with and without children, and the location of residential land uses.

Children's environmental opportunities

Cities include many places and spaces which by accident or design are used by children for various activities and a geography of urban children and youth inevitably includes a discussion of where these places are and their accessibility. The types of relevant places span most of the categories found on conventional land-use maps, but the traditional land-use designations provide insufficient detailed information to make them interpretable in terms of the use which children are likely to make of these areas. A retail furrier and a real-estate office may be in the same category as an ice cream store or a fast food outlet, but their relevance to children is hardly the same. Areas designated 'school' or 'church' on a land-use may have greatly different amounts and types of outdoor and indoor space facilities. That there is a school in a neighbourhood says almost nothing about its importance as a resource to children living there. Similarly, the existence of a public swimming pool says nothing about the opportunities it provides for swimming; we also need to know its size, hours and season of operation, user cost, any restrictions on its use, and what swimming programmes it offers if we are to have any idea about its significance as a resource for children in the neighbourhood.

Although an inventory of relevant environmental opportunities is a basic component of a geography of children and youth, this does not mean that places which are *not* used by children can be totally ignored. Their importance can be justified on several grounds: as moral influences (e.g. erotic cinemas, massage parlours); as sources of pollution; as traffic generators; as providers of services to parents; or simply as occupants of space which must be traversed or bypassed by children to reach places which *are* directly relevant to them. The residents of an adult-only apartment building may object to the expansion or creation of a park or playground proposed by residents of an adjacent building occupied by families with children, thereby influencing directly children's access to play opportunities. Just such a conflict is working its way through the City and Metropolitan governments in Toronto. 'Adult' land uses clearly can have an effect on children's lives.

The Whole City Catalogue project attempted to document the distribution of all the facilities, services, land uses, spaces, places, activities, and programmes relevant to children and teenagers throughout Metropolitan Toronto. To undertake such a massive data collection effort, the cooperation of the senior urban geography teachers in most high schools was enlisted and they arranged for their students to complete a curriculum exercise in which they compiled a map and inventory of all these resources for areas which were assigned to pairs of students. The intention was to compare the distribution of these resources with that of children of various ages and thereby measure neighbourhood differences in children's accessibility to resources. By including public, semi-public, semi-private and private facilities, a more realistic comparison of neighbour-hoods in terms of children's 'environmental opportunities' could be obtained. This supplemented the existing data for public facilities which in many cases were not comparable from one municipality to another in Metropolitan Toronto.

Though well received by students and teachers as a curriculum unit, this data gathering procedure involving so many participants was only a partial success and the Whole City Catalogue as originally conceived will not be completed. Problems of data reliability were greater than anticipated from the pre-tests, partly because of indirect communications between organizers and the students when the project was carried out all across Metropolitan Toronto; there were great variations among classes and students in terms of motivation and ability, also, and in the quality of teacher instruction and follow-up. Fortunately these deficiencies did not affect the other half of the project which yielded usable data. Figures 6.1 and 6.2 show the distribution of all the swimming pools and children in two mainly working class areas for which accurate information was assembled using the student inventories as a starting point. The maps distinguish between types of pools and, in the case of semi-private (apartment) pools, show whether non-residents can use them. Though still not a valid measures of opportunities for swimming since it ignores hours, seasons, sizes, programmes, and pools where an admission fee is charged, Figure 6.3 summarizes children's physical accessibility to swimming pools and shows that by considering apartment pools the *relative* levels of accessibility in the two areas are considerably altered. More valid indices of access to opportunities could certainly be calculated, however, and are a necessary step before any assertion that one area is better served in this respect than another. But by even considering private facilities at all, it can be argued that the survey has gone beyond what geographers and others concerned with urban service distributions typically consider: as noted by Rich (1979, p. 144), 'the distribution of public services has been studied largely without concern for private options for satisfying the same demands.'

Although geographers have contributed to the extensive literature on public facility location, much of their effort has been in the development and application of techniques for the optimal location of such facilities. Political scientists have studied the process whereby public bodies arrive at location decisions, but their interest is more in the process than in the impact on the urban landscape (Simmons and Huebert, 1970, p. 56). However, the growing interest among geographers in the public decision-making process and locational conflicts has ensured that at least some of this interest has been concerned with land uses relevant to children. The literature on school desegregation (Lord, 1977) provides an example of a conflict where the procedure for assigning students to schools has important consequences for residential structure and

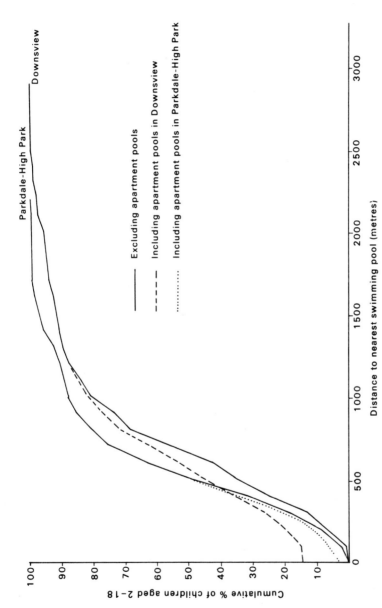

FIGURE 6.3. Accessibility of children in Downsview and Parkdale–High Park to free swimming pools

urban growth patterns. However, 'geographical studies of education in its social and environmental setting lack a strong research tradition' (Herbert, 1976, p. 123), in spite of the inherently spatial nature of important decisions about school facilities, expenditures, and programs made by local education authorities and central governments (Williamson and Byrne, 1979).

As far as a geography of children and youth is concerned, however, the principal lesson to be learned from this exercise is that a host of decisions made by private businesses and corporations, semi-public and semi-private bodies as well as public agencies determine the opportunities to which children living in an area have access. Not only the locational decisions—where a new McDonalds or a new Pentecostal church is to be located, and which schools (if any) should be closed in the face of declining enrolments—but also design considerations, the range and hours of services to be provided at each location, and the regulations regarding children's use of these opportunities must be taken into account if children's access to various opportunities is to be measured more than superficially. Furthermore, the range of government activity and the allocation of funds among various types of public services and facilities may well be more important than the geographical distribution of these services once the decision to fund them at certain levels has been made. Rich (1979, p. 148) maintains that it is in this supremely political activity, i.e., the budgetary process of the legislative body, that the highest stakes in urban politics are to be found. Once the budget has been set for playgrounds, natural ice rinks, group homes for retarded children, day care, or whatever facility or service is in question, the framework for deciding who gets what where has been set. Rich's (1979, p. 145) review concludes that while *public* facilities and services in American cities are not generally distributed in such a way that social classes or ethnic groups are treated very differently, private resources, residents' collective efforts, and abilities to obtain the particular resources desired by the community vary in such a way that the more-or-less equal distribution of public resources among neighbourhoods by no means implies an equality of *de facto* outcomes or an equitable distribution of public resources.

If neighbourhood differences in children's access to opportunities are to be examined in order that the allocation of public resources can redress inequalities and make children's 'life chances' and quality of life more equal than at present, then the data demands are formidable indeed. Not only is it necessary to know exactly where children live and what means of transportation exist for them to get around, but comprehensive information is also needed on a wide range of public and private facilities and services and their characteristics. Information on only a few types of opportunities or only publicly-provided facilities could lead to serious errors in judgment as to how well the present distribution of opportunities matches the distribution of children.

Since the manpower required to carry out a complete inventory of opportunities—public, private and in-between—in a large city, together with information about access, restrictions on use, hours, etc., is enormous, and since the relatively inexpensive method of utilizing high school students to collect data as part of their geography course work has proved too unreliable to yield readily usable data in the Toronto project, doubts exist on the feasibility of such an inventory for a large metropolitan area. With adequate resources, supervision and extensive follow-up checking, high school geography students *can* collect data about the environment, as the mammoth land-use survey in Britain in the 1930s and 1940s under Sir Dudley Stamp's direction demonstrated (Stamp, 1937–46). The existence and characteristics of the specific resources relevant to children and teenagers change so much more quickly than the categories used in conventional land use mapping in largely rural areas, however, that a large number of supervisory and checking staff would be required. The recommendation of Lindberg and Hellberg (1975, p. 19), first to select a *sample* of environments for study, and then a *sample* of children within them, for 'in no other way can we be reasonably confident of obtaining the necessary environmental data without spending the rest of our lives on the matter', points towards a manageable strategy for anslysis of selected city neighbourhoods or smaller cities.

Children's behaviour

As geographers have begun to pay more attention to the actual process whereby individuals decide how their time will be occupied and where and with whom they will pursue various activities, children's behaviour has captured the attention of at least a few. The two decisions which Johnston (1977, p. 121) identified as having received the most attention of behavioural geographers—where to shop and where to live—have been largely ignored as far as children are concerned, except insofar as parents take their children's needs into account in their residential location decisions. Other aspects of children's behaviour have been studied by professionals in various disciplines, but usually these studies have been concerned with particular types of behaviour such as children's play (e.g. Hayward, Rothenberg, and Beasley, 1974; Cooper Marcus, 1974), television watching (e.g. Greenberg and Dominic, 1969; Liebert, Neale, and Davidson, 1973), or delinquency (e.g. Herbert, 1977; Bagley, 1965), or with particular behaviour settings (e.g. Barker, 1968) such as basketball games, playgrounds, or classrooms.

Occasionally, however, researchers have studied a *wide* range of activities of the *same* children for the purpose of establishing the influence of the urban physical environment, including access to opportunities, on how and where children spend their time. Hart (1979), for example, based on extended research with 86 school children in a New England town, has gained much insight into how children experience their surroundings: how far boys and girls of various ages travel from home; how they use their environment; their 'place knowledge', and their 'place feelings'. Payne's (1977) study of children's use of the suburban environment in Calgary also includes an extensive philosophical and methodological discussion on approaches to the study of children's environments. The UNESCO-sponsored studies of adolescents in four countries provide similar types of information in various cultures, and a wealth of methodological suggestions (Lynch et al., 1977).

Farley's (1977) and van Vliet's (1980) attempts to relate teenagers' activities to aspects of the opportunity structure of their neighbourhood are both similar in intent to that part of the Whole City Catalogue project described in this section. The Children's Time Study at the University of California at Berkeley (Medrich, 1977) also shares the aim of evaluating the relative importance of the effects of the family environment and the physical and social components of the neighbourhood on children's activities. However, studies of activity systems have rarely been focused on children or teenagers, and the substantial literature on children and leisure has been more concrned with social class and cultural factors than with the neighbourhood opportunity structure (Rapoport and Rapoport, 1975).

Other approaches to the study of geographical aspects of children's behaviour and lives are found in the geographical literature. The new breed of 'humanistic geographers' has paid attention to adolescents, for example (Ley, 1975; Cybriwsky, 1978), complementing research done in sociology (e.g. Suttles, 1972; Popenoe, 1977). As in almost any subfield of geography, geographers interested in children have more to gain from outside their discipline than within it.

One of the primary purposes of the Whole City Catalogue project was to examine the exent to which children's (actully teenagers') activity patterns vary from one neighbourhood to another in Metropolitan Toronto and the effect access to a range of opportunities has on their behaviour. For this purpose, a questionnaire was completed by a sample of grade 9 students, primarily aged fourteen or fifteen, in most high schools in the metropolitan area. The questionnaire sought information on most types of out-of-school activities; all types of sports, lessons, hanging around in various types of places, going to the library, going to movies, playing pin-ball, visiting with relatives, spending time with friends at each others' homes, responsibilities at home, part-time jobs, etc. For most of these activities, questions were included to obtain information on frequency of participation, usual location, how they get there, with whom they do them, and how much they like doing them. Family background data—size, composition, social class, ethnicity, housing type—were also collected, along with students' attitudes towards and impressions of their neighbourhood.

Analysis of the data remains incomplete, but already some significant differences among neighbourhoods in terms of frequency of participation and modes of transportation have emerged from the questionnaires from two areas chosen for initial examination. As an example, Figure 6.4 shows the relationship between access to public libraries and frequency of visits. Students living closest

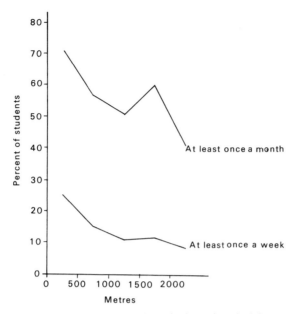

FIGURE 6.4. Frequency of grade 9 students' visits to public libraries by distance from their home to the nearest library, Downsview and Parkdale–High Park areas

go most often and students living more than about 2.0 km. from the nearest library go least. The spacing of libraries, therefore, seems to have an effect not only on *which* libraries teenagers go to, as demonstrated below, but on *how often* they go. The difference between access to libraries in the Parkdale–High Park area and Downsview as shown in Figure 6.5 is reflected in different frequencies of library usage in the two areas (Table 6.1). The actual patterns of travel to libraries shown in Figures 6.6 and 6.7, with 'desire lines' pointing in the direction of the library which each student usually visits, show the quite distinct library service areas. Teenagers almost without exception choose the public library nearest their home.

If it can be shown that access to suitable opportunities has a significant effect on levels of participation over a wide range of activities, as it apparently does in the case of library usage, this will indicate that public and private decisions about the location of opportunities and children are influencing their behaviour patterns. Access is not proposed as the only, or even the most important, influence on children's choice of activities; social class and ethnic background, for example, are probably more important, at least for some activities. Nevertheless, it is argued that if a child has poor access to a reasonable number of opportunities for constructive, purposeful activities, the consequence may

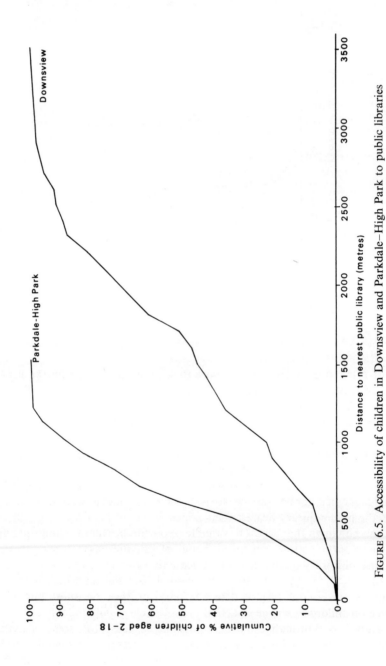

FIGURE 6.5. Accessibility of children in Downsview and Parkdale—High Park to public libraries

TABLE 6.1. Frequency of public library visits by grade 9 students living in Downsview and Parkdale–High Park

| Frequency of public library visits | Downsview | | | | Parkdale–High Park | | | |
| | Male | | Female | | Male | | Female | |
	Number	%	Number	%	Number	%	Number	%
At least once a week	16	9	19	10	20	23	14	20
Once or twice a month	69	38	78	43	38	44	29	42
Less than once a month	71	39	71	39	21	24	22	32
Never	22	12	12	7	7	8	4	6
Not stated	5	3	3	2	1	1	0	0
Total	183	100	183	100	87	100	69	100

be exessive amounts of time spent in passive ways such as simply hanging around streets or shopping centres or watching television. Few would argue against the suggestion that it is better for all concerned if children and youth experiment with and develop a variety of *constructive* pursuits, some of which will become sustaining life interests; and that if a fourteen-year-old does little outside school except hanging around, watching television, and perhaps playing pool and pinball, he is encountering only a very restricted sample of worthwhile experiences—to no-one's benefit. To the extent that a lack of opportunity for alternative pursuits in the neighbourhood contributes to this state of affairs, the public has an obligation to do what it can to rectify the situation by providing a reasonable range of conveniently located opportunities through direct or indirect actions.

A geographic epidemiology of children and youth

The measurement of children's wellbeing falls clearly within the purview of human geography conceived as the 'geography of welfare' or the geography of wellbeing (Smith, 1977). Measurement of wellbeing is most often captured by the documentation of its opposites—pathology and dissatisfaction. Daily life supplies specific reminders—of which adults are increasingly aware—of ways in which the millenium has not come. They monitor air and water quality, noise, and temperature, set standards, and plot distributions of dangers. But the differentiation of threats by age is all too rare. Although children are often threatened by the same factors as adults, their threshold of resistance to these factors is often lower and they come into contact with dangers in different ways. Diseases and deaths are inventoried and analysed with reference to age and location. In some instances, inferences have been justifiably made from correlations relating environmental causes and pathological effects among children. Nonetheless, many threats in the environment have not been analysed

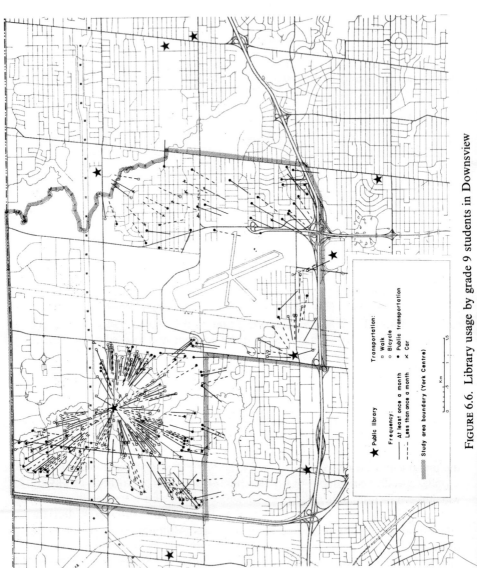

FIGURE 6.6. Library usage by grade 9 students in Downsview

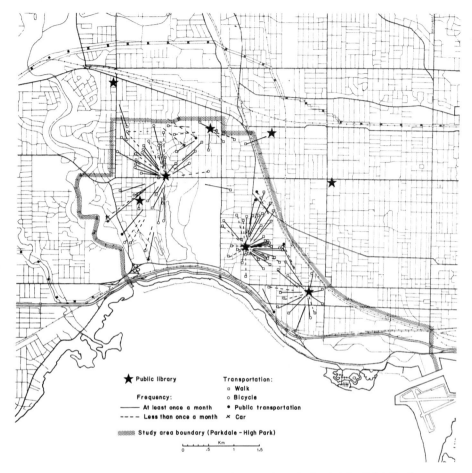

FIGURE 6.7. Library usage by grade 9 students in Parkdale–High Park

for their effects on children, particularly when such effects are not dramatic or deadly in the short run.

Some environmental factors of special concern to children's wellbeing are highlighted in this section. Kane (1976), for example, has sketched the particular sensitivity of children to airborne pollutants. As the result of intense activity, children inhale more outside air per unit of body weight than do adults. When this air is polluted, it has more impact on children than on adults. Furthermore, heavy pollutants are closer to the ground, with the result that children are closer to them both when breathing and when exposed to dirt. The monitoring of airborne particles does not customarily reflect the circumstances under which children are exposed to them. Thus, the serious study of the distribution of atmospheric pollution needs reorientation in order to cover the situation of children. Further, many of the effects of pollution are chronic rather than acute. What this means is that the effects of environmental dangers in this case are not readily apparent upon exposure (see Yankel et al., 1977); they build up and appear only years later, after intellectual, neurological, and motor development have been affected.

In some jurisdictions, children are warned to remain inside and be inactive when pollution levels are high. Nonetheless, a Tokyo study indicated some of the drawbacks of regulating the victim rather than addressing the causes by showing that children who live in more polluted regions and who engage less often in active outdoor play were in turn less healthy as a consequence of reduced outdoor activity (Hirosima, 1977).

There is a large and growing literature on the effects of environmental noise on adults and children alike. This literature suggests that continuous loud noises affect hearing and that intermittent and disruptive noises from uncontrollable external sources affect psychological wellbeing (Stevenson, 1972; Michelson, 1976, ch. 7). The data on children suggest their particular sensitivity to intrusions of noise. Parke (1978), for example, notes that the availability of a private room in which a child can retreat, free from intrusions of all kinds but particularly of noise, is emprically related to children's cognitive development. Cohen, Evans, Krentz, and Stokols (1980) document clearly the disruptive effect in thinking and discourse in schools brought on by intermittent but loud aircraft noise in the vicinity of schools. A now classic study on the effects of noise on children shows a strong relationship between distance from street noise (in this case measured by floor in a high rise building) and the development of auditory discrimination and hence reading ability (Cohen, Glass and Singer, 1973). Despite evidence of this kind, however, standards concerning noise are generally based on adult physiological tolerances, on the one hand, and on the practical marketability of office and residential buildings, on the other. Standards and forms of measurement which bear on children and their development are a challenge to be faced.

Accidents occur in non-random patterns. Even if accidents are, by definition, not intended, certain causes stand out for recognition. The general attitude among adults is that certain potential dangers in children's surroundings, like asphalt and automobiles, are also good and helpful and thus not to be eliminated; one attempts to minimize threats through a combination of vigilance by adults and early training of children. Research on children, however, suggests that vigilance and training are necessary but not sufficient, because children at certain stages of development lack the cognitive and physiological capacities to avoid specific dangers.

Traffic dangers represent a good example. Sandel's careful work for the Swedish Scandia Insurance Company (1974) indicates that, up to about the age of eleven or twelve, children do not see and move in reaction to potential traffic dangers as expected and taught by adults. Traffic is the greatest source of environmental fear for young persons (Moore and Young, 1978, p. 102), rationally enough, because five to nine year olds (old enough for active movement, but too young for adequate adaptation) have the highest pedestrian and bicycle fatality rates (see, for example, Rapoport, 1979a, p. 180; Michelson and Roberts, 1979, p. 435). Children are on foot more than most adults, yet they are more vulnerable than most adults realize. Practically, this suggests a greater need to separate pedestrian from vehicular traffic. More generally, this requires a much greater understanding of the various alternative pathways, how they are created or defined or both, how they are used at present, and how they might be created and (re)allocated in the future. Exploratory research by Bunge and Bordessa (1975), for example, documents the implications for children of different configurations of roads and traffic flow.

Another lesson about children's special safety needs comes from the study of automobile-related injuries. Contrary to expectations, at least one analysis has shown that the majority of automobile-related injuries occur to children, particularly pre-schoolers and older teens, not when they are vulnerable targets on the street but rather when passengers inside automobiles. Furthermore, seat-belt usage by children was shown to be inversely related to both the incidence and severity of injury (Michelson and Roberts, 1979, pp. 435–436). Such figures stress that automobile seats are not routinely designed for children's use, nor do adults and children routinely utilize even the safety equipment they have. Vigilance and training are wasted if routine measures against uncontrollable dangers are not followed. Hence, once again, research for the particular situation of the child is to be encouraged; data on how adults fare under these particular circumstances simply do not cover the same set of dynamics.

Crowding is another phenomenon typically viewed as a danger, and studied accordingly. Few studies have focused on children in this regard, and the weight of scientific evidence on the effects of residential crowding has not been established to any conclusive extent (Gilmore, 1978; Baldassare, 1979). Recent research, however, suggests that density considerations should be viewed with respect to *both* extremes: high and low. Fischer (1976), for example, suggests that much behaviour typically considered as 'urban' is a function of the ability of areas with large clusters of people with particular backgrounds to provide the necessary manpower or clientele for specialized activities, commerce, or services. In other words, cities are more likely to possess the *critical masses* for many more pursuits than areas of smaller scale. The children's literature suggests the need to understand how many other persons are a functional minimum for particular activities, as well as how many others become too many, depending on the situation or activity in question. Barker's theories of overmanning and undermanning may represent a particularly fruitful perspective with which to deal with questions on the quantitative side of social environments and associated behaviours (for example, Barker and Gump, 1964; Wicker, 1979).

In this section, objective factors in wellbeing have been discussed; satisfaction and dissatisfaction, however, may also be addressed more directly through survey methods. The literature about attitudes towards neighbourhood, housing satisfaction, and the like, is almost entirely an adult-based literature (see Marans, 1975). The well-known opinion that families with children prefer suburbs (e.g. Bell, 1968) is based on what adults have said about what they believe their children to think and value, as well as the meaning of alternative environments to themselves as parents. More recent studies have indicated, on the other hand, that under some urban conditions, families with children divide into subgroups which emphasize different locational preferences and that, furthermore, different members of the same family may apply different criteria to the judgment of their residential surroundings (Michelson, 1977; Keller, 1979). Whereas there are no clear data indicating that parents' impressions of their children's opinions are incorrect (Michelson, 1977), there remains the methodological problem of assessing the reaction of children who have relatively little experience in judging alternative environments. The dictum that one should measure dissatisfactions and dangers may hold in this case, but more assessment is needed of the 'disfunctional' elements reported in the lives of respondents.

The survey instrument completed by grade 9 students for the Whole City Catalogue project included questions designed to elicit information on their assessment of safety in their neighbourhood and elsewhere in Toronto. Students were asked to rate their own neighbourhood on a five-point scale from very safe to very dangerous, and to indicate whether there was anywhere in their neighbourhood and anywhere else in Toronto where they were afraid to go and, if so, the reason for their fears. In the two areas for which data have been analysed to date (Downsview and Parkdale–High Park), respondents mentioned places outside their neighbourhood as dangerous much more often than places in their neighbourhood (Table 6.2). The one exception was girls living in Downsview who seemed to be more afraid in their neighbourhood than elsewhere. In both areas, however, only a minority of both sexes admitted to being afraid to go anywhere in their neighbourhood or elsewhere in the city.

TABLE 6.2. Environmental fears among grade 9 students in downsview and Parkdale–High Park

Place of Residence	Sex	Percentage reporting fear of going anywhere in their neighbour-hood	Percentage reporting fear of going anywhere else in Toronto	Sample size
Downsview	Boys	17	31	183
	Girls	40	40	183
Parkdale–High Park	Boys	9	31	87
	Girls	35	48	69

Girls had considerably more fears than boys about their own neighbourhoods, but this sex difference decreased with respect to other parts of town.

The reasons for these fears were overwhelmingly related to people, rather than to physical dangers such as dogs or traffic. Drunks, bums, bullies, gangs, rowdies, roughs, toughs, robbers, muggers, criminals, rapists, murderers, prostitutes, pimps, drug addicts, drug pushers, homosexuals, weirdos, specific ethnic groups, tenants of Ontario Housing, residents of group homes—all these and more instilled fear into substantial numbers of fourteen- and fifteen-year olds. By far the most common locations mentioned for threats were downtown streets. On the five-point safety scale, most students (around 70 per cent) rated their neighbourhood on the safe side, only about 10 per cent as dangerous, with the remainder in the 'neither safe nor dangerous' category. Somewhat fewer girls than boys considered their neighbourhood safe, thereby corroborating the evidence from the question concerning specific types of fears in their neighbourhood.

APPLIED GEOGRAPHY

All the foregoing geographical approaches, in which the dimensions concerning children and youth require increased emphasis, have applied aspects. Nonetheless, major recent thrusts in the field have had to do with environmental management and planning *per se*, indicating the interests and the kinds of persons who come into play in the rough-and-tumble process of establishing and allocating the uses and resources which make up the urban environment (e.g. Harvey, 1973; Sewell, 1971). In this section, therefore, some special consideration required for an intergration of children's environmental interests within this approach are suggested.

Children can, of course, be represented by their parents, and certain parents have more 'clout' than others, by whatever definition chosen. Adults do not systematically recognize the needs and perspectives of children, however, nor do they act for those requirements which emerge for the broad spectrum of children as a class.

A heavy emphasis on future research detailing *only* the *status quo* decision-making and allocation processes concerning children's environmental interests is not justified. It is hardly frivolous to analyse which segments of the adult population, representing which interests, play decisive roles in this regard. Some adult interests take the cause of children, as they perceive them, much more seriously and effectively than do others. Yet in terms of research work with potential impact on the amelioration of children's urban spaces, attention is focused on projects which document the effects of altered and enhanced ways of incorporating children's interests into public policies and procedures.

At all levels of environment which relate meaningfully to children's everyday lives, opportunities occur for experiments and alterations in planning, design, and decision-making. They occur for parents when allocating spaces for many activities, inside and outside their home, with their children. Those planning housing could benefit by the integration of additional child-oriented considerations. The many components of the private and public sectors concerned with the planning and management of neighbourhoods require immediate confrontation with the wide range of children's interests and their integration throughout these areas. At the municipal level, the setting of standards, the allocation of resources, the patterning and financing of public transportation, the initiation of specialized facilities, the preservation of unusual habitats, the mechanisms affecting social groupings and the resultant social climate, and the origin and maintenance of programmes and facilities are all areas subject to innovation, experiment and study. Higher levels of government, while less frequently concerned with specific urban initiatives are, nonetheless, in a position to play supportive roles for lower levels of government and the citizenry itself. In short, the areas for study and application are many and varied in scale and nature.

A particular challenge in this regard lies in how adults can utilize the direct input of children themselves. Research *involving* children is a start, as is sensitive and skilled personal consultation. Although children and youth are less advanced developmentally, there is evidence that their insights and suggestions about those aspects of the world which affect them most directly can be uniquely insightful and helpful (see for example, Pfluger and Zota, 1974). The extent to which young people can assume full partnership is particularly challenging. At present, though, children and youth have little opportunity to exercise control over space, whether at home or elsewhere, and hence to adopt proprietary attitudes towards particular places. It is small wonder that so much youthful rebellion takes the form of vandalism and other property damage. Indeed, it is not beyond the range of scholarly curiosity to inquire about the extent and process of proprietary attitudes towards urban settings on the part of adults who lacked such experience as children and who largely lack feelings of control and identification with regard to many places as adults; the study of place-related civic responsibility is not confined to a single generation, and family dynamics cannot be ignored.

Parallel to the earlier discussion of children's environmental opportunities it is argued that purely spatial phenomena, even when including aspects of design and resources allocation, are not sufficient. Management and supervision of spatial entities should not be forgotten. Much of the debate about adventure playgrounds, for example, reflects the added dimension of low-key, but continuous, supervision which these land uses require. The surveillance and guidance given by supervisors in adventure playgrounds help transform relatively small pieces of land, which have not undergone great amounts of capital improvement, into busy areas involving many children (Cooper Marcus, 1970). One of the pitfalls in the creation of adventure playgrounds comes when municipal departments with traditions of designing and allocating space cannot deal with the incorporation of personnel to the picture, even though initial capital costs are lower.

The way is clear for many types of persons besides children to enter into decisionmaking, design, and allocation bodies which incorporate children's interests in the management of urban space. Parents are an obvious group. So are persons with expertise in the many different areas of knowledge germane to the overall context. These may well include persons not traditionally involved, such as political scientists and lawyers, to cope with both *de facto* and *de jure* aspects of the decision-making involved. Parents and children more clearly reflect knowledge of how things are in a particular place and for a particular group; they can and should be taken into consideration and collaboration regarding the ongoing functioning of the element under consideration, since it is they who are most closely involved and affected. Representatives of higher levels of government or finance or both can reflect, on the other hand, the interests of equity and the distribution of knowledge and resources to those who need them. Academics and others with pertinent knowledge can do more in the interests of children by (1) raising consciousness by facilitating education and the exchange of information, (2) critically reviewing legislation, regulations, and procedures to identify areas requiring improvement, and (3) participating in ameliorative action 'directly' (Michelson and Michelson, 1980).

One traditional approach which has already involved academics, lay people, and decision-makers to some extent on behalf of children has been the setting of standards for open space, recreational facilities, and the like. Many standards have been put forward, including some recent innovations (Esbensen, 1980; Knight, 1980). Research consistent with our earlier discussions would insist on empirically grounded standards which include not just total amounts of required space but also a firm consideration of distributions together with degrees and means of access. These latter considerations deal in a more realistic way with actual use of city space, not just *pro forma* requirements.

A final research consideration is the necessity to take the various considerations of the preceding sections and to deal with them in an *integrated* way. Decision-making, to be effective, must be comprehensive; so, too, must be the data base which supports it. There is no *deus ex machina* in this regard. The Toronto experience indicates just how hard this can be, because the individual elements which go into a 'whole city catalogue' of environmental opportunities for children and youth are themselves often complex and detailed. Macro models, the individual boxes of which have had to be simplified so much as to then reflect contents insensitively, cannot be recommended. Yet, the logic and rationale of integration are inescapable. Integration may represent the most difficult technical challenge to researchers, whilst individual demonstration projects present a social challenge to the *status quo* in urban planning, design, and management.

The plurality of disparate interests and philosophical approaches in urban geography shows little signs of convergence (Johnston, 1980), and it would be foolish to suggest that a geography of urban children and youth could provide a better integrative focus then any other sub-speciality. Nonetheless, the variety of topics, approaches, and considerations represented in this review suggests that many traditional and emerging geographical techniques and approaches can be applied to the study of the geography of children and youth—a group whose very numbers and unique characteristics cry out for more attention than geographers have given them in the past. Such application, furthermore, adds to the completeness and accuracy of the corpus of geographic knowledge. To those whose academic interests will remain exclusively on the adult population, a reminder is given that an *explanation* of adult behaviour must recognize the enduring influence of attitudes, perceptions, and experiences which arise from experiences in urban environments during infancy, childhood, and adolescence (Gold, 1980, pp. 62–75; Mercer, 1975). Whether one is concerned with leisure, environmental perception, residential structure, or a host of other urban geographical interests, researchers who ignore the importance of children and youth do so at the risk of overlooking the contributions which a focus on the world and experience of 'future adults' can provide.

ACKNOWLEDGEMENT

This paper and the research reported in it were made possible by a sustaining grant to The Child in the City Programme at University of Toronto by the Hospital for Sick Children Foundation. Specific research grants from the Ministry of State for Urban Affairs and the Ministry of Employment and Immigration (Canada), and from the Ontario Ministry of Culture and Recreation are gratefully acknowledged.

A UNESCO-sponsored symposium on 'Managing Urban Space in the Interests of Children' was convened by The Child in the City Programme in Toronto, June, 1979. This discussion reflects many of the papers and much of the discussion from that symposium. Edited proceedings are available from the Canadian Commission of UNESCO, Ottawa, Canada, in English and French. An abridged version, appeared as a special issue of the periodical, *Ekistics* in March/April, 1980.

The authors are grateful to Sue Ray and Sandra Knight for typing drafts of this paper and to their other colleagues at The Child in the City Programme, for helpful suggestions and criticisms. Whereas the paper was written under joint authorship, Frederick Hills main contribution is contained in the section on components of a geography of urban children and youth, pp. 202–215.

REFERENCES

Altman, I., and Wohlwill, J., Eds. (1978). *Children and the Environment,* Plenum, New York.
Andrews, H. F. (1973). Home range and urban knowledge of school-age children. *Environment and Behavior,* **5**. 73–86.

Bagley, C. (1965). Delinquency in Exeter; an ecological and comparative study. *Urban Studies*, **1**, 33–50.

Baldassare, M. (1979). *Residential Crowding in Urban America*, University of California Press, Berkeley.

Barker, R. G., (1968). *Ecological Psychology: Concepts and Methods for Studying the Environment of Human Behavior*, Stanford University Press, Stanford.

Barker, R., and Gump, P. (1964). *Big School, Small School*, Stanford University Press, Stanford.

Becker, F. D. (1976). Children's play in multifamily housing. *Environment and Behavior*, **8**, 545–574.

Bell, W. (1968). The city, the suburb, and a theory of social choice. In *The New Urbanization* (Eds. S. Greer *et al*), pp. 132–168, St. Martin's Press, New York.

Boocock, S. (1978). Unpublished report to The Russell Sage Foundation, New York.

Bronfenbrenner, U. (1977). Towards an experimental ecology of human development. *American Psychologist*, **32**. 513–531.

Bruner, J. (1976). The nature and uses of immaturity. In *Play—Its Role in Development and Evolution* (Ed. J. Bruner), pp. 28–64, Penguin, Baltimore.

Bunge, W. W., and Bordessa, R. (1975). The *Canadian Alternative: Survival, Expeditions and Urban Change*, York University Geographical Monographs, No. 2, Toronto.

Chombart de Lauwe, M. J., *et al.* (1976). *Enfant En-Jeu*, Edition du Centre Nationale de la Recherche Scientifique, Paris.

Churchman, A. (1980). Children in urban environments: the Israeli experience. In *Managing Urban Space in the Interest of Children* (Eds. W. Michelson and E. Michelson), Canadian Commission on UNESCO, Ottawa.

Cohen, S., Evans, G. W., Krantz, D. S., and Stokols, D. (1980). Physiological, motivational and cognitive effects of aircraft noise on children. *American Psychologist*, **35**, 231–243.

Cohen, S., Glass, D. C., and Singer, J. E. (1973). Apartment noise; auditory discrimination and reading ability. *Journal of Experimental Social Psychology*, **9**, 407–422.

Cooper Marcus, C. (1970). Adventure playgrounds. *Landscape Architecture Quartly*, **10**, 18ff.

Cooper Marcus, C. (1974). Children's play behaviour in a low-rise, inner-city housing development. In *Childhood City*, Part 12 of *Man–Environment Interaction, EDRA 5* (Ed. R. C. Moore), pp. 197–211, Environmental Design Research Association, Milwaukee.

Cybriwsky, R. A. (1978). Social aspects of neighbourhood change, *Annals, Association of American Geographers*, **68**, 13–33.

Dahlén, U. (1977). *Smahusbarnen*, Liber Förlag, Stockholm.

Durlak, J. G., Layman, J., and McClain, J. (1973). *The School Environment: A Study of User Patterns*, York University Division of Social Sciences, Toronto.

Esbenson, S. (1980). Legislation and guidelines for children's play spaces in the residential environment. In *Managing Urban Space in the Interest of Children* (Eds. W. Michelson and E. Michelson), Canadian Commission on UNESCO, Ottawa.

Farley J. (1977). *Effects of Residential Settings, Parental Lifestyles and Demographic Characteristics on Children's Activity Patterns*, Ph.D. Dissertation, University of Michigan, Ann Arbor.

Fischer, C. S. (1976). *The Urban Experience*, Harcourt, Brace, and Jovanovich, New York.

Gold, J. R. (1980). *An Introduction to Behavioural Geography*, Oxford University Press, Oxford.

Gilmore, A. (1978). *Crowding; An Anatomy of a Spurious Paradigm*, unpublished doctoral dissertation in Sociology, University of Toronto.

Gray, L. , and Brower, S. (1977). *Activities of Children in an Urban Neighbourhood*, unpublished paper, Baltimore City Department of Planning.

Greenberg, B. S. and Dominic, J. R. (1969). Racial and social class differences in teenagers' use of television. *Journal of Broadcasting*, **13**, 331–344.

Gump, P. (1975). *Ecological Psychology and Children*, University of Chicago Press, Chicago.

Hart, R. (1979) *Children's Experience of Place*, Irvington Publishers, New York.

Harvey, D. (1973). *Social Justice and the City*, Edward Arnold, London.

Hayward, D. G., Rothenberg, M., and Beasley, R. R. (1974). Children's play and urban playground environments: a comparison of traditional, contemporary, and adventure playground types. *Environment and Behaviour*, **6**, 131–168.

Herbert, D. T. (1976). Urban education: problems and policies. In *Social Areas in Cities: Volume II, Spatial Perspectives on Problems and Policies* (Eds. D. T. Herbert and R. J. Johnston), pp. 123–158, Wiley, London.

Herbert, D. (1977). Crime, delinquency, and the urban environment, *Progress in Human Geography*, **1**, 208–239.

Hirosima, K. (1977). Natural Conditions for Infants—Their Outdoor Play Environment and Healthiness in Urban Ecosystem. In *Tokyo Project Interdisciplinary Studies of Urban Ecosystems in the Metropolis of Tokyo*, (Ed. M. Numata), pp. 235–50, Chiba University, Chiba.

Johnston, R. J. (1971). *Urban Residential Pattens*, Bell, London.

Johnston, R. J. (1977). Urban geography: city structures. *Progress in Human Geography*, **1**, 118–129.

Johnston, R. J. (1980). Urban geography: city structures. *Progress in Human Geography*, **4**, 81–85.

Kane, D. N. (1976). Bad air for children, *Environment*, **18**, 26–34.

Keller, S. (1979). Planning for children in new communities. In *The Child in the World of Tomorrow* (Eds. S. Doxiadis, J. Tyrwhitt, and S. Nakau), pp. 447–451, Pergamon Press, Toronto.

Knight, J. (1980). Guidelines for planning play spaces. In *Managing Urban Space in the Interest of Children* (Eds. W. Michelson and E. Michelson), Canadian Commission on UNESCO, Ottawa.

Ley, D. (1975). The street gang in its milieu. In *The Social Economy of Cities* (Eds. G. Gappert and H. M. Rose), pp. 247–274, Urban Affairs Annual Reviews, Volume 9, Sage Publications, Beverly Hills.

Libert, R. M., Neale, J. M., and Davidson, E. S. (1973). *The Early Window: Effects of Television on Children and Growth*, Pergamon Press, New York.

Lindberg, G. and Hellberg, J. (1975). Strategic decisions in research design. In *Behavioral Research Methods in Environmental Design* (Ed. W. Michelson), pp. 9–40, Dowden, Hutchinson, and Ross, Stroudsburg, Pennsylvania.

Lord, J. D. (1977). *Spatial Perspectives on School Desegregation and Busing*, Resource paper 77–3, Association of American Geographers, Washington.

Lynch, K., *et al.* (1977). *Growing Up in Cities*, MIT Press and UNESCO, Cambridge and Paris.

Lynch, K. (1978). The spatial world of the child. In *The Child in the City: Today and Tomorrow* (Eds. W. Michelson, S. Levine, and E. Michelson), pp. 102-127, University of Toronto Press, Toronto.

Marans, R. (1975). Survey research. In *Behavioral Research Methods in Environmental Design* (Ed. W. Michelson), pp. 119–179, Dowden, Hutchinson and Ross, Stroudsburg, Pennsylvania.

Medrich, E. A. (1977). *The Serious Business of Growing Up: A Study of Children's Lives Outside of School*, Childhood and Government Project, School of Law, University of California, Berkeley.

Mercer, D. (1975). Perception in outdoor recreation. In *Recreational Geography* (Ed. P. Lavery), pp. 51–69, David and Charles, Newton Abbott, England.

Meyer, D. R. (1971). Factor analysis versus correlation analysis: are substantive interpretations congruent? *Economic Geography*, **47**, 336–343.

Michelson, W. (1976). *Man and His Urban Environment*, Addison-Wesley, Reading, Massachusetts.

Michelson, W. (1977). *Environmental Choice, Human Behavior and Residential Satisfaction*, Oxford University Press, New York.

Michelson, W. (1980). Spatial and temporal dimensions of childcare. *Signs: Journal of Woman in Culture, and Society*, In Press.

Michelson, W., and Michelson E., Eds. (1980). *Managing Urban Space in the Interest of Children*. Canadian Commision on UNESCO, Ottawa.

Michelson, W., and Roberts, E. (1979). Children and the urban physical environment. In *The Child in the City: Changes and Challenges* (Eds. W. Michelson, S. Levine and A. R. Spina), pp. 410–477, University of Toronto Press, Toronto.

Moore, R. (1980). Collaborating with young people to assess their landscape values. In *Managing Urban Space in the Interest of Children* (Eds. W. Michelson and E. Michelson), Canadian Commission on UNESCO, Ottawa.

Moore, R., and Young, D. (1978). Childhood outdoors: towards a social ecology of the landscape. In *Children and the Environment* (Eds. I. Altman and J. Wohlwill), pp. 33–81, Plenum, New York.

Morgan, B. S. (1973). Why families move: a re-examination. *The Professional Geographer*, **25**,124–129.

Parke, R. D. (1978). Children's home environments: social and cognitive effects. In *Children and the Environment* (Eds. I. Altman and J. Wohlwill), pp. 33–81, Plenum, New York.

Parke, R. D., and Sawin, D. B. (1979). Children's privacy in the home, *Environment and Behavior*, **11**, 87–104.

Payne, R. J. (1977). *Children's Urban Landscape in Huntington Hills, Calgary*, Ph.D. Dissertation, University of Calgary, Calgary, Alberta.

Pettyjohn, L. F. (1976). *Factorial Ecology of the Los Angeles—Long Beach Black Population*, Ph.D. Dissertation, The University of Wisconsin, Milwaukee.

Pfluger, L. W., and Zota, J. M. (1974). A room planned for children. In *Design for Childcare*, p. 45, Urban Design Centre, Vancouver.

Piaget, J. (1952). *The Origins of Intelligence in Children*, International Universities Press, New York.

Piaget, J. , and Inhelder, B. (1956). *The Child's Conception of Space*, Humanities Press, New York.

Pollowy, A. M. (1977). *The Urban Nest*, Dowden, Hutchinson, and Ross, Inc. , Stroudsburg, Pennsylvania.

Popenoe, D. (1977). *The Suburban Environment: Sweden and the United States*, The University of Chicago Press, Chicago.

Rapoport, A. (1979a). Balancing safety with adventure. In *The Child in the World of Tomorrow* (Eds. S. Doxiadis, J. Tyrwhitt, and S. Nakou), pp. 479–89, Pergamon Press, Toronto.

Rapoport, A. (1979b). The home range of the child. In *The Child in the World of Tomorrow* (Eds. S. Doxiadis, J. Tyrwhitt, and S. Nakou), pp. 427–428, Pergamon Press, Toronto.

Rapoport, R., and Rapoport, R. N. (1975). *Leisure and the Family Life Cycle*, Routledge and Kegan Paul, London.

Rich, R. C. (1979). Neglected issues in the study of urban service distributions: a research agenda. *Urban Studies*, **16**,143–156.

Rossi, P. H. (1955). *Why Families move*, The Free Press, Glencoe, Illinois.

Sandels, S. (1974). *The Skandia Report II: Why Are Children Injured in Traffic?* Skandia Insurance, Stockholm.
Sewell, W. D. (1971). Environmental perceptions and attitudes of public health officials. *Environment and Behavior,* **3**, 23–49.
Sharonov, Y. (1980). Designing children's spatial environments. In *Managing Urban Space in the Interest of Children* (Eds. W. Michelson and E. Michelson), Canadian Commission on UNESCO, Ottawa.
Siegel, A. W., Kirasic K. C., and Kail, R. V. Jr. (1978). Stalking the elusive cognitive map. In *Children and the Environment* (Eds. I. Altman and J. Wohlwill), pp. 223–258, Plenum, New York.
Simmons, J. W., and Huebert, V. H. (1970). The location of land for public use in urban areas. *The Canadian Geographer,* **14**, 45–56.
Smith, D. M. (1977). *Human Geography: A Welfare Approach,* Edward Arnold, London.
Social Planning Council of Metropolitan Toronto (1979). *Metropolitan Social Profile,* Toronto.
Stevenson, G. N. (1972). Noise and the urban environment. In *Urbanization and Environment* (Ed. T. R. Detwyler), pp. 195–228, Duxbury Press, Belmont, California.
Stamp, L. D. (1937–46). *The Land of Britain,* 9 Volumes, Geographical Publications Ltd., London.
Suttles, G. D. (1972). *The Social Construction of Communities,* University of Chicago Press, Chicago.
Timms, D. W. G. (1971). *The Urban Mosaic: Towards a Theory of Residential Differentiation,* Cambridge University Press, Cambridge.
Tuan, Y-F. (1978). Children and the natural environment. In *Children and the Environment* (Eds. I. Altman and J. Wohlwill), pp. 5–32, Plenum, New York.
Van Vliet, Willem. (1980). Use, evaluation, and knowledge of city and suburban environments by children of employed and non-employed mothers. *Unpublished Ph.D. Thesis,* Department of Sociology, University of Toronto.
Verwer, D. (1980). Planning residential environments according to their real use by children and adults. In *Managing Urban Space in the Interest of Children* W. Michelson and E. Michelson, (Eds.) Canadian Commission on UNESCO, Ottawa.
Ward, C. (1978). *The Child in the City,* Architectural Press, London.
Wicker, A. (1979). *An Introduction to Ecological Psychology,* Brooks/Cole, Monterey, California.
Williamson, W., and Byrne, D. S. (1979). Educational disadvantage in an urban setting. In *Social Problems and the City: Geographical Perspectives* D. T. Herbert and D. M. Smith, (Eds.) Oxford University Press, Oxford.
Wolfe, M. (1978). Childhood and privacy. In *Children and the Environment* I. Altman and J. Wohlwill, (Eds.) pp. 175–222, Plenum, New York.
Yankel, A. J., von Lindern J. H., and Walter, S. D. (1977). The Silver Valley lead study: the relationship between childhood blood lead levels and environmental exposure. *Journal of the Air Pollution Control Association,* **27**, 763–767.

Geography and the Urban Environment
Progress in Research and Applications, Volume IV
Edited by D. T. Herbert and R. J. Johnston
© 1981 John Wiley & Sons Ltd.

Chapter 7

The Spontaneous Geography of the Urban Child

Denise Piché

The continuing task which faces adults of discovering the nature of the geographical environment, its formative processes and evolution, is one of considerable complexity. Of comparable difficulty is the tasks of representing geographical knowledge in cartographic or literary form. For the child with far more limited experience in either the semi-natural countryside or the built environment of the city, these task assume even greater complexity and elusiveness. Yet children have to occupy geographical space and to construct their cognition of the world; such tasks are essential components of their learning process. The term 'spontaneous geography' is used to describe ways in which the child acquires an awareness of geographical space. Research on this theme is limited and has been concerned mainly with urban children and with basic concepts of their use and awareness of space.

Such a perspective in the study of spontaneous geography is not as limited as it may appear at first sight. On the contrary, geographic space cognition presents researchers with a difficult problem that has revived an old debate between the supporters of two different views of development, the incrementalists and the constructivists. The former, such as Pick (1976), assume that children have an innate ability to generate knowledge which simply unfolds with experience. For them, the locus of cognition lies in figurative or abstract accommodations to reality (schema) that are often conceived of as extensions of perception. The latter, best represented by Piaget (1926), states that children actively construct their means of understanding by assimilating the environment and accommodating to it: cognition is located in assimilation *schemes*, that is to say in transformations operated by the child rather than in images of reality. Hence, for the constructivists, cognitive processes involve the *sensori-motor stage* when the infant defines his place in the world in action, the *stage of concrete operations* when the child effectuates his first complete transformations of reality, thus surpassing its appearance, and the *stage of formal operations* when the pre-adolescent begins to elaborate complex rules and relationships.

Developmental stages	Logical operations (classes)	Infralogical operations (space)	Causality	Geographical experience (Piaget and Weil)	Orientation (Hart and Moore)
Sensori–motricity (0–2 years)	object permanence	enacted euclidian space			
Pre–operations: (2–7 years) I Preconcepts II Intuitive representations	graphic collections unstable classes	topological space	{ animism nominalism artificialism	intuitive notions	egocentric
Concrete operations (7–11 years) III a III b	part/whole relationships hierarchical systems	qualitative projective and euclidian space distance, proportion	immanent artificialism	socio–centrism	fixed frame of reference
Formal operations (11–16 yrs)	propositional logic	complex spatial relationships	experimentation	Reciprocity between notions	coordinated system of reference

FIGURE 7.1. Piaget's concept of sequences of a child's development and some associated ideas

A transitory stage is added after the sensori-motor stage, namely the *stage of pre-operations* when the child intuitively begins to represent reality and to relate different observations without yet achieving real concepts (see Figure 7.1 for a more detailed presentation which is based upon Piaget's stages and corresponding chronological ages of children).

Although favouring the constructivist approach with its focus on processes of understanding in a dynamic perspective and its awareness of the integrated nature of development, this essay will nevertheless take into account the arguments of the incrementalists in discussing the development of geographic space cognition and will also consider structuralist views. Space cognition is defined as *the process of creating geographical space and of establishing spatial relationships between positions (placements) and displacements.* There are various methods of approaching this subject. Geographic space cognition will be examined first at the regional scale and secondly at the local urban scale, with the intention of showing the congruence of all aspects of geographic space cognition with Piaget's description of cognitive development.

THE SPONTANEOUS REGIONAL GEOGRAPHY
OF THE URBAN CHILD

In its concern with the description of the Earth's surface, geography is more than a figurative knowledge solely interested in location, diffusion and relationships in space. It has also developed its own 'objects' by separating the continuous surface of the Earth into parts and by assembling various phenomena into units, it has defined distinctive hierarchies of concepts, and it has interested itself in causal processes. In their daily lives, children have in part to re-invent this geographical knowledge and to assimilate the geographical information diffused by their culture. Indeed, in order to make sense of their experience, they actively compare different places, spatially relate places that are disconnected in their temporal experience, question the origin of these places, and learn the names of these and other geographic concepts. If the hypothesis of a general sequence of development is valid, the development of this spontaneous geography should follow the cognitive stages described in Figure 7.1.

Before turning to the literature relevant to an examination of this hypothesis, the dearth of studies on geographic cognition must be explained. Researchers involved in the field of environmental cognition have generally evoked three reasons for turning away from this topic. First, many developmentalists have misgivings about children's verbal behaviour—often thought of as an incorrect index of their real cognitive ability. In seeking to understand geographic knowledge, they would feel unable to rely upon the evidence of verbal behaviour, or indeed of graphic behaviour, which is also considered an inappropriate medium for young children. Within a structuralist approach, this fear is not justified, as, although they are conceived as pertaining to the accommodation side of intelligence rather than to its assimilation side, verbal and graphic responses can always be interpreted in close relation to operative cognitive abilities. As a corollary to the first argument, it can be argued therefore that the best approach to cognitive development is by examination of the child in the process of solving a problem through the active manipulation of the environment. As it is obviously difficult to study children manipulating the Earth's surface, the topic has been largely ignored. The objection is a major one: it is certain that spontaneous geography is not the best subject for studying the way in which the child develops. However, considering the corpus of knowledge on children's assimilation schemes, the assimilation of geographical information and experience within these schemes is possible. The third hypothesis, more typical of environmentalists, suggests that during cognitive development geographic knowledge expands concentrically outward from home to larger regional entities. Of some heuristic value in the elaboration of a curriculum in geography (Hart, 1971), this hypothesis has limited experimental basis in societies where the child is liable to travel, to see images of many places and to come into contact with persons identified by adults as coming from foreign territories.

Despite these caveats, three types of studies have provided evidence that geographic knowledge changes with children's development. Normative studies (for instance, Gesell and Ilg, 1946; Ames and Learned, 1948; Gould and White, 1974) have investigated children's geographic knowledge simply in terms of their ability at answering questions about locations and places. Other normative studies (e.g. Jahoda, 1963; Klinenerg and Lambert, 1967; Hess and Torney, 1967; Eicher, 1977) have examined children's ideas of nationality, foreign people and countries and have focused mainly on the development of political attitudes and prejudices. Finally, research has been concerned with children's experiential apprehension of their local environment (e.g. Spencer and Lloyd, 1974; Parenteau and Pollowy, 1976; Chombart de Lauwe, 1976; Hart, 1979; Becchi and Riva, 1979; Piché, 1979) with a particular focus on the development of their intimate attachment to local space. All these studies have shown that, as they become older, children learn more of the geographic information elaborated by their culture and that they become more flexible in their reference to space. They have not, however, described the Earth's surface as it is understood and constructed by the child. An exception is Hart (1979), who concludes that the local community is the only geographic place of importance to the young child and thus supports Howe's (1931) and Lee's (1963) suggestion that, for the child, places beyond 'home' lie in an 'elsewhere' schema.

Although Hart's interpretation of development in which the young child refers to places where events happen and later progressively fixes them in space is acceptable, an empirical test (Piché, 1977) shows that even young children have images of distant places and that their representation of 'home' is never conceptualized before that of 'elsewhere'. The implications are many but only the very few studies (Piaget, 1924; Piaget and Weil, 1951; Jahoda, 1963; Rand, 1973) that have focused exclusively and deeply upon the structural basis of geographic knowledge constitute a valid demonstration of its congruence with Piaget's main sequence of development.

Piaget, as early as 1924, investigated the notion of 'country' by asking children if they were Genevese or Swiss: he found that pre-operational children thought of Switzerland as a simple unit besides the place where they lived, while, at the stage of concrete operations, they visualized a country as an area surrounding cities such as Geneva. It is only in the stage of abstract operations that they finally attain correct geographic notions and relationships. The author character-ized the pre-operational attitude as 'nominal realism', since for the child a name gives an exclusive identity to a geographical element. Piaget (1926) has also partly examined children's spontaneous geography from the point of view of geomorphology and found that children's conceptions of the origins of the Earth progress from attitudes of *animism*, whereby everything is considered alive, and *artificialism*, whereby everything is explained as being man-made, to an idea of *immanent artificialism*, whereby nature becomes an explanation in itself, albeit a purposeful explanation, until the child develops formal operations. *Egocentricism*, or the privileged place the child reserves for himself in his conception of the world, is another attitude that has been studied by Piaget and Weil (1954), who found that the intuitive child does not yet understand the notions of country and foreigner. However, as soon as the notion of country appears, the child develops an affective relation to the 'terra patria' and begins to judge foreigners; but it is not until the age of eleven years that he will understand the reciprocity of these notions and that he himself is a foreigner to others.

Following Piaget, Jahoda (1963) questioned children aged six to eleven years about Glasgow, Scotland, Britain, and other towns and countries. He classified children's verbal answers into four classes: (1) no conception of Glasgow as a unitary whole; (2) conception of Glasgow, but not as a part of Scotland; (3) conception of Glasgow as a part of Scotland, but not of Britain; and (4) correct conception. However, in checking his subjects' verbal answers against their representation of spatial relationships, Jahoda did not duplicate this elegant concentric development of geographic thought. It appeared rather that children at stages 1 and 2 had no organized spatial representation (6–7 years old), that at stage 3 very few were really understanding their own verbal formulation (8–9 years old) and that in stage 4 (10–11 years old) around 12 per cent retained characteristics of stage 1.

As an extension of these studies, Piché (1977) studied children's progressive objectification of the Earth's surface through clinical interviews with 5 to 8 year olds in London, involving drawing and mapping exercises and geographic puzzles. Questioning first surveyed their experience of place in their neighbour-hood and 'elsewhere' and subsequently developed in different ways for each individual but with the same objectives of examining how they divided the continuity of space into places, interpreted names of places and land-uses, structured the continuity of geographic space and comprehended hierarchies of geographic concepts and, finally, explained, identified with, and judged the world.

The analysis confirmed the general hypothesis of a main sequence of development. It suggested that there is no difference in the comprehension children have of proximate space and distant space: a correct conceptualization of 'here' is necessarily related to a conception of 'elsewhere', and complete comprehension of the nature of urban land involves an understanding of rural land. In addition, it showed that children develop their notion of geographic space and their classification of geographical objects in tandem.

The pre-conceptual child experiences places where things happen and imagines them in terms of a few features related to personal activities, independently of a geographic frame of reference. These places are singular and therefore not comparable in their general aspects. The active, affective and cognitive aspects of the relationship with environment are intermingled.

From the age of five (stage of representation), the child tries to name places and to qualify them in terms of land use, but proceeds by comparing only two places at a time, never maintaining consistent criteria of comparison for each assessment. When confronted with contradictions, the child will return to the notion of 'singular places': for instance, a child says that 'here, the market, city, town, Germany and America' are all places because one could go there. Moreover, there is greater difficulty in classifying local territory as opposed to other places: for instance, though qualifying another area of London as townscape, a child will insist that his house is *on* a street and not *in* a town. None of the places referred to by the child has a spatial extension and relations between places in the local area are conceived of in terms of the child's own displacements in the same ways as relations between places 'elsewhere' are imagined in terms of vehicular displacements directed by omniscient persons.

During the transition to the stage of concrete operations, the child compares phenomena more actively and discovers more constant notions. There is an eagerness to solve contradictions and to order the world. As a result, land uses can be identified. Paying more attention to displacements in space, the child begins to conceptualize the continuity of the land even though these conceptual schemes are not yet in equilibrium. Under the pressure of socio-cultural surroundings, the child is forced to imagine place hierarchies such as 'home— London—England' and 'village—town—cities within countries', but then invents such solutions as 'my house is linked with London by roads' (Figure 7.2a), 'London surrounds Buckingham Palace', 'England is linked with London', 'England is fixed or juxtaposed to London'.

At the same time, the child imagines the continuity of the land in terms of long and complex displacements; for instance, London is big because one can drive

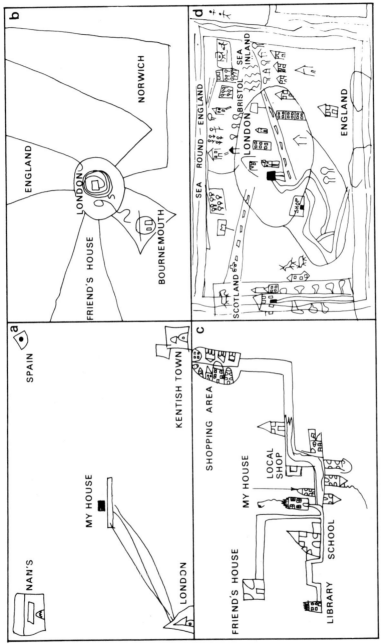

FIGURE 7.2. Children's representation of regional space

for a long time and still be in London, Bournemouth is far away because it takes a long time to get there, and the route between Bournemouth and London is represented as a spiral (Figure 7. 2b). At this stage, foreign places are imagined by the child as real places which can be visited but they are very personalized.

In the first half of the stage of concrete operations, there is an interesting lapse of time when the child seems to solve sub-logical problems such as the addition of places as continuous land and the seriation of displacements without yet solving logical problems such as the inclusion of places in regions and the coordination of locations and displacements. For instance, in the map in Figure 7.2(c) a child connects displacements and various places, but does not yet represent a road network. Another child (Figure 7.2(d)) maps England in a topographical conformity to reality but affirms that England surrounds London. There is no doubt that these representations are very important intermediary tools permitting the child to assimilate more adequate geographical concepts, but they are spatially correct only in appearance because, for the child, they are not yet spatial representations of reality. Such maps have been analysed quantitatively by Klett and Alpaugh (1976) for their scale, perspective and level of abstraction, but although the precision of this approach is appealing, it is rejected here because the observation of children while drawing gives access to better interpretations of their cognitive processes. A map at this stage is still a pure accommodation to the child's spontaneous ideas even though some of its elements may appear abstract. For example, when the author of Figure 7.2(d) was asked about the location of the sea at Bristol, she did not refer to the sea surrounding England; she simply drew another sea, inland.

Finally, towards the end of the stage of concrete operations children have developed notions of classification, seriation, and spatial continuity. Geographical imagination is then objective in its concrete form and the child is ready to tackle complex mapping problems and analytical questions.

In sum, the development of geographic knowledge does not present itself as being incremental, but it rather consists of the integrated construction by the child of all geographical notions in a parallel with Piaget's main sequence of development. This is not to say that the child experiences all places in the same way. On the contrary, Lee's 'elsewhere' schema was confirmed in the London study. This observation simply underlines that representations of proximate and distant places must be related together through operations before they are included in a single geographical space.

What is the relative influence of free exploration, travelling experience, verbal information, and operations on the observed sequence of development? Active exploration and manipulation of space have been at the centre of all explanations of the development of environmental cognition. These actions certainly develop the child's interest in the environment, but no comparison of more or less adventurous children has ever been attempted with respect to their geographical understanding. Piché's study of urban children has not identified any problematic feature of the urban experience involving representation of geographic space. Some of the evidence at least suggests that experience in the environment is not a sufficient explanation for development and the most experienced children did not in fact necessarily possess a more elaborate representation of the Earth's surface. It also appeared that the verbal and graphical information given to children stimulates their geographical imagination by attracting their attention to specific aspects of the environment and by facilitating comparisons between land uses, without constituting a sufficient condition of geographic understanding. An assessment of geographical lessons in books and educational television programmes has clearly demonstrated that they do not induce automatic understanding.

All evidence presently available shows that experience and information are structured by the child according to existing schemes of assimilation, although they can stimulate the transformation of unstable schemes. These assimilation schemes are general cognitive tools resulting from the composition of many different actions of the child, not simply actions in geographic space, and therefore explanation of geographic understanding does not reside solely in the latter. But the *interactive* effect of experience, assimilation and accommodation schemes such as language and images in the development of regional geographic cognition would require further attention, especially in the form of comparative studies and educational experimentations.

CHILDREN'S CONCEPTION OF URBAN GEOGRAPHICAL SPACE

As space is the fundamental organizational concept in geography, it is predictable that studies of children's geographic notions focus on their understanding of the location of places and the spatial relationships among them. Children's representation of geographical space at the national scale, as discussed in the preceding section, has important heuristic limits for the researcher because it can only be analysed qualitatively. Exact knowledge of this scale will only be acquired by the child through an examination of culturally-given representations, such as maps. In order to understand how the child learns to interpret such representations, it is necessary to examine how the correspondence between reality and these representations is established and how both qualitative and quantitative spatial notions are constructed. For this purpose, only the spatial scales that the child controls in action can be studied; the perceptual scale much studied by psychologists is inadequate because it does not conserve the *specific* property of geographical scale and urban space. We shall therefore now turn to the analysis of the child's representation of geographic space within its own exploration range according to two lines of inquiry: firstly, the study of children's representation through orientation and route problem-solving and, secondly, through their expression of spatial relationships in models and maps.

entation and way-finding in geographical space

on and finding one's bearing and way are basic 'geographical' skills.
ve by progressively determining positions in relation to landmarks,
ndmarks in relation to self and by learning sequences of displacements
betwee two landmarks. The mechanisms sustaining these operations have
received much attention (for good reviews see Howard and Templeton, 1966;
Shemyakin, 1962; and Paillard, 1974). Leaving aside the respective interests of
cerebral physiology and sensory modalities, this discussion will concentrate on
the hypothetical construct of 'mental representation' or 'mental map', which
has become the focus of recent research (Shemyakin, 1962; Kaplan, 1963;
Downs and Stea, 1973; Downs and Stea, 1977; Siegel *et al.*, 1978).

Since the beginning of the Hull-Tolman controversy, experimental psychologists have examined the relative validity of both Hull's sensorimotor connections and Tolman's mental maps as explanations of orientation. Amongst
students of behaviour in real environments, it seems that only the second of these
explanations has been considered and assessed. The concept of mental map
remains non-specific. Siegel *et al.* (1978 p. 225), in 'stalking the elusive cognitive
map', even admit to using it 'for the purpose of linguistic economy, knowing
that it is a convenient fiction'. Only Pailhous (1969; 1971; 1972), in his study
of urban space-learning in adults, has really demonstrated that the concept is
operational and valid but only if it is studied as a process and not as an image.
With respect to the child's geographic cognition, the role of representation in
orientation and way-finding must be analyzed to test the validity and necessity
of the mental map construct and to describe its development in terms of
process.

If Piaget's interpretation of development is correct, abstract representation
is not a necessary tool in order to find one's bearings and way. Indeed, he has
shown how sensori-motor adaptation can be a sufficient explanation of the
child's construction of space during the first two years of life. The infant
progresses from an egocentric confusion of self and the environment—when
space is entirely defined by the property of personal actions—to a practical
apprehension of Euclidian space whereby self and objects have positions in
space (Piaget, 1937; Acredolo, 1976; Lucaz and Uzgiris, 1977). In this context,
Bruner (1966) talks of *enacted* representation. In its achieved form, towards
the age of 18 months, this enables the child to view different routes in perceived
space (Piaget, 1937), to recognize modifications in the relative position of objects,
(Lyublinskaya cited in Shemyakin, 1962) and to orient self with reference to
the *objective* frame of reference of objects in space rather than according to
egocentric, learned motor habits (Acredolo, 1976). In this model of transperceptual space, the child directs itself step by step according to the perceived
environment and a sensori-motor scheme of general direction.

During the stage of pre-operations, the child progressively imitates internally actions *in* and *on* space, thus constructing an initial spatial representation, which is iconic and egocentric. As a figurative scheme, this gives way to the representation of topological relationships and sequences of displacements. How does this new acquisition affect performance on orientation and way-finding tasks? When are sensori-motor schemes, or quasi-automatic responses, a sufficient explanation of behaviour and when is representation a mediator? In order to answer these questions, researchers must find experimental situations in which the cognitive processes, especially representation, show through, a requirement that has kept most of them in laboratories.

Pick and Acredolo and their collaborators have reported interesting results with respect to the apprehension of positions in space and the selection of landmarks. *Pick et al.* (1973) have analysed four and five year-olds' representations of the spatial layout of their houses and found that, although the house is well known in practice, its representation is still intuitive. As regards orientation, the child is only beginning to identify unseen spaces behind the walls of various rooms. These representations are not yet abstract, but are an internalization of the child's perceptual activities; the same child fails when asked to point in the directions of rooms located in a different horizontal plan (Pick and Lockman, 1979), to identify adjacent rooms in settings where perceptual cues are limited to a minimum (for instance by sound-proof walls—Neumann, 1979), or to deduce the juxtaposition of rooms in a building other than that currently occupied (Pick *et al.,* 1973). These intuitive representations conserve only spatial topological relationships. Therefore the child forms an approximation of each position in space relevant to specific cues or landmarks rather than an exact position according to all information. In this way, Acredolo *et al.* (1975) found that space differentiation has a significant effect on the performance of three-to-five year old children in remembering where a key has been dropped along a corridor, but not on eight-year old children who possess rudimentary metric and Euclidian notions.

Acredolo (1976; in press, a) further tested the child's development of spatial frames of reference for orientation by examining the performances of three, four, five, and ten year-old children in experimental conditions which created conflicts between egocentric (in a sensori-motor sense), object-related and container-related frames of reference. Results indicate that during the pre-operational stage children orient themselves according to the position of landmarks, but that, in difficult situations such as conflicting frames of reference, lack of differentiation in the environment and large spatial scales, three year-old children will often turn to egocentric sensori-motor responses. Acredolo also implies that between three and four years of age children acquire a greater competence in composing their displacements and therefore in keeping track of their own position in space. These findings suggest that the pre-operational child, through intuitive representations, can solve simple orientation problems, but that indexation to landmarks remains a main problem-solving process.

If pre-operational children direct themselves according to landmarks in a real environment, they face the problem of selecting relevant landmarks. A spatially competent child may well select improper landmarks as Acredolo's observations suggest that children's performances differ according to the landmarks they take into consideration. Direct landmarks (those in proximity to the aim of the subject) and objects (unstable landmarks) are selected more often by intuitive children than are indirect and container landmarks (those pertaining to the scene). Many studies (Spencer and Lloyd, 1974; Sandels, 1975; Piché, 1977; Hart, 1979) have observed a similar phenomenon in real settings, where children focus their attention on the objects they value rather than on landmarks which would be more useful for orientation. Siegel (1979) further confirmed that incompetence in selecting landmarks is an important trait among young children. When the attention of young children was on the landmarks usually selected by older children in order to learn a route, they performed much better than when they were selecting their own points of reference.

Orientation is mostly a function of the use of landmarks for young children, but studies have also shown that children can compose simple displacements in a small space (Kosslyn *et al.*; 1974, Acredolo, in press, b). On the other hand, Pick *et al.*, (1973), in their study of children's representation of their houses, report that the five year-old child cannot explain the route from bedroom to kitchen. It seems that pre-operational children can act out displacements without yet representing them efficiently. Moreover, these studies suggest a parallel evolution of the representation of placements and displacements: for instance, Acredolo's results imply a consistency in development of enacted displacements and placements whilst Pick *et al.*'s findings imply a coherence in the development of their representation.

Pinol-Douriez (1975), in one of the few other studies of this topic, led blindfolded children aged four to fifteen years through a series of paths and afterwards asked them to reproduce their displacements in action (posturo-kinetic response) and graphically. Such tasks are very difficult from evidence of low global performances observed. Analytical scoring indicated that a four year-old can only enact simple displacements but that, a few months later, graphic representation develops rapidly and overtakes posturo-kinetic responses. It is only towards the age of fifteen that performances will be equal on the two tasks. The rapid growth of graphic representation was ascribed by Pinol–Douriez to an internalization of displacements in an intuitive manner that makes possible an analysis of the sequence of displacements. This occurs first in terms of straight segments and right angles and much later in terms of oblique segments and other angles, but is not powerful enough for the task of orienting and guiding complex practical displacements. It becomes a useful tool only when it is completely *semiotized* as a result of a complete composition of displacements. The author observed the same turning points in development as Acredolo: at about four years of age, children can relate a few simple displacements in the same way that they rely more efficiently on a few landmarks for orientation and at about the age of eight begin to represent complex displacements in the same way as they rely on Euclidian properties of space for orientation. This similarity confirms once more the reciprocal development of the representation of placements and displacements and partly disqualifies Siegel and White's (1975) hypothetical sequence of development which stated that landmarks are represented by the child *before* routes.

None of the studies reported so far has dealt with urban space. Following Pick *et al.*'s findings on the difficulty children experience in pointing out directions on the vertical axis and Pinol-Douriez's findings on the composition of displacements, it is possible to hypothesize that *representation in abstract terms will not be a mediator of orientation and way-finding in such space before the child is eight years of age.* Consequently, if this hypothesis is correct, we must examine how intuitive internal imitations of displacements and topological indexation to landmarks can explain urban orientation and if there are orientation problems that cannot be solved at the pre-operational stage.

With this purpose in mind, twenty children (selected from the first part of a study on spontaneous geography according to stage of development, were taken to a typical London residential area, well differentiated by a number of landmarks, with the aims of (a) examining how they would learn their way about in the site (Figure 7.3(b)) how they would discover new routes, and (c) how

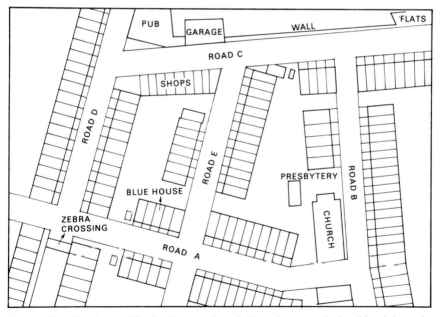

FIGURE 7.3. The site used for basic tests of spatial learning: a typical residential area in London which is well differentiated by landmarks

they would orient themselves. Each child was taken individually around the site twice and, during a third walk, directed into the middle road (E). A trinket was hidden in front of a landmark (a blue house) which was the point of both departure and arrival for the three walks. Besides being asked to map the way, the child was asked—at four stopping points—to explain verbally the route already followed, to point in the direction of the trinket, and to suggest a new route, to reach the trinket.

The results indicated that early intuitive children learn routes as a series of practical displacements coordinated with a few landmarks. They can neither explain nor predict routes, nor can they point at unseen places. On the other hand, they have already developed *algorithms* which facilitate their learning: for instance, they index places not only relative to landmarks but also to whole scenes (gestalt) and they construct sequences of displacements into *patterns* such as 'round the block'.

During the intuitive stage, children begin to organize routes into segments and to imagine general directions. They predict the route to follow by degrees and they find the trinket at the end of the walk as a result of indexation to landmarks. However, they are still referring to landmarks and displacements within *egocentric* intuitive representations and their cognitive schemes are not yet flexible and reversible. As a result, even though they realize that the shops are at the end of road E when standing at the corner of road A and E, they cannot predict the way to the trinket through road E when positioned in road C.

At the beginning of the stage of concrete operations, they often fail at tasks achieved earlier: for instance, they will not find the trinket at the end of the walk, a regression that seems partly due to their concern with trying to represent the site and the consequent neglect of concrete cues such as landmarks. These children are obviously coordinating portions of space, because they can point at directions in simple cases. They also possess schemas representing typical urban land-use because they can predict part of a new route: for instance, they try to use their representation of 'round the block' as a predictive tool, but they do not yet succeed in closing the network at the trinket, often passing by the blue house and looking for the trinket further down road A. Their main achievement is the representation of the road network (a topological transformation) in such a way that they can predict the shorter route through road E.

To summarize, if imitative representation of displacements, perceptual images of the environment and ability to conserve simple topological properties of space are sufficient conditions for learning one's way in urban space, coded representation of 'projective' and Euclidian space seems important for finding new ways and acknowledging general directions. However, at the stage of development studied, these coded representations are not yet refined: indeed, as we have already seen, children do not succeed at complex compositions and, as we shall see later, they do not yet reproduce the site in all its Euclidian properties.

With respect to geographical space, development seems to take on a spiral form alternating assimilation and accommodation schemes in the following succession: practical co-ordination of displacements and landmarks (assimilation); internal imitation of displacements (accommodation); simple composition of displacements (assimilation); more semiotical representation (accommodation); first real cognitive transformations of spatial relationships (assimilation); and more abstract representation (accommodation). This hypothesis should however be tested further as, in addition to the overall direction of development, many points of detail have been observed. These include the discrepancy between orientation based on topological indexation to landmarks and the achievement of strategies for remembering relevant landmarks and also between the construction of algorithms such as 'round the block' and the representation of a long sequence of displacements.

Research is still in its early stage. Apart from Pinol-Douriez, nobody has investigated orientation or way-finding along the whole developmental period of representation (from age two to sixteen). However, the multiplicity of strategies adopted by children and the specific effect of different urban forms on their development is already evident (Parenteau and Pollowy, 1976). The problem-solving approach is an excellent means for studying further the representation of geographic space; theoretical interpretations of children's performance in terms of representation can be cross-checked with their expression of these representations in the form of maps and models. Neglect in the use of this procedure to date is probably because it is cumbersome and inconvenient.

Children's representation of local space

Because a problem-solving approach is inconvenient for studying children's representation of geographic space, researchers have turned to children's expressions of their representation in models and maps. The validity of this approach is indisputable, but results have emphasized the contrast between Piaget's constructivist theory and empirical incrementalism. Whereas constructivists have focused their attention on the operative (transformative) aspects of representation, incrementalists have analysed its figurative side.

Piaget was probably the first to report data on children's ability to represent geographical space in maps and models. In a first experiment (Piaget and Inhelder, 1948), he asked children to represent a model village in drawings (bird's eye and 45° views) and in models (at a similar scale and at a smaller scale). In a second experiment (Piaget et al., 1948), he instructed children to draw the route from their school to their house and to model in a sandbox their familiar urban environment including their house and school; subsequently he examined ways in which they could reorganize part of the model when the school was rotated 180°. Similar patterns of development were observed in both cases, with a difference of two years in favour of the first. Pre-conceptual children usually play with the model. Intuitive children reproduce small areas of a site, bringing together objects in pairs at the geographical scale, but they cannot locate metrically and projectively each element according to a comprehensive frame of reference. They remember routes in urban space through internal imitations of practical displacements, at times ordering unidimensionally landmarks along their course. At the beginning of the stage of concrete operations, the child tries, in the model village situation, to locate each object according to the whole site, though he is unable yet to gauge distances, reduce the scale, and recognize a model after one of its components has been subjected to a 180° rotation. At the geographical scale, similar objective spatial relationships can be represented, but only for part of the site at a time. In the second part of the stage of concrete operations, the child takes into account distance and a comprehensive frame of reference and can reduce the scale of a model. From there on, the child will develop an ability to represent a layout in a completely formal manner calling on conventions and symbols.

Many authors (Asmussen, 1971; Mark, 1972; Maurer and Baxter, 1972; Thornberg, 1973; Hart, 1979) have confirmed Piaget's main sequence of development in their study of children's models of different large-scale settings. Towler (1970) also discovered a similar form of development—with a delay of two years by comparison to Piaget's observations—in his analytical examination of the transformations implied in mapping, that is to say distance, reference-system, direction, and scale (Towler and Nelson, 1968).

Among the incrementalists, Stea and Blaut (Blaut et al., 1970; Blaut and Stea, 1974; Stea and Blaut, 1973; Stea and Taphanel, 1974) have been the most active advocates of very young children's skills at mapping and modelling; for them, 'the child is already a mapmaker at the age of three'. By way of demonstration, Blaut et al. (1970) report that a three year-old can model an urban landscape and drive a toy-car in it. A similar achievement has been observed at the same age by Piaget (1946), who interpreted it, however, as play rather than as representation, because the task consisted of imaginary assimilation without any accommodation to reality. On asking children to reproduce a real environment, Pick et al. (1973) and Siegel and Schadler (1977) observed behaviour much more similar to that reported by Piaget. For instance, Siegel and Schadler asked five year-olds to reproduce their classroom with model furniture within a model of its architectural shell and found that intuitive children could duplicate local areas with accuracy but not the whole classroom. However, at the same time they proved their hypothesis of incremental development by showing that children more familiar with the classroom obtained significantly higher global scores. On the other hand, their argument in favour of familiarity and experience as an explanation of representation further confirms Piaget's theory. Indeed, familiarity is more effective since intuitive topological indexing is an inefficient intellectual strategy. Operational schemes allow the older child to overcome space and time difficulties in representations of architectural and geographical spaces.

Observed discrepancies in performance at isomorphic spatial problems can also be interpreted in terms of facilitating characteristics. Acredolo (in press, b) and Herman and Siegel (1978) compared different situations and show how environmental scale and complexity may facilitate topological indexation strategies. Context, in a similar way to familiarity, has more influence on intuitive children than on operational children who can manipulate projective and Euclidian transformations.

Although most research can be understood within Piaget's model of development, one important question concerning the representation of geographic space has not really been discussed in the past—Why can children represent small groups of objects in space but not the relationships between these groups? In order to answer this question, the ways in which children construct a representation of small portions of space will be examined and the possibilities of applying these mechanisms to large scale space will be explored. Piaget suggests that topological indexation explains the intuitive representation of small spatial areas, but this is an insufficient explanation in the context of geographical space. It is not topology as such that is easy for the child, but rather the intrafigural properties of space that can be apprehended through perception and constructed through intuition. In Piaget's scheme of modelling, intuitive and early operational children may assemble a few buildings correctly because these buildings belong to the same place in their experience. According to Hart's (1979) analysis of models of their small town by four to ten year-old children, even those aged six years or less are able to use a fixed-frame of reference, in this case a 'domocentric' one, in order to position all familiar objects relative to one another in the cluster of their home. However this ability to represent the home cluster does not warrant an explanation in terms of a fixed-frame of reference that implies Euclidian and projective transformations. The child at this stage is simply able to deal with the intrafigural character of the 'home cluster' and with the anthropomorphic character of the architectural object (a house has a front and a back). Moreover, familiarity will facilitate topological indexation.

If children cannot structure places such as their neighbourhood or town, it is obviously because displacements have a role to play in the representation of transperceptual space. On the other hand, we have seen that children during the intuitive stage can compose simple displacements (Acredolo, in press a; Piaget et al., 1948) and Piaget has shown that at the beginning of the stage of concrete operations children seriate landmarks along their routes. Why then can they not structure their representation of urban space? A few analyses (Appleyard, 1970; Moore, 1975) of adults' maps of urban areas have described many as 'partially co-ordinated'; such maps are in fact linearly connected, a consequence of the form of urban space where one usually travels back and forth along linear road segments. Children are similarly confronted with linear order; this may well explain the *dislocation* in their representation of urban space. What will happen if they have to learn a portion of urban space where roads are part of a circular network, as in Figure 7.3? This is one of the questions examined in a project already described (Piché, 1977). Of primary interest was the relevance of actions in geographical space to the development of cognition as it is postulated by Piaget *et al.* (1948), Hart and Moore (1973), and Hart (1979). After the series of walks in the site, the children were asked to build a model of the area using a complete set of model elements.

The results showed that the children used topological relationships in order to represent their displacements as well as the position of elements within small clusters. Their models were not linear and positional, but were usually circular and connected in terms of a network, yet they could not co-ordinate representation of placements and displacements. Pre-conceptual children retained only a vague impression of the site once they had left and therefore modelling was considered a play activity. Already during the intuitive period, however, they had developed images of placements and displacements: most children at this stage first gave to their model the form of a square according to their 'round the block' scheme, though they placed the landmarks arbitrarily, with the exception of the cluster of the shopping area (Figure 7.4a). During this stage, they perfect this use of their displacements as a frame of reference and the placement of landmarks according to the linear and circular order of their displacements, although they do work in *one* of these two perspectives at a time as Figure 7.4(b) shows. At the beginning of concrete operations, the child has achieved a rather good topological representation of the site (Figure 7.4(c)), which is an excellent figuration for reflecting space on a more abstract level but does not yet conserve any projective and Euclidian relationships. This intuitive scheme is the missing link in explaining the transition from intuition to operation with the development of geographic space cognition. It is on representation of this type that the child will carry out the first concrete operations, which will enable the construction of an overall model of the site using a general frame of reference (Figure 7.4(d)).

Although this review has been limited to modelling tasks, these have often been proposed in preference to mapping as the best means for studying children's representation of geographic space. Comparisons of the alternative approaches, however, have never received formal attention. Mapping has been relegated because of perceived difficulties in the interpretation of graphical representations. It has been claimed that because it is a projective medium, has a culturally developed form and calls for technical skill it may hide the child's real intellectual competence. Both Lemen (1966) and Goodnow (1977), however, have demonstrated how drawing, instead of obscuring cognition, is 'truly visible thinking' when it is considered as a process rather than as a product; with care the difficulties of interpretation can be overcome.

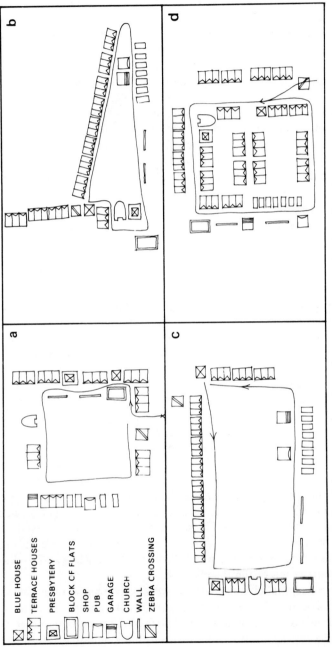

FIGURE 7.4. Attempts by children to model the urban site

Figure 7.4 provides a further argument in favour of the legitimacy of this approach. Children clearly find it difficult to model roads with discontinuous elements. Drawing is certainly a better way to show displacements because the micro-action of the hand provides the most suitable medium of representation. Descriptions and classification of children's drawings of geographic and urban space are numerous: Shemyakin (1962), for example, says that six to eight year-olds represent a locality by a method of tracing familiar routes, without making any reference to other roads, but that eight year-old children represent other roads as off-shoots of their own routes and by the age of twelve years can interconnect them (for other descriptions, see Klett and Alpaugh, 1976; Stea, 1976; Catling, 1978; 1979). However, the interest of children's maps resides in their mode of production and Pinol-Douriez (1975) presents the best interpretation of the representation described by Shemyakin and others.

The assumption is that between five and eight years of age, children draw maps of displacements by projecting their internal imitations of macro-actions into their graphic response rather than as perfectly semiotic representations. By way of demonstration, the interactive effects of graphic (G) and posturo-kinetic (P) responses are examined by comparing the performances of children who initially represented their displacements graphically ($G_1 P_2$) with children who gave graphic responses only after posturo-kinetic responses ($P_1 G_2$). Besides finding that children perform better graphically ($G > P$) from the age of four and a half years to the age of twelve years, between the ages of five and eight years there is no positive transfer from graphic responses to posturo-kinetic responses ($P_1 \nprec P_2$), but something more resembling a confusion effect of posturo-kinetic responses on graphic responses ($G_1 > P_1 > G_2$). A positive transfer from graphic responses to posturo-kinetic responses ($G_1 > P_2 > P_1$) will occur only with semiotic representation at the age of nine years. Direct transfer from the child's representation to posturo-kinetic in addition to graphic responses does not occur until the stage of formal operations. Only after they are eight years of age will children succeed in representing difficult displacements.

Blind displacements as used in Pinol-Douriez's tests and displacements in urban space are similar in that they must both be composed without the aid of perception. Piché (1977) confirms the interpretation put forward by Pinol-Douriez. One aim of the London study involved evaluating children's competence in learning how to map. Therefore, before the exercise already described each child was given a short training in mapping, and, during the exercise on the site, was asked to *draw* the way followed about the site and to draw a map of the site after each of the three walks.

The pre-conceptual children imbued with syncretism were unable to analyse the sequence of their displacements (Figure 7.5(a)). During the intuitive period, immense progress occurs because the child is beginning to separate the segments of the displacements, even though this is initially tentative and often confuses different kinds of movements such as change in direction and crossing a road.

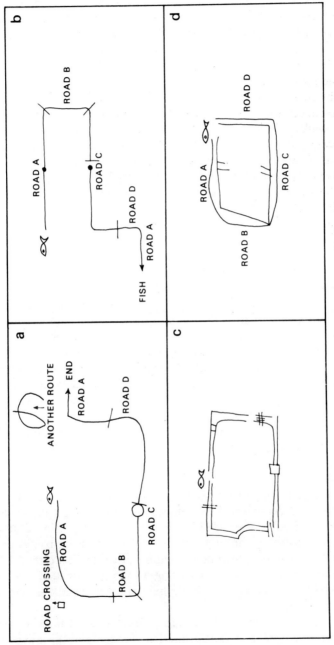

FIGURE 7.5. Children's maps of their route in the urban site

However, on the threshold of the stage of concrete operations, the child disentangles various moves and can reproduce them. Unfortunately, left and right hand turns are still confused and distance is not taken into account. One result is that points of departure and arrival cannot be synchronized (Figure 7.5(b)). At this stage experience is still beneficial. When questioned about the latter incongruity between start and finish, the child tries to map the whole site with the intention of linking points of arrival and departure while taking into account an analysis of displacements (Figure 7.5(c)). Such reflexion leads the child to concentrate on projective and Euclidian relationships over second and third walks. Figure 7.5(d) suggests that the child may produce an approximately correct map of the route, but this is not yet a road map, which shows good positioning of placements and displacements, because every suggestion that the two off-shoots of road E should be linked will be resisted. Only one child reproduced the network topologically at a first attempt; residual errors are not likely to be corrected until the age of ten (Hart, 1979) or fifteen (Pinol-Douriez, 1975).

Would the child perform better at map-reading—a decoding task—than at map making—an encoding task? Blaut, McCleary, and Blaut (1970) answer affirmatively for first-year schoolers and pre-schoolers since their subjects could work at simple tasks on aerial photographs and on their sketches of routes based on these. On the other hand, it is not clear that their subjects understood the basic nature of a map. Their results simply show that pre-operational children can work on images, that they have already acquired some graphic skills, and that they can make sense of an aerial photograph as well as other images. This finding underlines that mapping is not difficult because it involves reading an unusal point of view, but rather because it implies transformations from one point of view to another and is an abstract rather than an iconic representation. Hart (1971) complemented Blaut et al.'s findings in developing a method for teaching geography based on these basic skills among very young children. This relates to capacities for reading iconic representation and interpreting a variety of points of view but not for carrying out projective transformations.

Pinol-Douriez, in opposition to Blaut et al., has shown that decoding a representation in order to orientate actions in reality is a late achievement (after the age of nine years). Piché's (1977) training in mapping included an exercise in land-use map reading and all children were able to trace routes on a map and interpret the iconic representation. On the other hand, it cannot be denied (Parenteau and Pollowy, 1976) that using a map is difficult. Even the most developed child in the London sample could not yet translate the map in terms of the real environment.

All data reported so far contribute to a description of intuitive and early concrete operational children's representation of geographic space as perceptual, practical, egocentric and inflexible. This early representation nevertheless constitutes an excellent basis from which the older child can develop operations. It is interesting to note, by way of conclusion, that during the transition between intuitive and concrete operations many researchers (Blaut *et al.*, 1970; Blaut and Stea, 1974; Pinol-Douriez, 1975; Klett and Alpaugh, 1976; Piché, 1977) have observed regressions in the performance of spatial tasks. Some have attributed this regression to the school system, which would discourage children's spontaneous visual activity in favour of the development of verbal abilities. Constructivists see in this phenomenon an artifact of a transition in cognitive structures; between the age of seven and nine children are so absorbed in developing a conceptual view of the world that they put aside their pre-operational strategies and images, and, because their new way of thinking is still in its infancy, their performance often regresses. Such regressions are so general in development at this age that the constructivists' hypothesis is by far the most acceptable. Children at the beginning of the stage of concrete operations develop a new means of accommodation, a semiotic figuration rather than an imitative one, but, until it is in equilibrium with assimilation schemes through operations, they will not perform well at practical tasks.

Although the literature on the topic of geographic space representation is growing, much more work is needed. From the evidence already existing, it is obvious that the environment affects the strategies of children and it is important to examine how they learn various spatial forms. Further research should therefore continue to examine the representation of placements and displacements in isolation in real environments, but attention should also be focused on their synchronous development.

SUMMARY AND CONCLUSION

The purpose of this essay has been to discuss ways in which the child acquires an awareness of geographical space. Such an awareness and knowledge is not simply the product of successive spatio-temporal contacts with the environment, it is also moulded by the pressure of socio-cultural and adaptive forces.

The most fascinating outcomes of early research on this aspect of children's development concern the *coherence* of the development process, whatever spatial scale is considered, and the way it is structured into *stages*. In brief, the pre-conceptual child experiences and represents different geographic spaces that are tied to a world of perceptions and concrete behaviours in spaces. The intuitive child then begins to co-ordinate these representations of different spaces in an incremental way. At this stage, for example, the child will juxtapose places and try to relate them conceptually and will also engage in an analysis of displacements. Because iconic images are used and the relationships established are always partial and often obscured by a highly personalized image, this notion of geographic space, although it becomes substantial, is often deformed by the spatial transformations admitted in topology and is consistent only within experienced places. *Socio-cultural forces*, such as a pressure to explain that one is both a Londoner and an Englishman; *adaptive forces*, such as the necessity of finding one's way; and the development of operational *cognitive schemes*, such as inclusion and seriation characterized by their reversibility and transivity: all are combined during the stage of concrete operations and lead the child to more stable constructions. Therefore, space becomes homogeneous with the result that the concept of country is understood as the hierarchical addition of places and displacements and placements are reciprocally reported on one another.

Geographic space before the age of ten is represented by the child in qualitative and concrete terms: the child draws a map as a projection of personal activities and not yet as a one to one correspondence with reality within a general reference system. This means that the developmental process has not been entirely completed, but it is on the later stages of development when such completion might occur that research is most limited. One central need is to examine the development of projective, Euclidian and metric transformations of geographic space, along the lines followed by Towler (1970) and Pinol-Douriez (1975).

The analysis described in this chapter, and particularly the project with children in London, cannot yet be generalized upon; it requires further testing with children from various backgrounds. Already, however, it throws considerable light on ways in which children perform quite different tasks such as modelling, map-reading, map-drawing (at local and regional scales), and way-finding. Morever, it shows how the representation of placements in space and of displacements as a network evolve in a parallel way even though they are of a different nature. The concept of 'mental map' is clarified and its role in spatial cognition discussed. Here it is interpreted as a figurative representation of a construction that may be initiated by various cognitive processes and its characterization as a tool facilitating the transformation of these processes into more and more abstract and adapted schemes is another asset of this constructivist interpretation of development. This particular view should stimulate new research in didactics aimed at perfecting mapping exercises, in which maps would be drawn by the child and would then assume a corrective or re-equilibriating role on the cognitive system. Mental maps used in this way could stimulate geographical awareness by increased observation of varied places and land uses and more focused imagination of places located 'elsewhere'.

Study of the spontaneous geography of children was initiated as an investigation of spatial cognition. One clear finding is that enormous scope exists to deepen the efficiency of spatial strategies, both perceptual and intellectual, to improve evaluation of distances and directions, and the extent to which information about foreign places is assimilated. It should be clear that the investigations have only dealt with part of the problem and there are many more topics that should be seriously examined. There is a paucity of evidence at a regional scale but that available indicates that notions of place and explanations of natural and man-made environments are an integral part of children's spontaneous geography. These are issues which have intrinsic interest and may also throw more light on other stages in the development of spatial cognition. It is recognized that cognition does not encompass all of human experience: affectivity is another major facet that must be incorporated. The phenomenological perspective emphasizes this dual reality: it can be developed as an analytic tool to study early territorial identity and sense of place in children. If the importance of understanding the adaptive interactions between human beings and their geographic world is accepted, there is a considerable amount of research needed on the way in which geographical cognition develops.

REFERENCES

Acredolo, L. P. (1976). *New Directions for Environmental Psychology: We Can Get There from Here,* Paper presented at the Eastern Psychological Association, New York.

Acredolo, L. P. (in press, a). The development of the ability to coordinate perspective and maintain orientation in large-scale space. *Developmental Psychology,* in press.

Acredolo, L. P. (in press, b). Small-and-large-scale spatial concepts in infancy and childhood. In L. Liben, A. Patterson, and N. Newcombe (Eds), *Spatial Representation and Behavior Across the Lifespan,* Academic Press, New York.

Acredolo, L. P., Pick, H. L. and Olsen, M. (1975). Environmental differentiation and familiarity as determinants of children's memory for spatial location. *Developmental Psychology,* **11**, 495–501.

Ames, L. B., and Learned, J. (1948). The development of verbalized space in the young child, *Journal of Genetic Psychology,* **72**, 63–84.

Appleyard, D. (1970). Styles and methods of structuring a city, *Environment and Behavior,* **2**, 100–117.

Asmussen, D. G. (1971). *Children's Cognitive Organization of Space,* Unpublished doctoral dissertation, University of Washington, Washington, DC.

Becchi, E., and Riva, G. (1979). *Modèle dè vie des adultes et des enfants en deux milieux (urbain et en voie d'urbanisation),* Paper presented at Congrès International de Psychologie de l'Enfant, Paris.

Blaut, J. M., and Stea, D. (1974). Mapping at the age of three, *Journal of Geography,* **73**, 5–9.

Blaut, J. M., McCleary, G. S., and Blaut, A. S. (1970). Environmental mapping in young children, *Environment and Behavior,* **2**, 335–350.

Bruner, J. S. (1966). On cognitive growth. In J. S. Brunner, R. R. Olver and P. M. Greenfields (Eds.), *Studies in Cognitive Growth,* Wiley, New York, pp. 1–67.

Catling, S. (1978). The child's spatial conception and geographic education, *Journal of Geography,* **77**, 24–28.

Catling, S. (1979). *Children's Maps of Place,* Paper presented at the International Conference of Environmental Psychology, Guildford, Surrey.

Chombart de Lauwe, M. J. (1976). *Enfant en-jeu,* Centre National de la Recherche Scientifique, Paris.

Downs, R. M. and Stea, D. (1973). Cognitive maps and spatial behavior: process and products. In R. M. Downs and D. Stea (Eds.), *Image and Environment: Cognitive Mapping and Spatial Behavior,* Arnold, London, pp. 8–26.

Downs, R. M., and Stea, D. (1977). *Maps in Minds: Reflections on Cognitive Mapping*, Harper and Row, New-York.

Eicher, C. E. (1977). An investigation of elementary children's perceptions of selected countries of the world, *Education*, **98**, 82–90.

Gesell, A. L., and Ilg, F. L. (1946). *The Child from 5 to 10*. Harper and Row, New-York.

Goodnow, J. (1977). *Children's Drawings*, Fontana, London.

Gould, P., and White, R. (1974). *Mental Maps*, Penguin, Harmondsworth.

Hart, R. A. (1971). *Aerial geography: An experiment in elementary education*. Place Perception Research, No. 6, Clark University, Worcester, Massachusetts.

Hart, R. A. (1979). *Children's Experience of Place*, Irvington, New-York.

Hart, R. A., and Moore, G. T. (1973). The development of spatial cognition: a review. In R. M. Downs, and D. Stea (Eds.), *Image and Environment: Cognitive Mapping and Spatial Behaviour*, Arnold, London, pp. 246–288.

Herman, J. F., and Siegel, A. W. (1978). The development of cognitive mapping of the large-scale environment. *Journal of Experimental Child Psychology*, **26**, 389–406.

Hess, R. D., and Torney, J. V. (1967). *The Development of Political Attitudes in Children*, Aldine, Chicago.

Howard, I. D., and Templeton, W. B. (1966). *Human Spatial Orientation*, Wiley, London.

Howe, I. D. (1931). The teaching of directions in space. *Journal of Geography*, **31**, pp. 207–210.

Jahoda, G. (1963). The development of children's ideas about country and nationality. *British Journal of Educational Psychology*, **33**, 47–60 and 143–153.

Kaplan, S. (1973). Cognitive maps in perception and thought. In R. M. Downs and D. Stea (Eds.), *Image and Environment: Cognitive Mapping and Spatial Behavior*, Aldine, Chicago, pp. 63–78.

Klett, F. R., and Alpaugh, D. (1976). Environmental learning and large scale environments. In G. T. Moore and R. G. Golledge (Eds.), *Environmental Knowing*, Dowden, Hutchinson and Ross, Stroudsburg, Pa., pp. 121–130.

Klineberg, O., and Lambert, W. E. (1967). *Children's Views of Foreign Peoples: A Cross-National Study*, Appleton–Century–Crofts, New York.

Kosslyn, S. M. Pick, H. L., and Fariello, G. R. (1974). Cognitive maps in children and man, *Child Development*, **45**, 707–716.

Lee, T. R. (1963). Psychology and living space. *Transactions of the Bartlett Society*, **2**, 11–36.

Lemen, J. (1966). *L'Espace Figuratif et les Structures de la Personnalité*. Presses Universitaires de France, Paris.

Lucaz, T. C., and Uzgiris, I. C. (1977). Spatial factors in the object concept. *Developmental Psychology*, **13**, 492–500.

Mark, L. S. (1972). Modeling through a toy-play: methodology for eliciting topographical representations in children. In W. J. Mitchell (Ed.), *Environmental Design: Research and Practice*, University of California Press, Los Angeles, 1.3.1.–1.3.9.

Maurer, R., and Baxter, J. C., (1972). Images of the neighborhood and city among Black, Anglo-and-Mexican-American Children, *Environment and Behavior*, **4**, 351–388.

Moore, G. T. (1975) The development of environmental knowing: an overview of an interactional—constructivist theory and some data on within—individual developmental variations. In D. Canter and T. Lee (Eds.), *Psychology and the Built Environment*, Architectural Press, London, pp. 184–194.

Neumann, N. S. (1979). *La Compréhension des Liens Verticaux dans l'Espace Architectural*, Ecole d'Architecture, Report no. 11, Université Laval, Québec.

Pailhous, J. (1969). Représentation de l'espace urbain et cheminements. *Le Travail Humain*, **32**, 87–140 and 239–270.

Pailhous, J. (1971). Elaboration d'images spatiales et de règles de déplacement: une étude sur l'espace urbain, *Le Travail Humain*, **34**, 299–324.

Pailhous, J. (1972). Influence de l'ordre de présentation des données sur la constitution de l'image spatiale: une étude sur l'espace urbain. *Le Travail Humain*, **35**, 69–84.

Paillard, J. (1974). Le traitement des informations spatiales. In F. Bresson (Ed.), *De l'Espace Corporel à l'Espace Écologique*. Presses Universitaires de France, Paris, pp. 7–88.

Parenteau, R., and Pollowy, A. M. (1976). *Exploration Spatiale Chez les Enfants d'Âge Scolaire en Milieu Urbain*, Centre de Recherches et d'Innovation Urbaines, Universite de Montréal, Montréal.

Piaget, J. (1924). *Judgement and Reasoning in the child*, Routledge and Kegan Paul, London, 1926.

Piaget, J. (1926). *The Child's Conception of the World*, Paladin, London, 1973.

Piaget, J. (1937). *The Construction of Reality in the Child*, Basic Books, New-York, 1954.

Piaget, J. (1946). *Play, Dreams, and Imitation in Childhood*, Routledge and Kegan Paul, London, 1962.

Piaget, J. and Inhelder, B. (1948). *The Child's Conception of space*, Routledge and Kegan Paul, London, 1956.

Piaget, J. and Weil, A. M. (1951). Le développement, chez l'enfant, de l'idée de patrie et des relations avec l'étranger. *Bulletin International des Sciences Sociales*, **13**, 605–621.

Piaget, J., Inhelder, B. and Szeminska, A. (1948). The Child's Conception of Geometry, Norton, New York, 1967.

Piché, D. (1977). *The Geographical Understanding of Children Aged 5 to 8 years*. Doctoral dissertation, University of London, London.

Piché, D. (1979). *L'Environnement comme Média de Transmission de l'Identité Sociale et Régionale*. Paper presented at Congrés International de Psychologie de l'Enfant, Paris.

Pick, H. L. (1976). Transactional-constructivist approach to environmental knowing. In G. T. Moore and R. G. Golledge (Eds.), *Environmental Knowing*, Dowden, Hutchinson and Ross, Stroudsburg, Pa., pp. 185–188.

Pick, H., and Lockman, J. (1979). *Development of Spatial Cognition in Children*. Paper presented at Mind, Child, and Architecture, Rutgers University, Newark, N. J.

Pick, H. L., Acredolo, L. P., and Gronseth, M. (1973). *Children's Knowledge of the Spatial Layout of their Homes*. Paper presented at the Society for Research in Child Development, Philadelphia, Pennsylvania.

Pinol-Douriez, M. (1975). *La Construction de l'Espace*, Delachaux et Niestlé, Neuchâtel.

Rand, D. C. (1973). *The Relationship Between Children's Classification–Class Inclusion and Geographic Knowledge as Measured by Piaget's Spatial Stages*. Unpublished doctoral dissertation, Purdue University, Lafayette, Indiana.

Sandels, S. (1975). *Children in Traffic*, Paul Eler, London.

Shemyakin, F. N. (1962). Orientation in space. In B. G. Anany'ev (Ed.), *Psychological Science in the USSR*, US Office of Technical Reports, Washington, DC, pp. 186–255.

Siegel, A. W. (1979). *Development of Cognitive Mapping of Large-scale Environments*. Paper presented at Mind, Child, and Architecture, Rutgers University, Newark, N. J.

Siegel, A. W. and White, S. H. (1975). The development of spatial representations. In H. W. Reese (Ed.), *Advances in Child Development and Behavior*, Vol. 10, Academic Press, New York, pp. 10–55.

Siegel, A. W., and Schadler, M. (1977). Children's representations of their classrooms, *Child Development*, **48**, 388–394.

Siegel, A. W., Kirasic, K. C., and Kail, R. V. (1978). Stalking the elusive cognitive map: the development of children's representations of geographic space. In I. Altman and

J. F. Wohlwill (Eds), *Children and the Environment,* Plenum Press, New York, pp. 223–258.

Spencer, D., and Lloyd, J. (1974). *A Child's Eye View of Small Heath.* Centre for Urban and Regional Studies, University of Birmingham, Birmingham.

Stea, D. (1976). Program notes on a spatial fugue. In G. T. Moore and R. G. Golledge (Eds.), *Environmental Knowing*, Dowden, Hutchinson and Ross, Stroudsburg, Pa., pp. 106–120.

Stea, D., and Taphanel, S. (1974). Theory and experiment on the relation between environmental modelling and environmental cognition. In D. Canter and T. Lee(Eds.), *Psychology and the Built Environment*, Architectural Press, Tonbridge, pp. 170–178.

Stea, D., and Blaut, J. M. (1973). Some preliminary observations on spatial learning in school children. In R. M. Downs and D. Stea (Eds.), *Image and Environment: Cognitive Mapping and Spatial Behavior*, Arnold, London, pp. 226–234.

Thornberg, J. M. (1973). Child's conception of places to live in. In W. F. E. Preiser (Ed.), *Environmental Design Research*, Dowden, Hutchinson and Ross, Stroudsburg, Philadelphia, pp. 178–189.

Towler, J. O. (1970). The elementary school child's concept of reference systems, *Journal of Geography*, **69**, 89–93.

Towler, J. O., and Nelson, L. D. (1968). The elementary school child's concept of scale, *Journal of Geography*, **67**, 24–28.

Geography and the Urban Environment
Progress in Research and Applications, Volume IV
Edited by D. T. Herbert and R. J. Johnston
© 1981 John Wiley & Sons Ltd.

Chapter 8

The Social Geography of the Nineteenth Century US City

John P. Radford

In the cities of the nineteenth century United States, a set of principles, first worked out largely in Britain, was taken to something approaching a logical conclusion. Beatrice Webb, an acute if not impartial observer, wrote during a visit in 1898 of the universal acceptance by Americans of 'the old fallacy of the classical economists that each man will best serve the interests of the community by pursuing his own gain', a view which she claimed had never been fully accepted in England (Shannon, 1963, p. 149). Had Mrs. Webb probed more deeply into the American social fabric, she would have discovered a range of social philosophies if anything rather wider than that to be found at home. Yet it is fair to claim that the prevailing views 'universally acted upon' by the major decision makers of significance at the turn of the century owed much to Herbert Spencer and his American popularists Sumner, Fiske, and Small.

The importance of laissez-faire attitudes within the nineteenth century US has been recognized by writers from a wide range of ideological persuasions. Mumford (1938, pp. 152–3) described 'Coketown'—the paleotechnic US city— as being governed by a belief that order would somehow emerge from the unrestricted activities of private interests. Polanyi (1944) wrote of the operation of a self-regulated market, free from the fabric of social control. Berthoff (1960) characterized a self-made plutocracy of US industrialists as the agents of disorder and the proponents of a heartless and irresponsible society. On a more positive note, Hays (1957) has described attempts to cope with the 'shock' of industrialization between 1885 and 1914. Warner (1968a) has used the theme of privatism—the search for and use of personal wealth—to describe a continuity in the US urban experience from the late eighteenth to the early twentieth centuries.

US cities were above all else the nerve centres of a rapidly expanding market economy. In only a few cases, such as Salt Lake City and some older Southern cities, did other kinds of activities rival or even ameliorate this function. It was a role performed with great efficiency, evolving a rational urban economy across most of the continent between the 1830s and 1920s. If 'take-off' occurred over half a century later than in England, as has been suggested (Rostow, 1960), American technology acquired an early sophistication (Vance, 1977, pp. 324–349) which first became evident in Britain at the Great Exhibition (*Punch*, 1851). The half-century following the Civil War was one of rapid innovation and cumulative industrial-urban growth (Pred, 1966). City expansion occurred in bursts which were dependent on levels of demand exerted by waves of in-migrants, and supply emanating from large credit institutions through countless small developers (Hoyt, 1933). Transportation innovations were linked to the building cycle (Isard, 1942) with a simplicity that should be the envy of urban land economists everywhere. While the streetcar system of Leeds was encumbered by municipal constraints and somewhat muddled demand factors, that of Boston evolved in bursts of growth related directly to the quantitative forces of the national economy, the urban land market, and rates of in-migration (Ward, 1964).

The culmination of the industrial-urban upsurge occurred, not in the nineteenth century, but during the first three decades of the twentieth. It was in the 1920s that the manufacturing share in the total economy stabilized in favour of an expanding service sector, marking the end of 'industrial revolution' (Anderson, 1977). The beginnings of intervention in the laissez-faire city date from a little earlier, but not significantly before the turn of the century. Reform elements existed, of course, and made notable contributions to American thought and literature, but they scarcely dented the onward march of 'progress'.

Even the celebrated antebellum reform movements, except for the special case of slavery abolition, were essentially failures (Ware, 1924; Hugins, 1972). After the Civil War, urban reform movements remained in the background until at least the Progressive Era. There existed a widespread impatience with regulations which might restrict individual ambition (Scott, 1971). It is true that urban designer and booster collaborated successfully at times, most notably in the layout of urban parks and in the City Beautiful movement, but it was not until after 1906 that there was any discernible trend towards 'planning' (Hancock, 1967). Even then, although half of the largest fifty cities and several smaller ones embarked on what was called 'comprehensive planning' between 1907 and 1917, there was no effective Federal coordination until the Depression. At the national level, and laissez-faire attitude of government binds 1929 very firmly to 1870 (Ross, 1968).

The human ecologists at the University of Chicago were well placed to observe the results of this urban-industrial explosion. Robert Park was both fascinated and horrified by what seemed to be a society operating largely outside the realm of social controls, and in a state of shock stemming from the rapid increase of a heterogeneous population. From this spectre of distorted equilibrium there arose a plan for the systematic study of the effects of a city's growth upon its inhabitants. The concentric zone diagram drafted by Burgess (1925) was based upon empirical studies and was designed almost as a sampling framework to guide future work. Its influence on future generations of urban students has proved to be greater than that of any other construct. Selected items from the accompanying text have also been repeatedly seized upon. As is well known, ecological theory has also prompted almost continual criticism. Sociologists have largely abandoned it, whether because of its assumptions of rationalism (Firey, 1947), its focus on pathology, or its inadequacy as an environmental model (Michelson, 1976), and in recent years it has largely been left to urban geographers to use as a research framework. Harvey (1973, p. 133) has lamented the fact that urban geographers have turned to Burgess rather than Engels for guidance, and certainly there is considerable room for the exploration of Marxian themes in urban structure. Yet it is unclear whether a Marxian framework offers the most useful perspective on a society in which the control of government by business interests was as extreme as it became in the US by the opening of the twentieth century (Kolko, 1963). Ecological theory, including the Burgess model, is, on the other hand, a product of that era. Harvey is correct in labelling it a cultural rather than an economic interpretation. The very failures which make it deficient as a general model—the Social Darwinism and biological analogies, the equating of biotic with economic competition and of urbanization with disorder—anchor it firmly to the context from which it was derived.

Viewed historically, classical ecology can be regarded as the most vivid, systematic interpretation of the climax of urban-industrial expansion in the US, and our most coherent, if flawed, spatial theory. From it we can learn a considerable amount about urban growth, and even more about contemporary views of the social consequences of industrialization. Indeed, it is not difficult to argue that the Burgess model has more relevance to developments in the half-century preceding its formulation than to the half-century since. Warner (1972) and Handlin (1963), among others, have described an urban cultural continuity extending from the 1870s to the 1920s, a period characterized by the evolution of the 'segregated city' (Warner, 1972, pp. 85–112). A case for the application of Park's concept of the 'natural area' in the Victorian city has been made by Goheen (1970), though perhaps not in the most convincing of contexts, and possibly for a period extending too far back into the nineteenth century. Bearing in mind Ward's reservations about the retrospective application of urban models, but following his conclusion that *late* Victorian cities qualify as 'modern' (Ward, 1975), it can be suggested that human ecology is, at least at a superficial level, our most useful frame of reference for the period from about 1880 onwards. This observation can be taken to apply to Hoyt's model which shares a common set of assumptions with that of Burgess and is in many ways simply a variant of it (Johnston, 1971, pp. 79–81). For the beginning of the century, models of the mercantile or commercial city would seem appropriate (Davey and Doucet, 1975), and the middle decades can be regarded as a transition period (Muller and Groves, 1979).

The evolution of the US city from commercial to industrial might seem to offer a ready-made framework for reviewing its social geography. However, such a format would lend a false simplicity to the discussion, and confine our attention to a narrow section of the relevant literature. The usefulness of this framework will be explored in the final section of the chapter. First it is necessary to describe the major themes which dominate the wider literature on social space in the nineteenth century city. Such a task poses considerable problems of scale and definition. Whereas the literature on the nineteenth century US urban system is relatively contained, that on the social geography of the city is vast and disparate. Further, while geographers have to a large extent led investigations into the former, they have, with a few exceptions such as David Ward, had rather little impact on the wider literature of the latter. The 'social geography' of the nineteenth century US city is largely written in passing references to spatial or environmental changes by historians in the pursuit of other, more pressing, topics. Even the most important studies cannot all be cited in a single review. The emphasis here is therefore interpretative rather than encyclopaedic. Greater justice is done to the latter half of the century than to the antebellum era, and to the city-wide scale rather than to micro-patterns. An attempt is made to isolate and assess the most important spatial themes and statements, and to suggest directions for future research. This can be done under the headings of spatial mobility, ethnicity, class, and race, variables which, it need hardly be added, are closely inter-related and are separated here only for convenience.

SPATIAL MOBILITY

For the human ecologists, nothing symbolized the condition of the American city more appropriately than its high rate of population turnover. An earlier and more rural tradition had seen spatial mobility as a response to opportunity, and viewed the persistent individual as unenterprising. To the early ecologists, however, mobility was the cause of the pathological conditions endemic to the modern city because it undermined the influence of primary controls. As Burgess put it, 'the areas of the greatest mobility in the city have the greatest concentration of poverty, vice, crime, juvenile delinquency, divorce, desertion, abandoned infants, murder, and suicide' (Burgess, 1925, p. 153). So close was this inter-relationship that, in Burgess's view, a city's overall state of health could be gauged by measuring its mobility rates; geographical mobility was 'the pulse of the community' (Burgess, 1925, p. 59)

The pathological view of mobility dominated American social science for several decades. Studies found a close relationship between areas of high mobility and high incidences of psychoses and neuroses (for example, Sullenger, 1932; Tietze, Lemkan, and Cooper, 1942). Rapid urban growth seemed to stimulate social and mental disorders almost unheard of in a mythical past of rural stability (Faris and Durham, 1960). This view of residential mobility still survives in popular culture, receiving perhaps its most extreme expression in the 'pop sociology' of Vance Packard (1972).

Given this view, it is remarkable that one of the most important contributions of the 'new' urban history is the discovery of rates of mobility in the nineteenth century city substantially greater than those of today. About 20 per cent of the population changes residence each year in the contemporary US (Simmons, 1968), but this is less than half the rate uncovered by a number of researchers for several nineteenth century cities. Moreover, although there may have been some undesirable effects, most historians feel that the inhabitants of nineteenth century cities tended to view spatial mobility with as much approbation as those in rural areas. In the words of Thernstrom and Knights, 'the faith in spatial mobility as the key to virtue and success came into full flower in the nineteenth century' (Thernstrom and Knights, 1970, p. 7; also Chudacoff, 1972, pp. 97–9). Thernstrom and Knights were able to present a strong case for revising some long-standing views about the nature of nineteenth century cities in the light of their high rates of population turnover. The concept of racial and ethnic ghettoes, in particular, seemed to pale in the light of constant in- and out-migration of individuals and households. The net population figures clearly only skimmed the surface of some rather massive population shifts. For example, of the 67,000 householders who moved into Boston during the 1850s, over 61,000 left the city during the same period, and gross inmigration was thus about eleven times net inmigration (Knights, 1969, p. 262). Similar proportions, with much larger numbers, apply to the 1880s (Thernstrom, 1973, p. 17). It is possible that several of the characteristics of the nineteenth century American city resulted from attempts to ameliorate the otherwise damaging effects of high population turnover.

These high rates have long been mentioned in passing. As long ago as 1862, Frederick Law Olmsted, the pioneer park planner, found a high rate of turnover among merchants and dealers in San Francisco, and argued that a public park might prove to be a stabilizing influence (Bender, 1975). McKelvey noted that less than half of the people listed in the 1858 directory of Rochester, New York, could be found in that of 1859 (McKelvey, 1949). Curti's well-known study of a Wisconsin county cast doubt upon the notion of a former age of rural stability with his finding that three-quarters of the population could not be traced from 1860 to 1870 (Curti, 1959). It was, however, Thernstrom's study of Newburyport, Massachusetts which presented the first coherent study of a mobile nineteenth century urban population (Thernstrom, 1964). Although mainly concerned with social mobility, particularly the degree of upward mobility of the working class, this study delved into the question of population turnover. Thernstrom found that less than 40 per cent of the unskilled labourers and their children in Newburyport in 1850 were present in 1860. Almost 35 per cent of the labourers in the city in 1860 remained in 1870, and 47 per cent of these persisted until 1880. Confident that only a small proportion of the drop-out was due to death, or indeed to data problems, Thernstrom painted a picture of a volatile working class, largely made up of inmigrants from Ireland and New England. The major differential was between those who owned property, 80 per cent of whom persisted between 1850 and 1860, and those who did not, for whom the comparable figure was 31 per cent (Thernstrom, 1964, p. 90). Interestingly enough, those who left Newburyport did not seem particularly well equipped to succeed elsewhere, raising the picture of a group of permanent transients—a 'floating proletariat'—continually shifting in response to the labour market and not substantially improving their occupational status.

The plethora of mobility studies which poured forth between the mid-1960s and mid-1970s found high mobility rates throughout the nineteenth century in cities of all sizes, in every region of the United States. For example, Hopkins (1968) found evidence in late nineteenth century Atlanta of the existence of a floating population of manual workers similar to that of antebellum Newbury-port, and confirmed the existence of a correlation between persistence rates and occupational status, particularly among native whites. All groups, however, had high turnover rates. Within occupational categories, immigrants were the most mobile element in the population, but differences were slight. The major discrepancy was racial: the black population was much more persistent than both native and immigrant whites. A study of turn of the century Omaha examined the mobility experience—emigration, permanence, or intra-urban migration—of two sample groups, one between 1880 and 1900, the other between 1900 and 1920 (Chudacoff, 1972). Here too there was a correlation between low persistence rates and high occupational status among native whites, but again differences were small. Although members of manual occupational groups moved more frequently within the city than did those of non-manual groups, the rates of out-migration were about the same. There is little evidence here of a 'floating proletariat' to be contrasted with a more persistent skilled and non-manual population. A 'geographical restlessness' was universal, perhaps reflecting the newness, diversity and rapid growth rate of the city at this time. Likewise, differences in ethnicity produced no significant discrepancies in mobility rates. The use of probit analysis as a supplement to the more traditional methods in the body of the work also failed to isolate any variable which consistently influenced an individual's mobility pattern. However, since no income or wealth variable was included in the analysis, the possibility of financial status affecting mobility rates must be left open (Chudacoff, 1972, pp. 151, 165–7).

Two studies of mobility in Boston represent the high tide of a first generation of mobility studies, and demonstrate the existence of considerable methodological diversity in the field. Knights' study of antebellum Boston (1971) can be criticized for failing to set mobility in a wider social and geographical context but nevertheless provides a rigorous approach to the dissection of data, and a critical appraisal and careful use of quantitative source materials. Following through a carefully compiled list of basic questions about the population of Boston 1830–1860, Knights finds turnover rates averaging about 30 per cent per annum, and reaching a peak during the late 1840s. The foreign-born population was less mobile than the native-born, and less likely to move to the suburbs. Movements between core and periphery were much less numerous than movements into and out of the city. There is some suggestion that despite rapid turnover of individuals, the macro-patterns of socio-economic structure of the city as measured by core and peripheral regions showed a high degree of persistence. Finally, in following up outmigrants from the city, Knights found that a large proportion settled close to the city, and seemed to achieve slightly higher levels of success than those who remained.

Thernstrom's study of Boston between 1880 and 1930, although sharply criticized by Alcorn and Knights (1975) for its source materials and for projecting analysis of the persistent population into conclusions about the population of the city as a whole, is broadly based and interpretative. The final chapter provides a valuable summary of recent historical scholarship documenting the volatility of the US population: some two dozen studies of nineteenth century cities found persistence rates ranging between 39 and 64 per cent (Thernstrom, 1973, p. 222). Thernstrom is much less impressed with individual differences in the findings of these studies than with the fact that they appear to demonstrate the existence of 'a fairly constant migration factor operating throughout American society since the opening of the nineteenth century' (Thernstrom, 1973, p. 228). This observation is consistent with the migration patterns described in Zelinsky's development chronology, wherein the early nineteenth century US is viewed as an 'early transitional' society, becoming by late century a 'late transitional' society on the path towards modernization (Zelinsky, 1971). It is also given support in the continued appearance of case studies which broadly support the major findings (for example Griffen and Griffen, 1978; Decker, 1978).

Some of the more recent literature, however, having digested and to a large degree accepted the presence of these high turnover rates in nineteenth century America, nevertheless sounds some cautionary notes on their interpretation. Katz, Doucet and Stern (1978) warn that the acceptance of Thernstrom's view of a uniformity of mobility patterns may dull our appreciation of the effects of local circumstances. They emphasize the hazards of record linkage, a technique upon which all mobility studies rely, and note the difference between decennial population persistence and average length of residence as measures of population movement. The latter information can be obtained only in rare instances, such as in the New York State Census of 1855 of which use is made in their study. Among the conclusions stemming from the analysis is the effect of property ownership, and to a lesser degree large households and high occupational status, upon length of residence. The authors' point about local conditions is supported by a study of Canton, an industrial district of Baltimore (Beirne, 1979). Beirne finds very high persistence rates for the period 1880 to 1930, and argues that these were a result of a highly specific employment linkage in a small scale industrial setting with segmental labour forces which reinforced family and ethnic solidarity.

A final note of caution is directed at the tendency for mobility historians to infer rootlessness and community instability from data showing high turnover rates. In a study of the Italian community in Buffalo, New York, Yans-McLaughlin (1977) argues that the high mobility rates evident in the quantitative data sources do not clarify process, and should be viewed within a cultural context. Since family and village ties 'monitored the entire migration process' of Buffalo's Italians, high mobility rates did not undermine the strength of the Italian community, which was bound by emotional ties transcending place and distance.

After a decade and a half, the urban historians have given us a broad outline of mobility in the nineteenth century American city. Two types of study now seem to be required. First, there is a need for detailed case studies using smaller and more closely delimited spatial units within the city than those which have generally been adopted. Secondly, we cannot proceed very much further without some basic theory of nineteenth century intra-urban residential mobility. With recent evidence of high mobility rates in some British cities, a first step might be to test Pooley's Liverpool-based model of mobility in the English Victorian city within the North American context (Pooley, 1979, p. 274).

ETHNICITY AND CLASS

Michael Katz argues that the two great themes of nineteenth century history are transiency and inequality (Katz, 1975, p. 17). Having briefly surveyed the transiency of the nineteenth century urban population we turn now to three major dimensions of inequality: class, ethnicity, and race. The literature on race is sufficiently contained to be dealt with separately. Ethnicity and class are so intertwined, however, that they must be considered together.

The immigration of European peasants provided the United States with the bulk of its working class. Differences in ethnicity have been so striking that, both in popular and scholarly literature and in wider society, they have tended to obscure a deeper and perhaps more persistent class structure (Fried, 1973). Most immigrant groups underwent acculturation and urbanization simultaneously, with results which have often been described in the harshest of terms. The evils of an exploitive system were popularly exposed at the turn of the century by the 'muckrakers', and most notoriously in Upton Sinclair's novel *The Jungle* in which a family of Lithuanians is processed by industrial Chicago as inexorably as the hogs in the nearby stockyards—'everything but the squeal' (Sinclair, 1906, p. 38). Elements of this feeling appear in the work of the early ecologists, and more recently in the work of Handlin (1951). Contemporary social reformers, modelling their efforts on Charles Booth and Toynbee Hall, attempted to ameliorate the worst of the conditions, and, particularly in the case of Jane Addams and her collaborators at Hull House in Chicago, have left us valuable descriptive and cartographic records of late nineteenth century inner city neighbourhoods (Addams, 1895; Woods, 1898).

Although many immigrant groups experienced proletarian-like conditions, there is little evidence of a strong working class consciousness. In general there developed a positive response to American political symbols and institutions, which was seen as ideologically incompatible with working class movements (Parenti, 1968). Socialism remained, for reasons which are hotly debated (Leon, 1971), a comparatively uninfluential movement, entering the mainstream of economic decision-making on irregular and subsequently notorious occasions. The Socialist Party of America, preoccupied with an unsuccessful attempt to promote political reform at the national level, had little interest in municipal socialism. Perhaps the transiency of the working class population also contributed to the failure to develop a proletarian consciousness. Unlike the glass workers of Carmaux (Scott, 1969), the workers of the United States may have been too mobile to develop a deep-seated class consciousness (Thernstrom and Knights, 1970; Hirsch, 1978). Persuasive as this argument is, however, Griffen suggested almost the opposite in Poughkeepsie: the most settled workers had the greatest stake in the community and were the least inclined to social protest (Griffen, 1969). Katz (1975) has suggested a middle ground: where economic advancement was perceived to be possible, geographic stability may have prompted social and political stability, but where upward social mobility appeared unobtainable spatial stability may have encouraged the growth of militancy. One thing that no longer remains in doubt is the reality and persistence of inequality. In 1850–70, only forty per cent of adult males in the US owned real estate, and twenty to forty per cent were unable to accumulate any recorded estate, personal or real, in their lifetimes (Soltow, 1975).

At a general level, the most cogent overviews linking ethnicity with class formation in the nineteenth century city have come from attempts by political scientists to trace the nature of urban power structures. As part of his response to the 'power elite' school (Hunter, 1953; Mills, 1956) which maintained that all community decision making was controlled by small elites, Dahl presented an historical model of the power structure of New Haven, Connecticut (Dahl, 1961). A patrician oligarchy controlled the city in its earliest phase, but was replaced after 1842 by the 'new self-made men of business', who were in turn overtaken after 1900 by a new pluralism. Dahl maintained that it was possible to trace individual ethnic groups through three stages of development within the city. On arrival, a group would constitute the city's proletariat (Germans 1840–1880, Irish 1840–1890, Italians 1880–1930). A second stage was marked by increasing heterogeneity within the group, with some advancement into white collar jobs (Germans 1840–1920, Irish 1890–1930, Italians 1930–1950). In a final stage of twentieth century adoption of middle class ideas, lifestyles, marriage patterns, and neighbourhoods, the groups achieved assimilation from which perspective the traits of their fathers seemed meaningless or even embarrassing.

A useful extension of this model, and one more applicable to cities in the west, is suggested by Elazar (1970). The first settlers in an embryo prairie city (1815–1847) were normally native arrivals who founded the basic institutions— county government, schools, etc.—patterned on previous experience in New England, the Middle Atlantic States, or the South. Concurrent political structures were frequently created, but these merged before the end of the first generation, and class and reference group divisions remained slight. A second generation (1848–1876) brought new streams of in-migrants, usually from either one of seven European streams or from Canada. Conflict between old and new settlers tended to develop, with the intensity depending on the width of the cultural gap and the timing of inmigration. The third generation (1877–1916), bringing migration from other European streams, particularly Southern and Eastern Europe, was characterized by much greater conflict, with closed institutions, strong class and reference group differentiation, and a political split between the Republicanism of the old settlers and Democratic support from the new. After a period of quiescence (1917–1947), the mid-twentieth century saw the emergence of a new fluidity.

Initial attempts by urban historians to view urban populations 'from the bottom up' cast doubt upon the effectiveness of this apparently inevitable escalation process. Thernstrom's (1964) study of Newburyport, Massachusetts, sought in the social mobility patterns of manual workers a measure of the real basis of the myth of the 'open society'. This pervasive nineteenth century doctrine held that talent was distributed at random throughout the population, that American society was an 'open race', and that occupational mobility and property ownership were attainable by all who would practise industry and thrift. Thernstrom found that the reality was somewhat different. Some upward mobility occurred within manual occupational status categories, not so much for unskilled workers themselves as for their sons, but it was difficult even for the sons of manual workers to move into non-manual occupations. A pervasive pattern was to seek 'property mobility'—the ownership of a house, often achieved by making educational and other sacrifices which prevented occupational mobility.

Although Thernstrom's findings in Newburyport received some support, more recent studies have tended to be much less pessimistic. Gutman (1969), for example, found considerable basis in reality for the 'rags to riches' myth in Paterson, New Jersey. Thernstrom (1973) himself presented a markedly more optimistic view in his study of Boston. He found no evidence of a trade-off between property and occupational mobility which was apparently necessary in Newburyport. It should be noted in passing that much of this debate rests on the analysis of data necessarily confined to persistors in the population (Alcorn and Knights, 1975), and is complicated by reference to more than one time period. Although he surveys several possible factors which might account for the differences in levels of achievements, Thernstrom is so impressed by the success of the Russian Jewish population in achieving high rates of educational, occupation and income mobility in contrast to the Irish, that he turns reluctantly to cultural values as perhaps the major variable (Thernstrom, 1973, pp. 168–175). This change in emphasis in Thernstrom's work in Massachusetts epitomizes a more general shift towards findings of generally high rates of social mobility, varying with ethnicity. A recent review (Dinnerstein, Nichols, and Reimers, 1979) finds a tendency in the literature to distinguish between groups which evaluated their children's performance according to the values of 'American' achievement (East European Jews, Greeks, Germans, and most Protestant groups) and those whose goals revolved around family concerns, emphasizing early employment and minimizing the need to learn English (Italians, Poles, French, Canadians, Mexicans). Perhaps the strongest recent statement along these lines is Kessner's study of New York, the city which admitted three-quarters of American immigrants between 1880 and 1919 (Kessner, 1977). The study focuses on the two largest groups, and finds rates of upward mobility which are moderately high for Italians, and very high for Jews.

Ideally, this re-affirmation of the reality of social mobility, expecially when linked to ethnicity as the prime variable, might encourage us to seek a spatial expression in the invasion-succession processes of the ecological model. At a general level, such direction seems highly appropriate. There is no doubting the validity of the feeling that 'to move out was to step up' (Walter, 1975, p. 21), However, closer examination of the complex inter-relationships found in the general model suggests that their applicability in the nineteenth century city may be limited. No more concise statement of these relationships exists than that provided by Cressey:

The distribution of these various groups reflects a definite process of succession. Immigrant stocks follow a regular sequence of settlement in successive areas of increasing stability and status. This pattern of distribution represents the ecological setting within which the assimilation of the foreign population takes place. An immigrant group on its arrival settles in a compact colony in a low-rent industrial area usually located in the transitional zone near the center of the city. If the group is of large size several different areas of initial settlement may develop in various industrial sections. These congested areas of first settlement are characterized by the perpetuation of many European cultural traits. After some years of residence in such an area, the group, as it improves its economic and social standing, moves outward to some more desirable residential district, creating an area of second settlement. In such an area the group is not so closely concentrated physically, there is less cultural solidarity, and more American standards of living are adopted. Subsequent areas of settlement may develop in some cases, but the last stage in this series of movements is one of gradual dispersion through cosmopolitan residential districts. This diffusion marks the disintegration of the group and the absorption of the individuals into the general American population. The relative concentration or dispersion of various immigrant groups furnishes an excellent indication of the length of residence in the city and the general degree of assimilation which has taken place. (Cressey, 1938, p. 61)

In some cases these relationships seem empirically verifiable, especially in studies of the archtypical city of Chicago. For example, Beijbom's (1971) study of the Swedish population of Chicago documents what appears to be a clear case of initial clustering around Swedish institutions, followed by a general dispersal corresponding to assimilation into the wider community (Figure 8.1). However, Nelli's work on the city's Italian community casts doubt on the notion of a simple relationship between spatial change and group adjustment (Nelli, 1970). Groups of first generation immigrants could be found some distance

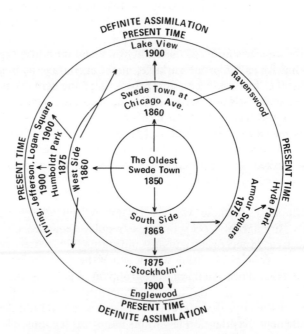

After Beijbom, 1971

FIGURE 8.1. Evolution of residential patterns of Swedes in Chicago. (Reproduced by permission of the author)

away from the centre of the city during the earliest periods of development, and the immigrant areas in general were constantly changing location, size, and membership.

Perhaps more important, doubt has been cast upon the whole notion of the immigrant ghetto. Ward (1970) has pointed out that in the antebellum era, before the advent of efficient transportation and the centralization of urban employment, immigrants found accommodation in a variety of locations. The Irish and Germans who made up the vast majority of non-British immigrants lived in peripheral shanty towns as well as forming clusters in areas adjacent to the central business district which had been vacated by residents of higher socio-economic status. Warner and Burke (1969) have gone further and argued that the ghetto is a special case in American urban history, and does not represent a typical residential form. Apart from Northern blacks, most urban dwellers have lived in heterogeneous neighbourhoods, and only eastern and southern Europeans in the late nineteenth century city have shown any marked tendency to cluster in exclusive areas. Zunz (1977), on the other hand, has argued that such observations are based upon impressions gained from aggregate data, especially ward totals. Using data for block sides, Zunz found pronounced ethnic clustering and coherent neighbourhoods in late nineteenth century Detroit, particularly of Irish, Germans, Poles, and native-born Americans. There was also evidence of clustering by occupational status, but it was not so strongly marked. A similar pattern has been described by Esslinger (1975) in South Bend, Indiana, where low indices of segregation by ward obscured small scale clusters by street which were especially marked among the Irish population.

These differences in viewpoint are recent examples of a lengthy debate which has in the past been obscured by a tendency to link ethnic clusters with pathological social conditions. Several studies have shown this association to be false. Ward (1969) has attempted a corrective to such stereotyping by proposing a model in the form of a Venn diagram which isolates particular variables associated with individual communities. Kessner, while content to describe the clusters of Italians and Jews in New York as 'ghettoes', emphasizes that they bore little resemblance to the European ghetto. Rather they had porous boundaries and acted as staging posts for upward mobility. In fact, because they provided the contacts necessary for immigrants to move into wider society, with an accompanying increase in place utility, they were highly functional 'mobility launchers' (Kessner, 1977, p. 174).

Perhaps the strongest statement of this type is Vecoli's (1964) well known critique of Handlin's *The Uprooted* (1951). Vecoli minimized the degree of disruption and isolation suffered by Italian immigrants and stressed the importance of family ties and the *padrone* system in maintaining relative order. He discounted the image of *contadini* from harmonious old world villages, retaining a sentimental attachment to the land, being thrust unwittingly into the maelstrom of American urban industrialism, with resulting social break-down. In reality, he claimed, intimate patterns of interaction were maintained, largely through the extended family and *padroni*. What seemed to the outsider a homogeneous community was actually made up of several local groups with intensely local loyalties (see also Parenti, 1968). To a large extent these immigrants recreated their native villages within the industrial city. The Italian immigrants in Chicago 'came to terms with life . . . within the framework of their traditional pattern of thought and behaviour' (Vecoli, 1964, p. 417). Similar sentiments are expressed in Yans-McLaughlin's (1977) study of Italian immi-grants in late nineteenth century Buffalo. The 'ghetto' areas existed because of the language barrier and the need for affordable accommodation, but also because intense local and family networks and shared values and ideology left little need for external contacts. The immigrant experience was marked by a successful adjustment of old country ways to the individual environment, with tradition acting as the mediator between the old and new environments.

Something of a middle ground between Handlin's interpretation and such viewpoints has been suggested by Bodnar (1977a), who has stressed that care should be taken to avoid structural determinism on the one hand and extreme views of cultural persistence on the other. While urbanization is a powerful process, it has always worked within a framework provided by the ethnic background and pre-immigration experiences of individual groups, and the inter-relationship is therefore not dichotomous but dialectical. The 'peasants into achievers' model is clearly an exaggeration, but a pathological approach is inappropriate in nearly all cases. A similar sort of middle position is taken by Hareven in her study of French Canadian families in Manchester, New Hampshire (Hareven, 1977). That such caution is also appropriate for the antebellum era is shown in Conzen's study of Milwaukee's German community which grew up with the city and maintained a high degree of institutional completeness. It is suggested that this group provides an example lying between the 'assimilative success of the British at one extreme and the saga of the "uprooted" on the other' (Conzen, 1976, p. 228).

Both Bodnar and Conzen have made valuable contributions to our under-standing of the detailed relationship between ethnicity and class. Bodnar (1977b) has suggested that the ethnic associations in Steelton, Pennsylvania immediately after the Civil War existed within the context of working class neighbourhoods. The role of ethnicity was to foster identity and community, and to provide a vehicle for adjustment to industrialization. Local dialects and customs persisted among the mainly Slavic working class population, and localism was expressed in fraternal organizations reflecting regional origins. In a study of more immediate interest to urban geographers, Conzen (1975) has factor analysed a 25 per cent sample, drawn from the manuscript schedules of the federal census, to investigate the social areas of Milwaukee in 1850 and 1860. Family structure emerged as the most significant factor in 1850 but formed no distinctive spatial pattern. By 1860 a decentralization trend was evident in the family status dimension, but it had been replaced as the most important factor by socio-economic status. An area of high status native-born inhabitants had emerged close to the lakeshore with an extension on the west side. In general, segregation by ethnicity was greater than by socio-economic status. Seventy-three per cent of Germans in 1850 and 83 per cent in 1860 lived in German neighbourhoods, defined on the basis of at least 60 per cent occupance by a particular group of grid squares the size of four city blocks. Forty-one per cent of the Yankees in 1850 and 53 per cent in 1860 lived in neighbourhoods of 'native-born'. About half of the Irish lived in Irish neighbourhoods at both dates. The trend was towards the consolidation of German and native born neighbourhoods, with the Irish tending to assimilate slightly. The relationship between ethnicity and socio-economic status was close, but was complicated by the fact that the German areas were microcosms of the economic divisions of the city while the Irish neighbourhoods were heavily biased in favour of low socio-economic status.

Some aspects of Irish working-class districting in Waltham, Massachusetts between the 1850s and 1870s have been examined by Gitelman (1974, pp. 136-7). Many of the themes touched on are reminiscent of the pioneering work of Vance in tracing the highly specific employment linkages of mill towns in New England (Vance, 1966). Beirne (1979) has found similar ties within working class areas in Baltimore. At a much more general level, Ward has neatly summarized the reasons for the attractiveness of the city centre for the in-migrant poor (Ward, 1971, pp. 106-9).

At the other end of the socio-economic scale, some attention has been paid to the residential patterns of urban elites, not only because of the more readily available data but because the upper class was most successful in developing a class consciousness (Hirsch, 1978). Pessen (1973), in elaborating upon his thesis that the Jacksonian era was far from being a democratic interlude between oligarchy and pluralism, has shown how centralized elite residential patterns were associated with closeness of community in antebellum New York, Philadelphia, and Boston. Local studies which map places of residence of the socially prominent abound, and there is general agreement that until about mid-century, central locations were favoured by local elites. An interesting case study of Pittsburgh in 1815 (Swauger, 1978) shows a disproportionate concentration of high status occupations in the core and low status groups in the periphery (Figure 8.2). This discrepancy is seen as being due primarily to access to workplace, an argument which is supported by the otherwise anomalous distribution of people with private means and no need to work.

As centralization in the economy culminated in a shift away from the independent merchant towards corporate capitalism later in the century (Porter and Livesay, 1971), much of the provincialism of the elites vanished, especially in the major centres. An inter-city upper class, bolstered by clubs, boarding

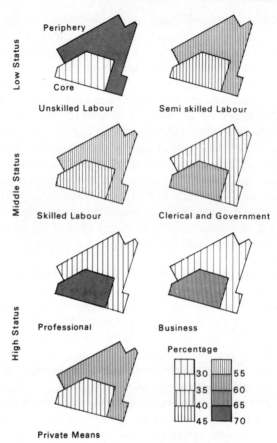

FIGURE 8.2. Residential distribution of occupational groups between core and periphery in
Pittsburgh in 1815. (Reproduced by permission from
the *Annals of the Association of American
Geographers*, **68**, 1978; Figure 2, p. 273)

schools and social registers, emerged in the last two decades of the century
(Baltzell, 1958). There is much agreement that, with the onset of industrialization, the upper class made use of transportation innovations to escape the
confines of the central area. Certainly there is no lack of accounts of the
foundation of high income suburbs and exurbs. However, Baltzell found that as
late as 1940, 88 per cent of Philadelphians listed in *Who's Who* gave an address in
the Main Line–Chestnut Hill neighbourhood (Baltzell, 1958).

Apart from the attempts to gauge social mobility mentioned earlier, many
of the efforts of the new urban historians in the area of social class have been
directed towards constructing measures of socio-economic status. Occupation

seems to provide the most satisfactory and accessible surrogate measure. Much attention has been given to devising suitable occupational status groups into which individual or household data from censuses and city directories can be classified (reviews in Katz, 1972; and Griffen, 1972). Extension of these investigations into a spatial dimension has been attempted in some cases, perhaps most notably by members of the Philadelphia Social History Project (Hershberg et al., 1976), and in isolated studies of other cities. Other evidence has also been used on occasion. For example, Johnston (1966) has used church membership records as a basis for a spatial analysis of social differentiation of Philadelphia in 1838 and 1856, and Bastian (1975) has investigated class segregated patterns of late nineteenth century Terre Haute, Indiana, especially the division between blue- and white-collar workers, as expressed in its residential architecture. Yet, among the major variables which differentiate the social landscape of the nineteenth century US city, social class remains the least comprehensively covered.

RACE

Perhaps the most spectacular product of the laissez-faire US city was the so-called black ghetto. Consistent with the chronology outlined above, the culmination of a trend towards patterns of macro-segregation did not occur until after 1900. The ghetto in its extreme form is largely a twentieth century phenomenon, although the decade of the 1890s was an important transition period. While 'emergent concentrations' were probably to be found somewhat earlier, particularly in the border cities between North and South (Groves and Muller, 1975), 'it seems doubtful that anything even remotely resembling a real black ghetto existed in American cities, north or south, prior to the 1890s' (Kusmer, 1976, p. 12). Much more characteristic of the nineteenth century were the scattered patterns of the older Southern cities and varying degrees of black clustering found elsewhere. E. Franklin Frazier (1957) distinguished between old Southern cities, in which the distribution of the black population approximated that of the white, newer Southern and border cities, where a mixture of clustering and scattering was found, and large Northern cities in which the black population was confined to a small part of the city. Such a classification, while obviously too simple, suffices as a framework for discussion.

Although older Southern cities are commonly believed to have been characterized by 'mixed' racial residential patterns, detailed studies are rare. The substantial literature on race in the South has been concerned with matters other than residential patterns, except in passing. Some of the most useful observations come from sociological studies seeking an historical dimension to contemporary situations (Frazier, 1957; Taeuber and Taeuber, 1965). It is significant that even in the mid-twentieth century the age of a Southern city was the most powerful factor in explaining its levels of segregation as measured by segregation indices (Schnore and Evenson, 1966). Those cities which were important before the Civil War had the highest levels of residential intermixture by census tract.

For the last quarter century, debate on the physical separation of the races in the nineteenth century Southern city has revolved around the thesis developed by C. Vann Woodward in *The Strange Career of Jim Crow*. Sharp criticism following the first publication of this book in 1955 led to a series of disclaimers in the second edition (1957) but the essential argument remained unchanged and was subsequently enlarged and updated (1966). In this influential work, Vann Woodward accurately demonstrated that Jim Crow segregation laws enforcing separation of the races did not exist before 1890. With somewhat less justification, he went on to argue that this reflected an absence of systematic physical separation of the races until a so-called 'capitulation to racism' in the 1890s. This marked deterioration of racial tolerance by whites was reflected not only in new segregation laws but in exclusionary tendencies in such national institutions as churches and unions, in violently racist attitudes in scientific and popular literature, and in a newly aggresive foreign policy. These trends were reinforced by the US Supreme Court decision in the case of *Plessy v. Ferguson* in 1896 which, in declaring that 'legislation is powerless to irradicate racial instincts', sanctioned the principle of 'separate but equal' which remained the official legal position for over half a century.

Debate over this view of systematic segregation as a relatively recent phenomenon has been lengthy, focusing particularly on the need to distinguish between *de jure* and *de facto* segregation. Critics have found segregation in the antebellum North (Litwack, 1961), in the antebellum South (Fischer, 1969), and in the Reconstruction South (Williamson, 1965). On the other hand, several studies have corroborated the thesis, and some rather critical ones have only modified the timing (review in Vann Woodward, 1964). There is no doubt that by the turn of the century the practice of using restrictive convenants to reinforce the so-called racial purity of neighbourhoods was widespread (Vose, 1959) and residential segregation laws reached a peak in the years 1910–1917 (Rice, 1968). This congruence between law and practice undoubtedly contributed to the ghetto formation process in the early twentieth century. The picture before 1890, however, remains unclear, a situation which is aggravated by the traditional lack of interest by historians in residential as opposed to other forms of segregation.

The cities of the antebellum South offer a particularly interesting situation because of the existence of large numbers of urban slaves, in some amounting to almost half of the total population. The well known study by Wade (1964), although advancing several arguments which are by no means universally accepted (Goldin, 1975), nevertheless represented a landmark contribution to the social geography of the antebellum Southern city because it included discussion of residential patterns, recognized the importance of scale factors, distinguished between social distance and spatial distance, and examined differences in the distributions of whites, slaves, and free Negroes. Wade's thesis was that slavery was incompatible with urbanization. Urban slavery was undercut by the opportunities of the urban economy and was in decline by 1860. The practices of 'hiring out' and 'living out' weakened the tie between master and slave. Provision of slave accommodation on the same lot as the main house, which resulted in highly scattered patterns of slave residence at the city-wide scale, was declining during the late antebellum period. It was replaced by a looser ownership system which allowed payment of wages in lieu of accommodation and produced clusters of slaves and former slaves, particularly near wharf areas and on the peripheries of cities. According to this view, it is in the weakening of the institution of slavery that the origins of residential segregation in Southern cities are to be found.

The most highly segregated element in the antebellum Southern city, however, was the free Negro. Berlin has computed the following indices of dissimilarity: white/slave 11.4; white/free Negro 23.2; slave/free Negro 25.3 (Berlin, 1974, p. 250). Even so these blacks remained less segregated than their counterparts in Northern cities. Almost non-existent at the time of the American Revolution, the free Negro group emerged through escape and in-migration from the West Indies. Most of them settled in cities where they sought opportunity, or in the case of runaways, anonymity. They were much more urbanized than either whites or slaves, but never occupied a secure place in the white social system. In reaction to increasing pressures during the antebellum decades their number declined and the gap between them and the slaves narrowed. It may well be that such a deterioration of status was accompanied by increased levels of residential segregation. Certainly Hershberg found such an association in Philadelphia during the period 1838 to 1860 when 'all social indicators—race riots, population decrease, disfranchisement, residential segregation, per capita wealth, ownership of real property, family structure and occupational opportunities—pointed toward socio-economic deterioration within Philadelphia's antebellum black community' (Hershberg, 1971, p. 192).

Some of the separation of free Negroes in Southern cities may be regarded as voluntary as blacks sought to escape the surveillance of whites and the necessity of conforming to the deferential modes of behaviour which whites required. Access to employment opportunities also encouraged clustering. Such clusters were usually near to and frequently overlapping poor white areas in the least desirable sections of cities. Kellogg (1977) has suggested a useful typology of black settlement enclaves in the antebellum city which illustrates the variety of patterns to be found: (i) back-alley dwellings—rows' of servants' houses behind those of masters or employers; (ii) clusters on out-of-the-way streets; (iii) clusters of better-off skilled free Negroes forming communities with institutions such as churches; and (iv) shanty towns near the edge of the city.

It is not clear whether any marked changes took place in racial residential patterns in the South during Reconstruction. The attention of historians has focussed overwhelmingly on the politics of the era, including the political role of the black population. Even where a deliberate attempt has been made to emphasize the social history of the urban black, as, for example, in Blassingame's (1973a) study of New Orleans, residential segregation is scarcely mentioned. The same author's observations on Savannah suggest that mixed patterns remained the rule and that the ghetto model is inappropriate to the Southern city until the twentieth century (Blassingame, 1973b, pp. 483–4), an observation closely in tune with the Vann Woodward thesis. Detailed mapping of racial patterns in another seaport city, Charleston, South Carolina, for 1880 showed little clustering and no tendency towards ghetto formation (Radford, 1976). In contrast, a recent study of six inland centres argues that segregated neighbourhoods grew up almost immediately after the Civil War (Rabinowitz, 1978, pp. 97–124). Rabinowitz's study of Atlanta, Montgomery, Nashville, Raleigh, and Richmond, documents a pattern of post-bellum segregation of blacks in institutions and public facilities, and finds a parallel creation of distinct black housing areas. Well before the end of the century, it is claimed, these cities were made up of two separate but unequal racial societies, reflected in the existence of black ghettoes by 1890. Yet segregation, it is argued, was introduced by white Northerners, and actually represented an improvement in most areas of life over what preceded it. Its forerunner was, in fact, exclusion, a concept which may account for some of the all-Negro towns described by Rose (1965). Rabinowitz's interpretation shifts the search for ghetto origins away from the early twentieth century North, where it has been directed since the mid-1960s, to the Reconstruction South. A middle view is expressed by Kellogg (1977) who has suggested that the large black clusters now visible in Lexington, Atlanta, Richmond, and Durham emerged during two post-bellum periods. The inner cores of these clusters were formed on low land either within the city or at the city's edge, between 1865 and 1880, largely by rural in-migrant freedmen. Subsequent expansion has been achieved both through the addition of new black housing on the edges of the core clusters (a uniquely Southern process), and through invasion–succession processes familiar in the North (Kellogg, 1977, pp. 320–1).

The border cities between North and South have generally been regarded as showing the influence of both regions. Slavery was abandoned here much earlier than in the South, and after the Civil War these cities became increasingly identified with the North, or in some cases the West. Given this, Groves and Muller (1975) hypothesized that scattered patterns would have been abandoned in Baltimore and Washington by 1880 in favour of substantial black residential concentrations. Their conclusions indicate broad acceptance of this hypothesis. Other studies, however (Radford, 1967; Borchert, 1972; Groves, 1974) have emphasized the persistence of micro-segregated racial patterns in Washington, DC up to the end of the century.

The evolution of the black ghettoes in Northern cities has traditionally been attributed to the in-migration of blacks during the twentieth century. This assumption paralleled a view of migration which emphasized the massive Northward shift of the black population after 1914 (Hart, 1960). Since the mid-1960s it has become increasingly clear, first, that a substantial migration of blacks to Northern cities was occurring well before 1910, and secondly, that, in any case, numbers alone do not produce ghettoes. Attention has come to focus upon 1890–1910 as the main period of ghetto inception and on racial dynamics as an active agent in the process. Osofsky's (1965) study of Harlem was the first large-scale study in this vein, and because of a level of spatial awareness unusual in social history, it remains of outstanding interest to geographers. In brief, Osofsky argued that the ghetto emerged in the period 1890–1920 as a necessary response to increasing racial antagonism in an era of rapid black in-migration. The actual location for the ghetto was an unlikely one: a new, largely middle class suburb with a greater percentage of old, wealthy and native-born among its population than among New Yorkers in general. In 1900 the relatively small numbers of blacks were mainly employed in domestic service, and, like the peripheral clusters of Italian immigrants, were treated by the host community as 'curiosities, sources of minor annoyance or objects of charity' (Osofsky, 1965, p. 85).

The extension of the subway system to Harlem in the 1890s created a wave of land speculation, and the area became much in demand, particularly by upwardly mobile East European Jewish immigrants seeking to move out of the Lower East Side. Substantial investments by large companies and small tradesmen alike produced a wave of speculative building ranging from luxury apartment blocks to small houses of frame construction. Property changed hands rapidly, sometimes more than once in a single day, and prices sky-rocketed. Even peripheral garbage dumps became objects of speculation. In 1904–5 the bottom dropped out of the market as it became clear that overbuilding had been rampant and rental levels had become too high to be sustained. Financial institutions withdrew from the loan market, and foreclosures proliferated. Many landlords were forced to choose between financial ruin and renting to blacks. Many took the latter course, often subdividing apartments in an attempt to sustain rent yields. The white population, apprehensive at what they saw as a black invasion, and seeing even racial covenants collapse in the face of economic pressures, resorted to panic selling at substantial losses, a practice often induced by block-busting realtors. In 1914, when an Urban League survey found that blacks occupied 1,100 houses in a twenty-three block area of Harlem, it was already the 'largest colony of colored people, in similar limits, in the world' (Osofsky, 1965, p. 122).

Although Osofsky's explanation of the ghetto-forming process rests heavily on economic factors, particularly the nature of the land market, deteriorating race relations in New York City between 1890 and 1914 are seen as an essential ingredient. Most spatially aware studies have been less concerned with racial attitudes. The classical ecologists, for example, could find little difference between racial and ethnic prejudice, assuming that both would eventually melt away. Park, for all his experience as assistant to Booker T. Washington, remained over-optimistic in this regard (Wilson, 1974, pp. 104–5). McKenzie (1933) recognized that because the 'badge' of skin colour could not, like language and cultural traits, dissipate over time, the black community would expand *in situ* rather than migrating towards the suburbs. However, the framework itself is rooted in ethnic, not racial terms. This tradition has received more recent expression in the work of Oscar Handlin, particularly his earlier work (Handlin, 1941) where he argues a high degree of volunteerism in the establishment of separate black society. Spear's study of ghetto inception in Chicago (Spear, 1967), while carefully evaluating this viewpoint, concludes that separate black institutions were established only after the spatial ghetto had formed, and that the rhetoric on the desirability of erecting a separate society was largely a rationalization. The physical ghetto was 'a product of white hostility'. Katzman is critical of both Osofsky and Spear for underestimating the caste nature of American society (Katzman, 1973, p. 216). Unfortunately, his own study of Detroit, while providing valuable insight into social processes is little concerned with spatial change in the pre-ghetto period, only briefly describing the black clusters in the near east side of the city (Katzman, 1973, pp. 75–80). Deskins (1972) found that, between 1873 and 1965, Detroit blacks consistently recorded lower rates of residential mobility than whites, and also had far less tendency to disperse. The races remained separated by a considerable social distance.

The effects of institutional racism on residential patterns remains an open question, and one to which geographers have much to contribute. Most spatial studies have either underestimated racism, as distinct from ethnic prejudice, as a spatial force, or else have tended to regard it as a powerful constant against which technical and transport changes have operated to produce spatial change. Yet, while rapid in-migration and the streetcar provided essential ingredients for the change from micro to macro segregation patterns, they are not a complete explanation for the transformation. And although it may be useful in present day studies to view white racism as unchanging, it is more accurate in historical study to recognize changes in intensity of racial feeling on both sides. While Vann Woodward's thesis remains controversial, it does provide the basis of a plausible model of the effects of racial dynamics on urban residential patterns. Further articulation and testing of this model promises to advance our knowledge of racial patterns in the nineteenth century city, as well as contributing tangible evidence to the wider debate on the intensity and periodicity of racial residential segregation practices in American society.

THE SEARCH FOR THEORY

The literature surveyed here offers little encouragement to any who would seek a general theory of the changing social geography of the US city. The area is clouded by that mixture of contemporary impression and modern interpretation which Ward has grappled with in the specific case of the Victorian slum (Ward, 1976). There is considerable evidence that by the close of the century some observers had developed an awareness of the nature of the urban expansion process. Richard T. Ely's work in land economics from 1892 onwards, and Hurd's *Principles of City Land Values*, published in 1905, foreshadowed much of the more modern work on urban growth dynamics. Other turn of the century commentators stressed the lack of any deep sense of community in American society, a theme which some modern historical scholars have also found attractive. Lemon (1978) has described an absence of community feeling in Pennsylvania even in the colonial era. More commonly, urban industrial growth in the nineteenth century has been blamed for the erosion of a previously flourshing matrix of local preindustrial communities (Warner, 1972; Bender, 1975). The trend in studies of the sociology of present-day American cities, however, has been towards an emphasis upon the intimacy of urban social networks (Gans, 1962; Suttles, 1968). Further, some recent studies of nineteenth century cities have cast doubt upon the role of industrialization and immigration as agents of disorganization. Hoffecker has characterized her study of Wilmington, Delaware, as 'a partial corrective for . . . the view that urban communality was prevented by excessive individualism' (Hoffecker, 1974, p. xii). Blumin presents a picture of Kingston, New York, experiencing most of the trends current in the middle nineteenth century US, and yet growing *towards* community because of increased social participation (Blumin, 1976; see also Frisch, 1972).

To those willing to adopt a relatively narrow focus on spatial relationships, with perhaps only a superficial consideration of process, such issues present no obstacle to the adoption of the Burgess diagram as a reasonable model of the US industrial city. True it is a partial model. It is based upon Chicago, and cannot account for regional variations. It is bounded temporally by technological stages. The concentric form does not apply to all variables, and the dimension which it fits best may be family status rather than socio-economic status as in the original model. Such partiality is not however the issue, and in any case all but the last of these reservations were readily admitted in the original version. The major difficulty associated with the adoption of the Burgess model is the set of ecological assumptions which, although not evident in either of the two diagrams (Burgess 1925, pp. 51 and 55), form the foundation of the accompanying discussion. The fundamental idea is that population movements and distributions at all scales are ultimately caused by changes in the complex relationship between human communities and their natural environments (Faris, 1967). They are part of an adjustment to disequilibrium, a process which also encompasses social changes of all kinds. An important aspect of the ecological quest was to find out what rate of change could be absorbed by a city without inducing a disequilibrium which would weaken the moral order and leave rampant competition as the only principle governing social and spatial organization. Biotic and economic competition were equated. The neo-ecologists, reacting to criticism of this view, argued that the biotic undercurrents could be safely ignored, and study of the spatial aspects of society could proceed on similar bases as before. A similar position has been taken by Goheen (1972) in his adoption of Park's concept of natural area. Anyone reluctant to separate the spatial patterns of the ecological constructs from the assumptions which underlay them is, however, forced to ponder the validity of the notions of equilibrium, shock, disorganization, survival of the fittest mechanisms, and so on, all of which are important human ecological notions. It is quite possible to regard anomie and other apparent symptoms of disorganization as a direct outcome of laissez-faire processes, rather than stemming from some, perhaps illusory, ecological imbalance (Powell, 1962). Unfortunately, such a viewpoint leaves the spatial models of the ecologists without any obvious *modus operandi* (Firey, 1947).

Nevertheless, the group of hyperactive sociologists (Wilson, 1974, p. 92) at the University of Chicago in the 1920s produced a formulation which is at least a powerful social analogy to the politico-economic phenomenon of laissez-faire. If the Burgess model did not reflect some fundamental truths about modern urban structure, it would not have persisted as our most useful model at the city-wide scale. It describes a highly differentiated city, with specialized land uses, in which residence is ordered according to class and ethnicity, and in which socio-economic status increases from centre to periphery. A set of pervasive themes running through the historical and geographical literature is compatible with the adoption of the Burgess model as our most adequate representation of the end-product of nineteenth century urbanization. As expressed by Goheen (1970), these themes are changing scale, changing heterogeneity of small areas within the city, and changing orientation. The effect of the impact of industrialization on the city was to increase size and distance out of all proportion, to intensify if not initiate a process of sorting leading to the functional specialization of land use, and to reverse the direction of the social gradient.

The problems confronted in attempting to identify a construct to represent the *antecedents* of the industrial city in the US are even greater. The changes outlined above are almost identical to those implied in the work of Sjoberg (1960). The preindustrial city was characterized by an institutional and residential gradient across concentric zones from centre to periphery, within-zone clustering by occupation and family, and an absence of other kinds of differentiation found in the industrial city (Sjoberg, 1960). Yet the adoption of the Sjoberg construct as a model of cities in the US before the industrial revolution can hardly be justified. In addition to the general defects of the construct (Wheatley, 1963), it depends on a set of assumptions which cannot be demonstrated in most of the US. Even in an old Southern city, dominated by a genuine non-mercantile elite, its success in linking process to pattern is only moderate (Radford, 1979). When Thernstrom (1964) writes of the transformation of Newburyport from a small town controlled by a centrally located elite into an industrial town from which the upper class has escaped, it is tempting to view the differences between empirical history and a Sjoberg-to-Burgess construct as more of degree than of kind. Indeed, this framework is often called upon to do service as an introduction to studies of contemporary cities, for example by Ottensman (1975), and occasionally as an organizational framework (as in Deskins, 1972). Nevertheless, although attractive as a pedogogical device for assessing the impact of industrialization on the city, such a construct is seriously deficient as a research hypothesis.

Three of the most attractive alternatives to such a scheme remain in unpublished form: Walker (1977) has related internal structural changes in the US city since 1780 to three stages of industrial accumulation, and provided a detailed Marxian interpretation of the suburbanization process; Weiss (1970) has applied the orthogenetic—heterogenetic typology of Redfield and Singer (1954) to the evolution of Boston from Puritan to modern times, suggesting a link between the internal structure of a city and its cultural role; and Bowden (1972) has proposed a detailed model of the colonial replica city, and argued more generally for the recognition of the commercial city, rather than the preindustrial city, as the main antecedent to the industrial city in the United States. The latter viewpoint echoes sentiments which have been expressed elsewhere in the geographical literature (Pred, 1966; Davey and Doucet, 1975; Vance, 1977). It suggests that the evolution of the industrial city is best regarded as proceeding, not from a preindustrial city dominated by a gentry, but from a commercial city based on mercantile pursuits. The fullest general statement of this process is that of Warner (1968a; 1968b), who suggested that changing relationships between jobs, housing and transportation largely define the American urban experience and provide a scaffolding for comparative study. In a recent review of the new urban history, Hershberg (1978) concludes that Warner's suggestions have not been followed up, and that they form perhaps the most promising research frontier. It is this very area to which many of the most valuable contributions by geographers have been addressed, and from which the makings of a descriptive model emerge.

In simple terms, the changes in scale, heterogeneity and orientation which accompanied industrialization can largely be accounted for by the operation of three sets of forces. The first and most widely discussed is the impact of intra-urban transportation innovations. The horse car diffused rapidly down the urban hicrarchy in the 1850s (Krim, 1967), as did the electric streetcar after 1887 (general overview in Ward, 1970). Ward (1964) and Warner (1962) have described streetcar suburbanization in Boston, and their work has been taken a step further in Pittsburgh by Tarr (1972). These and similar studies elsewhere have emphasized the close relationship between the private street railway companies and the residential property market. In essence, improved transportation increased the residential options for those who could afford to use it. The relationship between fares and wages made streetcars essentially a white-collar mode of transportation until late in the nineteenth century. It was the upper and middle classes who were first able to leave the increasingly unattractive environment of the downtown, pulled both by a deep seated rural ideal (Muller, 1977) and by cheaper per unit land costs on the urban periphery.

A second set of forces contributing to the urban transformation was the advent of factory industry. Vance (1966) has traced the linkages between place of work and residence in industrializing New England. Following the highly specific employment linkages of the dormitories and tied houses of the early milltowns came Holyoke, Massachusetts, which represented a departure from the paternalistic mode of housing provision. The physical and psychological separation of work and residence led to the development of a housing market distinct from the market for productive land, and thence to functional districting, a functional hierarchy, urban sprawl and working class residential areas. This pattern was imported into the industrializing mercantile cities. Although this early work of Vance can be faulted for overstating the role of industry as the initiator rather than the major catalyst of such changes, it nevertheless provides considerable insight into the impact of factory employment on urban structure. Further, in viewing transportation as the agency by which the stretching of the employment linkage was accomplished rather than the cause of the separation, it acts as a corrective to interpretations of changing urban structure which depend too heavily on the impact of the streetcar (see also Zunz, 1972). In addition to providing a new type of employment linkage, factory industry also contributed to the deteriorating environment of the central areas, thus providing additional impetus to the out-migration of high income groups.

A third set of forces contributing to these structural changes involved the expansion of the central business district. Bowden (1975) has examined in great detail the dynamics of CBD differentiation and growth. Rapid expansion in bursts of growth had considerable impact upon surrounding residential areas, giving rise to the so-called zone of transition of the Burgess model. Ward has attempted a refinement of this idea by linking particular edges of the expanding CBD with particular types of central residential area (Figure 8.3). Only the edge of the retail area fits the residential displacement stereotype, the others abutting more or less durable communities. A particularly lucid case study of the effect of CBD expansion on residential succession is provided for late nineteenth century Nashville by Marshall (1975).

Intra-urban transportation innovations, the impact of factory employment, and CBD differentiation and growth, then, account in large part for the urban transformation process. Other factors, including changing residential tastes in the rising middle class, changing family size, and repulsive forces between certain ethnic and racial groups, also played a role. The most dramatic result was the

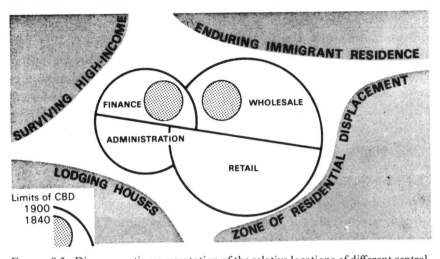

FIGURE 8.3. Diagrammatic representation of the relative locations of different central residential areas. (Reproduced by permission of Oxford University Press)

reversal of the social gradient: 'The social geography of the big city of 1860 was almost the reverse of the late nineteenth and early twentieth-century metropolis' (Warner, 1968b, p. 56). By the latter period the city was split between a white, native, Protestant, Republican, middle class periphery, and a poor, blue collar, black and immigrant core run according to the 'boss system' (Wade, 1968).

CONCLUSION

An integration of the major sections of this essay makes possible the identification of certain broad trends in the social geography of the nineteenth century US city. In essence, the most important changes can be interpreted as a set of transformation processes involving the increasing socio-spatial differentiation of the population according to class, ethnicity, and race. The main agents of spatial change were intra-urban transportation innovations, the rise of the factory system, and the expansion of the CBD, augmented by the impact of a new inmigrant population and an evolving class structure. Cities became much larger, their social gradients were reversed, and districts within them showed increasing homogeneity. All of these changes were accomplished through high rates of spatial mobility during periodic bursts of growth related to the economic cycle.

If these broad generalizations can be taken to represent something of a consensus within the literature, it is also true that behind them lie considerable gaps in our knowledge and wide differences in the interpretation of specific aspects of the urban transformation. Even in the area of ethnicity, with its vast literature, fundamental issues remain unresolved. The lack of 'an appropriate paradigm for ethnic research' exists, not because of 'a lack of interest and effort, but rather . . . because the subject is broad and multi-dimensional' (Raitz, 1979). Two decades or so of comparable effort in the study of race in the nineteenth century city have failed to produce even the shaky consensus reached by ethnic historians, while the study of social class remains an underdeveloped area.

Within the discussion of class, ethnicity, race, and mobility in the nineteenth century city, the spatial patterning of the population occupies a potentially important but as yet largely undefined position. Traditionally regarded by historians as among the least important aspects of cities, the spatial arrangement of demographic variables has proved in many cases to be among the easiest to verify empirically. While there is much evidence that interest in spatial patterns is growing among urban historians (see, for example, the recent text by Goldfield and Brownell, 1979) it is still unusual for spatial arrangements to be used as direct evidence of social process. The spatial perspective and techniques of the geographer have much to offer in this respect. On the other hand, it would be a mistake for geographers to limit their contribution to spatial insights alone. Historical geographers have maintained a firm commitment to the cultural and landscape traditions of the discipline which largely eluded urban geography for several years. The comparatively small group of urban historical geographers in the US has brought to urban studies a sensitivity to the role of culture in the evolution of urban morphology and the allocation of functional and residential space, thereby viewing the American city not *sui generis* but as a part of American society.

The perpetuation of this tradition requires, for the nineteenth century US, a full appreciation of the increasing pervasiveness of the ideology of laissez-faire. This doctrine held no monopoly on American thought, especially among intellectuals. However, while not always so explicitly 'anti-urban' as has sometimes been claimed (White and White, 1962), the intellectual community tended to be remarkably disinterested in urban affairs. City development was conducted within the ideological context of the free market, and no force other than that of the market bound together the myriad decisions which, in aggregate, produced city growth and change. Peterson's (1979) recent study shows how deeply the development of urban sanitary reforms between 1840 and 1890 was affected by suspicion of concentrated governmental authority and a strong tradition of professional autonomy. Architects, engineers, designers, and several other professionals worked, quite independently, to produce innovations, while such regulation as existed was divided among local, state and federal bodies. The resulting absence of an overall conception resulted in unevenness and unpredictability. In several areas of reform, even during the Progressive era, efforts tended to be either absorbed or deflected. When Upton Sinclair wrote graphic descriptions of the industrial accidents which could befall immigrant workers in the Chicago meat-packing houses (Sinclair, 1906) he could hardly have forseen that the resulting public outcry would ensure passage, not of labour reform measures, but of the Pure Food and Drug Act of 1906. Likewise, business interests were successful in stalling until after 1916 state legislation which would allow cities to introduce zoning ordinances. Even then planning objectives remained a long way from radical intervention. When R. M. Haig, in his eloquent statement of 1927, identified the chief goal of planning as the minimization of the costs of friction, he successfully characterized the dominant planning philosophy of a whole era (Haig, 1927, pp. 31–44).

Recognition of the pervasiveness of laissez-faire values should not lead us to assume a uniformity of urban structure in the nineteenth century US. In fact the opposite was the case. Laissez-faire attitudes encouraged diversity by sanctioning the implementation of individual conceptions of urban expansion. Certain morphological innovations diffused widely through the urban system, but there was room for an infinite variety of detail which was later to be criticized as a lack of coherence in the urban landscape. Similarly, varying ethnic and racial mixes, class structures and employment bases produced considerable inter-urban variations in social geography. In addition the forces of laissez-faire themselves showed great temporal and regional contrasts. It would be a mistake, for example, to project the excess of the 1880s back to the antebellum era. Yet the 'vogue for Spencer' was clearly grafted onto a much older tradition of individualism, to which it lent the authority of a philosophy uniquely suited to the Darwinian era (Hofstadter, 1959). The broader continuity of individualism is perhaps better conveyed in Warner's concept of 'privatism' which unites on the basis of a common attitude towards property the otherwise very different urban environments of 1780 and 1920. Middle and late nineteenth century industrialization can be seen as accelerating rather than initiating major trends, casting doubt upon the validity of the notion of a 'preindustrial' era in the United States. The most commonly recognized regional deviant in the march of nineteenth century 'progress' is the South, which is often viewed as defining its identity in opposition to the excessive individualism of a grasping North. By mid-century the West was becoming fully integrated functionally and ideologically with an expanding northeast core, but the South, by most accounts, remained apart until the New South movements later in the century. Here again, however, there are those who emphasize continuity and uniformity throughout the US. Certain urban historians (especially Goldfield, 1977) have departed from precedent in viewing even the antebellum Southern city as substantially conforming to the American norm. Such a view leaves unanswered several questions relating to process and pattern in early- and mid-nineteenth century cities. Comparative studies of the spatial structure of the US commercial city, focusing on regional contrasts in ideology as well as economic and demographic variables, present a major research frontier for the historical geographer.

A second research frontier is the transformation process itself. Ward (1975) has reminded us most forcefully that transformation was neither simple nor sudden. Different elements underwent change at different rates and times, and it was only late in the century that the various transformation processes produced a highly differentiated 'modern' city. Geographers would seem well equipped to chart temporal and regional variations in the onset of transformation among members of the urban hierarchy. At present our knowledge is highly impressionistic. A reversal of the social gradient seems to have occurred early in the century in Newburyport (Thernstrom, 1964) and late in the century in Cincinnati (Miller, 1968). Yet position in the urban hierarchy may have been as important as location (Jackson, 1975), and it may prove possible to identify critical population thresholds. Finally, the mix of process and pattern found within individual transitional cities would repay close attention at the micro-scale. The best recent study of this type (Muller and Groves, 1979) stresses local variations in the speed and sequence of change, giving the transitional city almost a cellular structure. The detailed study of neighbourhood responses to the vast changes in nineteenth century urban society may prove to be the most rewarding research direction of all.

ACKNOWLEDGEMENTS

I wish to thank my colleagues J. U. Marshall, R. A. Murdie, and J. O'Mara for commenting on an earlier draft of this paper.

REFERENCES

Addams, J. (1895). *Hull House Maps and Papers*, Thomas Y. Crowell & Co., New York. Reprint edition Arno Press, 1970.

Alcorn, R. S. and Knights, P. R. (1975). Most uncommon Bostonians: a critique of Stephen Thernstrom's *The Other Bostonians*. *Historical Methods Newsletter*, **8**, 98–114.

Anderson, A. N. (1977). *The Origin and Resolution of an Urban Crisis*, Johns Hopkins Press, Baltimore.

Baltzell, E. D. (1958). *Philadelphia Gentlemen*, The Free Press, Glencoe, Illinois.

Bastian, R. W. (1975). Architecture and class segregation in late nineteenth century Terre Haute, Indiana. *Geographical Review*, **65**, 166–179.

Beijbom, U. (1971). *Swedes in Chicago* (trans. Donald Brown), Laromedelsforlagen, Stockholm.

Beirne, D. R. (1979). Residential growth and stability in the Baltimore community of Canton during the late nineteenth century. *Maryland Historical Magazine*, **74**, 39–51.

Bender, T. (1975). *Toward an Urban Vision: Ideas and Institutions in Nineteenth Century America*, University Press of Kentucky, Lexington, Kentucky.

Berlin, I. (1974). *Slaves Without Masters: The Free Negro in the Antebellum South*, Pantheon Books, New York.

Berthoff, R. (1960). The American social order: a conservative hypothesis. *American Historical Review*, **65**, 495–514.

Blassingame, J. W. (1973a). *Black New Orleans: 1860–1880*, University of Chicago Press, Chicago.

Blassingame, J. W. (1973b). Before the ghetto: the making of the black community in Savannah, Georgia, 1865–1880. *Journal of Social History*, **6**, 463–488.

Blumin, S. M. (1976). *The Urban Threshold: Growth and Change in a Nineteenth Century American Community*, University of Chicago Press, Chicago.

Bodnar, J. (1977a). The immigrant and the American city. *Journal of Urban History*, **3**, 241–250.

Bodnar, J. (1977b). *Immigration and Industrialization*, University of Pittsburgh Press, Pittsburgh.

Borchert, J. (1972). The rise and fall of Washington's inhabited alleys: 1852–1972. *Records of the Columbia Historical Society*, 276–288.

Bowden, M. J. (1972). The internal structure of the colonial replica city: San Francisco and others. *Paper presented to the Annual Meeting of the Association of American Geographers, Kansas City.*

Bowden, M. J. (1975). Growth of the central districts of large cities. In L. F. Schnore (Ed.), *The New Urban History*, Princeton University Press, Princeton, New Jersey.

Burgess, E. W. (1925). The growth of the city: an introduction to a research project. In R. E. Park, E. W. Burgess, and R. D. McKenzie, *The City*, University of Chicago Press, Chicago, pp. 47–62.

Chudacoff, H. P. (1972). *Mobile Americans: Residential and Social Mobility in Omaha, 1880–1920.* Oxford University Press, New York.

Conzen, K. N. (1975). Patterns of residence in early Milwaukee. In L. F. Schnore (Ed.), *The New Urban History*, Princeton University Press, Princeton, New Jersey.

Conzen, K. N. (1976). *Immigrant Milwaukee, 1836–1860: Accommodation and Community in a Frontier City*, Harvard University Press, Cambridge, Mass.

Cressey, P. F. (1938). Population succession in Chicago: 1898–1930. *American Journal of Sociology*, **44**, 59–69.

Curti, M. (1959). *The Making of an American Community*, Stanford University Press, Stanford, California.

Dahl, R. A. (1961). *Who Governs? Democracy and Power in an American City*, Yale University Press, New Haven, Connecticut.

Davey, I. and Doucet, M. (1975). The social geography of a commercial city, ca. 1853. In Katz, M. *The People of Hamilton, Canada West*, Harvard University Press, Cambridge, Massachusetts.

Decker, P. R. (1978). *Fortunes and Failures: White Collar Mobility in Nineteenth Century San Francisco.* Harvard University Press, Cambridge, Mass.

Deskins, D. R. (1972). Residential mobility of Negroes in Detroit, 1837–1965. Michigan Geographical Publications No. 5, University of Michigan, Ann Arbor.

Dinnerstein, L., Nichols, R. L., and Reimers, D. M. (1979). *Natives and Strangers*, Oxford University Press, New York.

Elazar, D. S. (1970). *Cities of the Prairie*, Basic Books, New York.

Esslinger, D. R. (1975). *Immigrants and the City: Ethnicity and Mobility in a Nineteenth Century Midwestern Community*, Kennikat Press, Port Washington, New York.

Faris, R. E. L. (1967). *Chicago Sociology: 1920–1932.* Chandler Publishing Co., San Francisco.

Faris, R. E. L. and Dunham, H. W. (1960). *Mental Disorders in Urban Areas*, University of Chicago Press, Chicago. Reprinted.

Firey, W. (1947). *Land Use in Central Boston*, Harvard University Press, Cambridge, Massachusetts.

Fischer, R. A. (1969). Racial segregation in antebellum New Orleans. *American Historical Review*, **74**, 926–937.

Frazier, E. F. (1957). *The Negro in the United States*, MacMillan, New York.

Fried, M. (1973). *The World of the Urban Working Class*, Harvard University Press, Cambridge, Massachusetts.

Frisch, M. H. (1972). *Town into City: Springfield, Massachusetts and the Meaning of Community, 1840–1890*. Harvard University Press, Cambridge, Mass.

Gans, H. J. (1962). *The Urban Villagers: Group and class in the Life of Italian–Americans*, The Free Press, New York.

Gitelman, H. M. (1974). *Workingmen of Waltham: Mobility in American Urban Industrial Development, 1850–1890*, Johns Hopkins Press, Baltimore.

Goheen, P. G. (1970). *Victorian Toronto*, University of Chicago, Department of Geography Research Paper No. 127.

Goheen, P. G. (1972). Human ecology at Chicago. *Geographical Review*, **62**, 419–420.

Goldfield, D. R. (1977). Pursuing the American dream: cities in the old South. In B. A. Brownell and D. R. Goldfield (Eds.), *The City in Southern History*, Kennikat Press, Port Washington, N. Y.

Goldfield, D. R., and Brownell, B. A. (1979). *Urban America: From Downtown to No Town*, Houghton Mifflin, Boston.

Goldin, C. D. (1975). Urbanization and slavery: the issue of compatibility. In L. F. Schnore (Ed.) *The New Urban History*, Princeton University Press, Princeton, New Jersey, pp. 231 246.

Griffen, C. (1969). Workers divided: the effect of craft and ethnic difference in Poughkeepsie, New York, 1850–1880. In S. Thernstrom and R. Sennett, *Nineteenth Century Cities*, Yale University Press, New Haven, Connecticut, pp. 49–93.

Griffen, C. (1972). The study of occupational mobility in nineteenth century America: problems and possibilities. *Journal of Social History*, **5**, 310–330.

Griffen, C., and Griffen, S. (1978). *The Ordering of Opportunity in mid-Nineteenth Century Poughkeepsie*, Harvard University Press, Cambridge, Massachusetts.

Groves, P. A. (1974). The 'hidden' population: Washington alley dwellers in the late nineteenth century. *Professional Geographer*, **26**, 270–276.

Groves, P. A., and Muller, E. K. (1975). The evolution of black residential areas in late nineteenth-century cities. *Journal of Historical Geography*, **1**, 169–191.

Gutman, H. G. (1969). The reality of the rags-to-riches 'myth': the case of the Paterson, New Jersey, locomotive, iron and machinery manufacturers, 1830–1860. In S. Thernstrom and R. Sennett (Eds.), *Nineteenth Century Cities*, Yale University Press, New Haven, Connecticut.

Haig, R. M. (1927). *Major Economic Factors in Metropolitan Growth and Arrangement*, Regional Plan of New York and its Environs, New York.

Hancock, J. L. (1967). Planners in the changing American city, 1900–1940. *Journal of the American Institute of Planners*, **33**, 290–304.

Handlin, O. (1941). *Boston's Immigrants*, Harvard University Press, Cambridge, Massachusetts.

Handlin, O. (1951). *The Uprooted*, Little, Brown, Boston.

Handlin, O. (1963). The modern city as a field of historical study. In O. Handlin and J. Burchard (Eds.) *The Historian and the City*, MIT Press, Cambridge, Massachusetts, pp. 1–26.

Hareven, T. K. (1977). The laborers of Manchester, New Hampshire, 1880–1940; the role of family and ethnicity in adjustment to urban and industrial life. In R. L. Erlich (Ed.) *Immigrants in Industrial America, 1860–1920*, University Press of Virginia, Charlottsville.

Hart, J. F. (1960). 'The changing distribution of the American Negro. *Annals of the Association of American Geographers*, **50**, 242–266.

Harvey, D. (1973). *Social Justice and the City*, Arnold, London.

Hays, S. P. (1957). *The Response to Industrialism: 1885–1914*, University of Chicago Press, Chicago.

Hershberg, T. (1971). Free blacks in antebellum Philadelphia: a study of ex-slaves, freeborn, and socio-economic decline. *Journal of Social History*, **5**, 189–190.

Hershberg, T. *et al.* (1976). The Philadelphia social history project. *Historical Methods Newsletter*, **9**, passim.

Hershberg, R. (1978). The new urban history: toward an interdisciplinary history of the city. *Journal of Urban History*, **5**, 3–40.

Hirsch, S. E. (1978). *Roots of the American Working Class*, University of Pennsylvania Press, Philadelphia.

Hoffecker, C. E. (1974). *Wilmington, Delaware: Portrait of an Industrial City, 1830–1910*, University Press of Virginia, for the Eleutherian Mills–Hagley Foundation, Wilmington.

Hofstadter, R. (1959). *Social Darwinism in American Thought*, Rev. ed., New York, George Brazilier.

Hopkins, R. J. (1968). Occupational and geographic mobility in Atlanta, 1870–1896. *Journal of Southern History*, **34**, 200–213.

Hoyt, H. (1933). *One Hundred Years of Land Values in Chicago: The Relationship of the Growth of Chicago to the Rise in its Land Values, 1830–1933*, University of Chicago Press, Chicago.

Hugins, W. (Ed.) (1972). *The Reform Impulse: 1825–1850*, Harper and Row, New York.

Hunter, F. (1953). *Community Power Structure: a Study of Decision Makers*, University of North Carolina Press, Chapel Hill.

Hurd, R. M. (1905). *Principles of City Values*, The Record and Guide, New York.

Isard, W. (1942). Transport developments and building cycles. *Quarterly Journal of Economics*, **57**, 90–112.

Jackson, K. T. (1975). Urban deconcentration in the nineteenth century: a statistical enquiry. In L. F. Schnore (Ed.) *The New Urban History*, Princeton University Press, Princeton, New Jersey, pp. 110–144.

Johnston, N. J. (1966). The caste and class of the urban form of historic Philadelphia. *Journal of the American Institute of Planners*, **32**, 334–350.

Johnston, R. J. (1971). *Urban Residential Patterns: An Introductory Overview*, G. Bell, London.

Katz, M. B. (1972). Occupational classification in history. *Journal of Interdisciplinary History*, **3**, 63–88.

Katz, M. B. (1975). *The People of Hamilton, Canada West*, Harvard University Press, Cambridge, Massachusetts.

Katz, M. B., Doucet, M. J., and Stern, M. J. (1978). Migration and the social order in Erie County, New York 1855. *Journal of Interdisciplinary History*, **8**, 669–701.

Katzman, D. M. (1973). *Before the Ghetto: Black Detroit in the Nineteenth Century*, University of Illinois Press, Urbana, Illinois.

Kellogg, J. (1977). Negro urban clusters in the postbellum South. *Geographical Review*, **67**, 310–321.

Kessner, T. (1977). *The Golden Door: Italian and Jewish Immigrant Mobility in New York City, 1880–1915*, Oxford University Press, New York.

Knights, P. R. (1969). Population turnover, persistence, and residential mobility in Boston, 1830–1860. In S. Thernstrom and R. Sennett (Eds.) *Nineteenth Century Cities*, Yale University Press, New Haven, Connecticut.

Knights, P. R. (1971). *The Plain People of Boston, 1830–1860*, Oxford University Press, New York.

Kolko, G. (1963). *The Triumph of Conversatism*, The Free Press, Glencoe, Illinois.

Krim, A. J. (1967). The innovation and diffusion of the street railway in North America. *Unpublished M. A. Thesis,* Department of Geography, University of Chicago.

Kusmer, K. L. (1976). *A Ghetto Takes Shape: Black Cleveland, 1870–1930,* University of Illinois Press, Urbana, Illinois.

Lemon, J. T. (1978). The weakness of place and community in early Pennsylvania. In J. R. Gibson (Ed.) *European Settlement and Development in North America,* University of Toronto Press, Toronto.

Leon, D. H. (1971). Whatever happened to an American socialist party? a critical survey of the spectrum of interpretations. *American Quarterly,* **23,** 236–258.

Litwack, L. F. (1961). *North of Slavery: The Negro in the Free States, 1790–1860,* University of Chicago Press, Chicago.

McKelvey, B. (1949). *Rochester: The Flower City 1855–1890,* Harvard University Press, Cambridge, Massachusetts.

McKenzie, R. D. (1933). *The Metropolitan Community.* Russell and Russell, New York.

Marshall, J. M. (1975). Residential expansion and central city change. In J. F. Blumstein and B. Walter (Eds.) *Growing Metropolis: Aspects of Nashville,* Vanderbilt University Press, Nashville, Tennessee, pp. 33–64.

Michelson, W. H. (1976). *Man and his Urban Environment,* 2nd ed. Addison–Wesley Publishing Company, Reading, Massachusetts.

Miller, Z. L. (1968). *Boss Cox's Cincinnati: Urban Politics in the Progressive Era,* Oxford University Press, New York.

Mills, C. W. (1956). *The Power Elite,* Oxford University Press, New York.

Muller, E. K., and Groves, P. A. (1979). The emergence of industrial districts in mid-nineteenth century Baltimore. *Geographical Review,* **69,** 159–178.

Muller, P. O. (1977). The evolution of American suburbs: a geographical interpretation. *Urbanism Past and Present,* **4,** 1–10.

Mumford, L. (1938). *The Culture of Cities,* Secker and Warburg, London.

Nelli, H. S. (1970). *Italians in Chicago: 1880–1920,* Oxford University Press, New York.

Osofsky, G. (1965). *Harlem: The Making of a Ghetto,* Harper and Row, New York.

Ottensman, J. R. (1975). *The Changing Spatial Structure of American Cities,* D. C. Heath and Co., Lexington, Massachusetts.

Packard, V. (1972). *A Nation of Strangers,* David McKay, New York.

Parenti, M. (1968). Immigration and political life. In F. C. Jaher (Ed.) *The Age of Industrialism in America,* The Free Press, New York, pp. 79–99.

Pessen, E. (1973). *Riches, Class, and Power Before the Civil War,* D. C. Heath and Co., Lexington, Massachusetts.

Peterson, J. A. (1979). The impact of sanitary reform upon American urban planning, 1840–1890. *Journal of Social History,* **13,** 83–103.

Polanyi, K. (1944). *The Great Transformation,* Farrar and Rinehart, New York.

Pooley, C. G. (1979). Residential mobility in the Victorian city. *Transactions, Institute of British Geographers,* (N.S.), **4,** 258–277.

Porter, G., and Livesay, H. C. (1971). *Merchants and Manufacturers,* Johns Hopkins Press, Baltimore.

Powell, E. H. (1962). The evolution of the American city and the emergence of anomie: a culture case study of Buffalo, New York, 1810–1910. *British Journal of Sociology,* **13,** 156–168.

Pred, A. R. (1966). *The Spatial Dynamics of US Urban–Industrial Growth, 1800–1914,* MIT Press, Cambridge, Massachusetts.

Punch (1851). *Last Appendix to 'Yankee Doodle'.* 117.

Rabinowitz, H. N. (1978). *Race Relations in the Urban South: 1865–1890.* Oxford University Press, New York.

Radford, J. P. (1967). Patterns of White–Nonwhite Residential Segregation in Washington, DC in the Late Nineteenth Century. Unpublished M. A. Thesis, University of Maryland.

Radford, J. P. (1976). Race, residence and ideology: Charleston, South Carolina in the mid-nineteenth century. *Journal of Historical Geography*, **2**, 329–346.

Radford, J. P. (1979). Testing the model of the pre-industrial city: the case of ante-bellum Charleston, South Carolina. *Transactions, Institute of British Geographers*, (N.S.), **4**, 392–410.

Raitz, K. B. (1979). Themes in the cultural geography of European ethnic groups in the United States. *Geographical Review*, **69**, 79–94.

Redfield, R., and Singer, M. B. (1954). The cultural role of cities. *Economic Development and Cultural Change*, **3**, 53–73.

Rice, R. L. (1968). Residential segregation by law, 1910–1917. *Journal of Southern History*, **34**, 179–199.

Rose, H. M. (1965). The all-Negro town: its evolution and function. *Geographical Review*, **55**, 362–381.

Ross, H. N. (1968). Economic growth and change in the United States under laissez-faire: 1870–1929. In F. C. Jaher, *The Age of Industrialism in the United States*, pp. 6–48.

Rostow, W. W. (1960). *The Stages of Economic Growth*, Cambridge University Press, Cambridge.

Schnore, L. F. and Evenson, P. C. (1966). Segregation in southern cities. *American Journal of Sociology*, **72**, 56–67.

Scott, J. W. (1969). The glassworkers of Carmaux, 1850–1900. In S. Thernstrom and R. Sennett, *Nineteenth Century Cities*, Yale University Press, New Haven, Connecticut, pp. 3–48.

Scott, M. (1971). *American City Planning Since 1890*, University of California Press, Berkeley and Los Angeles.

Shannon, D. A. (Ed.) (1963). *Beatrice Webb's American Diary: 1898*, University of Wisconsin Press, Madison.

Simmons, J. W. (1968). Changing residence in the city: a review of intra-urban mobility. *Geographical Review*, **58**, 622–651.

Sinclair, U. B. (1906). *The Jungle*, Grosset and Dunlap, New York.

Sjoberg, G. (1960). *The Preindustrial City*, The Free Press, New York.

Soltow, L. (1975). *Men and Wealth in the United States, 1850–1870*, Yale University Press, New Haven, Connecticut.

Spear, A. H. (1967). *Black Chicago: The Making of a Negro Ghetto, 1890–1920*, University of Chicago Press, Chicago.

Sullenger, T. E. (1932). A study in intra-urban mobility. *Sociology and Social Research*, **17**, 16–24.

Suttles, G. D. (1968). *The Social Order of the Slum: Ethnicity and Territory in the Inner City*, University of Chicago Press, Chicago.

Swauger, J. (1978). Pittsburgh's residential pattern in 1815. *Annals of the Association of American Geographers*, **68**, 265–277.

Taeuber, K. E., and Taeuber, A. F. (1965). *Negroes in Cities: Residential Segregation and Neighbourhood Change*, Aldine Publishing Co., Chicago.

Tarr, J. L. (1972). *Transportation Innovation and Changing Spatial Patterns: Pittsburgh, 1850–1910*, Carnegie–Mellon University, Pittsburgh.

Thernstrom, S. (1964). *Poverty and Progress: Social Mobility in a Nineteenth Century City*, Harvard University Press, Cambridge, Massachusetts.

Thernstrom, S. (1973). *Other Bostonians: Poverty and Progress in the American Metropolis, 1880–1970*, Harvard University Press, Cambridge, Massachusetts.

Thernstrom, S. and Knights, P. R. (1970). Men in motion: some data and speculation about urban population mobility in nineteenth century America. *Journal of Interdisciplinary History*, **1**, 7–36.

Tietze, C., Lemkan, P. and Cooper, M. (1942). Personality disorder and spatial mobility. *American Journal of Sociology*, **48**, 29–39.

Vance, J. E. (1966). Housing the worker: the employment linkage as a force in urban structure. *Economic Geography*, **42**, 294–325.

Vance, J. E. (1977). *This Scene of Man*, Harper, New York.

Vecoli, R. J. (1964). Contadini in Chicago: a critique of *The Uprooted*. *Journal of American History*, **54**, 1964, 404–417.

Vose, C. (1959). *Caucasians Only: The Supreme Court, The NAACP, and the Restrictive Covenant Cases*, University of California Press, Barkeley and Los Angeles.

Wade, R. C. (1964). *Slavery in the Cities: the South, 1820–1860*, Oxford University Press, New York.

Wade, R. C. (1968). Urbanization. In C. V. Woodward (Ed.), *The Comparative Approach to American History*, Basic Books, New York.

Walker, R. A. (1977). The Suburban Solution: Urban Geography and Urban Reform in the Capitalist Development of the United States. Unpublished Ph.D. dissertation, The Johns Hopkins University.

Walter, B. (1975). Ethnicity and residential succession: Nashville, 1850 to 1920. In J. F. Blumstein and B. Walter (Eds.), *Growing Metropolis: Aspects of Development in Nashville*, Vanderbilt University Press, Nashville, Tennessee, pp. 3–32.

Ward, D. (1964). A comparative historical geography of streetcar suburbs in Boston, Massachusetts and Leeds, England. *Annals of the Association of American Geographers*, **54**, 477–489.

Ward, D. (1969). The internal spatial structure of immigrant residential districts in the late nineteenth century. *Geographical Analysis*, **4**, 337–353.

Ward, D. (1970). The internal spatial differentiation of immigrant residential districts. Northwestern University, Department to Geography, *Special Publication No. 3*, 24–42.

Ward, D. (1971). *Cities and Immigrants: A Geography of Change in Nineteenth Century America*. Oxford University Press, New York.

Ward, D. (1975). Victorian cities: how modern? *Journal of Historical Geography*, **1**, 135–151.

Ward, D. (1976). The Victorian slum: an enduring myth? *Annals of the Association of American Geographers*, **66**, 323–336.

Ware, N. (1924). *The Industrial Worker 1840–1860*, Houghton, Mifflin Co., Boston.

Warner, S. B. (1962). *Streetcar Suburbs*, Harvard University Press, Cambridge, Massachusetts.

Warner, S. B. (1968a). *The Private City: Philadelphia in Three Periods of Its Growth*, MIT Press, Cambridge, Massachusetts.

Warner, S. B. (1968b). If all the world were Philadelphia: a scaffolding for urban history, 1774–1930. *American Historical Review*, **74**, 26–43.

Warner, S. B. (1972). *The Urban Wilderness*, Harper and Row, New York.

Warner, S. B., and Burke, C. B. (1969). 'Cultural change and the ghetto', *Journal of Contemporary History*, **4**, 173–187.

Wheatley, P. (1963). What the greatness of a city is said to be: reflections on Sjoberg's 'Preindustrial City'. *Pacific Viewpoint*, **4**, 163–188.

White, M. A., and White, L. (1962). *The Intellectual Versus the City*, Harvard University Press, Cambridge, Massachusetts.

Weiss, E. T., Jr. (1970). The City and its Cultural Role: Spatial and Conceptual Implications. Unpublished M.A. Thesis, Clark University.

Williamson, J. (1965). *After Slavery: The Negro in South Carolina During Reconstruction, 1861–1877*, University of North Carolina Press, Chapel Hill.

Wilson, W. H. (1974). *Coming of Age: Urban America, 1915–1945*, John Wiley and Sons, Inc., New York.

Woods, R. A. (1898). *The City Wilderness*, Houghton Mifflin and Co., Boston.

Woodward, C. V. (1964). *American Counterpoint*, Little, Brown, and Co., Boston.

Woodward, C. V. (1966). *The Strange Career of Jim Crow*, 2nd rev. ed., Oxford University Press, New York.

Yans-McLaughlin, V. (1977). *Family and Community: Italian Immigrants in Buffalo, 1880–1930*, Cornell University Press, Ithaca, New York.

Zelinski, W. (1971). The hypothesis of the mobility transition. *Geographical Review*, **61**, 219–249.

Zunz, O. (1972). Technology and society in an urban environment: the case of the Third Avenue elevated railway. *Journal of Interdisciplinary History*, **3**, 89–102.

Zunz, O. (1977). The organization of the American city in the late nineteenth century: ethnic structure and spatial arrangement in Detroit. *Journal of Urban History*, **3**, 443–466.

Geography and the Urban Environment
Progress in Research and Applications, Volume IV
Edited by D. T. Herbert and R. J. Johnston
© 1981 John Wiley & Sons Ltd.

Chapter 9

The American Urban System in the Nineteenth Century

Michael P. Conzen

America is the 'land of mushroom cities'
A. F. WEBER (1899)

INTRODUCTION

Every age is said to rewrite history to its own ends, placing the present in a rational context of long-term change and giving meaning to current trends. Urbanization is now so far advanced in most western countries that interpretations of modern history can no longer afford to disregard or undervalue this fundamental social transformation. The role of industrialization in redefining the functions and character of cities in the nineteenth century is also beyond question. The opportunities and dislocations associated with the largest-scale transformations stimulated scholarly comment and study from an early period. But it is only with the realization in the second half of the twentieth century that the problems of urban change in one community are inextricably linked with the workings of the larger urban system of which an individual town or city is a small part that concerted efforts have been made to understand the evolution and nature of the national system of cities as an object of enquiry in its own right. That the relation between general economic growth of large regions and particular cities within them has become highly complex, none would doubt, but it is less clear through which forces and by what sequence the fortunes of one place have become so tied together with those of another. Because so many contemporary questions of city-system organization must deal with locational and functional characteristics laid down during the last century, this essay seeks to explore this topic from the perspective of urban and historical geography with special reference to the United States system of cities during the nineteenth century.

To students of general urban systems evolution, the significance of considering the American urban system in this period is threefold. To begin with, this is the era in which the urbanization of the United States 'caught up' with that of Western Europe, starting from a decidedly modest base. In 1800, for example, when London was outranked as a world city only by Peking, Philadelphia ranked 119th, and New York occupied the 133rd rank. By the end of the century, New York had become the second-largest city in the world (behind London), Chicago was fifth, and seven American cities were among the top fifty world cities (compared with six for Britain). The massive urban transformation implied in these statistics affected the whole array of American urban places and was predicated upon the rapid formation of a highly-articulated city-system.

Secondly, insofar as cities were vital to national development, the sheer scale of territorial expansion and settlement destined the urban network to be far-flung and complex. This brought into being hundreds of urban places created *de novo*, large numbers of which grew at phenomenal rates, many to become cities of over 100,000 inhabitants within two or three decades of founding. The newness of these additions to the urban system meant that it could evolve unfettered by many of the regional and human constraints that characterized regions of much older settlement.

Thirdly, given the large geographical scale on which urbanization developed, American cities were particularly quick to adopt innovations of all kinds, most notably industrial enterprise of every complexion (with an early shift to the factory system), deployment of transport improvements, both regional and internal, and commitment to consumer production. The urban system that resulted from these stimuli developed a locational structure nevertheless strongly biased by the pervasive influence of 'initial advantage' that favoured a number of its older cities. Innovations in production and communications, however, could not possibly maintain the early locational *status quo* of the city-system, indeed, they were instrumental in redefining it severely. The large scale of the expanding settled area and the organizational changes in economic life imposed a continuous sorting and reformulation of functional roles among cities in different localities, and 'comparative advantage' in one function or another shifted with remarkable alacrity from place to place.

But if one is to look at the American city-system in the nineteenth century, it is necessary to consider the historical and cultural conditions that have shaped in fundamental ways the theories advanced to explain urban systems growth in the United States and more generally. After considering the implications of the historical context, the essay will then discuss major conceptual work relevant to the changing geographical structure of the American urban system, and conclude with a brief interpretation of the system's evolution suggested by the conceptual work just reviewed.

The American context

It is clear that cities played an important role in modernizing the economic and social life of the United States during the course of the nineteenth century, and that such 'modernization', however defined, in turn made possible and indeed powerfully stimulated certain forms of urban growth. On the one hand, cities in their capacity as regional nodes of one sort or another served as articulation points for exchanges in the non-urban realm and by redistributing agrarian production augmented the total expansion of the rural sector and its social increase through demographic response. Such relatively passive functions, seemingly facilitating the growth of a large rural nation, were balanced on the other hand by essential 'middleman' functions, which connoted extensive influence and control of various types. Thus, while the city as 'middleman' was neither 'handmaiden' nor 'dictator' to the countryside, elements of both co-existed to different degrees throughout the urban system and among the regions. It is a commonplace observation that in late twentieth century America the national culture is substantially defined by reference to urban values, interests, and outlook. That it was not always so, and indeed was radically different at the beginning of the nineteenth century is beyond doubt, and raises long-term questions of the precise role of cities in engendering and extending change of this magnitude.

From a geographical perspective four factors stand out as fundamental to any discussion of the emergence of the national urban system: political independence, demographic growth, national expansion, and modernization (Table 9.1). These factors share a common context of basic social values, such as liberal capitalism, individualism, the Protestant work ethic, and support of education, but in their implications for urban settlement growth differ in the types and distribution of functions they have directly stimulated.

The colonial origins of European settlement in America created a pattern of somewhat discrete regions that had been colonized with varying motives and certainly were endowed with different natural resources. By the time of the Revolution these differences were somewhat muted through growing intercolonial contacts that were becoming articulated through the major port cities that had served as erstwhile colonial administrative capitals in addition to their obvious foreign trade functions. Hence the colonial heritage of numerous port towns was a rich one, particularly in the northern colonies lacking major staple exports. The largest of these centres were poised for continental trade penetration once political independence under a federal system with strong local authority was to lay the groundwork for a remarkable proliferation of government functions at all levels, consequently stimulating the growth of towns and villages by the thousands. Add to this a steady growth in national population throughout the nineteenth century through massive immigration and natural increase, and both the need for a rational geographical distribution of services for this expanding population and a demand for networks of central places is not difficult to predict.

National policies emerged quickly to encourage settlement expansion into the continental interior that opened up one resource frontier after another. Central to this strategy was the forging of interregional communications that tied the

TABLE 9.1. Conceptualization of the major sources of long-term urban change

General	Specific	Urban settlement consequences

1. Political independence	• Changes in mercantile patterns (still staple-based)
	• New brand of nationalism (manifest destiny)
	• Governmental accoutrements of democracy (multiplicity of functions at small scale)
	• Government policies that strongly encouraged but did not direct growth
		• Inheritance of urban networks from previous empires
		• Major support from old articulation points in expanding nation
		  —commerce: internal improvements
		  —political: government apparatus (capitals, county seats; forts; clearing houses, etc.)

2. Demographic growth (by immigration and high birth rates)	• New population size thresholds • Wider (more dispersed) population distribution	• Continuous increase in service functions (with returns to scale) —central place networks in areas of high population density
3. Spatial expansion of natural resource exploitation	• Sequence of staple production relations (cumulative, but varies with nature of staple)	• Forging of regular accessibility (transport and communications) • Wholesaling networks (for export or internal distribution)

4. Modernization	• Industrialization (small-scale craft to factory urban industry)
	• Business revolution
	• Change in purchasing power, living standards, expectations
		• Emergence of industrial cities
		  —metropolitan type
		  —specialized medium and small type
		• Elaboration of service networks
		  —incr. frequency and range of central places
		  —growth of specifically cultural functions (colleges, hospitals, prisons, etc.)

fortunes of towns and cities inevitably to their relative location in transport and wholesaling terms. Lastly, technological and organizational innovations brought changes in material production and standards of living, which resulted in a large number of highly industrial cities being introduced to the urban network and a multiplication of central place activities up and down the settlement hierarchy. These fundamental changes in nineteenth century America were not unique to the continent in themselves, but the geographical scale at which they occurred, together with ratios between land, capital, and labour markedly different from those in Western Europe, produced favourable conditions for the rapid evolution of the nineteenth century's largest politically unified urban system.

THE EVOLUTION OF AMERICAN CITY-SYSTEM RESEARCH

The study of the evolution of the American urban system has a comparatively long history, although concerted efforts to interpret the nature of the system *qua* system have been made only in the last several decades (Bourne and Simmons, 1978, p. 3). Distinguishing between interest in simple population growth of cities as a component of general urbanization on the one hand, and the relations among cities in the geographical distribution of that growth on the other (the latter being the key to a systems approach), it is evident that scholarly attention to the relative growth performance of sets of cities in the United States and the reasons behind it emerged only in the last decade of the nineteenth century. In a sweeping overview of the rise of American cities, Albert Bushnell Hart (1890) accounted for the exceptional and differential growth among the nation's cities by reference to seven chief causes: peaceable conditions, convenience of commerce, manufactures, other amenities (site conditions), artificial creation (political functions), 'momentum', and the reinforcing effect of transport innovations (particularly railways) on older eastern cities. His conception of city fortunes was clearly focused upon individual cities, drawing heavily on factors of site and situation to account for rapid or slow growth over time. The notion of viewing cities as a group producing a general urbanization effect was more clearly developed in Adna F. Weber's monumental study of city growth (1899), though his treatment of American cities was mostly confined to broad population change.

The elements of locational advantage such as break-of-bulk points and gateways were well understood by the end of the century (Ratzel, 1893, pp. 336–42; Semple, 1903, Ch. 16), but a clear and detailed analysis of the multiplicity of urban functions and their relative distribution among cities was still a long way off. A useful benchmark was a brief examination by Tower (1905) of major urban roles that could be used as single characterizations of individual cities, such as commercial (domestic or foreign), industrial (located for power or raw materials), political, and social (especially health) functions.

Though concerned with contemporary rather than historical classification of city types, Tower's study remained for long the only explicit statement of differential urban roles within an implicitly understood urban network.

But if cities specialized their functions and competed against each other on the basis of different locational advantages, then they must draw on different and changing territorial bases of support. This implied the concept of trade areas and hinterlands, which soon received some early attention by American geographers (Genthe, 1907; Emerson, 1908–9). Frederick Emerson, for example, found in the history of commercial relations between New York and the northern continental interior, particularly during the nineteenth century, a useful distinction between local and extra-regional hinterland relations which explained different rates of growth for the metropolis (Emerson, 1908–9, pp. 601 ff., 726 ff.). Almon E. Parkins (1918) added the regional competitiveness of urban industry to that of commerce in his classic historical study of Detroit as an explanation of urban strategies that arose to cope with declining locational advantage within the nation. These studies, however, focused mainly on the performance of single cities, even when viewed comparatively.

Another approach also appeared in these productive years of the early twentieth century. While the term 'urban hierarchy' was not employed until later decades, Mark Jefferson (1915) and Lawrence V. Roth (1918) contributed the first discussions of American city growth rates with an eye to systematic classification and ranking. Jefferson's urban typology, based on long-term trends in decadal growth rates, classified cities as vigorous, halting, or exuberant; it may seem superficially descriptive today, but his comparative graphical analysis and mapping of types suggested some obvious locational explanations, and more importantly, treated the nation's major cities as a single collectivity—a sound basis for systems thinking. Roth's contribution was to explain urban growth behaviour even more strongly by reference to historical development regions (e.g. Atlantic coast, Great Lakes), and to graph historical population ranks so that patterns of inter-city and interregional competition and stability emerged clearly. Significant though these developments were, however, the systematic relations of cities were seen only as simple competition between the largest agglomerations, and the nascent idea of urban hierarchy was not cross-fertilized with the notion of an urban functional array.

An extraordinary hiatus of nearly two decades then occurred before geographical studies of American urban networks gained any appreciable theoretical sophistication, and meaningful historical application of new concepts had to wait much longer. It is a measure of the intellectual isolation of the interwar period that American urban geographers remained apparently oblivious to the analyses of settlement hierarchy and trade areas by American rural sociologists (Galpin, 1915; Kolb, 1933), the definition and mapping of metropolitan spheres of influence by the new urban sociologists (Park, Burgess, and McKenzie, 1925;

McKenzie, 1933), and the theoretical breakthrough in central place formulation made by the economist–geographer Walter Christaller (1933) which was disseminating rapidly among German geographers.

These developments trickled into American urban geography only during and after the Second World War (Ullman, 1941; Dickinson, 1947), though not apparently fast enough to have immediate impact. An isolated article by Lewis F. Thomas (1949) presented a nice empirical portrait of the historical shrinkage of St. Louis' wholesale hinterland, and James S. Matthews (1949) charted the settlement history of northeastern Ohio, including tantalizing data on differential urban growth within the 14-county study area, but eschewing theoretical inferences. Although Chauncy D. Harris (1943) had suggested a bold new scheme for contemporary functional classification of American cities and thereby emphasized urban roles in the national city system in the early 1940s, neither his conceptualization nor his methodology spurred any historical explorations of urban functional specialization. The application of central place postulates to American small town networks in the 1950s, however, produced useful schematizations of evolving low-order central place hierarchies in southwestern Iowa and southwestern Wisconsin as prologues to contemporary analyses (Brush, 1951; Laska, reported in Berry, 1967, pp. 5–9). In these studies competitive initial sorting thinned a dense field of low-order villages and towns as a few selected places grew to larger size and functional importance. These findings have proven reasonably representative of areas where a low-order central place hierarchy has not been complicated by other functional developments such as manufacturing or long-distance trade. Morrill (1962) later offered a simple simulation strategy for generating a hierarchy of service centres in a hypothetical field over time, showing that central place postulates could be applied to a dynamic model of settlement evolution.

A final important element, the relationship between urban system growth and regional economic growth, emerged in the 1960s as an outgrowth of urban hierarchy questions posed in the context of the national rank-size distribution of urban places. Carl H. Madden (1956) had already drawn attention to the remarkable stability of the overall rank-size curve for US cities plotted logarithmically from 1790 to 1950. Demonstrating that a log-normal distribution of city sizes held for over a century and a half, he also argued, however, that sufficient number of cities declined relatively and were replaced in the distribution by others to make growth prediction problematical, and furthermore that great inter- and intra-regional variations in growth were necessarily occurring simultaneously to maintain the smooth curve. It was a short conceptual step, then, to study this question comparatively among nations, and argue that observed differences in the form of the urban rank-size curve were related to stages of national economic development (Berry, 1961). Although this line of investigation, a species of 'social physics', left much intermediate theoretical ground uncultivated, it set the scene indirectly for later integration of regional economic development as a necessary dimension in influencing the rate and distribution of growth within the city system and its subsystems.

Recent literature in this field falls fairly simply into five types. The first deals with general overviews of urban growth and expansion of the city network, and is characterized by varying but generally emphatic periodizations and choice of driving forces. The most celebrated treatment is that of John R. Borchert (1967), which emphasizes the role of energy use and transport technology in differentiating four major epochs of urban growth (with terminal dates seen in 1830, 1870, and 1920) that witnessed successive waves of expansion and recentralization of the urban network in each period. Accessibility to resources and markets provides the emphasis in the discussion by Berry and Neils (1969) that rests upon a similar historical periodization. Less sharply organized by specific periods, the interpretations of Duncan and Lieberson (1970) and Ward (1971) focus more clearly on regional strategy, the former from the sociological perspective of metropolitan dominance and the latter from the development economist's perspective of core-periphery relationships.

A second type of research is exploring regional economic growth as a determinant of city system development, at least in its gross aspects, and is by far the least developed. Stimulated in part by the Callender–Schmidt–North interregional trade model (North, 1966), in which northeastern deficits in raw materials and surplus manufactures complement southern cotton and western grain surpluses, with the west also feeding the south, a considerable debate has developed over the differential economic base for urbanization among the three super-regions (Earle and Hoffman, 1976; Lindstrom, 1978), some of it examined in the light of general location theory and regional incomes (Lampard, 1968).

A third class of work might be termed the 'city biography' approach in that it refers to the numerous studies dealing with the external relations of individual cities. This includes research devoted to city-hinterland development (e.g. Albion, 1939; Reisser, 1951), and to a special sub-class recognized specifically as urban rivalry. The classic studies have been those of historians (e.g. Belcher, 1947; Livingood, 1947; Rubin, 1961), and nearly all works of this type, while focusing well on a single centre or two or three rivals, fail to give enough attention to inter-settlement dependencies and complementarities among a whole set of cities. The various geographical vignettes of selected major cities that make up part of the *Comparative Metropolitan Analysis Project* (Adams, 1976) belong to this tradition insofar as they give partial consideration to historical external relations of their central cities.

The fourth category is composed of studies investigating city growth rate behaviour and rank-size distribution. Madden's challenge to explain the regional growth dynamics underlying the serene progress of the rank-size curve (1956, p. 252) was answered inconclusively by Lukermann (1966) at the national level and Williamson and Swanson (1966) in the case of the northeast region (see also Higgs, 1969), for this approach has consciously avoided direct consideration of hinterland and interurban relations.

The last type of writing is concerned explicitly with the evolution of the urban settlement hierarchy as an integral system of interdependent parts in which relations between cities assume major importance. It is allied with the first and second categories of literature in its comprehensive approach to the geographical structure of the urban system, but stands somewhat apart for its emphasis on functional interrelations within the national network of cities, albeit at a variety of geographical scales. It is this research tradition that will be drawn upon most heavily and discussed in more detail in the remainder of this essay.

THEORETICAL APPROACHES TO THE DEVELOPING AMERICAN CITY-SYSTEM

If the recent literature pertinent to city-system development can be distinguished by the scope of enquiry, the choice of key variables, and the geographical scale of examination, as has just been argued, the specific theories drawn upon for conceptual support must be identified in separate terms, for elements of several theoretical approaches can be found interwoven in much of the work currently contributing to the analysis of nineteenth-century city-system evolution. At least five recognizable theoretical traditions have emerged, in which the conceptual insight applies either directly to the organizational nature of the urban system and its geographical expression in network structure, or indirectly through specifying the growth determinants and sectoral biases in economic change without necessarily specifying the settlement system implications. For brevity's sake these traditions will be discussed only for the light they cast on the changing character of the American urban system in the nineteenth century.

Imperial colonization and mercantile theory

There is no question that American cities at the opening of the nineteenth century owed most of their size, functional composition, and geographical arrangement to two centuries of European settlement of eastern North America governed by policies reflecting imperial ambitions. If mercantilism was the dominant strategy in colonial arrangements, towns were essential to its implementation of monopoly trading channels. As control points for assemblage of raw materials for export to and distribution of manufactured goods from the metropolitan centre in Europe, colonial entrepôts were intentionally few in number and coastal in location. Only as deeper penetration of the resource hinterland proceeded might interior centres be encouraged for efficient accumulation of supply for bulk shipment to the coastal entrepôts for forwarding (Vance,

1970, pp. 150–55). In terms of geographical development of this basic premise, the best statements are contained in the Meinig-Vance models of colonial implantation and mercantile establishment (Meinig, 1969, 1976; Vance, 1970, pp. 68–79). Vance's 'mercantile model' extends the theory of continental settlement penetration by specifying the founding of wholesaling chains made up of 'depôts of staple collection' and coordinated in time by a few, larger 'entrepôts of wholesaling,' containing the most highly specialized of wholesale functions. In its final stage of elaboration, the mercantile model posits significant lateral linkages between interior wholesaling routes and centres as more of the total long-distance trade involves destinations within the expanding national settlement frame, producing a network geometry strikingly reminiscent of that in the Taaffe, Morrill, and Gould (1963) model of African transport development. The notion of gateway cities positioned at the margins of resource regions such as commodity belts to assemble exports for long distance shipping fits the mercantile model well in the American case (Burghardt, 1971). The primacy accorded wholesaling over local trade in settlement evolution and therefore the factor of external demand in regulating the growth and complexity of trading functions in American towns is particularly important in mercantile theory as applied to urban growth in the American context.

It would be misleading to imply, however, that Vance's mercantile model is satisfactorily developed for general application. While considerable empirical data from the past and present support Vance's discussion, Vance neither tested the model systematically enough with eighteenth and nineteenth century evidence to avoid the charge of selecting only convenient evidence, nor did he indeed specify with sufficient precision the emergence of particular wholesale specializations in centres of given sizes and locations to offer a clear and detailed evolutionary picture of wholesaling's role in urban growth. Notably missing is historical evidence on patterns of wholesale firm structure and the behaviour of individual entrepreneurs, as well as on the changing relations between wholesaling and manufacturing during the later nineteenth century. This was a period in which Porter and Livesay (1971, pp. 2–4) see fundamental alterations in wholesale distribution networks favouring specialized and large-scale manufacturers at the expense of independent middlemen. Such changes likely affected differently the wholesaling contribution to certain types of large and medium-sized cities. Nevertheless, the importance of interregional chains of cities based on wholesale functions dating from the beginning of a region's development can no longer be ignored, and together these chains form the basic geographical superstructure of the American system of cities. In addition, Vance's model accounts explicitly for the divergence of wholesaling functions from a strict central place principle of organization (Vance, 1970, pp. 202–5), and such other characteristics as, for example, the location of highly specialized medium- and small-sized wholesaling centres on newly developing through-routes in response to changing transport conditions.

Mercantile operations, however, break down not only into wholesale and retail functions, but involve a distinction in the wholesaling phase between control of exchange and the performance of physical movement. This distinction has been taken up by Meyer (1980a) to expand Vance's model and provide substantial new insights concerning the evolving spatial structure of the mercantile network. Significant trade cannot emerge until centres develop to control the exchange. Such control implies the power to allocate payments and stocks between producers and consumers, thus capturing a portion of the exchange value. Depending on communication techniques, costs of control do not rise steeply with distance, and so large amounts of trade can be controlled from a few major centres. Conversely, costs of physical movement do rise sharply with distance, and in the nineteenth century produced more localized dendritic networks of supply lines. Hence there developed a hierarchy of points of exchange control ('metropolises') superimposed upon a more extensive network of transport nodes commanding more localized control of physical movement. Meyer's exchange–transport control model awaits systematic testing with historical evidence, but the distinction is a valuable one, and holds important implications for the phasing of urban system expansion and integration, some implications of which have been considered in the development of the national and regional banking exchange system (Conzen, 1977).

Regional growth theory

If mercantilism serves to explain the initial morphology of the continental urban system, it is not comprehensive enough to account for variations in rates of regional economic development and therefore regional differences in the number of early 'points of attachment', nor indeed differential growth in the longevity and robustness of wholesaling chains. Concepts of regional economic specialization have been employed to fill the gap, and two variants have emerged, On the one hand, Ward (1971, pp. 18–46) has adopted the core-periphery concept of Friedmann (1963) to characterize the changing relations between more and less developed areas between 1790 and 1910. By 1870 the core could be construed as roughly co-terminus with the present extent of Megalopolis (Gottmann, 1961), having earlier supplanted what was an American colonial periphery to an English core, and by 1910 it had enlarged to cover the traditional manufacturing belt (Hartshorne, 1936). Ward's delineation of the periphery over time is vague in light of the regional relations he discusses, but makes the important point that Friedmann's core-periphery relationships were supplemented in the American case by significant intra-peripheral complementarities, as large variations in transport connectivity and the nature of staple exports influenced differential overall rates of regional urbanization.

On the other hand, economic historians have long regarded economic regionalism in the United States as a simple system comprising three elements, the east, south, and west. The orthodox Callender–Schmidt–North model is based on the premises that antebellum food and raw material deficiencies in the east were paid for by manufacturing exports to the west and south, that manufacturing demands not satisfied locally within the west were balanced by food exports to the south and east, and that the south in turn paid for its food and manufacturing deficits through exports of plantation staples abroad and to the east (North, 1966, p. 103).

There are two immediate objections to this thesis regarding its utility for urban growth explanations. First, debate has cast substantial doubt on the symmetrical relationships offered. The south, for example, was not generally deficient in foodstuffs (Hilliard, 1972), traded modestly with the west (Fishlow, 1964), and took less than a quarter of the east's exportable manufacturing (Uselding, 1976). Secondly, Lindstrom (1978) in a study of antebellum economic development in the Philadelphia hinterland has argued that explanations of eastern growth have rested too heavily upon interregional trade, and in so doing have underestimated the contribution of intraregional growth. According to her 'eastern demand model' which applies to the nation's economic core region (to use Ward's terminology), improved accessibility spread and intensified commercial relations within the immediate hinterlands of the major eastern urban centres, which in turn spurred increased primary production in agriculture and mining and some manufacturing. Hinterland towns then specialized their functions somewhat and so developed local complementarities. By these means growth was rapid and led to structural change in the regional economy.

Lindstrom's interest in intraregional economic arrangements represents a major advance in economic historians' understanding of the intricacy of changing spatial structure, but her model remains vague and unspecified with regard to the actual settlement interdependencies within a large urban region. More generally, the evidence on interregional trade does not yet lend itself to proper interpretation of the geographical structure of the national wholesaling complex as it affected the system of cities. Nevertheless, studies of regional production and trade have made it clear why gross differences in general levels of urbanization and numbers of large and medium-sized towns were so markedly lower in the south throughout the nineteenth century compared with other regions. As far as commercial centres were concerned, the contrasting nature of marketing cotton and grains (in terms of their physical requirements for handling and the potential for bulk-reducing, value-raising industrial processing within the regions) goes a long way in explaining the different urban employment multipliers they could generate, independent of other factors (Rothstein, 1966).

The trend in economic theorizing has been towards a finer spatial texture in model-building, but the regional entities treated from a development perspective are still gross and imprecise by geographers' standards. Recent work on the spatial structure of urban networks in developing small regions has sought to throw new light on the sequencing of economic change within metropolitan hinterlands with special attention to the nature of the settlement array (Conzen, 1975a; Muller, 1977). Whatever the verdict on interregional trade dependencies, there is no question that throughout the nineteenth century frontier regions required enormous capital investment for growth and that circulating capital within these areas was mostly in short supply (Davis, 1971). Therefore, large imports from established regions can be expected. However, as local development proceeded, interest rate differentials would have fallen and local sources of 'plough-back' capital should increasingly have replaced that from external sources (Conzen, 1975a). In a partial test of this notion, examination of selected bank capital flows into and within Wisconsin established not only a half-century process of regional substitution of capital, but a strong role for the local urban network in the capital flow system. Hierarchical downward filtering of capital in early years gave way to counter-hierarchical and 'lateral' flows from medium-sized centres as a result of the spatial diffusion of economic development and the probable attraction of metropolitan capital to regions of higher interest rates or more profitable local industrial investments.

If one can assume that capital flows, regardless of geographical origin, supplied frontier localities with development potential in a suitable form, then the pattern of improvements should follow a logical progression based on regional circulation and staple exports. Muller (1977) has proposed such a model in the light of evidence from the Middle Ohio Valley in the antebellum period. In a three-phase model an intial 'pioneer periphery' containing small scattered urban centres offering only basic goods and services over short distances, gave way as agriculture developed to a three-level hierarchy which included small centres, district trade centres, and the major entrepôt cities of the region. Selective town growth was a function mainly of position on a long-distance trade route, secondly of expanding service to a local hinterland with improving transport channels, and to a lesser degree some incipient industrial processing. A later 'specialized periphery' phase posits major growth of the regional entrepôt through continued interregional trade, and a selective pattern of smaller town growth allied to changing nodality within intensifying local hinterlands. Some district centres gained status in a new fourth urban level of sub-regional importance upon gaining access to wider markets that permitted more specialized services and partial manufacturing competition with imports and with the regional metropolis. A final 'transitional periphery' phase hinges on either the continuation or alteration of past trends. If broad industrialization occurred, the regional metropolis would benefit from expanding its industrial base, and the subregional centres would follow suit at a lower level, leaving small towns behind in an agricultural service capacity. If industrialization did not pervade the region, transport nodality would come to benefit medium-sized centres that gain from centralization and decentralization trends in services and processing at the upper and lower levels of the urban hierarchy.

The model's terminology presupposes that its type-region (the Cincinnati-centred urban region in Ohio–Indiana) would become part of the national economic core sometime after 1860, hence the careful calibration of 'periphery' phases. But if the model is ready for extension in time, it is less easily enlarged to account for the immediate external relations of this urban system with its own and neighbouring high-order metropolises, or indeed the possibility that various parts of this hypothesized subsystem could have been passing through the specified phases at different times and with varying speed (Muller, 1976). These limitations are heavily outweighed for the present, however, by the attractiveness of a selective growth model for a small region that recognizes the changing interplay between staple production, processing, long-distance commerce, central place functions, and the specific network of towns.

The role of industrialization

Neither the mercantile model, nor interregional trade interpretations, nor small-region multi-variate models are sufficient to account for broad change in the nineteenth century American urban system. In 1810 not one in thirty workers was engaged in manufacturing; but by 1840 almost one in every ten worked in that sector of the economy. After 1840 manufacturing expanded substantially to reorient the structure of the national city system in a major fashion. From a geographical point of view the phenomenon of industrialization revolves around several issues, primarily how it affected selective urban growth, what distribution it created in the spatial structure of the system, and what new interurban links it forged within the system. Conceptual work aimed at relating the evolution of manufacturing capacity to the progress of the urban system has been scarce (Lampard, 1968) and theories seeking to account for the changing spatial relations among industries and cities even scarcer.

The various forms of industrial activity have influenced urban growth with widely differing results. In the early nineteenth century some industrial types of production were ubiquitous, many were local in scale, and only some called into being specialized towns. Changes in power sources, raw materials, and labour needs helped greatly augment certain classes of manufacturing in rough proportion to city size at the same time that national expansion decentralized much production. A general shift from power and raw material sites to market locations helped concentrate industry to a considerable extent in large and medium-sized cities, while the growth and geographical expansion of the population allowed new natural resource fields to buttress the extension of large-scale manufacturing outside traditional east coast areas. Consequently, geographical theories of manufacturing development concerned at all with the urban system have tended to emphasize two aspects, the concentration of exceptional manufacturing capacity in the major cities, particularly in the northeast, and the emergence of specialized regional industrial urban complexes.

The most enduring concept of urban-industrial concentration is the model of circular and cumulative growth (Pred, 1966, pp. 24–46). Applicable in contexts of rapid industrial transformation, this model presupposes a generally mercantile city that benefits from the establishment of a new or enlarged industry. This event generates initial multiplier effects through new industrial and consumer demands from the extra workforce. Such increase in time develops new local or regional thresholds of demand which in turn stimulate further industrial expansion. In addition the multiplier effects increase the possibility of inventions or innovations bringing further efficiencies in production, some of which come into being, thereby also stimulating new industry. Add to this other 'stimulants' to urban size growth such as natural increase of the population, wage differentials encouraging migration, and external economies as well as scale economies, and a spiral growth effect is easily produced. It is Pred's contention that these conditions emphatically favoured the large east coast mercantile cities during the course of the nineteenth century (none more so than New York), and that, owing to the principle of 'initial advantage' (itself an amalgam of antecedence, inertia, and momentum), they were able to procure a disproportionate amount of industrial growth and in so doing ensure their high urban rank stability.

Pred's general model has not been challenged on its basic components, except for its simplicity and limited scope, and indeed it has been incorporated in later models of multiple-city relations (Pred, 1973). It applies very well to existing fairly large entrepôt cities that then undergo industrialization and deals usefully with the concept of market thresholds. However, while it contributes to an explanation of large-city rank stability, it implies little about the forces that create whole urban-regional industrial complexes. Although Pred (1966, pp. 46–83) discusses general urbanization and industrialization trends in the second half of the nineteenth century, interest now focuses upon conceptualizations that help explain the timing, regional extent and interregional spread of all the urban-industrial complexes that coalesced by the early twentieth century to form 'the manufacturing belt'. A model of the rise of regional industrial systems must incorporate factors behind the appearance and system-connectivity of small and medium-sized specialized industrial towns and cities as well as the industrializing mercantile metropolises.

Meyer (1977, 1980b) has suggested a developmental sequence both for the rise of an individual urban-regional industrial complex and for the development of multiple regional complexes in the northeastern United States. Regardless of coastal or interior location, a region containing an important mercantile city could industrialize under the following conditions. Expansion in local and regional demand for consumer products and processing would foster creation of market-serving and commerce-serving manufactures. These would locate in towns throughout the region, but with special concentration in the metropolis and nearby places. Such industry in turn would generate demand for producer durables such as machinery, iron foundries, and steam engines of particular relevance to transport and processing activities. Manufacture of producer durables could locate either in the mercantile centre or in a smaller hinterland city if it was an important processing centre. Over time, the processing industries may have declined, at least relatively (especially in eastern regions), but this did not affect the expanding producer durables sector, though the latter tended to remain regional in scope; meanwhile expanding demand, innovative production, and improved interregional accessibility (and presumably also new marketing techniques) would stimulate some traditional consumer goods to be manufactured for a national market and initiate the production of new goods on this enlarged scale. Robust local and regional market- and commerce-serving manufactures would continue to buttress the vitality of the regional complex (Meyer, 1977).

Three such regional industrial complexes emerged on the east coast (centred on Boston, New York, and Philadelphia). The sequence of events that led to a veritable manufacturing belt involved basically the replication of regional industrial systems in the newly populated regions immediately west of the Allegheny Mountains, following at a great distance the westward moving frontier (Meyer, 1980b). Over the long run, regionally-oriented manufacturing gave way in relative terms to extraregional and national market production. The sequence of basic settlement was critical in differentiating regional industrial experience. New regions developed local and regionally-oriented manufacturing and were often limited to this level by the greater accessibility to national markets that allowed older regions to reach wider markets first. Once industry oriented to extra-regional and national markets was well established it could rarely be supplanted by competing or later blossoming industry elsewhere. As Pred (1966) noted, such precedence could be reinforced by patents, concentration of technical skills, scale economies, and fixed capital investments. Then, Meyer goes on to argue, scale of markets and timing of regional emergence tended to arbitrate future developments. Regional manufactures emerged continuously in all industrial regions during the course of the century, but they were eclipsed increasingly by national market orientation. Some industrial localities made the scale shift from one to the other, often to the immediate disadvantage of competing regions. Once the shift to national markets was made in one or more regional complexes, however, later developing complexes could rarely participate in that type of manufacture. Older regional industrial complexes tended to support both old and new national market manufactures, whereas newer complexes could support mainly newer industries. A point came when the market scale shifts eroded the basis on which new industrial regions could emerge. Late developing regions were unable to incubate manufacturing skills and producer durables in a protected regional context since many products were already available or newly introduced at national-market competitiveness from older regions. Their only prospect was to compete with established regions at an immediately national market level for new kinds of manufacture (Meyer, 1980b).

These developmental models of urban-regional industrial growth open a new vista for research in urban systems work, since Meyer's theoretical formulations have not been accompanied by systematic empirical examination. Even the crudest regional demarcations of these industrial complexes and their stages of development at particular times have yet to be offered, but the outlook is promising for a substantially more sophisticated view of the relations between industrialization and the urban system in nineteenth century America.

Central place theory

There was a time when centrality was next to piety on the urban geographer's scale of moral rectitude. Hailed by some as geography's greatest single theoretical success, classical central place theory (Christaller, 1933; Berry, 1967) has suffered notably reduced status as a conceptual framework for interpreting the major lineaments of North American urban systems development. It came under shrill attack from Vance (1970, pp. 138–48, 162–4, 166 fn) who argued that, as an elaborate model of endogenic change in a closed system characteristic more of feudal or command economies than of areas of liberal settlement, it should be viewed primarily as a 'special case' in the American setting of a more general mercantile capitalist basis for urban systems in Western settlement expansion. Specifically, Vance regards central place concepts as most relevant in regions of staple production, to be interpreted as subordinately linked to and centred upon major nodes along the historical wholesaling alignments of the continent (Vance, 1970, p. 165). Considerable evidence has been offered in support of this proposition (Conzen, 1975b; Muller, 1976), and it is fast gaining the character of a new orthodoxy (Muller, 1980; Palm, 1981, p. 146).

There are three ways, it appears, in which central place theory remains useful in understanding the nineteenth century American urban system. Firstly, fairly strict application of central place principles does appear to account for the network structure of the lower orders of the settlement hierarchy in a number of regions, particularly in the Midwestern corn and dairy belts in which the most notable local-scale examinations of the historical record of urban functions have been conducted (Brush, 1953; Laska, reported in Berry, 1967; Muller, 1976). Despite great changes in transport conditions during the century, there is no reason to believe that the principles of retail gravitation, range of good, functional thresholds, and hierarchical ordering of settlements did not strongly influence the structure of local trade centres. Secondly, given the 'bottom-up' basis of consumer demand and competitive sorting of low-order central places over time, central place postulates contribute a useful tool in conceptualizing a sequence through which largely rural areas passed in establishing long-term locations for urban centres of certain functional importance and in establishing the order and location of new functions as they became feasible with rising or stabilizing population densities.

Thirdly, a number of central place concepts such as centrality, service area, threshold, and hierarchy are applicable in more or less limited ways to non-retail service provision within the settlement system. Hence urban hierarchies existed within the wholesaling network, the advanced urban services (such as banking), and in the industrial realm. Apart from the inapplicability of settlement geometry implied by strict central place theory, the greatest limitations in its analogous use may derive from the sometimes incompatible origins of 'control' within the structure. Central place theory hinges upon demand-side assumptions, whereas in the complex organization of the urban system even in the nineteenth century much of the settlement structure may derive as well from supply-side constraints.

Given the historically and regionally reduced scope for central place theory in American urban settlement it is tempting to view this research tradition as stagnant; but by introducing a new emphasis on conscious and 'imposed' design of low-order central place systems in the Great Plains, Hudson (1979) has recently breathed some new life into it. While others pursue still further the internal mathematics of abstract central place formulations, Hudson has become impressed with the extent of big-city and railway corporation 'planning' of vast small town networks in the Dakotas and beyond towards the end of the century when these 'designers' of the rural service system drew upon all the accumulated town development experience of older regions to the east. In stressing the institutional framework of central place network creation Hudson may be in a position to redefine central place concepts to cover the supply side more adequately, and elevate the entrepreneur to a position of centrality along with the consumer.

Metropolitan dominance

The last theoretical tradition to be considered here arises in part from one of the principal weaknesses of central place theory as applied in its heyday to the American urban system, namely, its inability to account properly for the unusual size and regional concentration of the nation's largest cities, and their particular power to distort the density and functional array of urban places within their 'metropolitan shadow'. The concept of metropolitan dominance, however, antedates modern central place theory and even has tenuous links with mercantile theory through its first formulation in the writing of Gras (1922) in connection with his notion of 'the metropolitan economy'. Refined subsequently by McKenzie (1933), Dickinson (1947), and Bogue (1950), the concept at its most fundamental level asserts that large territorial regions are economically and socially oriented towards the nearest of the nation's large multifunctional metropolises usually lying within and near the centre of the region for which it serves as the important node. Leaving aside problems of specification such as the criteria for recognizing when a given city constitutes a regional metropolis and the appropriate delimitation of boundaries between metropolitan regions, the essential insight is that for reasons of proximity and convenience large regions are tied to or indirectly influenced by major cities. This has been demonstrated in one way through the existence of gradients of urban influence that decrease with increasing distance from the metropolis, expressed in such characteristics of areas as land values, population density, agricultural intensity, human fertility, migration, and other variables. Such measures are indirect but undeniable. Other measures involve the extent to which economic and social transactions over large areas must occur through the aegis of one metropolitan centre or another, generally detectable with direct flow data.

One of the attractions of this concept is the assumption that an urban hierarchy is established through time not from the 'bottom up' but rather from the 'top down', implying economic principles of centralization that initiate and organize a large system from a few source points. This may indicate, though it does not require, highly centralized control, which in any event in manpower terms could still (and during the nineteenth century mostly did) involve fragmented decision-making, and large numbers of more or less independent enterprises—however much they may have acted in unison on certain matters. In addition, metropolitan dominance, while it can be said to augment the role and stature of the large metropolises in the urban system, and may be viewed as a characteristic possessed by the high-order centres in a central place system, also fits well with mercantile theory. North American settlement would be difficult to interpret in the light of a fully settled continent slowly developing the demand for a centralized wholesaling network; indeed, the reverse was most likely true that the 'impulse to trade' spurred key urban centres of mercantile decision-making that have formed the backbone of the urban system ever since. Canadian historiography has even enshrined this form of metro-politanism as one of the interpretive keys to general Canadian history (Careless, 1954).

There are several theoretical levels at which metropolitan dominance can affect the urban-regional system and two will be discussed on the basis of work applied to the nineteenth century. At the level of a single region clearly 'tributary' to a given metropolitan centre, dominance in high-order functions and trade flows should be demonstrable from early settlement. As these flows transferred investment into regional resources and development, improved accessibility and productivity should benefit areas closest to the metropolis, extending outward in a wave-like fashion. Resulting gradients of metropolitan influence should thus be shallow at the outset of a region's growth, become steep during periods of maximum development, and then level off as the benefits of advanced development penetrated fringe areas to some extent. This sequence of gradient reversal was found for several metropolitan hinterlands in the Middle West, with the tipping point generally occurring between 1890 and 1910 (Conzen, 1974). Thereafter, while interregional and intraregional variations remained, gradients attributable to metropolitan influence continued to lessen through the early twentieth century.

From this single-region level the concept of metropolitan dominance can be broadened to encompass the theoretical dominance that large metropolises could exert over multiple regions and, indeed, over the nation as a whole. Pred's model of large-city rank stability fits into this intellectual category (if not the formal research tradition). To seek an explanation for the historic pre-eminence of New York and the other east coast metropolises throughout the nineteenth century by focussing on the mechanisms by which 'intial advantage' was not only maintained but enhanced is to pose a problem in the selectivity of national metropolitan dominance. Not concerned with the specific transformation of the hinterlands as a cause or result of metropolitan dominance, Pred has chosen to emphasize the growth that accrued to the metropolises themselves as a result of metropolis-hinterland dependencies.

Pred's model of large-city rank stability began as a design to explain the top rank maintenance of a major city like New York (Pred, 1966), but it has since been extended to apply to an interacting sub-system of large cities (Pred, 1973). The motor in the model is, once again, the principle of circular and cumulative growth establishing new thresholds that spur another round of expansion (see Figure 9.1). In casting the model in a fuller urban system context, however, Pred places crucial reliance on the role of spatial biases (regional differences) in the circulation of business information as the mechanism by which some cities could exploit additional economic opportunities and forge ahead of their competitors. Once again, circular reasoning applies to the question of the origin of the spatial biases: they develop because the larger cities are naturally in a better position than smaller ones to initiate improvements to their information environment, and such improvements will be designed primarily to benefit the larger cities. To them that hath, is given. Applied to the multi-regional context of the eastern seaboard before the Civil War this model works quite well because unusual changes in spatial biases in the communications systems were not common. For the larger context of the national system of cities later in the century, conditions under which competing interdependencies could emerge to the ones postulated would need to be added to the model. Although this has not been done, some additional light on the nature of the complex urban inter-dependencies that developed later in high-order urban functions can be gained from the spatial and hierarchical structure of the banking system by the century's end (Conzen, 1977). The forging of many 'lateral' links (i.e. non-dendritic) and

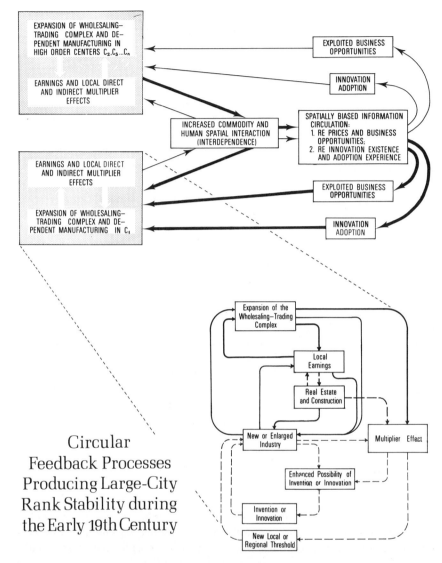

Circular
Feedback Processes
Producing Large-City
Rank Stability during
the Early 19th Century

FIGURE 9.1   (Reproduced from Pred (1966) by Permission of The MIT Press. © 1966, The MIT Press)

the rise of Chicago's influence were notable developments. Given that the major money metropolises served in Meyer's terms as centres of exchange control, a major step forward would entail a reformulation of the rank-stability model to accommodate the explicit regionalism of the exchange–transport control model.

Fundamental issues in tracing change in the urban system

The theoretical frameworks employed in the study of the American urban system in the nineteenth century remain somewhat disparate despite advances that cut across and occasionally unify certain theoretical themes. Borrowing from cognate fields has occurred with good results although not all formulations have made the geographical dimensions of system structure explicit. Even where they have, most models and concepts have been devised to explain structure and change in too limited a period or region, and, most frustrating of all, in too partial a segment of the whole urban system, using non-comparable criteria, variables, and scales. It is neither practicable nor even possible here to force a new synthesis, particularly since new contributions are appearing with a healthy frequency. However, a brief review of fundamental questions about city-system change may serve to highlight some of the current lacunae in the theoretical fabric of the subject.

Three basic questions must be answered at the outset. What is a city (or urban) system? What is 'structure' in an urban system? And, what is the role of individual cities in an urban system? A *city* (or urban) *system* may be regarded as a set of interdependent cities such that any change in the socioeconomic structure or functioning of one will directly or indirectly affect the socioeconomic structure or functioning of one or more other cities in the set (modified from Pred, 1973, p. 187). Further, one might add, *urban subsystems* are regional sets of cities within a national, continental, or intercontinental set of cities in which the interdependencies within the subsystem are greater than those between that subsystem and another subsystem. The *structure* of an urban system is the pattern of interdependencies between cities, composed of similarities and differences in size, location, and functional specialization. The *role* of individual cities is to exploit a particular location in order to maximize use of local resources and facilitate interaction between cities and regions within the larger geographical entity.

A fourth question builds naturally upon the last three: What is change in a system of cities? Change is any shift in the relative structure of forces shaping the organization and functioning of the urban system. Since change occurs in a myriad of ways and with variable timing, numerous changes can occur simultaneously, overlap partially in time, or occur in sequences. In a dynamic context such as nineteenth century America, it is difficult to envisage the urban system as anything but subject to continuous change, much of it rapid and most of it complex. A distinction also needs to be made between expansive change that brings 'more of the same' (particularly in terms of settlement extension into new areas), and transformative change that alters for good the essential mixture of forces operating within the system. Although technically even replication of urban growth in new areas brings inevitable change in the whole system through greater demand thresholds and larger geographical extent,

A Framework for Change in an Urban System

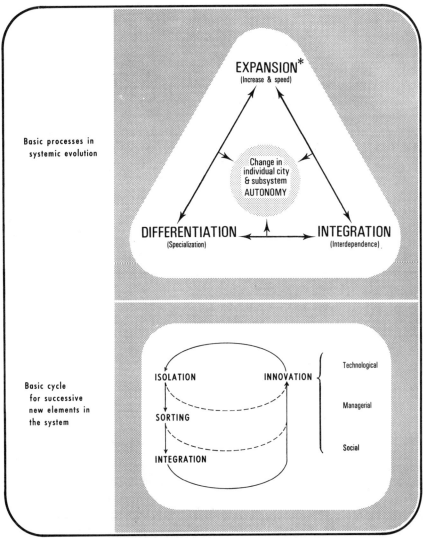

*In rare cases this process may be reversed and CONTRACTION (or IMPLOSION)
be the key process.

FIGURE 9.2

there is still a qualitative difference between replication upon a basically known pattern, such as planting familiar types of towns in new territory, and change in urban patterns brought about through a major new functional innovation.

Generalizing to a level of abstraction that encompasses varied change in evolving urban systems over long periods of time, three discrete processes seem to control the nature of system structure and change (Figure 9.2). Once the existence of a system of cities is beyond question (i.e. there is more than one urban centre in a region, no matter how large), expansion, differentiation, and integration of the system may occur in any combination and proceed at any pace, and the causal linkages may be direct or oblique between all three processes. If social and environmental circumstances favour a city in one location, another at some distance from the first may in time also be warranted. Expansion of a set of cities may result from migration or indigenous reorganization. If the cities perform identical local functions and nothing else they would not constitute a system. If they perform extralocal functions in addition, such as trade or political control, complementarity (interdependence) develops that may or may not encourage differentiation of system roles through specialization. If specialization and interchange occur then by definition integration proceeds, and expansion may be favoured by the increased transactions produced through either differentiation or integration. Likewise, differentiation can also be stimulated by integration.

These processes operate in combination to produce a growing network of urban places, the structure of which at any given moment is a partial equilibrium of various functional–spatial cycles in differing stages of completion or eclipse (Figure 9.2). The simultaneous contribution of successive innovations to structural change in the urban system is best illustrated by regional transport improvements. At an early developmental stage, a city-system adapts its regional exchange functions, for example, to a route network of coastal and navigable river corridors. In terms of other growth dynamics in the system this adaptation may not have run its course fully before a wave of canal building creates a subset of more convenient transport links that alters the pattern of trade flows. As this innovation passes from an isolated phenomenon through a diffusionary phase to a point where the transport network is integrated in a major new way, towns and cities grow, stagnate, or decline according to their locational advantages on or off this altered communications network. Then, when some growth of cities is still being generated by initial-phase (coastal–river) stimuli and other growth results from canal-phase stimuli, the railway spreads a new network and begins a new transformation while the remnants of earlier transformations are still in progress. Innovations that transformed the urban system occurred, of course, also in marketing practices, production techniques (especially energy shifts), administrative patterns and other spheres of economic and public life, as well as in the field of transport.

There is one final conceptual question, and that concerns the notion of autonomy within the urban system. In a strict sense interdependence discourages autonomy, but no matter how complex are the ties that bind, the notion of autonomy (or at least partial autonomy) has intuitive appeal because cities are not automatons. However much a city's function might appear to be dictated by location and site circumstances and its role within the larger city-system there are two reasons a degree of autonomy may exist in the city's purpose and future. On the one hand powerful entrepreneurial interests may succeed in so biasing local and external patterns of capital investment that the city develops in a different manner than it otherwise would. This is often referred to by historians as the 'leadership factor'. On the other hand, many individual urban roles within a regional or national city system are far from rigidly defined, even in terms of systemic pressures. Therefore in many cases a town might develop in one way or another without causing much friction within the larger system. Such systemic neutralism encourages autonomy, and in the broadest social and economic context of an evolving city-system, levels of individual place or subsystem autonomy become factors to measure in their own right.

To sum up, then, the fundamental theoretical issues in urban system evolution concern the interrelations of the three basic processes of expansion, differentiation, and integration as they proceeded through a complex sequence of temporally overlapping cycles of adaptation to new technological, managerial, and social innovations (nearly all with space-adjusting consequences for the geographical structure of the system). Industrialization, for example, may be seen from this viewpoint as a series of innovations that fundamentally changes the relations between urban expansion, differentiation, and integration during the nineteenth and early twentieth century, as far as North America is concerned. On this broad loom, needless to say, the theoretical model-building and interweaving with appropriate historical evidence appears skimpy indeed. Different investigators have tried their hands with different materials, colours, and techniques, and unsurprisingly the resulting conceptual image of the urban system is choppy, imprecise, and occasionally at odds. However, a critical mass of ongoing research on the historical urban system exists and the accompanying dialogue is substantial. One small example is Meyer's discovery of a Pred–Conzen anomaly in crude estimates of the progress of urban system integration during the nineteenth century—Pred arguing for significant integration by 1840 and Conzen not recognizing major integration until the end of the century (Pred, 1973, pp. 187–9; Conzen, 1977, p. 108). Meyer's observation that each writer was measuring different aspects of long-term integration is certainly true, through his proposed exchange–transport control distinction as the key may be only a partial solution (Meyer, 1980a, p. 135).

If the theoretical framework of urban system evolution in nineteenth century America resembles more a patchwork quilt than a tapestry, this is not to say that an informal picture of the system's character and evolution cannot be obtained. To sew together all the empirical fragments of research on the topic would stimulate a whole cottage industry in itself, but in the space remaining a brief attempt will be made to present some picture of the evolving urban system between 1790 and 1910.

SEQUENCES OF URBAN SYSTEM CHANGE IN THE UNITED STATES

A basic set of indices of urbanization at the national level yields three periods into which the evolution of the nineteenth-century urban system can be divided

TABLE 9.2   Indices of long-term urban change, 1790–1940

Census	Decade	Total number of cities (≥ 2,500)	Urban Population %Total population	Urban Population %Change	%Increase of urban population	Non-agriculture labour force %Total labour force	Non-agriculture labour force %Change
1790		24	5.1				
	1790–1800			1.0	59.9		
1800		33	6.1			26.3(17.4[a])	
	1800–10			1.2	63.0		−10.1
1810		46	7.3			16.2	
	1810–20			−0.1	31.9		4.9
1820		61	7.2			21.2	
	1820–30			1.6	62.6		8.2
1830		90	8.8			29.4	
	1830–40			2.0	63.7		7.5
1840		131	10.8	****	****	36.9	
	1840–50	****	****	4.5	92.1		8.3
1850		236	15.3			45.2	****
	1850–60			4.5	75.4	****	1.9
1860		392	19.8			47.1	
	1860–70			5.9	59.3		0.4
1870		663	25.7			47.5	
	1870–80			2.5	53.7		1.2
1880		939	28.2	****	****	48.7	****
	1880–90	****	****	6.9	56.5	****	8.6
1890		1,348	35.1			57.3	
	1890–1900			4.6	36.4		2.5
1900		1,737	39.7			59.8	
	1900–10			6.0	39.3		8.8
1910		2,262	45.7			68.6	****
	1910–20			5.5	29.0	****	5.5
1920		2,722	51.2			74.1	
	1920–30			5.0	27.3		4.3
1930		3,165	56.2	****	****	78.4	
	1930–40	****	****	0.3	7.9		4.6
1940		3,464	56.5			83.0	

Sources: US Census data; Lebergott (1964, Table A-1); [a] David (1967, p. 166).

for analytical purposes (Table 9.2); the general social and economic implications of trends in these indices have been discussed elsewhere (Lampard, 1968; Ward, 1971; Davis *et al.*, 1972). Clear breaks in the trends suggest 1840 and 1880 as useful dividing lines that separate periods of significantly different levels of urbanization, rates of new town founding, and shifts in the proportional importance of the non-agricultural labour force (Table 9.3). Because many earlier discussions have adopted similar period breaks but pegged them one decade earlier in each case then here (e.g. Borchert, 1967; Ward, 1971), the rationale for choosing 1840 and 1880, it should be clear, is based on growth trends reflected directly in the dimensions of the system, rather than imputed from indirect and partly independent variables such as the timing of various transport technologies. It is evident that 1910 does not represent a significant break in urban indices (1930 is a better terminal date for the period begun in 1880); the year 1910 is taken as an end point in this study only for convenience.

Such indices, of course, provide a mere backdrop against which to project the evolution of the urban system itself. A first glimpse of the system's structure is revealed in the graphical history of urban rank sizes (Figure 9.3). Lukermann's

TABLE 9.3 Summary urban indices

	1790	1790–1840	1840	1840–1880	1880	1880–1910	1910
Number of cities (≥2,500)	24		131		939		2,262
Average number of new cities per annum		2		20		44	
Urban population as percentage total population	5.1		10.8		28.2		45.7
Rate of increase in urban share		1.1		4.4		5.6	
Average decadal percentage change urban population		56.4		67.3		44.0	
Non-agricultural labour force as percentage total	–		36.9		48.7		68.6
Average decadal percentage change non-agricultural labour force		2.6		2.9		6.6	
Number of urban places:							
Over 1 million	–		–		1		3
0.5M–1 million	–		–		3		5
0.25M–0.5 million	–		1		4		11
100,000–0.25 million	–		2		12		31
50,000–99,999	–		2		15		59
25,000–49,999	2		7		42		119
10,000–24,999	3		25		146		369
5,000–9,999	7		48		249		605
2,500–4,999	12		46		467		1,060

Sources: See Table 9.2

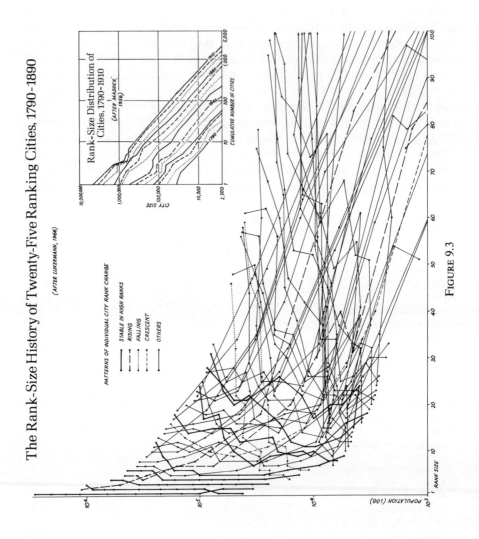

The Rank-Size History of Twenty-Five Ranking Cities, 1790-1890

(AFTER LUKERMANN, 1966)

Rank-Size Distribution of
Cities, 1790-1910

(AFTER MADDEN,
1956)

PATTERNS OF INDIVIDUAL CITY RANK CHANGE

STABLE IN HIGH RANKS
RISING
FALLING
CRESCENT
OTHERS

FIGURE 9.3

calculations of individual city rank profiles between 1790 and 1890 indicate that while the aggregate rank-size curve of the urban hierarchy varied little over time (Figure 9.3, inset), the rank history of particular cities did, so that a surface calm was maintained, as it were, at the expense of widespread individual rank volatility. Five patterns deserve mention. Most obvious was the rank stability in the face of competition of the upper echelon cities that spurred Pred to develop his eastern circular–cumulative growth model. Secondly, there was a pattern of 'dropouts', concentrated in two periods: small eastern port towns like Gloucester and Savannah succumbed early to loss of position followed several decades later by Salem and Charleston, unable to keep pace with more diversified and better-located competitors. Thirdly, late-blooming interior cities like St. Louis and Chicago burst through the rankings to take high positions by 1890. A fourth pattern characterized cities like Louisville that progressed well in the early years only to 'stall' and fall behind once their regional niche in the urban system had been found. A fifth pattern comprised those places that rose and fell in rank with little regular pattern. At best, these patterns in Figure 9.3 merely pose part of the question (the ageographical part) concerning the determinants of urban growth, and in so doing highlight the tremendous volatility endemic to an urban system undergoing such radical transformation. For further elucidation, they need to be placed in a clear spatial context.

The broader spatial context can be summarized in terms of the rank performance and locational structure of the top 30 cities during the course of the three growth periods (Figure 9.4). In the early period some major eastern seaports were still exchanging ranks, while widespread patterns of gains by new towns were balanced by concentrated patterns of drop-outs (the same stagnating town identified by Lukermann). In the middle period, westward extension of the national urban network to the Pacific allowed major western entrepôts to capture high rank at the expense of smaller eastern ports generally and some northeastern inland centres. The final period was marked by extensive high-rank stability along the Atlantic corridor, new western entrepôts becoming established, and a new basis for rank attainment in manufacturing. Such attention to the locational volatility of upper ranks in the city system provides a preliminary sketch of the system's evolution, but the picture can be filled in considerably more with the help of interpretations drawn from the conceptual work reviewed earlier.

Forging an autonomous American urban system (1790–1840)

The period that stretches from the aftermath of the American Revolution to 1840 may be characterized as one in which European colonialism was replaced by continental colonialism (Duncan and Lieberson, 1970, ch. 3). Colonial policies in Europe had encouraged the rise of an Atlantic seaboard wholesaling alignment anchored in the major entrepôts of Boston, New York, Philadelphia,

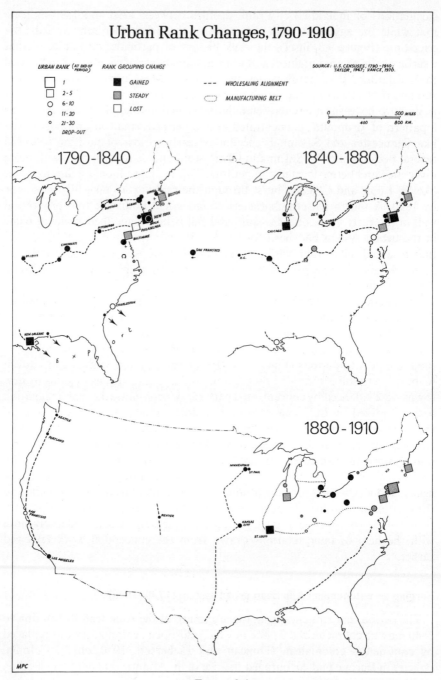

FIGURE 9.4

Functional Structure of the City-System

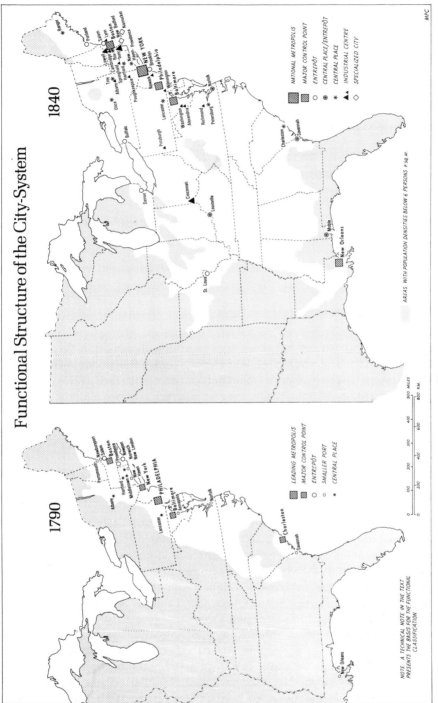

FIGURE 9.5

and Charleston (joined later by Baltimore). At the time of independence each of these ports had major links with London and other foreign ports and very few with its seaboard neighbours. Thus it is highly uncertain that one can properly refer to the entire eastern seaboard as an autonomous urban system in 1790 although it certainly comprised a dependent transatlantic subsystem of metropolitan Europe. More likely each major port acted as a semi-autonomous entrepôt, given diverse ocean trading patterns, and several (Boston, New York, and particularly Philadelphia) had begun or were beginning to organize hinterlands with rudimentary town networks (Figure 9.5(a)). Remaining towns, depending on their urban rôles, were either small ports, or incipient central places; Albany was an outpost of New York serving both local and long-distance river trade.

In the course of the next half-century, the processes of expansion, differentiation, and integration proceeded on an extensive scale (Figure 9.5(b)). Already by 1840 the four major northeastern ports had established a combined, long-term urban supremacy based on intensive development of their common immediate hinterlands and aggressive attempts to tap the wealth of the transmontane west (Rubin, 1961; Lindstrom, 1978). This was just as well, since foreign commerce began a long decline in its contribution to urban growth (Taylor, 1967). Transport improvements widened the sphere of superior information circulation, but these were exceptionally biased in favour of the four big ports, whose wholesale-trading sectors took full advantage of hinterland organization to spur metropolitan manufactures as well (Pred, 1973). The most significant regional developments were the emergence of two major wholesaling alignments roughly at right-angles to the coastal metropolitan corridor alignment, one reaching from New York up the Hudson and *via* the Erie Canal (1825) to the eastern Great Lakes, the other across the mountains to Pittsburgh and the Ohio Valley (Vance, 1970). New Orleans benefited from much Mississippi–Ohio river trade but could stimulate no major entrepôts between itself and St. Louis (Figure 9.4).

The urban subsystem that developed in the United States up to 1840 showed early signs of increasing differences among urban rôles (Figure 9.5(b)). Manufacturing was beginning to contribute both to the solid growth of the leading mercantile centres (which managed to monopolize most of the exchange control functions in the system), and also to more specialized industrial cities such as Lowell and Providence. Cincinnati capitalized on processing industry (Walsh, 1978, pp. 10–12), as the Queen City came to be known popularly as 'Porkopolis'. Beyond these emerging specialisms, smaller cities on the eastern seaboard acquired roles of either regional or long-distance significance. Many large towns (Petersburg, Virginia, Hartford, Charleston, Bangor) became frankly central places with little extraregional importance, while others (Portland, Salem, Brooklyn, Norfolk, Savannah, Mobile) became medium-sized wholesale headlinks as a more clearly articulated east-coast wholesaling network

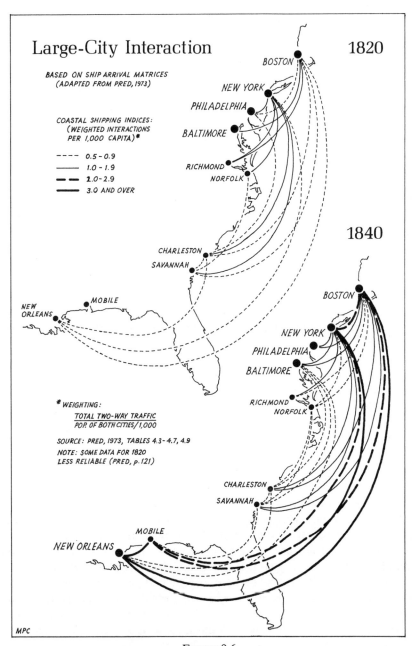

Large-City Interaction   1820

BASED ON SHIP ARRIVAL MATRICES
(ADAPTED FROM PRED, 1973)

COASTAL SHIPPING INDICES:
(WEIGHTED INTERACTIONS
PER 1,000 CAPITA)*

---- 0.5 - 0.9
—— 1.0 - 1.9
— — 2.0 - 2.9
—— 3.0 AND OVER

BOSTON

NEW YORK

PHILADELPHIA

BALTIMORE

RICHMOND

NORFOLK

CHARLESTON

SAVANNAH

MOBILE

NEW
ORLEANS

1840

BOSTON

NEW YORK

PHILADELPHIA

BALTIMORE

RICHMOND

NORFOLK

*WEIGHTING:
TOTAL TWO-WAY TRAFFIC
POP. OF BOTH CITIES/1,000

SOURCE: PRED, 1973, TABLES 4.3-4.7, 4.9
NOTE: SOME DATA FOR 1820
LESS RELIABLE (PRED, p.121)

CHARLESTON

SAVANNAH

MOBILE

NEW ORLEANS

MPC

FIGURE 9.6

emerged. Meanwhile, a few highly specialized centres developed or 'hung on', such as the small resorts of the Carolinas (Kovacik, 1978) or the large whaling ports of Nantucket and New Bedford.

Such extensive differentiation of urban functions among towns in the settlement system should imply an increasing amount of integration within the system as well. In general, while hard data are extremely difficult to assemble at this point (Pred, 1973), it appears that by 1840 one could begin to speak of a more-or-less autonomous and articulated American urban system. Coastal traffic between ports increased between 1820 and 1840 (Figure 9.6) and more ports became mutual trading partners. Inland, travel times for freight, news, and personal transport fell significantly, suggesting the basis for greater interaction (Pred, 1973, Ch. 5). But costs of travel remained high over long distances, and business channels maintained a largely dendritic focus on individual cities, although these large port hinterlands began to overlap and compete at their margins by the end of the period.

Within this national urban system several urban subsystems developed characteristics that were to define their rôles within the larger system for the remainder of the century. Four brief examples must suffice. The east coast contained many regions of relatively dense population (at least by western standards). Within the context of a powerful mercantile large-city axis along the seaboard, central place subsystems emerged in areas of solid agricultural settlement such as southeast Pennsylvania during the colonial period or Vermont and upper New York state in the early national period. Terrain and natural endowments in Vermont, however, could not duplicate the rich farming base of 'the best poor man's country' in Pennsylvania (Lemon, 1967), and central place competition among nascent trade centres in the former between 1790 and 1830 was fierce and often uncertain. Under these conditions a simple three-level local hierarchy emerged whereby initial sorting produced a rough matrix of first-order trade centres, from which regionally important third-order towns subsequently arose, and were surrounded by the in-filling of second-order places during a third phase (Bowden et al., 1970).

Rather different was the experience in the middle Ohio Valley, where a local urban network developed chronologically about two decades behind the Vermont case. While Vermont lay outside major trade routes and offered a somewhat restricted agricultural base, the Cincinnati hinterland was fertile, relatively flat, and adjacent to a major commercial thoroughfare, the Ohio River (Figure 9.7). In these circumstances a highly variegated urban subsystem grew up in which different levels of transport nodality worked and reworked the settlement hierarchy from a very linear long-distance pattern to a radial central place network centred on Cincinnati (Muller, 1976). The region's location astride major routes west destined its urban subsystem to alter even more drastically in a later period. What differentiated the Cincinnati hinterland system from many others further east was its provident physical setting, the

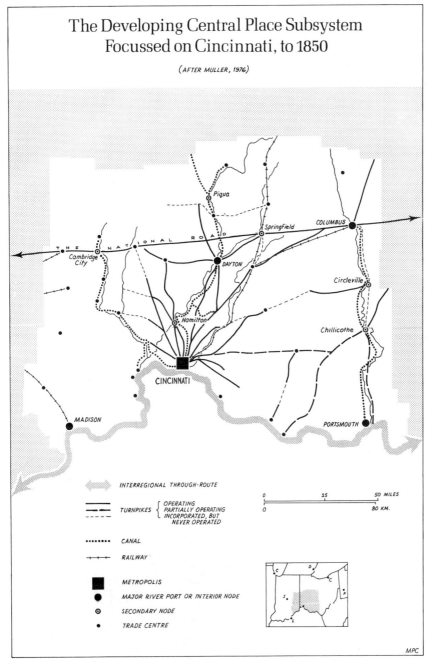

The Developing Central Place Subsystem
Focussed on Cincinnati, to 1850

(AFTER MULLER, 1976)

FIGURE 9.7

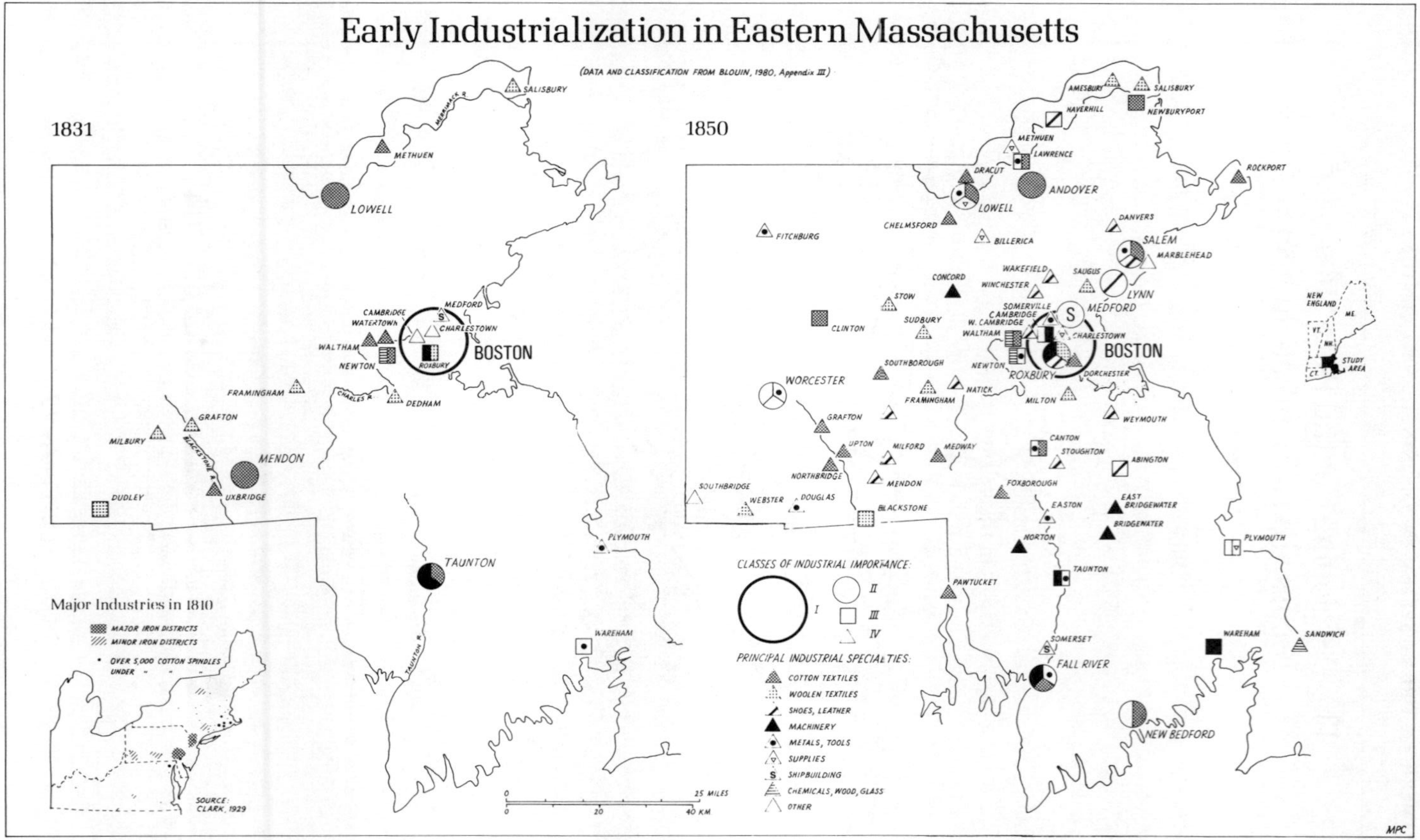
Early Industrialization in Eastern Massachusetts
(DATA AND CLASSIFICATION FROM BLOUIN, 1980, Appendix III)
1831
1850
SALISBURY
METHUEN
LOWELL
MERRIMACK R.
MEDFORD
CAMBRIDGE
WATERTOWN
CHARLESTOWN
WALTHAM
NEWTON
ROXBURY
BOSTON
FRAMINGHAM
CHARLES R.
DEDHAM
GRAFTON
MILBURY
BLACKSTONE R.
MENDON
DUDLEY
UXBRIDGE
PLYMOUTH
TAUNTON
TAUNTON R.
WAREHAM
Major Industries in 1810
MAJOR IRON DISTRICTS
MINOR IRON DISTRICTS
OVER 5,000 COTTON SPINDLES
UNDER
SOURCE: CLARK, 1929
25 MILES
40 KM
AMESBURY
HAVERHILL
NEWBURYPORT
LAWRENCE
DRACUT
ANDOVER
ROCKPORT
CHELMSFORD
FITCHBURG
BILLERICA
DANVERS
SALEM
MARBLEHEAD
WAKEFIELD
SAUGUS
CONCORD
WINCHESTER
LYNN
STOW
CLINTON
SOMERVILLE
W. CAMBRIDGE
SUDBURY
DORCHESTER
SOUTHBOROUGH
WORCESTER
NATICK
MILTON
WEYMOUTH
CANTON
STOUGHTON
ABINGTON
UPTON
MILFORD
MEDWAY
NORTHBRIDGE
FOXBOROUGH
SOUTHBRIDGE
WEBSTER
DOUGLAS
BLACKSTONE
EASTON
EAST BRIDGEWATER
BRIDGEWATER
NORTON
PAWTUCKET
SOMERSET
FALL RIVER
NEW BEDFORD
SANDWICH
NEW ENGLAND
ME.
VT.
NH.
CT.
STUDY AREA
CLASSES OF INDUSTRIAL IMPORTANCE:
I
II
III
IV
PRINCIPAL INDUSTRIAL SPECIALTIES:
COTTON TEXTILES
WOOLEN TEXTILES
SHOES, LEATHER
MACHINERY
METALS, TOOLS
SUPPLIES
SHIPBUILDING
CHEMICALS, WOOD, GLASS
OTHER
MPC

Figure 9.8

stimulus to transport improvements provided by its strategic location, and its capacity to develop processing and later fabricating industries at several levels of the urban hierarchy, much of it oriented beyond the region—a combination that mirrored only a few eastern regions, such as the urban hinterlands of upstate New York (e.g. Syracuse; see Miller, 1979).

In complete contrast were large parts of the South, where few large or even medium- or small-sized cities emerged in the nineteenth century. The roots of this situation lay in the colonial period (Earle and Hoffman, 1977), but little change occurred even later (Denecke, 1976; Adkins, 1973). Between the town-usurping character of many large plantations and the commerce-minimizing structure of cotton marketing, few towns found any long-term stability (LaRose, 1973).

If most regional subsystems in this early period were predicated on local trade and central place functions, the region centred on Boston altered radically by industrializing early and diversely. Eastern Massachusetts shifted between 1810 and 1840 to a manufacturing region with four grades of industrial towns based on output and entrepreneurial variety, under the stimulus of severe changes in agriculture and foreign trade, abundance of water, power, and local inventiveness (LeBlanc, 1969, pp. 12–41; Blouin, 1980). Most striking was the regionally diffused nature of the manufacturing and the seeming randomness with which local town and village industrial specialities were distributed within the region (Figure 9.8). Many towns participated in this early industrial revolution, although major water power and coastal locations (for cotton and coal imports) ultimately contained the largest enterprises.

Creating a continental network (1840–1880)

A phenomenal growth in the size of the urban system from 131 to 939 urban places occurred during the middle phase of the nineteenth century (Table 9.3). The successful establishment of wholesaling alignments into the continental interior opened up the Ohio Valley and Great Lakes regions to rural settlement as in-migration swelled. Co-ordinated with population growth and the rapid production of agricultural surpluses, a diverse regional programme of internal transport improvements created, first with canals and later with railways, vastly extended long-distance trading routes that after 1869 reached the Pacific and by 1880 had begun to organize the western prairies. As a result, the old wholesaling alignments were extended westward (railways and the Civil War having redirected much of the Upper Mississippi trade from New Orleans directly to the east), so that St. Paul and Kansas City became the depôts of staple collection (Figure 9.9). The centres they replaced in that capacity—Buffalo, Louisville—turned to more diversified regional functions, including upper-level central place service, while the largest cities (Chicago, St. Louis, and San Francisco) managed to capture both added processing functions (Walsh, 1978)

Functional Structure of the City-System in 1880

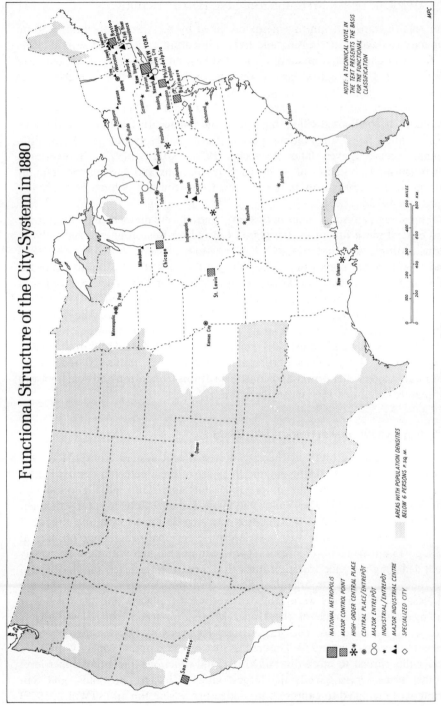

NOTE: A TECHNICAL NOTE IN THE TEXT PRESENTS THE BASIS FOR THE FUNCTIONAL CLASSIFICATION

NATIONAL METROPOLIS

MAJOR CONTROL POINT

HIGH-ORDER CENTRAL PLACE

CENTRAL PLACE/ENTREPÔT

MAJOR ENTREPÔT

INDUSTRIAL/ENTREPÔT

MAJOR INDUSTRIAL CENTRE

SPECIALIZED CITY

AREAS WITH POPULATION DENSITIES BELOW 6 PERSONS P. SQ. M.

500 MILES

800 KM

FIGURE 9.9

and significant exchange control functions. This control of exchange was not so much a change at New York's absolute expense but rather a case of fast-growing metropolises with regional proximity as a factor garnering some of the new economic articulation needs of the enlarged country. The ability of entrepreneurs in New York to capture most of the increase in exchange control certainly helped it maintain its national pre-eminence (Conzen, 1977). Few regional centres could break into these exalted functional ranks, and indeed New Orleans lost its earlier importance as a control centre through the new reorientations (Lewis, 1976). Thus medium-sized cities increasingly settled into the rôle of regional central-place hubs (Richmond, Columbus, Indianapolis, Nashville, Atlanta, Denver) while their counterparts in the northeast combined similar functions with more developed manufacturing (Hartford, Scranton; Figure 9.9).

In these changes the dual processes of expansion and differentiation redefined the macro-system. They also made room for new specialization within old areas, such as the rise of Washington as a major government centre, Jersey City as a specialized wholesale terminal, and a host of burgeoning industrial cities like Cleveland, Reading, Dayton, and Newark. By 1880, too, the railway network had become extremely dense so that patterns of multi-directional interaction were possible as never before, and the telegraph made instant communication possible. Nevertheless, interdependence developed most intensely among the most important cities across the nation, and below that level most clearly within a framework of regional subsystems that nevertheless allowed non-hierarchical 'lateral' links between similarly-sized places, often for reasons of industrial or wholesale linkage (Conzen, 1975b, 1977; Vance, 1970).

With an expanding urban system developing complex inter- and intraregional interdependencies it was inevitable that new types of urban-regional subsystems emerged. Space permits only passing reference to two midwestern examples. At a sub-metropolitan level, central place factors played an important role in all new areas of rich agricultural settlement. Unlike Vermont and the middle Ohio Valley, on the prairies of Illinois the iron horse 'caught up' with the frontier settling process and became an inseparable part of it. Central Illinois between 1830 and 1880 therefore provides a key illustration of a central-place subsystem evolving upon a bold new transport principle.

The early efforts at town promotion in Central Illinois resembled those of older regions, although the flatness of the terrain and the neutrality of the land survey grid may have encouraged an even more excessive wave of 'lost cause' locations (Figure 9.10(a)). Significantly, the distribution and particularly the timing of townsite failures suggest that for some areas at least, 'sorting' continued to proceed far beyond the 'initial' phase (*contra* Berry, 1967, pp. 6–7; Bowden *et al.*, 1970), with attempts to add new nodes to the network still being made late in its maturing stages. By 1900 differentiation among central place levels had emerged as a clear response to railway conditioning of town spacing

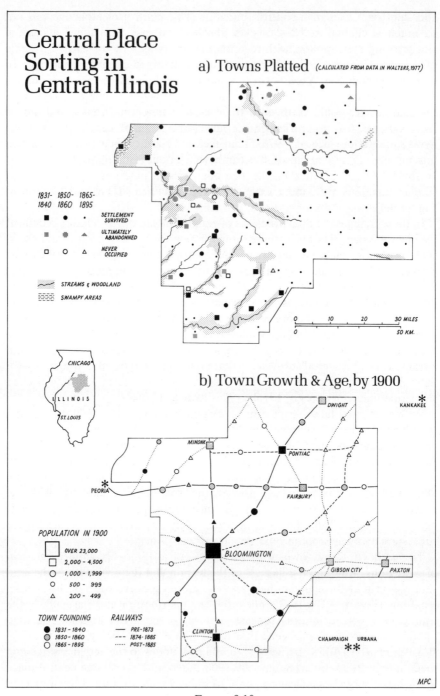

Central Place Sorting in Central Illinois

a) Towns Platted (CALCULATED FROM DATA IN WALTERS, 1977)

	1831-1840	1850-1860	1865-1895	
SETTLEMENT SURVIVED	■	●	·	
ULTIMATELY ABANDONNED	▦	▦	⚞	
NEVER OCCUPIED	□	○	△	

STREAMS & WOODLAND

SWAMPY AREAS

0   10   20   30 MILES
0   50 KM.

CHICAGO
ILLINOIS
ST. LOUIS

b) Town Growth & Age, by 1900

DWIGHT
KANKAKEE *
MINONK
PONTIAC
PEORIA *
FAIRBURY
BLOOMINGTON
GIBSON CITY   PAXTON
CLINTON
CHAMPAIGN URBANA **

POPULATION IN 1900

□ OVER 23,000
□ 2,000 - 4,500
○ 1,000 - 1,999
○ 500 - 999
△ 200 - 499

TOWN FOUNDING	RAILWAYS
● 1831 - 1840	— PRE-1873
◉ 1850 - 1860	--- 1874 - 1885
○ 1865 - 1895	···· POST-1885

MPC

FIGURE 9.10

and selective urban growth (Figure 9.10(b)). Only one out of eight second-order centres in that year had not enjoyed railway linkage since the earliest period, and no trade centre rose to third-order status without at least fifteen years of railway service to help it. Not a single settlement over 200 population survived in 1900 off the railway network.

The operation of centralizing forces and accessibility worked at another scale by affecting large hinterlands associated with major metropolises. Railway service frequency in metropolitan hinterlands supported urban gradient characteristics so strong that the incipient autonomy of middle-order central places within the hinterland was compromised by the long reach of metropolitan influence (or dominance), thereby limiting the extent to which middle-order service areas could expand (Conzen, 1975b). Chicago, for example, easily checked the putative spread of local urban influence from centres like Peoria, Springfield, and Freeport in Illinois, and Fort Wayne and Crawfordsville in Indiana, between 1872 and 1890, and put great pressure on the dominance fields of larger neighbours like Indianapolis, St. Louis, and Milwaukee. The increasing strength of these metropolitan fields in the Middle West is reflected also in steepening gradients of metropolitan influence (Figure 9.11) that interfered with and overrode the central-place-forming processes operating in territory lying between such major metropolises (Conzen, 1974). These gradient measures represent, in addition, oblique reflections of the increased integration of the urban system at all levels during the later nineteenth century.

Weaving the complex urban pattern (1880–1910)

Between 1880 and the First World War the urban system expanded to more than double its earlier size (Table 9.3), as 1,323 new urban places appeared at an annual average rate of 44 per annum (twice the rate of the preceding period). This expansion included frontier settlements in new regions and substantial infilling of settled areas as population densities reached their historic plateaus. The westward extension of wholesaling alignments was essentially completed during this phase with the appearance of a Pacific coast wholesale chain, and a Great Plains alignment from Duluth to San Antonio (Figure 9.12). West of this line settlement developed from isolated nucleii into small regional complexes that remained mostly discontinuous (Meining, 1972, p. 163; Sargent, 1975; Luckingham, 1979) and thus tended to combine long-distance and regional central place functions with little differentiation in the few large centres the regional population thresholds could sustain. Nevertheless, the west coast urban subsystems, despite their fragmentation, reflected the salience of wholesaling links with the rest of the national urban system.

In the older regions east of the Mississippi River the growth of towns and cities at all levels was accompanied by further spatial and functional differentiation in urban rôles. While the 'big-four' ports on the east coast remained

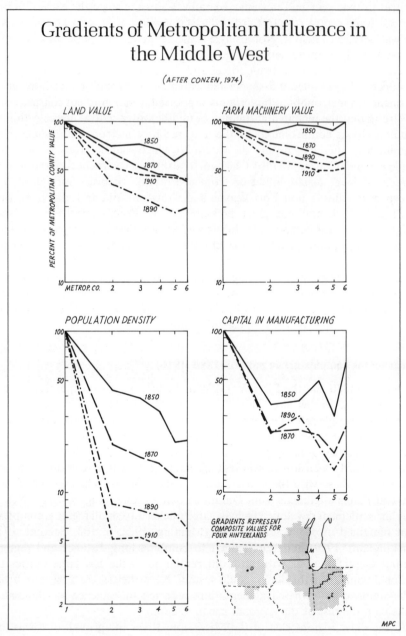

FIGURE 9.11

Functional Structure of the City-System in 1910

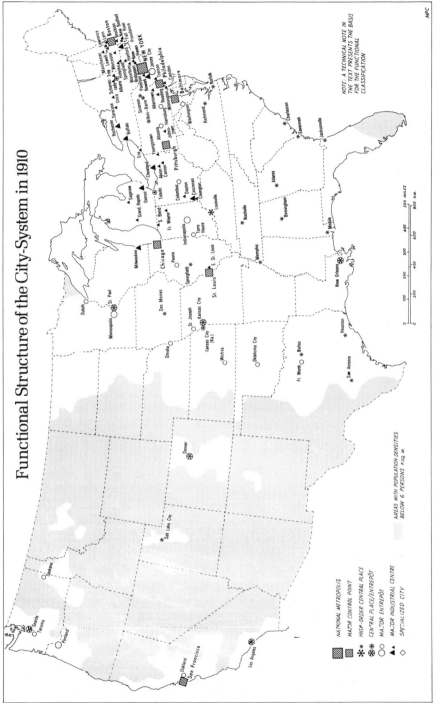

NOTE: A TECHNICAL NOTE IN
THE TEXT PRESENTS THE BASIS
FOR THE FUNCTIONAL
CLASSIFICATION

NATIONAL METROPOLIS
MAJOR CONTROL POINT
HIGH-ORDER CENTRAL PLACE
CENTRAL PLACE/ENTREPÔT
MAJOR ENTREPÔT
MAJOR INDUSTRIAL CENTRE
SPECIALIZED CITY

AREAS WITH POPULATION DENSITIES
BELOW 6 PERSONS P.SQ. M.

FIGURE 9.12

the chief centres of economic control in the urban system, the period witnessed the final emergence of a complex national manufacturing belt covering nearly all the northern states. Within this belt, major cities differentiated further so that Buffalo, Detroit, and Milwaukee became heavily industrial, while high-level central place functions became scattered at various urban levels—split among the densely-packed industrial cities that offered thresholds for services otherwise not warranted in any but the largest regional centres. Another significant shift was the emergence of a specialized wholesale alignment running east–west through the very heart of the manufacturing belt. Represented by a string of centres from Jersey City, through Harrisburg, Altoona, Columbus, Indianapolis, Terre Haute, Peoria, and St. Joseph, this alignment arose to facilitate local distribution within the Northeast and offer a 'bypass' route through the industrial belt for some commodities moving between the transmississippi West and the east coast (Vance, 1970; Meyer, 1980a).

The Civil War and Reconstruction may have altered the economic and social fabric of the South, but played little part in redefining the basis for urbanization in that section of the country. Urban places grew, but in a balanced way so that most large southern cities developed broad central place functional structures. Old towns revived, such as Savannah, Charleston, Mobile, and Nashville, and newly growing ones like Jacksonville, Memphis, and Houston evolved similar regional niches in the national urban system (likewise Birmingham, for its industrial rise had barely begun). Finally, the forces of differentiation had produced by 1910 a considerable list of highly specialized functional city types such as state-level administrative centres, educational centres, and resorts (Mahnke, 1972; Vanderhill, 1973). Because so many of these towns were single-function centres, their size was not sufficient to appear on Figure 9.12.

Traditional networks of urban connectivity, such as the railway system, telegraph, and other channels of physical movement, had achieved a high degree of 'closure', that is, most places that needed to be interconnected to move people, freight, and ideas between any two points were indeed linked. Developments towards the end of the nineteenth century concerned more the spatial biases (to use Pred's term) in the use of the networks. The development of banking channels in the national financial system from the 1840s up to 1910 suggests that the period after 1880 was crucial in evolving a fully integrated national-regional hierarchy of bank exchange (Conzen, 1977), though the extreme dominance of New York and, to a lesser degree, Chicago, may reflect conditions more typical of the national financial sector than of the economic system as a whole.

If the complex nesting of subsystems found in the banking hierarchy indexed with any accuracy the more general pattern of subsystems within the national urban system, however, then more such regional systems in a greater variety of different historical and regional settings existed in 1910 than ever before.

Two subsystems provide examples of the new processes at work at the regional level. Firstly, the northern Great Plains, effectively settled following 1880, experienced the last surge of central place elaboration prior to the automobile. Unlike regions further east, however, the Great Plains were pioneered by the railway, and the corporate and institutional strategies and settlement design concepts of the railway companies were crucial in defining the spatial and functional structure of the resulting urban settlement system (Hudson, 1979). The railways had been significant in Illinois central place formation as providers of accessibility and sometimes a few townsites; by the time of Dakota settlement such elements as standardization of banking practices, large railway corporations, and specialization in wholesaling and retailing, made town planning a much more routine process carried out almost by blueprint (Hamburg, 1977). In the wheat-based Plains urban system railway officials literally dictated town densities by fixing distances between them along the lines; grain elevator companies and lumber dealers reinforced these decisions with all the independence of side-kicks; and innumerable local businessmen materialized to stock these towns with standardized functions—banks, hotels, hardware stores. This was the great age of assigned central places, and the coming of rural depopulation, the automobile, and mail-order merchandising after the turn of the century was to make it also seem in retrospect the great age of overbuilding.

Lastly, the American urban system had by the end of the nineteenth century created an industrial sector so large and geographically concentrated that the national core region (in Ward's terminology) was synonymous with the manufacturing belt (Figure 9.13). Like any large and complex settlement region, the roles of individual urban places within it varied immensely, but underlying all this there was a basic symmetry in the pattern of regional specialization within it. Measures of industrial specialization generalized from location quotients for the largest manufacturing cities (Duncan and Lieberson, 1970, p. 85) support a three-part segmentation of the manufacturing belt in 1900. Heavy biases towards consumer-goods production characterized Boston, New York, and Baltimore, while a producer-goods 'axis' connected Philadelphia to Cleveland, the latter itself anchoring a western cluster of diversified manufacturing cities slightly biased towards consumer goods. This zonation of highly generalized biases in production patterns is so abstract as to defy accurate explanation, but one can glimpse in the consumer orientation of the three eastern ports a reflection of the mercantile orientations historically associated with these old entrepots, as modelled by Pred. The producer bias of the 'Keystone' cities suggests the close association with the Pennsylvanian coalfields and lake importation of iron ore, whereas the mixed manufacturing of cities in the western manufacturing belt implies diversification and consumer orientation appropriate for a region intermediate between the heavy industrial core and the rest of the non-industrialized regions dependent on consumer goods. What bound the manufacturing belt together were the high-intensity information

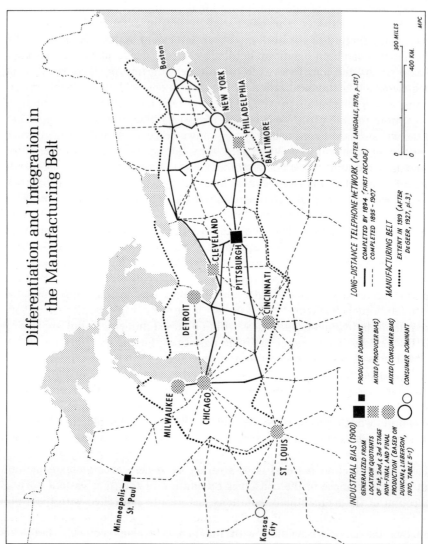

Differentiation and Integration in
the Manufacturing Belt

INDUSTRIAL BIAS (1900)
GENERALIZED FROM
LOCATION QUOTIENTS
OF 1st, 2nd, & 3rd STAGE
NON-FINAL AND FINAL
PRODUCTION (BASED ON
DUNCAN & LIEBERSON,
1970, TABLE 5-1)

PRODUCER DOMINANT
MIXED (PRODUCER BIAS)
MIXED (CONSUMER BIAS)
CONSUMER DOMINANT

LONG-DISTANCE TELEPHONE NETWORK (AFTER LANGDALE, 1978, p.151)
COMPLETED BY 1894 ("FIRST DECADE")
COMPLETED 1895 - 1907

MANUFACTURING BELT
EXTENT IN 1919 (AFTER
DeGEER, 1927, pl. 3)

0   300 MILES
0   400 KM.

MPC

FIGURE 9.13

channels and the external economies of corporate concentration (Langdale, 1978; Abler, 1977; Cohen, 1979; Meyer, 1980b).

CONCLUSION

The developmental history of the American urban system in the nineteenth century must be pieced together at present from an extremely diverse body of research, and many aspects remain obscure. But the steady stream of conceptual interpretation in recent years, while sometimes narrow and focused upon single dimensions of the system, holds out the possibility of further theoretical integration when placed in a larger framework of systemic evolution such as that attempted here. Such theoretical maturity is still a long way off, for a great deal of empirical research will need to accompany the formulation of more complex models. But summary maps that begin to outline the enormous change in the nineteenth century urban system show clearly the multiplication in the number of urban subsystems, their increased hierarchical ordering, and the high-intensity linkages that bound together the most important regional metropolises in a complex web of management within the national urban system (Figure 9.14).

As research continues, to cite only a few examples of gaps that need closing, the assumptions of hypercommercial instincts on the part of producers (agricultural and others) could benefit from closer examination. So too could the reasons why 'initial advantage' evaporates in some localities but lives on in others to trigger repeated cycles of urban growth models; the role of entrepreneurs and other individuals in historical industrial location patterns; industrial product cycles and industrial linkage; the varied role of government activity in support of, and bias for or against certain types of urban system development; the importance of city-system structure in the minds of urban 'prime movers'; the realm of social interactions within the urban system, e.g. connectivity of social and business elites, interurban migration in an historical setting, and travellers' perceptions of urban system structure; and finally, concepts to tie together changes in the internal spatial structure of cities with their position in the evolving system of cities. If the trend of slowly rising interest in the historical evolution of the American urban system continues, we can look forward to a time when the conceptual baggage we currently carry will seem thoroughly outmoded. But such understanding should not end with the nature of the urban system itself, rather it should penetrate the significance it holds for the workings of the larger social system.

TECHNICAL NOTE TO FIGURES 9.5, 9.9, AND 9.12

The typology is based on three criteria, applied in the following order of precedence: (1) above-average representation in any of three occupational

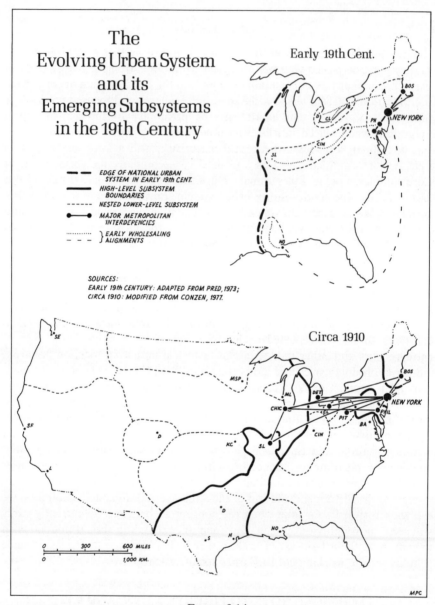

FIGURE 9.14

categories (trade and transport, mining and manufacturing, all other urban occupations); (2) designation as national metropolis or major control point if financial transactions in the banking system surpassed the mean for the top 50 cities; and (3) identification as highly specialized in some other respect, e.g. government, whaling port, based on varied historical evidence. Adjustments to these criteria were made in the following instances: (a) bank capital rather than clearing house volume was used to define major control points in 1840, and in the absence of financial measures for 1790, general population size for that year; and (b) lacking occupational data for all the towns in 1790, more general distinctions in size, location and function were drawn from previous research (particularly Taylor, 1967). Smaller symbols in some categories indicate centres of lesser importance.

REFERENCES

Abler, R. (1977). The telephone and the evolution of the American metropolitan system. In I. deS. Pool (Ed.), *The Social Impact of the Telephone*, MIT Press, Cambridge, Massachusetts, pp. 318–341.

Adams, J. S. (Ed.) (1976). *Contemporary Metropolitan America: Twenty Geographical Vignettes*, Ballinger, Cambridge, Massachusetts.

Adkins, H. G. (1973). The geographic base of urban retardation in Mississippi, 1800–1840. *West Georgia College Studies in the Social Sciences*, **12**, 35–49.

Albion, R. G. (1939). *The Rise of New York Port, 1815–1860*, Charles Scribner's Sons, New York.

Belcher, W. W. (1947). *The Economic Rivalry between St. Louis and Chicago, 1850–1880*, Columbia University Press, New York.

Berry, B. J. L. (1961). City size distribution and economic development. *Economic Development and Cultural Change*, **9**, 573–588.

Berry, B. J. L. (1967). *The Geography of Market Centers and Retail Distribution*, Prentice-Hall, Englewood Cliffs.

Berry, B. J. L. and Neils, E. (1969). Location, size, and shape of cities as influenced by environmental factors: the urban environment writ large. In H. S. Perloff (Ed.), *The Quality of the Urban Environment: Essays on 'New Resources' in an Urban Age*, Resources for the Future, Baltimore.

Blouin, F. X. Jr. (1980). *The Boston Region 1810–1850: A Study of Urbanization*, UMI Research Press, Ann Arbor.

Bogue, D. J. (1950). *The Structure of the Metropolitan Community: A Study of Dominance and Subdominance*, University of Michigan, Ann Arbor.

Borchert, J. R. (1967). American metropolitan evolution. *Geographical Review*, **57**, 301–332.

Bourne, L. S., and Simmons, J. W. (Eds.) (1978). *Systems of Cities: Readings on Structure, Growth, and Policy*, Oxford University Press, New York.

Bowden, M. J., LaRose, B. L., and Mishara, B. (1970). The development of competition between central places on the frontier: Vermont, 1790–1830. *Proceedings, Association of American Geographers*, **3**, 32–38.

Brush, J. E. (1951). *The Trade Centres of Southwestern Wisconsin: An Analysis of Function and Location*, unpublished Ph.D. dissertation, University of Wisconsin, Madison.

Brush, J. E. (1953). The hierarchy of central places in southern Wisconsin. *Geographical Review*, **43**, 380–402.

Burghardt, A. F. (1971). A hypothesis about gateway cities. *Annals, Association of American Geographers*, **61**, 269–285.

Careless, J. M. S. (1954). Frontierism, metropolitanism, and Canadian history. *Canadian History Review*, **35**, 1–21.

Christaller, W. (1933). *Die Zentralen Orte in Süddeutschland*, Gustav Fischer, Jena.

Clark,V. S. (1929). *History of Manufactures in the United States*, Vol. I, McGraw-Hill, New York.

Cohen, R. (1979). The changing transactional economy and its spatial implications. *Ekistics*, **274**, 7–15.

Conzen, M. P. (1974). Historical change in the gradient structure of American metropolitan regions. Paper presented at the annual meeting of the Association of American Geographers, Seattle.

Conzen, M. P. (1975a). Capital flows and the developing urban hierarchy: state bank capital in Wisconsin, 1854–1895. *Economic Geography*, **51**, 321–338.

Conzen, M. P. (1975b). A transport interpretation of the growth of urban regions: an American example. *Journal of Historical Geography*, **1**, 361–382.

Conzen, M. P. (1977). The maturing urban system in the United States, 1840–1910. *Annals, Association of American Geographers*, **67**, 88–108.

David, P. A. (1967). Growth of real product in the US before 1840: new evidence, controlled conjectures: *Journal of Economic History*, **27**, 151–197.

Davis, L. E. (1971). Capital mobility and American growth. In R. W. Fogal and S. Engermann (Eds.), *The Reinterpretation of American Economic History*, Harper and Row, New York. pp. 285–300.

Davis, L. E. *et al.* (1972). *American Economic Growth: An Economist's History of the United States*, Harper and Row, New York.

DeGeer, S. (1927). The American manufacturing belt. *Geografiska Annaler*, **9**, 233–359.

Denecke, D. (1976). Prozesse der Entstehung und Standortverschiebung zentraler Orte in Gebieten hoher Instabilität des räumlich-funktionalen Gefüges: Virginia und Maryland vom Beginn der Kolonisation bis heute. *Marburger Geographische Schriften*, **66**, 175–200.

Dickinson, R. E. (1947). *City Region and Regionalism: A Geographical Contribution to Human Ecology*, K. Paul, Trench, Trubner, and Co., London.

Duncan, B. and Lieberson, S. (1970). *Metropolis and Region in Transition*, Sage Publications, Beverly Hills.

Earle, C. V., and Hoffman, R. (1976). Staple crops and urban development in the eighteenth-century south. *Perspectives in American History*, **10**, 7–78.

Earle, C. V., and Hoffman, R. (1977). The urban south: the first two centuries. In B. A. Brownell and D. R. Goldfield (Eds.), *The City in Southern History: The Growth of Urban Civilization in the South*, Kennikat Press, Port Washington. pp. 23–51.

Emerson, F. V. (1908–09). A geographic interpretation of New York City (Pts. I, II, and III). *Bulletin of the American Geographical Society*, **40**, 587–612, 726–738; **41**, 3–21.

Fishlow, A. (1964). Antebellum interregional trade reconsidered. *American Economic Review*, **54**, 352–364.

Friedmann, J. (1963). Regional economic policy for developing areas. *Papers and Proceedings of the Regional Science Association*, **11**, 41–61.

Galpin, C. J. (1915). *The Social Anatomy of an Agricultural Community*. Research Bulletin 34, University of Wisconsin Agricultural Experiment Station, Madison.

Genthe, M. K. (1907). Valley towns of Connecticut. *Bulletin of the American Geographical Society*, **39**, 513–544.

Gottman, J. (1961). *Megalopolis: The Urbanized Northeastern Seaboard of the United States*, Twentieth Century Fund, New York.

Gras, N. S. B. (1922). *An Introduction to Economic History*, Harper and Brothers, New York.

Hamburg, J. F. (1977). Papertowns in South Dakota. *Journal of the West*, **16**, 40–42.

Harris, C. D. (1943). A functional classification of cities in the United States. *Geographical Review*, **33**, 86–99.

Hart, A. B. (1890). The rise of American cities. *Quarterly Journal of Economics*, **4**, 129–157, 241–244.

Hartshorne, R. (1936). A new map of the manufacturing belt of North America. *Economic Geography*, **12**, 45–53.

Higgs, R. (1969). The growth of cities in a midwestern region, 1870–1900. *Journal of Regional Science*, **9**, 369–375.

Hilliard, S. B. (1972). *Hogmeat and Hoecake: Food Supply in the Old South, 1840–1860*, Southern Illinois University Press, Carbondale.

Hudson, J. C. (1979). The plains country town. In B. W. Blouet and F. C. Luebke (Eds.), *The Great Plains: Environment and Culture*, University of Nebraska Press, Lincoln. pp. 99–118.

Jefferson, M. (1915). How American cities grow. *Bulletin of the American Geographical Society*, **47**, 19–37.

Kolb, J. H. (1933). *Trends in Town-Country Relations*. Research Bulletin 117, University of Wisconsin Agricultural Experiment Station, Madison.

Kovacik, C. F. (1978). Health conditions and town growth in colonial and antebellum South Carolina. *Social Science and Medicine*, **12**, 131–136.

Lampard, E. E. (1968). The evolving system of cities in the United States: urbanization and economic development. In H. S. Perloff and L. Wingo, Jr. (Eds.), *Issues in Urban Economics*, Johns Hopkins University Press, Baltimore. pp. 81–138.

Langdale, J. V. (1978). The growth of long-distance telephony in the Bell system: 1875–1907. *Journal of Historical Geography*, **4**, 145–159.

LaRose, B. L. (1973). Urbanization in the antebellum South, 1800–1860. Paper delivered to the Historical Urbanization of North America Conference, York University, Downsview, Ontario.

Lebergott, S. (1964). *Manpower in Economic Growth: The American Record since 1800*, McGraw-Hill, New York.

LeBlance, R. B. (1969). *Location of Manfacturing in New England in the 19th Century*, Dartmouth College, Dartmouth.

Lemon, J. T. (1967). Urbanization and the development of eighteenth-century southeastern Pennsylvania and adjacent Delaware. *William and Mary Quarterly*, 3rd Series, **24**, 501–542.

Lewis, P. F. (1976). *New Orleans: The Making of an Urban Landscape*, Ballinger, Cambridge, Massachusetts.

Lindstrom, D. (1978). *Economic Development in the Philadelphia Region, 1810–1850*, Columbia University Press, New York.

Livingood, J. W. (1947). *The Philadelphia–Baltimore Trade Rivalry, 1780–1860*, Pennsylvania Historical and Museum Commission, Harrisburg.

Luckingham, B. (1979). The southwestern urban frontier, 1880–1930. *Journal of the West*, **18**, 40 50.

Lukermann, F. (1966). Empirical expressions of nodality and hierarchy in a circulation manifold. *East Lakes Geographer*, **2**, 17–44.

Madden, C. H. (1966). On some indications of stability in the growth of cities in the United States. *Economic Development and Cultural Change*, **4**, 236–252.

Mahnke, H. -P. (1972). Hauptstadtverlegung in den USA. *Geographische Rundschau*, **24**, 366–370.

Matthews, J. S. (1949). *Expressions of Urbanism in the Sequent Occupance of Northeastern Ohio*. University of Chicago Department of Geography Research Paper No. 5, Chicago.

McKenzie, R. D. (1933). *The Metropolitan Community*, McGraw-Hill, New York.

Meinig, D. W. (1969). A macrogeography of western imperialism: some morphologies of moving frontiers of political control. In F. Gale and D. H. Lawton (Eds.), *Settlement and Encounter: Geographical Studies Presented to Sir Grenfell Price*, Oxford University Press, New York. pp. 213–240.

Meinig, D. W. (1972). American wests: preface to a geographical introduction. *Annals, Association of American Geographers*, **62**, 159–184.

Meinig, D. W. (1976). Spatial models of a sequence of transatlantic interactions. In *International Geography '76: Section 9, Historical Geography*, International Geographical Congress, Moscow. pp. 30–35.

Meyer, D. R. (1977). Model of nineteenth century urban–regional industrial complexes. Paper presented at the annual meeting of the Association of American Geographers, Salt Lake City.

Meyer, D. R. (1980a). A dynamic model of the integration of frontier urban places into the United States system of cities. *Economic Geography*, **56**, 120–140.

Meyer, D. R. (1980b). Emergence of the American manufacturing belt: a conjectural hypothesis. Paper presented at the annual meeting of the Association of American Geographers, Louisville.

Miller, R. B. (1979). *City and Hinterland: A Case Study of Urban Growth and Regional Development*, Greenwood Press, Westport.

Morrill, R. L. (1962). Simulation of central place patterns over time. *Lund Studies in Geography, Ser. B, Human Geography*, **24**, 109–120.

Muller, E. K. (1976). Selective urban growth in the middle Ohio valley, 1800–1860. *Geographical Review*, **66**, 178–199.

Muller, E. K. (1977). Regional urbanization and the selective growth of towns in North American regions. *Journal of Historical Geography*, **3**, 21–39.

Muller, E. K. (1980). Review of Lindstrom's *Economic Development in the Philadelphia Region*. *Journal of Historical Geography*, **6**, 346–349.

North, D. C. (1966). *Growth and Welfare in the American Past*, Prentice-Hall, Englewood Cliffs.

Palm, R. (1981). *The Geography of American Cities*, Oxford University Press, New York.

Park, R. E., Burgess, E. W., and McKenzie, R. (1925). *The City*, University of Chicago Press, Chicago.

Parkins, A. E. (1918). *The Historical Geography of Detroit*, University of Chicago Libraries, Chicago.

Porter, G., and Livesay, H. (1971). *Merchants and Manufacturers: Studies in the Changing Structure of Nineteenth-Century Marketing*, Johns Hopkins University Press, Baltimore.

Pred, A. R. (1966). *The Spatial Dynamics of US Urban-Industrial Growth, 1800–1914*, MIT Press, Cambridge, Massachusetts.

Pred, A. R. (1973). *Urban Growth and the Circulation of Information: The US System of Cities, 1790–1840*, Harvard University Press, Cambridge, Massachusetts.

Ratzel, F. (1893). *Politische Geographie der Vereinigten Staaten von Amerika*, R. Oldenburg, Munich.

Reisser, C. E. (1951). *Pittsburgh's Commercial Development, 1800–1850*, Pennsylvania Historical and Museum Commission, Harrisburg.

Roth, L. V. (1918). The growth of American cities. *Geographical Review,* **5**, 384–398.

Rothstein, M. (1966). Antebellum wheat and cotton exports: a contrast in marketing organization and economic development. *Agricultural History,* **40**, 91–100.

Rubin, J. (1961). Canal or railroad? Imitation and innovation in the response to the Erie Canal in Philadelphia, Baltimore, and Boston. *Transactions, American Philosophical Society,* n.s. **51** pt. 7, Philadelphia.

Sargent, C. S. (1975). Towns of the Salt River valley, 1870–1930. *Historical Geography Newsletter,* **5**, 2, 1–9.

Semple, E. C. (1903). *American History and its Geographic Conditions,* Houghton, Mifflin and Co., Boston.

Taaffe, E. J., Morrill, R. L., and Gould, P. R. (1963). Transport expansion in underdeveloped countries: a comparative analysis: *Geographical Review,* **53**, 503–529.

Taylor, G. R. (1967). American urban growth preceding the railway age. *Journal of Economic History,* **27**, 309–339.

Thomas, L. F. (1949). Decline of St. Louis as midwest metropolis. *Economic Geography,* **25**, 118–127.

Tower, W. S. (1905). The geography of American cities. *Bulletin of the American Geographical Society,* **37**, 577–588.

Ullman, E. (1941). A theory of location for cities. *American Journal of Sociology,* **46**, 853–864.

Uselding, P. J. (1976). A note on the interregional trade in manufactures in 1840. *Journal of Economic History,* **36**, 428–435.

Vance, J. E. Jr. (1970). *The Merchant's World: The Geography of Wholesaling,* Prentice-Hall, Englewood Cliffs.

Vanderhill, B. G. (1973). The historic spas of Florida. *West Georgia Studies in the Social Sciences,* **12**, 59–77.

Walsh, M. (1978). The spatial evolution of the mid-western pork industry, 1835–75. *Journal of Historical Geography,* **4**, 1–22.

Walters, W. D. Jr. (1977). The making of the urban pattern in central Illinois: 1831–1895. *Bulletin, Illinois Geographical Society,* **19**, 3–15.

Ward, D. (1971). *Cities and Immigrants: A Geography of Change in Nineteenth Century America,* Oxford University Press, New York.

Weber, A. F. (1899). *The Growth of Cities in the Nineteenth Century,* Columbia University Press, New York.

Williamson, J. G. and Swanson, J. A. (1966). The growth of cities in the American northeast, 1820–1870. *Explorations in Entrepreneurial History,* 2nd Ser., **4**, Supplement.

Index